Mitrovice/Kosovska Mitrovica June 18, 1999.
Kosovo Albanians shout at Serb civilians in filled vehicles,
leaving for Serbia. In spite of the presence of 40,000 armed
soldiers, the international community failed to stop a new
wave of ethnic cleansing in Kosovo. As the Yugoslav army
pulled out of Kosovo, many Serbs left in their wake. After the
summer of 1999 only half of the Serb population was left.
The approximately 100,000 remaining Serbs are living in
enclaves or divided cities.
PHOTO: JEAN-PHILIPPE KSIAZEK/PRESSENS BILD

*Cover:*
Kosovo Albanian refugees in Kukes, Albania.
During the period March 24—June 19, 1999 approximately
863,000 refugees, most of them Kosovar Albanians, fled
Kosovo and an additional 590,000 were internally displaced.
PHOTO: PAOLO PELLEGRIN

# THE KOSOVO REPORT

## CONFLICT
*
## INTERNATIONAL RESPONSE
*
## LESSONS LEARNED
*

### THE INDEPENDENT INTERNATIONAL
### COMMISSION ON KOSOVO

OXFORD
UNIVERSITY PRESS

# OXFORD

UNIVERSITY PRESS

Great Clarendon Street, Oxford OX2 6DP

Oxford University Press is a department of the University of Oxford
It furthers the University's objective of excellence in research, scholarship,
and education by publishing worldwide in

Oxford New York

Athens Auckland Bangkok Bogotá Buenos Aires Calcutta
Cape Town Chennai Dar es Salaam Delhi Florence Hong Kong Istanbul
Karachi Kuala Lumpur Madrid Melbourne Mexico City Mumbai
Nairobi Paris São Paulo Singapore Taipei Tokyo Toronto Warsaw

with associated companies in Berlin Ibadan

Oxford is a registered trade mark of Oxford University Press
in the UK and in certain other countries

Published in the United States
by Oxford University Press Inc., New York

British Library Cataloguing in Publication Data

Data available

Library of Congress Cataloging in Publication Data

ISBN 0-19-924308-5
ISBN 0-19-924309-3 (PBK)

1 3 5 7 9 10 8 6 4 2

The royalties for this book go directly to The Humanitarian Law Center,
founded and led by Natasa Kadic. HLC works in both Serbia and Kosovo,
documenting violence against all victims—without regard for their ethnic
origins—and works for peace and reconciliation among the different
ethnic groups in Kosovo and Serbia.

Cover design and typeset by
Cecilia Medin/Global Reporting Sweden
Printed in Great Britain
on acid-free paper by
Biddles Ltd, www.biddles.co.uk

# TABLE OF CONTENTS

Executive Summary • 1
Address by former President Nelson Mandela • 14
Map of Kosovo • 18
Introduction • 19

**PART I: WHAT HAPPENED?**

Preface • 29
1. The Origins of the Kosovo Crisis • 33
2. Internal Armed Conflict: February 1998–March 1999 •67
3. International War Supervenes: March 1999–June 1999 • 85
4. Kosovo under United Nations Rule • 99

**PART II: ANALYSIS**

5. The Diplomatic Dimension • 131
6. International Law and Humanitarian Intervention • 163
7. Humanitarian Organizations and the Role of Media • 201
8. Kosovo: The Regional Dimension • 227
9. The Future Status of Kosovo • 259

**PART III: CONCLUSION**

10. Conclusion • 283

**ANNEXES**

1. Documentation on Human Rights Violations • 301
2. Kosovo—Facts and Figures • 319
3. The Rambouillet Agreement—a Summary • 320
4. The Ahtisaari-Chernomyrdin Agreement—a Summary • 324
5. UN Resolution 1244 • 325
6. The Commission's Work • 331
7. Endnotes • 342
8. Literature on Kosovo and the Crisis • 364
9. Acronyms • 367
10. Index • 369

www.kosovocommission.org

# MAIN FINDINGS

**PREVENTION** ⋆ The origins of the crisis have to be understood in terms of a new wave of nationalism that led to the rise of Milosevic and the official adoption of an extreme Serbian nationalist agenda. The revocation of Kosovo's autonomy in 1989 was followed by a Belgrade policy aimed at changing the ethnic composition of Kosovo and creating an apartheid-like society.

From the early 1990s onwards, governments and international institutions were aware of the impending conflict in Kosovo. There were plenty of warnings, and moreover, the Kosovo conflict was part of the unfolding tragedy of the break-up of Yugoslavia. Yet prior to 1998, the international community failed to take sufficient preventative action. There were some diplomatic initiatives especially in 1992–3, but they were confused and not backed by sufficient high-level pressure. More importantly, insufficient support was provided to the non-violent resistance movement, which created its own parallel institutions and which managed to prevent large-scale violence in Kosovo up to 1997. The decision to exclude the Kosovo question from the Dayton negotiations, and the lack of results achieved by the strategy of non-violence, led many Kosovar Albanians to conclude that violence was the only way to attract international attention. It was during this period that the KLA groups first made their appearance. Until late

1997 they were small resistance groups who pursued hit and run, low level guerrilla warfare, hoping for international intervention. The Serbian response to the initial KLA attacks was, as expected, brutal and was also directed against civilians. The Serbian massacre of 58 people in Prekazi/Prekaze in February 1998 became a turning point. The internal war escalated.

The general conclusion to be drawn from this experience is that much more effort needs to be devoted to prevention. It is not necessarily a matter of early warning; it is a matter of political will, readiness to expend resources, and having a presence on the ground.

**ARMED CONFLICT** * This armed conflict between the KLA and the FRY lasted from February 1998 to June 1999 although it escalated after March 1999 when the NATO air campaign supervened. It can be characterized both as an armed insurgency and counter-insurgency, and as a war (against civilians) of ethnic cleansing.

The Commission has collated information from a wide variety of sources in order to assess the extent of atrocities. In the first phase of the conflict from February 1998 to March 1999, casualties were relatively low: around 1,000 civilians were killed up to September although the evidence is uncertain; the number of victims between September and March is unknown but must be lower. More than 400,000 people were driven from their homes during this period, about half of these were internally displaced. Most of these internal refugees returned after the Holbrooke-Milosevic agreement of October 1998. There were also widespread arrests and detentions during this period.

In the period March 24, 1999 to June 19, 1999, the Commission estimates the number of killings in the neighborhood of 10,000, with the vast majority of the victims being Kosovar Albanians killed by FRY forces. Approximately 863,000 civilians sought or were forced into refuge outside Kosovo and an additional 590,000 were internally displaced. There is also evidence of widespread rape and torture, as well as looting, pillaging and extortion.

The pattern of the logistical arrangements made for deportations and the coordination of actions by the Yugoslav army, paramilitary groups and the police shows that this huge expulsion of Kosovo-Albanians was systematic and deliberately organized. The NATO air campaign did not provoke the attacks on the civilian Kosovar population but the bombing created an environment that made such an operation feasible.

**THE DIPLOMATIC EFFORT** ★ The most promising window of diplomatic opportunity was prior to 1998. At each stage of the conflict, the diplomatic options narrowed. However, the political will to mount a major diplomatic effort could only be mobilized *after* the conflict escalated into full-scale violence.

The diplomatic effort throughout 1998, culminating in Rambouillet, was characterized by confusion and mixed signals. In the face of Milosevic's ruthless strategy of oppression and the maximalist demands of both the LDK and KLA, there was little chance that diplomacy would prevail. The Holbrooke-Milosevic agreement of October 1998 led to the introduction of unarmed international monitors and did succeed in reducing the level of violence. However, KLA units took advantage of the lull in the fighting to reestablish their control of many positions vacated by the redeployed Serbian troops. Violence escalated again in December 1998 also after Serbian forces reentered the province.

The Commission believes that there are important lessons to be learned about the role of unarmed monitors in reducing the level of civilian suffering, if not averting humanitarian catastrophe.

The overall narratives of the international response are inherently inconclusive, and hence without clear "lessons" beyond the prudential observations in favor of early engagement and greater attentiveness to nonviolent options. Certain key conclusions are worth emphasizing.

1 Multiple and divergent agendas and expectations and mixed signals from the international community impeded effective diplomacy,

2 The international community's experience with Milosevic as not amenable to usual negotiations created a dilemma. The only language of diplomacy believed open to negotiators was that of coercion and threat. This lead to legal and diplomatic problems—such threat diplomacy violates the Charter and is hard to reconcile with peaceful settlement. The credibility of the threat must, in the final analysis, be upheld by the actual use of force.

3 It is impossible to conclude, however, despite these weaknesses, that a diplomatic solution could have ended the internal struggle over the future of Kosovo. The minimal goals of the Kosovar Albanians and of Belgrade were irreconcilable.

4 Russia's contribution to the process was ambiguous. Its particular relationship with Serbia enabled crucial diplomatic steps, but its rigid commitment to veto any enforcement action was the major factor forcing NATO into an action without mandate.

**THE NATO AIR CAMPAIGN** * The Commission concludes that the NATO military intervention was illegal but legitimate. It was illegal because it did not receive prior approval from the United Nations Security Council. However, the Commission considers that the intervention was justified because all diplomatic avenues had been exhausted and because the intervention had the effect of liberating the majority population of Kosovo from a long period of oppression under Serbian rule.

NATO believed that a relatively short bombing campaign would persuade Milosevic to sign the Rambouillet agreement. That was a major mistake. NATO also underestimated the obvious risk that the Serbian government would attack the Kosovo Albanians. NATO had to expand the air campaign to strategic targets in Serbia proper, which increased the risk of civilian casualties. In spite of the fact that NATO made substantial effort to avoid civilian casualties there were some serious mistakes. Some 500 civilian deaths are documented. The Commission is also critical of the use of cluster bombs, the environmental damage caused by the use of depleted-uranium tipped armor-piercing shells and missiles and by toxic leaks caused by the bombing of industrial and petroleum complexes in several cities, and the attack on Serbian television on April 17, 1999. The Commission accepts the view of the Final Report of the ICTY that there is no basis in the available evidence for charging specific individuals with criminal violations of the Laws of the War during the NATO campaign. Nevertheless some practices do seem vulnerable to the allegation that violations might have occurred and depend, for final assessment, on the availability of further evidence.

The Commission argues for a higher threshold of protective standards in any future undertaking and proposes the negotiation of a "Protocol III" to make this explicit and mandatory.

In conclusion, the NATO war was neither a success nor a failure; it was in fact both. It forced the Serbian government to withdraw its army and police from Kosovo and to sign an agreement closely modeled on the aborted Rambouillet accord. It stopped the systematic oppression of the Kosovar Albanians. However, the intervention failed to achieve its avowed aim of preventing massive ethnic cleansing. Milosevic remained in power. The Serbian people were the main losers. Kosovo was lost. Many Serbs fled or were expelled from the province. Serbia suffered considerable economic losses and destruction of civilian infrastructure. Independent media and NGOs were suppressed and the overall level of repression in Serbia increased.

**RESPONSE TO HUMANITARIAN CRISIS** ★ Both governmental and non-governmental agencies were unprepared for the scale of the refugee crises in the neighboring states of Albania and Macedonia.

There were obviously no warnings from NATO to either UNHCR or other organizations of a possible refugee flow. The lack of planning can be partly attributed to the under-funding of UNHCR. NATO peacekeeping troops based in Macedonia were brought in by governments to assist with the refugee crisis. Lack of cooperation and competition between the military and the main humanitarian agencies as well as with the numerous NGOs who rushed to the region to help, hindered the humanitarian effort.

Given these initial difficulties, the Commission commends the scale and effectiveness of the humanitarian response and proposes a number of measures, such as the screening of NGOs and more cooperation among military and civilian agencies, to improve planning and coordination in the future. To ensure more even-handed response to humanitarian crises and to promote preparedness and coordination, the international community must provide more funds for UNHCR.

The extraordinary scale of the humanitarian response took place at a time when worldwide aid budgets were dwindling. This compromised the claim of impartiality and universality in the provision of humanitarian assistance and aid.

**ROLE OF THE MEDIA** ★ Both NATO and the Belgrade government engaged in a propaganda war and made exaggerated claims. Nevertheless, on the whole, journalists did not allow themselves to be "spun." Even in Belgrade, where the government cracked down on independent media, a few courageous journalists continued to speak out.

Just as the Commission has concluded that the conduct of military operations in humanitarian interventions should be conducted according to especially strict rules of engagement, it also concludes that media operations must be conducted under especially stringent rules of disclosure. The Commission strongly believes that open access to both sides of any humanitarian intervention is critical if military operations, on both sides, are to be kept under effective public scrutiny. The Commission believes there is no case for restricting the ability of journalists to operate in theaters of conflict where humanitarian interventions are taking place. The Commission strongly condemns the attempts by the Serbian government to place restrictions on their own media's coverage of the war and its aftermath, especially the detention of Miroslav Filipovic for his interviews with FRY soldiers who took part in operations in Kosovo, and for his publication of their admission of atrocities and war crimes.

**UNMIK RULE** ★ United Nations Resolution 1244 authorized the deployment of military forces, KFOR, to Kosovo and the establishment of a civilian administration, UNMIK. Dr. Bernard Kouchner was appointed by the UN Secretary General to head the mission.

After the summer of 1999, Kosovo was characterized by a high level of crime and agression, much of which was directed against the minority population, especially Serbs. The inability to stop a new wave of ethnic cleansing in Kosovo, in spite of the presence of 40,000 armed soldiers, was a major failure for the international community. More than half of the Serb population left the province together with departing Serbian forces or were later forced to leave. The remaining Serb population is living in enclaves or divide cities. In particular, the division of the northern city of Mitrovice/Kosovska Mitrovica represents a focal point for renewed conflict. In addition, those political forces among the Albanian population who had advocated violence were greatly strengthened by the war.

Although the international authorities can claim some achievements in establishing an administration and starting to solve some of the problems of the economy and of law and order, they still face serious challenges. The establishment of UNMIK was slow and its work has been seriously hampered by a number of obstacles, notably the absence of police and of judicial processes, and the slowness of donors to implement their funding commitments. Although KFOR troops did undertake civilian tasks, only some national contingents were ready to undertake police work. Moreover, the contradictory character of 1244 which includes commitments both to "substantial autonomy and meaningful self-administration" for Kosovo and to the sovereignty and territorial integrity of FRY, greatly complicates policy-making on a range of issues such as security, currency, trade etc.

The lessons of UNMIK rule for other UN operations include the need to create an international policing capability, the need to increase funding for post-conflict operations, and the importance of supporting and strengthening moderate democratic political groupings.

EFFECTS ON THE SURROUNDING REGION * The conflict in Kosovo cannot be understood except in the broader regional context. The Kosovo conflict produced shock waves affecting neighboring states as a result of the influx of refugees, the economic damage caused by disruptions to trade and production and the growth of criminality, and the political impact on fragile states such as Albania, Macedonia and Montenegro.

The Commission welcomes the initiative for a Stability Pact, which opens up new opportunities to create a post-conflict zone of stability and cooperation in the Southeast European region as a whole. The Pact has generated high expectations but has achieved relatively little in its first year. The combination of extensive conditionality and Brussels red tape has kept disbursement on a low level. There is a risk of failure or fading into irrelevance if it were to remain essentially a concept imposed on the region from above without adequate input from, and identification within, the region. It will work only if the desire to join Europe prevails over nationalistic agendas and corrupt practices. The destination of the Balkans as a whole must be European integration.

Two important obstacles to regional integration are weak state institutions and widespread criminalization of the economy. It is important to strengthen civil society in the region as a whole and to assist state-building processes. There also needs to be much greater international cooperation in fighting organized crime, including adequate legislation and improved enforcement capacity.

The Commission is deeply concerned about the deteriorating political situation in Serbia and the risk of a new violent conflict between Montenegro and Serbia. It recommends greatly increased political and economic support for Montenegro and an expanded international presence in that country. It also recommends a long-term project of promoting civil society in Serbia, including NGOs, alternative or independent media, municipalities and universities, while maintaining targeted sanctions against the Belgrade regime.

**FUTURE STATUS** ★ Resolution 1244 created a unique institutional hybrid, a UN protectorate with unlimited power whose purpose is to prepare the province for autonomy and self-government—but in the framework of FRY. There is also a sharp division in the UN Security Council concerning if and how the resolution should be implemented. It is however very clear that, after what the Kosovo Albanians have experienced at the hands of the FRY authorities, they are absolutely unwilling to accept any meaningful or even symbolic expression of FRY sovereignty on the province.

The Commission has concluded that the best available option for the future of Kosovo is "conditional independence". This means expanding the autonomy and self-government promised by 1244 in order to make Kosovo effectively self-governing outside the FRY, but within an international framework. The international community would take responsibility for an initial security guarantee and for overseeing the protection of minority rights and would also integrate Kosovo into an effective stability pact.

The status of "conditional independence" would have to be reached through an "internal agreement" between representatives of the international community in Kosovo and the Kosovo majority, as well as representatives of ethnic minorities, and an "external agreement" negotiated with Kosovo's neighbors. Eventually, this will also have to include the Serbian government but a refusal of the Serbian government to engage in dialogue should not constitute a veto on this process.

**THE FUTURE OF HUMANITARIAN INTERVENTION** ★ Experience from the NATO intervention in Kosovo suggests the need to close the gap between legality and legitimacy. The Commission believes that the time is now ripe for the presentation of a principled framework for humanitarian intervention which could be used to guide future responses to imminent humanitarian catastrophes and which could be used to assess claims for humanitarian intervention. It is our hope that the UN General Assembly could adopt such a framework in some modified form as a Declaration and that the UN Charter be adapted to this Declaration either by appropriate amendments or by a case-by-case approach in the UN Security Council. We also suggest a strengthening of the level of human rights protection contained in the UN Charter—aware of course of the political problems of implementing such a change.

Our proposed principled framework includes three threshold principles, which must be satisfied in any legitimate claim to humanitarian intervention. These principles include the suffering of civilians owing to severe patterns of human rights violations or the breakdown of government, the overriding commitment to the direct protection of the civilian population, and the calculation that the intervention has a reasonable chance of ending the humanitarian catastrophe. In addition, the framework includes a further eight contextual principles which can be used to assess the degree of legitimacy possessed by the actual use of force.

The implication of our framework is that governments and international institutions also need to possess the appropriate means for carrying out this kind of operation. This means expanding the international peacekeeping capacity to protect civilians on the ground.

The Commission is aware that in many countries of the world there is a much stronger commitment to the protection of their sovereignty than currently exists in the West. Given the dual history of colonialism and the Cold War, there is widespread concern about Western interventionism. The growing global power of NATO creates a feeling of vulnerability in other parts of the world, especially in a case such as Kosovo where NATO claims a right to bypass the United Nations Security Council.

The Commission, composed as it was of citizens of many non-European, non-Western societies, puts great emphasis on the continued importance of the United Nations. It advocates increased funding and the need to consider ways to reform the main bodies of the United Nations, especially the Security Council, so that they are better suited to the post-Cold War environment.

The proposal for a new framework for humanitarian intervention should not detract from the need to prevent humanitarian catastrophes in the future. The Commission takes the view that much more political effort and economic resources need to be devoted both to pre-conflict and post-conflict situations. In the case of Kosovo, far more attention and money was spent on Kosovo during the intervention than before or after.

The Commission also advocates greater emphasis on the gender dimension of humanitarian intervention. In Kosovo, insufficient attention has been paid to the impact of the conflict on women, in particular, the use of rape as a weapon of war, and the rise of trafficking in the post-conflict period. Moreover, women have a crucial role to play in post-conflict reconciliation and reconstruction.

Finally, the Commission is acutely aware that the world has not given the same priority to humanitarian catastrophes outside Europe as it gave to Kosovo. It is the Commission's hope that, after the Kosovo experience, it will be impossible to ignore tragedies such as the genocide in Rwanda in other parts of the world, and that the lessons of the Kosovo conflict will help us to develop a more effective response to future humanitarian catastrophes wherever they occur.

# ADDRESS BY FORMER PRESIDENT
# NELSON MANDELA

*Delivered at the Independent International Commission on
Kosovo's final seminar, University of the Witwatersrand,
South Africa, August 25, 2000*

In his opening address to the General Assembly in September
1999 Secretary-General Kofi Annan made a plea for United
Nations intervention in cases of gross violations of human rights.
We know that few states endorsed the remarks of the Secretary-
General, and even fewer supported the Swedish position that
"the collective conscience of mankind demands action."

The reluctance on the part of states is perhaps understandable
due to a wariness of intervention too readily initiated; but we
must all admire the determination of Secretary-General Annan
and Sweden to end the conflicts which continue to plague so
many regions of our world. It is hardly surprising that both had
given their support to the Independent International Commission on Kosovo—a commission established to examine the events
in Kosovo. Both Prime Minister Persson and Secretary-General
Annan believe that to end conflict we must better understand it.

We must say to Secretary-General Annan that, at a time when
the quest for peace demands greater accountability on the part of
states and international organisations for their actions, we are
fortunate to have a man like him at the helm of the United Nations Organisation. In Africa we take particular pride in him.

The quest for peace has created a need for even more dialogue
on the international plane. The report of the Kosovo Commis-

sion will provide an independent assessment of conflict and intervention that can assist in advancing dialogue amongst all leaders, scholars and interested parties. It is vitally important that we engage in this discourse and discussion. The century behind us was one of great wars and conflicts. As we start this one, we need to understand the lessons of those conflicts and learn from them for our future.

We find it most fitting that the Kosovo Commission has decided to host its final meeting and seminar here in South Africa. It is equally fitting that it chose as its focus for this seminar the lessons to be learnt from Kosovo for dealing with conflicts in regions like Africa and Asia. While we are not convinced that it is only a lack of schooling on the part of the international community that has made it so reluctant to act to halt conflicts in Africa, this disparity of treatment does desperately require attention. And the Kosovo Commission can play an important part in addressing also that issue.

It has now become so customary to point to the failure of the international community to intervene and end the genocide in Rwanda that it is almost forgotten that this relative neglect of Africa in these matters is much more general than only the Rwanda case. For example, while NATO prepared itself for action in Kosovo, Sierra Leone seemed a virtually forsaken place from an international perspective. As atrocities were carried out in Sierra Leone, Nigeria, under the aegis of an ECOMOG peacekeeping mandate, sent in troops, but the weaponry, funding, communications and intelligence promised by Western powers failed to materialise.

And even in Rwanda itself, once the genocide had ended, there was and is more that the international community could do than merely repent about its failures. The dynamics that ignited the genocide in Rwanda today continue to play a role in the conflicts in neighbouring Burundi and Democratic Republic of Congo.

We are not suggesting that these and other African conflicts can be subjected to the same template of conflict resolution or that the actions of Kosovo can simply be transplanted to the conflicts on this continent. We in Africa and Asia must, however, envy the readiness and willingness on the part of the international community to intervene and commit resources to the reconstruction of Kosovar society.

It is therefore particularly encouraging to us to note the interest of the international community in the Burundi Peace Process to which we have been the Facilitator since the beginning of this year, building on the sterling work done by Mwalimu Julius Nyerere. A number of leaders from both Africa and the broader international community have given their time to attend some of the plenary sessions of the peace process held in Arusha. On Monday 28, August we shall again have such a plenary, this time with the intention to have a peace agreement signed. Once more a number of heads of states and governments, or their representatives, will be in attendance, signalling a renewed interest of the world in the affairs of Africa.

Even more encouraging has been the indications from Western leaders of their willingness to actively assist in the rebuilding and development of the Burundi economy once a peace agreement had been reached. We shall ourselves remain actively involved in mobilising the international community for that project. We would wish to see Burundi as a showcase of peace bringing its dividends through the actions of the international community.

We have quite often in the past made the comment that in this contemporary world of globalisation, we have indeed again become the keepers of our brother or sister. The global village cannot only be such where it concerns the accessibility and penetrability of markets; it must surely also mean that the ills and woes of one are the shared concern of all.

We speak here today to support the Kosovo Commission as potentially a powerful means of promoting and consolidating that sense of one-ness amongst ourselves. As we learn to understand that destructive part of our human condition that has caused so much pain and suffering throughout our human history, we may advance in the knowledge that we share so much— bad or good. Together, and only together, can we make of the world a better place for our children to grow up in.

I wish you well, and thank you for the opportunity of sharing with you. And thank you for thinking specifically of Africa in your deliberations.

I thank you.

# INTRODUCTION

The war in Kosovo is the most recent tragedy in the Balkan conflict—the decade-long implosion of the old Yugoslav Federation
that left a quarter million dead, many thousands more displaced
and much of the region in ruins. Yet the war will be remembered
as a turning-point: compelling a collective armed intervention for
the express purpose of implementing UN Security Council (UNSC)
resolutions but without UNSC authorization. NATO, deploying for
the first time its armed forces in war, placed the controversial
doctrine of "humanitarian intervention" squarely in the world's eye.

Unsurprisingly, several demanding international issues were
framed by the intervention: reconciliation of the commitment to
international protection of human rights with respect for national sovereignty and legal restrictions on the non-defensive use of
force; the continued legitimacy of the post World War II world
order as set forth in the United Nations charter; the capacity of
the United Nations to act as global peace keeper and the ramifi-
cations of the right to self-determination. But the war's course
also specifically provoked a number of questions fundamental to
the way in which future conflicts will be treated. Why was the
international community unable to act earlier and prevent escalation of the conflict? Why did diplomacy fail? Did NATO act
rightfully in launching a military campaign without Security

Council approval? Could agreement only be secured by resorting to armed intervention? How can the international community ensure future peace and security for the region?

These questions have focused global attention and initiated a heated debate. They demand sustained study and detailed analysis. The establishment of the Independent International Commission on Kosovo and the compilation of this report came about in recognition of that demand.

Understanding the action taken in Kosovo requires that the conflict be placed in context. It occurred at the end of a decade of particularly savage conflicts. Civilians, not soldiers, are increasingly recognized as the primary targets and victims of modern war; civilian suffering is often the direct objective of military action. The war in Bosnia culminating in the massacre at Srebrenica is emblematic of this brutal trend. The atrocities that amounted to genocide in Rwanda represented the ultimate targeted attack on civilians. These events were tragic not only for the suffering inflicted but because of inaction and non-intervention on the part of the international community. Kosovo, on the other hand, is a case of collective intervention, but it presents its own dilemmas.

During the past year, two groundbreaking reports have been issued under the auspices of the United Nations. The first, *The Report of the Secretary-General Pursuant to General Assembly Resolution 53/35 (1998)* documents the manner in which and the reasons for the United Nations failure to deter the Bosnian-Serb attack on Srebrenica in July 1995 and the subsequent massacre of 8000 Muslim men and boys. The second, *The Report of the Independent Inquiry into the Actions of the United Nations during the 1994 Genocide in Rwanda* was commissioned by the Secretary-General, Mr Kofi Annan, under authority of a Security Council resolution. Each of these reports focused on circumstances in which the United Nations has been accused of doing less than it could to prevent tragedies. Neither report shied away from apportioning blame to particular organs of the United Nations. These reports demonstrated the willingness of the United Nations Secretariat to take seriously its own shortcomings. A third report, produced by the Panel on United Nations Peace Operations and published in August 2000, highlights the need for a more robust peacekeeping doctrine including more realistic mandates.

This report, by the Independent International Commission on Kosovo, is not the work of a commission appointed by any governmental or non-governmental organization. The members of this Commission have participated solely in their personal capacities. The Commission was the initiative of the Prime Minister of Sweden, Mr Göran Persson, concerned by the absence of independent analysis of the conflict in Kosovo and any real attempt to research the lessons to be learned from the conflict. The Secretary-General of the United Nations, Mr. Kofi Annan, with whom he informally discussed the idea, endorsed the project.

Prime Minister Persson announced the establishment of the Commission on August 6, 1999. Direct involvement by the Swedish government in the Commission extended only to the invitation to Justice Richard Goldstone of South Africa and to Mr. Carl Tham, Secretary-General of the Olof Palme International Center in Stockholm to act as chairman and co-chairman respectively.

Appointment of the remaining 11 members of the Commission was made after invitations had been extended to particular individuals by Justice Goldstone and Mr Tham. Given the sensitive nature of the initiative—the very many international actors who stood to be scrutinized by the Commission—selection was made on the basis of known expertise and with due regard for the gender and geographical composition of the Commission.

The eleven members appointed are:

Dr Hanan Ashwari from Palestine[1]

Professor Grace d'Almeida from Benin

Senator Akiko Domoto from Japan

Professor Richard Falk from the United States of America

Ambassador Oleg Grinevsky from the Russian Federation[2]

Mr Michael Ignatieff from Canada

Professor Mary Kaldor from the United Kingdom

Professor Martha Minow from the United States of America

Professor Jacques Rupnik from France

Mr Theo Sommer from Germany

Mr Jan Urban from the Czech Republic

This report is to be handed over to the Secretary-General of the United Nations Mr. Kofi Annan. The Commission appreciates the Secretary-General's undertaking to receive the report. The Commission believes that the United Nations is best suited to implement and learn from many of the lessons of the Kosovo conflict. It should not be inferred, however, that the UN is the primary focus of this report. On the contrary, the scope of the report is very broad, comprising an assessment of the actions of all the major players involved in the conflict, including but certainly not limited to the United Nation's involvement. Nor was it ever intended that the lessons be only imparted to the United Nations. The Commission hopes that the report will be widely read, intensely debated and its findings seriously considered.

During the period of the Commission's twelve month appointment it has met on five occasions: in Stockholm September 21, 1999, in New York December 5–6, 1999, in Budapest April 5–6, 2000, in Florence June 26–30, 2000 and in Johannesburg

---

1 Unfortunately commitment to peace initiatives in the Middle East has prevented Dr Ashwari from participating in more than the first of the Commission's meetings and she is, therefore, not associated with the report.

2 Unfortunately ill-heath prevented Ambassador Grinevsky from participating in more than the first of the Commission's meetings and he is not associated with the report.

August 27–28, 2000. Prior to each of the meetings in New York, Budapest and Johannesburg, seminars were held to inform and facilitate the work of the Commission by gathering a wide range of experts who could offer insight into the Kosovo crisis.

The work of the Commission members has, however, continued throughout the year. Two delegations of the Commission visited Kosovo and met with representatives of the Serb and Albanian communities who had witnessed the conflict, as well as international administrators charged with overseeing the peacekeeping operations. The chairman and co-chairman sought meetings with State representatives from within and outside the NATO alliance. Other members of the Commission were invited to and, on several occasions did join, these meetings. Of the states approached, only two governments refused to cooperate with the work of the Commission. The United States of America, represented by senior officials of the State Department, was prepared to lend support only on condition that the Commission would restrict its investigation to human rights abuses perpetrated by the Federal Republic of Yugoslavia during the conflict. The FRY was unwilling to enter into discussion with the Commission on the basis of Justice Goldstone's alleged anti-Serb bias, demonstrated during his tenure as Chief Prosecutor of the International Criminal Tribunal for the former Yugoslavia, and because they were opposed to commissions in principle.

The war in Kosovo has sparked an extraordinary amount of commentary: books, articles, websites and official documents about the crisis abound. Facts and figures are often contradictory and ambiguous. The Commission has not attempted to tap secret sources. It has worked entirely with documents available in the public domain, and has endeavored to present only verifiable information. The Commission has noted where uncertainties exist. It has made a special effort to obtain the most reliable facts relating to human rights violations and to this end has worked closely with a group of experts compiling human rights data. Their documentation is presented in Annex 1 to this report and the most important findings are used in the report itself. The Commission's investigation extended until August 28, 2000, and does not take into account any developments or information released after that time.

Hostility in Kosovo has played itself out largely between two identifiable ethnic groups–Serbs and Albanians–each using their own language. Any assessment of conflict involving ethnic identity requires delicate treatment of language and an analysis of Kosovo would be particularly short-sighted were it to forego consideration of language sensitivities. The Commission has attempted to use a system that is both practical and inoffensive. The term "Kosovo" is used throughout the report because it is the form used in the English language. For place-names within Kosovo, the report gives both the Albanian and Serbian versions (e.g. Peje/Pec), but, following the convention adopted by the Organization for Security and Cooperation in Europe, does not make use of any accents.

The final product of the Commission's work is this report. It represents the collective efforts of all the members of the Commission. Every effort has been made to ensure that the analysis reflects the discussions of participating Commission members. Nevertheless, the Commission's chairman and co-chairman accept responsibility for the final wording of this report.

The Commission's Mission Statement has guided the structure of this report. That statement reads as follows:

> The Independent International Commission on Kosovo will examine key developments prior to, during and after the Kosovo war, including systematic violations of human rights in the region. The Commission will present a detailed, objective analysis of the options that were available to the international community to cope with the crisis. It will focus on the origins of the Kosovo crisis, the diplomatic efforts to end the conflict, the role of the United Nations and NATO's decision to intervene militarily. It will examine the resulting refugee crisis including the responses of the international community to resolve the crisis. The effect of the conflict on re-

gional and other states will also be examined. Furthermore, the Commission will assess the role of humanitarian workers, NGOs and the media during the Kosovo war. Finally, the Commission will identify the norms of international law and diplomacy brought to the fore by the Kosovo war and the adequacy of present norms and institutions in preventing and responding to comparable crisis in the future. In addition the Commission will take up: the future status of Kosovo; Lessons learned for Kosovo; and Lessons learned for the future

The report is divided into three sections: narrative, analysis, and conclusion. The structure is intended to simplify presentation but makes a degree of overlap and repetition inevitable. Part 1, "What Happened?" documents the factual chronology of the Kosovo crisis, beginning with its origins. The war in Kosovo is distinguished in two parts. The first part encompasses the fatal spiral of repression and resistance: the second was initiated by NATO's intervention and ended with the peace agreement of June 1999. The final chapter in the narrative presents Kosovo today—a province administered by the United Nations under Security Council Resolution 1244.

Part II provides an analysis of aspects of the intervention most fiercely contested. It examines the failure of diplomacy, particularly that attempted at Rambouillet, to end the conflict, and considers the alternatives to intervention. Questions of international law, specifically the legitimacy of humanitarian intervention—in both form and substance—are assessed in detail. The third chapter in this section subject the role of organizations offering humanitarian assistance and that played by the media in the Kosovo conflict to scrutiny. Specific attention is paid to the adequacy of the response evoked by the hundreds of thousands of refugees who fled Kosovo and massed on the borders of Albania, Macedonia, Italy and Montenegro. Effects of the conflict on the region, however, extend beyond reception of refugees. A chapter is devoted to the political and economic impact of the crisis on the region, the position and prospects for Serbia, in particular, and the reinvigorated attempts at reconstruction and regional cooperation brought about by the European Stability Pact. The final chapter in this section plots a map of the road ahead: examining the options for Kosovo's future status.

Part III of the Report sets out the Commission's conclusions. These conclusions have been formulated with the express goal of ensuring lasting peace and security for Kosovo in particular, and the Balkan region in general. But the Commission believes that many of its conclusions may be beneficially applied to the treatment of conflict the world-over. To this end the Commission has located its findings in a wider historical and political context. It has also sought specifically to identify the lessons from Kosovo which may assist in resolving conflicts in Africa and Asia— regions which have too long suffered the effects of a world drawn between developed and developing.

# PART I

# WHAT HAPPENED?

*

# PREFACE

The changing character of contemporary political violence calls into question some of the traditional ways of categorizing forms of violence. The traditional distinction between "times of peace" and "times of war" is increasingly blurred, as is the distinction between "internal" and "external" conflict. The several phases of the conflict in Kosovo raise these issues in a vivid form.

It is traditional to associate violations of human rights with peacetime, violations of international humanitarian law with wartime. Such a distinction may be misleading given the nature of the conflict that unfolded in Kosovo. The Belgrade government exerted its oppressive authority in Kosovo over the years through the mechanism of persistent abuses of human rights to such an extent that it can be argued that a right of resistance on the part of the targeted minority came into existence. In effect, the narrative of atrocities and human rights violations underpins the resistance of Kosovar Albanians, both in the form of the LDK non-violent activities and later in the form of KLA armed struggle. With respect to the latter phase of armed struggle, and counterinsurgency violence organized by the FRY, it is possible to describe the facts either from the perspective of human rights violations or from the perspective of international humanitarian law, the latter being more appropriate to the extent that the relationship between state and society is characterized as one of "armed conflict." With the internationalization of the conflict, certainly from the commencement of the NATO campaign, a condition of "war" existed, and the apprehension of unacceptable behavior on either side would most generally be treated under the rubric of international humanitarian law (what used to be called the "laws of war").

However, these considerations do raise questions about the appropriateness of traditional definitions. In effect, there were two types of conflicts. There was an internal armed conflict on the ground in Kosovo, in which military strategy took the form of widespread and systematic human rights violations. This conflict lasted from February 1998 to June 1999, although it escalated from March 1999. There was also an international conflict between NATO and Yugoslavia, which lasted from March 24, 1999 to June 10, 1999.

Chapter 1 covers the period from the abrogation of Kosovo's autonomous status in 1989 through February 1998. In it, we refer to violations of international human rights standards.

Chapter 2 deals with the first phase of organized armed conflict on the ground in Kosovo, involving FRY forces and the KLA, between February 1998 and March 1999. Wrongful behavior by each side is covered by Protocol II of the Geneva Conventions codifying international humanitarian law, applying to "Victims of Non-International Armed Conflicts" and by applicable standards of the customary law of war. Restraints on sovereign governments are minimal in this setting even as embodied in Protocol I, and states remain reluctant to accept their accountability.

Chapter 3 deals with the continuation and escalation of the internal armed conflict and the supervention of international armed conflict when NATO launched its attacks. The four 1949 Geneva Conventions on the Law of War are relevant, as supplemented by Protocol I signed in 1977, applicable for the *Protection of Victims of International Armed Conflicts*.[1] This Report also argues for a higher threshold of protective standards in any future international undertaking justified as "humanitarian intervention," and proposes the negotiation of a "Protocol III" to make this explicit and mandatory. In the interim, the report encourages the UN General Assembly to adopt a Declaration of Principles on Humanitarian Intervention. (See the Chapter on "Law and Humanitarian Intervention" for further discussion).

Chapter 4 covers the period of KFOR/UNMIK rule up to August 2000. The Security Council Resolution 1244 in legal terms resembles the period covered in Chapter 1, although the role of international institutions creates ambiguity in a period of peace building after the occurrence of war.

Early warnings: from the late 1980s onwards, Kosovo exhibited all the signs of a catastrophe waiting to happen.
PHOTO: PAOLO PELLEGRIN

# 1

# THE ORIGINS
# OF THE KOSOVO CRISIS

The origins of ethnic conflict are often claimed to date back hundreds of years. Protagonists refer to great migrations, epic battles, and holy sites. The conflict over Kosovo is no exception. Although it is true that stories and myths surrounding Kosovo were kept alive for centuries in ballads and legends, it was only in the late nineteenth century that they were resurrected as part of the narratives of rival Serb and Albanian national movements. The twentieth-century history of Kosovo has been bloody, with episodes of mass expulsions and atrocities conducted both by Slavs and Albanians. Nevertheless, the latest round of violence cannot be explained merely by reference to this history.

The origins of the current crisis have to be understood in terms of a new wave of nationalism in the 1970s and 1980s, which made use of this history. Although Kosovo was populated mainly by Albanians, it was a symbol of nationalist aspirations for both Albanians and Serbs. The Albanian national movement was launched in Prizren/Prizren in 1878, and the incorporation of Kosovo into Serbia in 1912 was one of the bitter memories conjured up in subsequent years. For the Serbs, Kosovo was viewed as the holy place of the Serb nation, the place where the Serbian Army was defeated by the Turks in the famous Battle of Fushe Kosove/Kosovo Polje of June 1389 and the site of many of Serbia's historic churches. Also, Belgrade nationalist intellectuals exploited discrimination against Serbs living in Kosovo during the 1980s.

It was nationalism that led to the rise of Slobodan Milosevic and the official adoption of an extreme Serbian nationalist agenda. Once the nationalist agenda had become governmental policy, war became a real possibility. Indeed, perhaps the most salient question to ask is why the war was postponed until 1998, and whether the international community could have done anything to make use of this borrowed time to prevent it.

The conflict in Kosovo also has to be understood in the context of the disintegration of Yugoslavia. Kosovo was one of the eight constituent units of Yugoslavia; there were six republics (Serbia, Croatia, Slovenia, Montenegro, Macedonia, and Bosnia-Herzegovina) and two autonomous provinces in Serbia (Vojvodina and Kosovo). The removal of autonomy from Kosovo and Vojvodina in 1989 was a key moment in a series of events leading to demands for independence from other republics, the wars in Slovenia, Croatia, Bosnia-Herzegovina, and eventually Kosovo. The final settlement of the former Yugoslavia has still not been determined.

## THE RISE OF MILOSEVIC

After the Second World War, the new communist leadership of Yugoslavia declared Kosovo to be an autonomous "constituent part" of Serbia. Under Tito's rule, Kosovar Albanians experienced both harsh persecution and glimpses of freedom. The effects of three decades of government-sponsored colonization by Serbs of almost half of Kosovo's arable land were mitigated when Tito returned a third of the land to its Albanian owners after 1945. Also, some of the prewar measures employed to stifle the Albanian language were lifted. The immediate post-war period was, however a period of repression in Yugoslavia and, after Tito broke with Moscow in 1948, Kosovar Albanians experienced particularly harsh repressive measures, since they were suspected of sympathizing with Albanian president and loyal Stalinist, Enver Hoxha.

One of the most public acts of repression during this period was a show trial held in Prizren/Prizren in 1956 at which leading Albanian communists were accused of being part of a network of spies supposedly infiltrating Kosovo from Albania, and were given long prison sentences. During this period Islam was suppressed, and Albanians and Slav Muslims were encouraged to declare themselves Turkish and to emigrate to Turkey. Serbs and Montenegrins dominated the administration, security forces, and industrial employment. Public investment was low, and levels of production and income grew more slowly than in the rest of Yugoslavia.

The situation began to change in the 1960s. In 1966 Aleksandar Rankovic, the person most associated with the Serbianization policy, was dismissed from the Central Committee.[1] In 1968 there were student demonstrations, as in the rest of Europe. A new Europeanized generation was demanding greater freedoms in general, although some of the slogans included "Kosovo-Republic", "We want a University", "Down with colonial policy in Kosovo", and "Long Live Albania". Although the demonstrations were dealt with harshly, a series of measures were taken during this period which greatly improved the situation of Kosovar Albanians. These included the establishment of a university in Prishtina/Pristina, rapprochement with Albania, the use of Albanian professors and Albanian textbooks to teach Albanian language and literature, rapid Albanization of administration and security, and increased public investment.

The culmination of these improvements was the 1974 Yugoslav constitution, under which Kosovo, like Vojvodina, was declared an autonomous province of Serbia. The status of autonomous province was almost the same as the status of republic. As an autonomous province, Kosovo had its own administration, assembly, and judiciary, and it was a member of both Serbian institutions and federal institutions—the collective Presidency and the federal Parliament, in which it had the right of veto. The main difference between an autonomous province and a republic was that provinces did not have the right to secede from the federation and were not considered the bearers of Yugoslav sovereignty, as were the republics. This difference was explained by the fact that the Albanians, like the Hungarians of Vojvodina, were classified as a nationality *(narodnost)* rather than a nation *(narod)*. Supposedly this was because their nation had a homeland elsewhere. Nations had the right to their own republic but nationalities did not. In the national pecking order, there was an even lower category of national minority, which applied mainly to Roma, Vlachs, and Jews.

When students and other demonstrators took to the streets in 1981, arguably the issue was primarily one of status rather than a desire for independence. It was true that the rapid growth of the university and the influence from Tirana had fed nationalist aspirations; in 1978 there had been festivities all over Kosovo to celebrate the centenary of the founding of the League of Prizren—the so-called Albanian "national awakening." But the dominant emotion underlying the demand for republic status seems to have been resentment that nationalities, i.e. Albanian or Hungarian, were somehow inferior to nations i.e. Serbs or Croats. In other words they felt like second-class citizens. Among the demonstrators, there were members of clandestine radical groups, generally declaring themselves Marxist–Leninist, who favored unification with Albania. But interviews and commentaries suggest that these were marginal.[2]

The 1981 demonstrations were brutally crushed. Police and military units and even the newly created territorial defense units were brought to Kosovo from all over Yugoslavia and a state of emergency was declared. Hundreds of people were arrested, tried, and imprisoned.[3] A Communist Party purge was undertaken, euphemistically labeled "differentiation". Thousands of university professors and schoolteachers were sacked. The provision of Albanian professors and Albanian textbooks was stopped.

This was the period of political uncertainty just after Tito's death, which may account for the vehemence of the reaction at a Serbian and federal level to the demonstrations. The period of the late 1960s and 1970s, which are often considered the apogee of the Tito period and to which both Albanians and Serbs were to look back nostalgically, were over. The consequence was a growing polarization between the Albanian and Serbian communities in Kosovo during the 1980s.

It was also a period of austerity for the whole of Yugoslavia, when reforms were introduced as part of a debt-rescheduling package. Kosovo had always been the poorest region of Yugoslavia. Despite high levels of public investment after 1957, and despite receiving the largest share of the Fund for Underdeveloped Regions, the gap between Kosovo and the rest of Yugoslavia grew over the period. In 1952 Kosovo's Gross Material Product (GMP)[4] per capita was 44% that of the Yugoslav average. It had declined to 29% in 1980 and to 22% in 1990. Unemployment had reached 27% in 1980 and was to increase to 40% in 1990.[5] Student numbers also increased rapidly; high student numbers were said to be a kind of "safety valve" for unemployment, but they were also a source of political agitation.

The austerity pressures of the 1980s, directly contributed to the tensions because the way in which resources were distributed became part of the nationalist debate. Typically, bureaucratically regulated economies are characterized by competition for resources rather than competition for markets. Thus, Serbia as well as the other northern republics increasingly resented the monies being taxed to support the development of Kosovo. Long before the rise of Milosevic, Serbian political debate included demands for recentralizing control of economic policy and budgetary resources in Belgrade away from Vojvodina and Kosovo—directly parallel to the reforms for the country as a whole in the IMF program and the policy recommendations of market reformers. The withdrawal of Kosovar autonomy corresponded to pressures for government reform toward a market economy and export-oriented investment program. At the same time, Albanian activists believed that their underdevelopment, unemployment, and poverty was a result of insufficient control over their economic life. Republic status would surely give them greater economic control, with which they would introduce more favorable policies. Their capacity to mobilize support on ethno-national lines, using family structures, rural culture, foreign assets (their workers abroad), and university students facing unemployment, cannot be understood except in the context of a social structure created by administrative arrangements combined with liberalization.

Another critical factor in the development of the conflict has been the demographics of Kosovo. Over the period 1961–81, the proportion of Albanians in the population of Kosovo rose from 67% to 78%. This was due both to the very high birth rate of Albanians and to outmigration of Serbs and Montenegrins. Between 1961 and 1981 the Serb and Montenegrin population declined by around 30,000, and fell by a further 20,000 during the 1980s. Actual emigration by Serbs and Montenegrins between 1961 and 1981, was probably around 100,000, although much higher figures were circulating in Belgrade. In fact, emigration among all communities was high, mainly for economic reasons: Kosovo was stagnating while other parts of Yugoslavia were booming. But among the Serbs, there were additional reasons; many complained of harassment and discrimination. Undoubtedly, the Serbian community was becoming smaller both absolutely and relatively and was losing its privileges. Surveys and interviews indicate that the Serbs who left, who were often of an older generation, were genuinely afraid of physical violence and damage to their property; they also experienced institutional and ideological discrimination. In interviews, they suggested that the physical threats came from younger Albanians, often immigrants from Albania, and not from friends and neighbors.[6] At the same time, some of the wilder claims that were circulating in Belgrade, especially about rape and murder, are not substantiated by official figures. Crime rates including rates of rape were considerably lower in Kosovo than in the rest of the Yugoslavia. Likewise, the Serb nationalist argument that the Albanian birth rate was politically motivated is belied by the fact that the birth rate of Albanians in towns was the same as the birth rate of the rest of the urban population—it was only in the countryside, where there was poverty and low levels of education, that the birth rate was so high, (see Table 1).

From the mid-1980s, Serb intellectuals began openly to publish nationalistic tracts and to discuss the "genocide" of Serbs in Kosovo. By 1983, the funeral of Serb hard-liner Rankovic had already turned into a nationalist event. Kosovar Serbs and Montenegrins began to make public protestations in the mid-1980s and were supported by Belgrade intellectuals. These sentiments were further inflamed by the Martinovic case, in which a 56-year-old Kosovar Serb, Djordje Martinovic, claimed to have been attacked by two Albanians who forced a bottle into his rectum.[7]

In January 1986, 216 prominent Serbian intellectuals, including Dobrica Cosic, who had been expelled from the Central Com-

| | Total population | Serb population | Share of Serb population (%) |
|---|---|---|---|
| 1948 | 728,436 | 171,911 | 23.6 |
| 1953 | 804,530 | 189,869 | 23.6 |
| 1961 | 966,026 | 227,016 | 23.5 |
| 1971 | 1,247,344 | 228,264 | 18.3 |
| 1981 | 1,585,333 | 209,498 | 13.2 |
| 1991 | 1,961,515 | 194,190 | 9.9 |

Source: Marina Blagojevic, "Kosovo In/visible Civil War" in Thano Veremis and Evangelos Kofos, Kosovo: *Avoiding Another Balkan War,* ELIAMEP, University of Athens, 1998.

Table 1: Share of Serb Population in Total Population of Kosovo

mittee in 1968 for favoring the Rankovic policy towards Kosovo, presented a petition to the Serb and Yugoslav Assemblies. They declared that: "The case of Djordje Martinovic has come to symbolize the predicament of all Serbs in Kosovo." Later, in the same year, a memorandum published by the Serbian Academy of Arts and Sciences sent shock waves through Yugoslavia. The memorandum talked about the "physical, political, legal and cultural genocide" of Serbs in Kosovo and argued that the "remnants of the Serb nation (...) faced with a physical, moral and psychological reign of terror (...) seem to be preparing for their final exodus." Likewise, the memorandum suggested that the position of the Serbs in Croatia was "jeopardized" and that if "solutions are not found, the consequences might well be disastrous, not only for Croatia but for the whole of Yugoslavia."[8] It was also claimed that the Martinovic case was "reminiscent of the darkest days of the Turkish practice of impalement."[9]

These nationalist ideas were criticized by the Yugoslav authorities, especially the President of the Serbian Socialist League, Ivan Stambolic, but nothing like the harsh measures imposed on Albanian nationalists was applied. A turning point was the visit of Slobodan Milosevic, then deputy-president of the Serbian Party, to Kosovo on 24 April 1987. Milosevic arrived at the meeting place in Fushe Kosove/Kosovo Polje in the middle of a scuffle between Serbs and the police. He then uttered the famous words: "No one should dare to beat you," and proceeded to give a speech about the sacred rights of Serbs. He became a national hero overnight. With the support of Radio TV Belgrade, and with mass rallies throughout the country known as "Meetings of Truth", he was able to mobilize popular feelings and to take control of the party leadership. First he displaced his old friend and patron Stambolic. Then he forced the resignation of the party leaders in Vojvodina and Montenegro, and finally he removed the two main party leaders in Kosovo. An incident in 1987, that helped his cause was the case of an Albanian army recruit who went berserk and shot four other recruits (two Bosniak, one Croat, and one Serb) and then committed suicide. The case was considered a deliberate attack on Yugoslavia, and eight Albanians were accused of planning the attack. The incident helped to bring the JNA, the Yugoslav Army, into the ambit of Milosevic.

At a rally in Belgrade in November 1988, attended by 350,000 people, Milosevic declared: "Every nation has a love, which eternally warms its heart. For Serbia, it is Kosovo."[10] And in June 1989, on the 600th anniversary of the Battle of Kosovo, Milosevic declared to 1 million people: "Six centuries later, again, we are in battles and quarrels. They are not armed battles although such things cannot be excluded."[11] There followed a series of steps, including in 1989 the Serbian assembly taking more direct control over Kosovo's security, judiciary, finance, and social planning,[12] which led finally in July 1990 to the revoking of the autonomy of Kosovo. As early as 1989 and early 1990, the Serbian government had already passed a series of decrees aimed at changing the ethnic composition of Kosovo: these included restrictions on the sale of property to Albanians, incentives for Serbs and Montenegrins to return, family planning for Albanians, and encouragement to Albanians to seek work elsewhere in Yugoslavia. In July the Kosovo Assembly was dissolved, despite provisions in the 1974 Constitution requiring Assembly consent for its own dissolution. Arguably, this act signaled the end of the 1974 Constitution, and, according to some, the dissolution of Yugoslavia.

The revocation of Kosovo's autonomy spawned an increase in human rights abuses and discriminatory government policies designed to Serbianize the province.[13] These included discriminatory language policies: the closure of Albanian language newspapers, radio, and television; the closure of the Albanian Institute; and the change of street names from Albanian to Serbian.[14] In particular, the introduction of a new Serbian curriculum for universities and schools:

> resulted in the closing down of the Educational Administration of Kosovo
> (...) and of other institutions and facilities in the field of education (...)
> [M]ore than 18,000 teachers and other staff of Albanian-language class-
> room facilities (...) were summarily dismissed when they rejected the text-
> books of the uniform curricula.[15]

Thousands of Albanians were dismissed from public employment; according to the independent Kosovar Albanian Association of Trades Unions, 115,000 people out of a total 170,000
lost their jobs. Attempts were also made to colonize the province.
Special privileges were granted to Serbs who resettled or returned
to Kosovo, including loans and free plots of land.[16] Legislation
was also passed which made it illegal for Kosovar Albanians to
buy or lease property from Serbs, and refugees from Croatia were
sent reluctantly to Kosovo. Above all, there were widespread
human rights abuses—arbitrary arrest, torture, detention without trial. Albanians were accused of "verbal crimes" and taken to
police stations for "informative talks." The scale of these abuses
has been documented by Amnesty International, Human Rights
Watch and the Council for the Defense of Human Rights in
Kosovo.[17] It is said that at least one member of every Albanian
family had been called to a police station, or had spent some time
in jail, or was waiting for a trial.

## THE ALBANIAN RESISTANCE

Many commentators, especially among the Kosovar Albanians,
expected a war in Yugoslavia to begin in Kosovo. Many Kosovar
Albanians anticipated ethnic cleansing in the context of violent
conflict. Indeed, there were acts of apparent provocation in
Kosovo, including random shootings of villagers in central Kosovo and the alleged poisoning of schoolchildren in March and
April 1990.[18]

Prior to 1990, the majority of Albanians supported the Yugoslav framework. Their demands were primarily about constitu-

tional rights. In November 1988, the miners of Trepce/Trepca marched 55 kilometers from Mitrovice/Kosovska Mitrovica to Prishtina/Pristina in the freezing cold, in protest at the removal of the party leaders. In Prishtina/Pristina they were joined by factory workers and students. They carried Yugoslav and Albanian flags, as well as pictures of Tito, and hailed the 1974 constitution. They shouted Titoist slogans like "Brotherhood and Unity" and even (to show they were not anti-Serb) "Long Live the Serbian people!" And in February 1989, the miners of Trepce/Trepca went on hunger strike to protest the imposition of provincial officials. These demonstrations were probably the last Titoist demonstrations in Yugoslavia. The Slovene President Kucan commended the Albanian miners for trying to save Yugoslavia.

Among Kosovar Albanians, there was also a much smaller Enverist political strand consisting of small underground Marxist-Leninist groups. The best known person was Adem Demaqi, who founded the Revolutionary Movement for Albanian Unity during the 1960s; he was arrested in 1964 and spent many years in prison.

One reason why a war did not begin in Kosovo was developments elsewhere in Yugoslavia, especially in Slovenia and Croatia; indeed, up to 1995 Milosevic was preoccupied with the wars in Croatia and Bosnia. The other reason was the adoption of a strategy of non-violence — something that was quite contradictory to Kosovar Albanian traditions. According to Rugova, the dominant figure in the Albanian movement: "The Serbs only wait for a pretext to attack the Albanian population and wipe it out. We believe that it is better to do nothing and stay alive than be massacred."[19]

In 1990 the various strands of Albanian political movements — former officials and former revolutionaries —came together to form a mass movement which was to operate a self-organized parallel system in Kosovo. On July 2, 1990, three days before the Kosovo Assembly was dissolved, 114 of the 123 Albanian delegates in the Kosovo Assembly met on the steps of the Assembly building, which had been locked. There were enough of them to constitute a quorum and they issued a declaration giving the Albanians the status of a nation entitled to their own republic. On September 7 they met again at Kacanik/Kacanik and agreed on the proclamation of a constitutional law for a "Republic of Kosovo," including provisions for a new assembly and elected presidency. After the Slovene and Croatian declarations of independence in June 1991, the demand for a republic was changed to a demand for independence. In September 1991, a self-organized referendum on independence took place. It is said that 87% of voters took part, including some minorities, and the vote was 99% in favor. And in May 1992 Kosovo-wide elections were held, using private homes as polling stations, for a new republican government and assembly.

The non-violent character of the movement was not only tactical; it was also principled. First of all, the ideas of the democratic opposition in Eastern Europe had a profound influence in intellectual circles. The Association of Albanian Writers, whose president was Dr Ibrahim Rugova, the Association of Philosophers and Sociologists, and the Prishtina/Pristina branch of the Union for a Yugoslav Democratic Initiative, whose representative was Veton Surroi, held many public meetings in 1988 and 1989 and organized a petition "For Democracy Against Violence" which collected 400,000 signatures. The idea of a parallel system or a "shadow" government was deeply influenced by the notions of autonomy and self-organization developed among Central European intellectuals, and especially Polish Solidarity.

Secondly there was a spontaneous reaction among ordinary Albanians who wanted to show that they were different from the "primitive and uncivilized" stereotype portrayed by Serbs. At the very height of the tension in the early 1990s, the Kosovar Albanians decided to abolish the traditional practice of blood feud. Some 2000 families were reconciled, and some 20,000 people were able to move outside their homes. A "Council of Reconciliation" was established which tracked down Albanian families (even those living abroad) and brought them together for a mass reconciliation; this event then spawned the Pan-National Movement for the Reconciliation of Blood Vendettas.[20] A related factor was the increasing self-identification of Kosovar Albanians as European. Around a third of the Albanian population had spent some time abroad, mostly in Western Europe. Many houses had and have satellite dishes, enabling them not only to receive the Diaspora Albanian language broadcasts from Geneva but also to watch MTV, Eurosport, etc. As travel to Albania became easier and the people became aware of the depressing reality of life in Albania, aspirations to be European came to replace fantasies of returning to Albania. Nevertheless, it should not be forgotten that it was the Kosovar Albanians in the Diaspora who became the most radicalized part of the Kosovar Albanian community and were to create the KLA.

The dominant political organization was the League for a Democratic Kosovo (LDK). It spread rapidly in 1990 and 1991 and claimed 700,000 members by the spring of 1991. The LDK drew on village organizations and the traditional clan structure of Kosovar Albanian society. It was also able to fill the void left by the collapse of the previous Albanian political movement, the Socialist Alliance. In the May 1992 elections, the LDK won 96 of the 100 single constituency seats. (Of the other 4 seats, 2 were won by independents who were members of LDK, 1 by the SDA, the Bosniak party, and 1 by the Turkish Peoples Party.) A further 42 seats were distributed by proportional representation, giving the Turkish party 12 seats, the Christian Democrats 7 seats, the Social Democrats 1 seat and the SDA 3 seats; 13 seats reserved for Serbs and Montenegrins were left empty.

The LDK, under the leadership of Rugova, set about developing a historically unique parallel state apparatus. A government was established on October 19, 1991; initially it was based in

Ljublijana, but it moved to Bonn in 1992. The Prime Minister was Bujor Bukoshi. "Voluntary" taxes were levied on all Kosovar Albanians. Suggested guidelines were: for employed individuals, 5%, for businesses, between 8% and 10%, and for landowners, according to the productivity of their land; workers in the Diaspora were expected to contribute 3% of their income. Computerized databases were maintained that tracked the "tax" records of individual families; non-compliance was low.[21] As for expenditure, 90% of the funds were spent on the parallel education system and the remainder went on sports, some cultural activities, the LDK administration and some health care. In 1993, the parallel education system employed 20,000 teachers, lecturers, professors and administrative staff; it included 5291 pre-school pupils, 312,000 elementary school pupils, 65 secondary schools with 56,920 pupils, two special schools for disabled children, 20 faculties and colleges with about 12,000 students, and several other educational establishments such as the Institute for Publishing Textbooks. The elementary schools were allowed to use their own buildings but received no finance; the other 204 facilities, such as homes and garages, were donated by Kosovar Albanians.

Other organizations close to the LDK made important contributions. The Mother Theresa Society was established in 1990 and provided humanitarian assistance and health care for Albanians afraid to use the Serb-dominated facilities, especially after the alleged mass poisoning. (As a result, many children did not receive vaccinations and the incidence of diseases such as polio, tetanus, and tuberculosis increased.) The Council for the Defense of Human Rights set up a monitoring system throughout the province using local people to provide detailed information on human rights abuses. Another significant organization was the Association of Independent Trades Unions. The "Councils for Reconciliation" provided a sort of parallel justice system, and there were also organizations for culture and sport. A number of non-governmental organizations (NGOs) dealing with women and young people were also established during this period. Indeed, like the Councils of Reconciliation, these NGOs reflected an interest, even at village level, in breaking with tradition and planting "the seeds of a different kind of state."[22] A Group for Women's Studies was established with support from the Belgrade Women's Group and a magazine called Kosovaria was started. Among the youth groups, the best known was the Post-Pessimist Club.

The only Albanian magazine that was permitted was the farmers' magazine *Bujko*. This became the mouthpiece of the LDK. Later, other independent media were founded with support from the Open Society Foundation, including *Zeri, Koha Ditore,* and *Forum* (the paper founded by Adem Demaqi) and some women's and youth magazines.

Alongside the development of the parallel state apparatus went the growth of the informal economy. Many of the Albanians who lost their jobs decided to start private businesses. Maliqi describes how, in just a few weeks, "fired Albanian workers, ex-civil servants and former policemen registered several hundred taxis, vans, lorries and minibuses (twice as many began operating without registration) taking over city and intercity lines. Their initiative made transport so cheap and efficient that the main state companies faced bankruptcy and after six months, Belgrade banned alternative transport and taxis."[23] Other initiatives included tourist agencies, coffee bars, and other small enterprises. As of 1993, the number of registered private enterprises was 27% of the total (up from 20% in 1990) and the informal economy was estimated to account for 70% of the total economy of Kosovo.[24]

During this period, some 400,000 Albanians are estimated to have emigrated from Kosovo to Western Europe, many to avoid conscription into the Yugoslav army. Skills acquired in Western Europe and remittances contributed to the thriving shadow economy. Many also emigrated to the United States. Nevertheless, poverty was still very widespread, as evidenced by the growing numbers dependent on the Mother Theresa Society. Moreover, the burden of double taxation by the LDK and the Serb authorities weighed heavily on many families.

The main goal of the LDK was independence for Kosovo. The strategy for achieving this goal was to influence the international community and to deny the legitimacy of Belgrade institutions, both through the parallel system and through boycotting elections — by refusing, as one person put it, "to dignify Milosevic with my vote."[25] Rugova pressed instead for the establishment of a temporary protectorate under UN auspices, which could oversee the transition to independence.

The LDK has been criticized for its combination of excessively passive tactics and maximalist political demands (nothing less than independence), and for its refusal to seek accommodation with Belgrade. Rugova, though extremely popular throughout Kosovo, has been paradoxically characterized as both an autocratic and an ineffectual leader. The boycott of the elections was also criticized by some as abdicating responsibility for opposition within Serbia while focusing all attention, somewhat ineffectively, on the international community.

There was, for example, a brief window of opportunity both for more direct political action by the LDK, and for the international community actively to intervene to shape a political compromise in Kosovo, when Milan Panic became prime minister of Serbia in July 1992. Panic met Rugova in London in August and promised "restoration of self-rule for the Kosovar Albanians, the re-admittance of Albanian students to Pristina University, the reinstatement of Albanian professors, freedom for the Albanian press, and free elections."[26] In October, Panic visited Kosovo and tried to make a deal with Rugova in exchange for support in the presidential elections. But his efforts failed, and in the elections of December 1992 he was defeated by Milosevic— had the Albanians voted, they might have tipped the balance. According to Fehmi Agami, vice president of LDK and perhaps the most respected intellectual among the Kosovar Albanians, who was killed during the 1999 war;

> Frankly, it is better [for us] to continue with Milosevic. Milosevic was very successful in destroying Yugoslavia and, in the same way, if he continues, he will destroy Serbia (...) [Panic] is offering enlightened hegemony (...) He thinks we will accept him because he is an opponent of Milosevic. It is not enough. He may offer us to take part in the elections but without offering anything concrete. We are against Milosevic but we also know he must fall, with or without Panic.[27]

And if the Kosovar Albanians believed that they were more likely to achieve their final goals with Milosevic in power, it seems as though Milosevic also preferred the status quo—the repressive toleration of the non-violent movement. The end result was what has been called "separate worlds" — a system of apartheid in which there was almost no communication between the two sides.[28] As a Kosovar Serb told Tim Judah,

> There are two parallel systems here. Each one has organized their own education. They control the private sector, the Serbs the public sector. There is even a double system of taxation. They have their own informal taxes. Our children don't play together any more (...) [And in the evening when people stroll out in Pristina] they have one side of the main road and we have the other.[29]

But it was, of course, an unequal parallelism. One of the factors that the Kosovar Albanians perhaps did not take into account was the toll the system took on everyday life and the difficulty of sustaining a shadow state over many years. The conflict in Kosovo, wrote Maliqi in 1996, "has turned into a kind of intense war of nerves, in which one side stops at nothing, committing the most brutal violations of human rights and civil liberties, completely ignoring the protests of the international organizations which for a while kept monitoring teams in Kosovo, while the other side bottles up its humiliation, despair, fury, rage and hatred —but for how long before it explodes?"[30]

## THE DESCENT INTO WAR

From the mid-1990s, the situation began to deteriorate. At the very moment when many ordinary Kosovar Albanians were losing patience with the strategy of passive resistance and were becoming exhausted from the struggle to sustain the parallel system under such difficult conditions, the Dayton Agreement over Bosnia was signed in which no mention was made of Kosovo. For many Kosovar Albanians, it seemed as though the strategy had failed. The conclusions to be drawn from Dayton, to quote Veton Surroi, were that "ethnic territories have legitimacy" and that "international attention can only be obtained by war."[31] Several leading Kosovar intellectuals, such as Adem Demaqi and Professor Rexhap Qosja, who was close to the politicians in Tirana, began to criticize Rugova for excessive passivity. Qosja talked about the need for active non-violent resistance and Demaqi called for civil disobedience.

A beacon of hope was the agreement on education reached in 1996 by representatives of the LDK and the Belgrade Ministry of Education, mediated by the Italian catholic organization Communita di Sant'Egidio. It was agreed that Albanians could return to the school and university buildings and that the pre-1990 curriculum would be used. There was no agreement, however, about paying teachers and professors. The significance of the agreement lay in the fact that Albanian negotiators had been implicitly recognized as legitimate representatives. This recognition suggested the possibility of negotiation as a feasible, albeit uncertain, path toward normalizing the situation in Kosovo.

A number of proposals were circulating among intellectuals both in Belgrade and Prishtina/Pristina for a compromise solution to the Kosovo question during 1996–7 and, it is in this context that the education agreement should be understood. The best known proposal was from the President of the Academy of Sciences, Aleksandr Despic, who proposed a partition and peaceful secession of Kosovo. He proposed that talks begin "with those who are insisting on secession of Kosovo about a peaceful and civilized separation and demarcation."[32] Other proposals included the "three republic" proposal; that Kosovo should be given equal status to Montenegro. The Kosovar Albanians in this period were being urged by President Berisha in Tirana to be more conciliatory and to open up talks with Belgrade. Had the international community been more attentive in these years, it could have put pressure on Milosevic to negotiate seriously with the LDK. If Western powers had treated the LDK with greater respect, they — like Berisha—also could have encouraged this nascent discussion of political options involving autonomy short of independence.

The agreement on education, however, was never implemented. Commentators suggested that both sides had an interest in the status quo because they feared a compromise solution. The continued status quo "allows both sides to harbor illusions of their own supremacy; Serbs in terms of police/military control, and Albanians in terms of running of society."[33] Despite Rugova's disapproval, students began to protest against the failure to implement the agreement in September 1997, just as the school year was about to begin. The demonstrators were treated harshly, and even today some student leaders are held in Serbian jails.

It was during this period that the KLA first made its appearance. The KLA grew out of a Marxist–Leninist–Enverist party formed in the Diaspora in the early 1980s called the LPK (Levizja Popullare e Kosoves). In 1992 and 1993, the LPK played a leading role in setting up a guerrilla group in secret meetings in Prishtina/Pristina and Tetovo (Macedonia). The first violent action taken was the killing of a Serb policeman in 1995. But it was not until 1996 that an organization based in Switzerland and calling itself the KLA claimed responsibility for these attacks. At the time most Albanians had not heard of the KLA, and many believed that the attacks were artificial provocations by the authorities.

The KLA is alleged to have received funding from illicit drug trade; in addition, many Kosovars in the Diaspora switched their support from the LDK to a fund called "Homeland Calling" set up by the KLA. The dominant figures in the KLA seem to have been a new generation of people, like Thaci (now prime minister of the provisional government established by the KLA), who had been students in the late 1980s and had subsequently worked or studied abroad. (Thaci, for example, holds a Masters Degree in International Relations from the University of Zurich.) The strategy of the KLA also seems to have been directed at the international community. Woefully unprepared for war, the KLA seems instead to have had the deliberate strategy of provoking an international intervention.

Indeed, until late 1997, active armed resistance groups in Kosovo were very small and without permanent bases in the province. They had few arms and do not seem to have had any clear leadership structure. Individual operations consisted of hit-and-run terrorist attacks on Serbian police outposts and supposed Albanian "collaborators". These operations were commanded and planned by KLA members coming from abroad with only a few days of preparation with local fighters. The collapse of the Albanian state system and institutions in 1997 changed the situation dramatically. Albanian Army and Interior Ministry warehouses and depots were looted and arms and ammunition were made available to the KLA. Because of the collapse of the security system and the ensuing lawlessness in Albania, it was possible, for the first time, to organize training facilities in northern Albania near the borders with Kosovo. This proved to be the most important precondition for creating permanent recruitment and training facilities, for organizing supply routes into Kosovo, and for the first efforts to coordinate different regional and even local fighting groups. As elsewhere in post-Yugoslav wars, organized crime played an important role in organizing and financing the conflict. The combination of large-scale Albanian political and economic emigration from Kosovo, the collapse of the Albanian state, and the criminal nature of Serbian police and para-military oppression, all contributed to the self-proclaimed "Robin Hood" image of Albanian organized crime.

With the rise of the KLA, the already pervasive police harassment increased. The Serbian government proclaimed the KLA a terrorist organization, thereby justifying searches, detentions, and political trials. The Humanitarian Law Center (HLC) documented numerous cases involving police mistreatment of ethnic Albanians, including arbitrary arrest, detention, physical abuse, illegal searches, and extra-judicial killing. In 1997 the HLC investigated the death of three ethnic Albanians who had been in police custody in Kosovo, concluding that police officers were responsible for physical abuse and extra-judicial killing.[34] Other human rights organizations, including the Council for the Defense of Human Rights and Freedoms, Amnesty International, Human Rights Watch, and the International Helsinki Federation for Human Rights, corroborate the prevalence of extensive beatings, including the use of electric shocks.[35] Albanians charged with membership in the KLA reported the use of torture to extract false confessions. In addition, the defense counsel for the accused reported that they were not given free access to their clients or to necessary information.[36] This police behavior was targeted not only at members of the KLA, but also at members of the LDK political party, activists, and other civilians.

If the status quo was being challenged on the Albanian side, it is also useful to speculate about the ways in which it was being challenged in Belgrade. During 1996-7, Milosevic's position was challenged both by the pro-democracy opposition and by the extreme right. In the municipal elections of November 1996, the opposition coalition Zajedno won the mayoral elections in 15 major towns and gained control of the Belgrade Assembly. The ruling elite tried to quash the election results, and this led to major demonstrations in Belgrade and other cities. In February 1997 the authorities finally conceded. At the same time, the ruling party in Montenegro split and a new government committed to democratization came to power. The mobilization of students and the spread of an independent radio network seemed to offer genuine hope for moves towards democratization including a more conciliatory approach towards Kosovo. Indeed, the students in Belgrade were making contact with the students in Prishtina/Pristina; the Post-Pessimists' club for example, developed branches throughout Yugoslavia.

Milosevic's party also lost votes in the Serbian Parliamentary elections of September 1997, while the Serbian Radical Party of Vojislav Seselj made important gains. Seselj, whose para-military group known as the "*Chetniks*" had been responsible for some of the most terrible atrocities in Bosnia, had always held an extreme position on Kosovo. Seselj's political program since 1991 had included the expulsion "without delay" of what were claimed to be 360,000 postwar immigrants to Kosovo from Albania "and their descendants". He proposed clearing a belt "20 to 30 km as the crow flies along the Albanian border" of Kosovars "as it has transpired that Albania is a state lastingly hostile to Serbia." He also demanded that no parliamentary elections be held in Kosovo "until the ethnic structure of the population is restored to the ratio which existed on 6 April 1941." [37] In February 1998 a new governing coalition for Serbia was formed which included the Radical Party, and Seselj himself became deputy prime minister.

Commentators at the time suggested that the victory of Seselj "does not imply wide support for Mr Seselj's "Greater Serbia" nationalism but rather reflects the strength of feeling against the Milosevic regime among an embittered and outcast section of the population, including hundreds of thousands of refugees and their families who are among the biggest losers of the turmoil in former Yugoslavia during the past decade." [38] Nevertheless, the success of Seselj and his inclusion in the government should have set alarm bells ringing in international circles. Moreover, it can be argued that that an increased atmosphere of tension was the method through which Milosevic had always neutralized his opposition, both progressive and extreme. Moreover, the power of both Milosevic and Seselj depends on criminalized networks that benefit from violence and related phenomena such as sanction breaking. Thus, at that time, there were extremist elements in the government and society that were resistant to moves towards compromise and had a vested interest (both political and economic) in an escalation of violence to sustain their positions.

The denouement came on February 28 1998, when the Serbs decided to arrest Adem Jashari, a local strongman in Prekazi/Prekaze, who had joined the KLA. Within a week, his extended family of 58 people was killed. At this point, village militias all over Kosovo sprang up to defend their villages. Many of them were linked to the parallel structures, but they called themselves the KLA, even though a number still considered Rugova to be their President.

This was the beginning of the war.

## THE ROLE OF THE INTERNATIONAL COMMUNITY

The first–and last–attempt to find a comprehensive negotiated settlement to the dissolution of Yugoslavia was the Brioni agreement, brokered by the EU in July 1991, and Lord Carrington's plan submitted in October of that year. The destruction of the town of Vukovar, Croatia, by the Yugoslav army in November 1991 and later the recognition of Croatia and Slovenia's independence put an end to such attempts to find a global approach to the Yugoslav crisis. From then on, separate and disjointed solutions were posed for each successive crisis.

Kosovo was not a priority for the international community before 1998. The province's troubles almost appear to have been an inconvenience, adding further complications to negotiations about the wars in Slovenia, Croatia, and Bosnia. Kosovo seems to have been regarded as secondary to these conflicts in terms of both urgency and status. Had the international community shown greater interest and commitment in these years preceding the rise of the KLA, the war in Kosovo might conceivably have been avoided. In this light, the escalation of armed violence in 1998–9 signals a dismal failure of "early warning" lessons.

The one strong statement that was made in official circles during this period was President Bush's Christmas warning. On December 24 1992, the US Ambassador to Belgrade read the following message to Milosevic: "In the event of conflict in Kosovo caused by Serbian action, the US will be prepared to employ military force against Serbians in Kosovo and Serbia proper."[39] The message was subsequently reiterated by Madeline Albright in the UN Security Council in August 1993.[40]

The quantitatively low level of deadly violence in Kosovo during the early 1990s was by and large misinterpreted by the international community. Milosevic had allowed the LDK to establish its parallel network, cracking down only sporadically to prevent direct challenges to Belgrade's authority, such as an attempt to set up a parallel police force. The LDK's passive strategy served Milosevic's purpose for apparently convergent reasons, since he seemed eager to avoid another conflictual front during the Bosnian hostilities. The international community, rather than recognize the temporary and still-volatile nature of this apparent truce, and the possibility for engagement offered by the LDK, instead responded complacently, pushing Kosovo further and further into the background.

None of the main international actors, including the International Conference on Former Yugoslavia (ICFY), the European Union (EU), the Organization of Security and Co-operation in Europe (OSCE) and the United Nations (UN), paid Kosovo more than sporadic attention. The little attention that was directed toward Kosovo by intergovernmental organizations seems to have been concentrated in the 1992–3 period when governments feared that war in Bosnia-Herzegovina would spill over into Kosovo.

The tone was set by the European Union (EU, then Community) Conference on Yugoslavia, chaired by Lord Carrington, which took place in the Hague in 1991. This conference went so far as to define Kosovo as an "internal" problem for Yugoslavia, thus discouraging international interest and involvement. At its second meeting in London in August 1992, Carrington put out very mixed signals, almost but not quite inviting Rugova to attend.[41]

Meanwhile, Rugova and other LDK leaders were managing to get increased attention from the international NGO community, and even arranged several high-level diplomatic meetings with foreign governments. The international message given to Rugova was nearly unanimous praise for his movement, especially for its non-violent character, but this praise was never translated into concrete support.

The EC Conference became the International Conference on Former Yugoslavia (ICFY) under the joint chairmanship of David Owen and Cyrus Vance. Under the auspices of ICFY, a Working Group on Ethnic and National Communities and Minorities was established in August 1992, chaired by Geert Ahrens, and this Working Group in turn established a Special Group on Kosovo. The Special Group concluded that it was important to normalize the situation in Kosovo and that the Group should focus on negotiations about education. The Group tried to mediate, and a Common Statement by the Kosovar Albanians and the federal government was agreed in October 1992. However the dialogue collapsed after the rector of the parallel university, Ejup Statovici, was arrested in late 1992. The Working Group continued in existence and was later transferred to the Dayton Peace Implementation Council and subsequently the Contact Group,[42] but very little was achieved.

The low priority of the Kosovo issue was also reflected in the EU's deliberations about the recognition of Slovenia and Croatia in the autumn of 1991. European governments accepted the distinction between republics and provinces or between nations and nationalities enshrined in the Yugoslav constitution. Rugova had appealed to the EU for recognition of independence in December 1991 when the EU was discussing the issue of recognition of Slovenia and Croatia. The Badinter Commission, which reported in early 1992, proposed that republics of Yugoslavia should have the right to become independent provided certain preconditions were met. Autonomous provinces were not offered the same option. In November 1993 the European Union endorsed a proposal for the re-establishment of autonomy for Kosovo in its European Action Program on Yugoslavia. But leading politicians, including David Owen, the co-chair of ICFY, continued to insist on the integrity of Yugoslavia. The fear was, of course, a never-ending process of political fragmentation sometimes referred to as Balkanization. There is a real question to be asked about whether Badinter itself committed the original sin, permitting the disintegration of Yugoslavia, or whether, having decided to accept the breakup into constituent units, it was right to treat provinces differently from republics.

The Helsinki Summit of the newly established OSCE in July 1992 adopted a Declaration on the Yugoslav Crisis, calling for "immediate preventative action" and urging "the authorities in Belgrade to refrain from further repression and to engage in serious dialogue with representatives from Kosovo in the presence of a third party."[43] In August 1992 it was decided to establish Missions of Long Duration to Kosovo and Vojvodina. These Missions did try to open a dialogue on the ground, especially concerning education. However, in 1993 Milosevic refused the renewal of visas for members of the Missions and they had to leave the country on July 28. This may have been a response to the suspension of Yugoslav membership in the OSCE. Human rights violations were reported to be lower when the Missions were present; and they rose immediately after the withdrawal of the Missions.

The UN Special Rapporteurs for Human Rights, Tadeusz

Maziowiecki and subsequently Elizabeth Rehn, both reported on the situation in Kosovo. Mazowiecki tried unsuccessfully to establish an office in Kosovo. Various resolutions were passed by the UN General Assembly, and in July 1993 the UN Security Council passed a resolution calling for the return of the OSCE Mission. Other UN efforts included attempts by UNESCO to mediate an education agreement and, in 1996, a joint initiative by UNICEF and WHO to carry out a polio vaccination program together with both the government and the parallel system.

Most of these efforts were concentrated in the years 1992–93. Clearly, the intransigence of the Belgrade regime hampered any international attempts to deal with Kosovo. However, little was done to counter this intransigence up to late 1997. On the contrary, in the desperation to halt the war in Bosnia-Herzegovina, Kosovo was deliberately sidelined. Kosovo was not included in the Dayton negotiations because Tudjman and Izetbegovic were not interested in Kosovo and Milosevic would have refused to consider it. Milosevic was viewed as a key player, and the international community did not want to jeopardize the chances of reaching agreement. The result of this caution, however, was indirectly to legitimate Milosevic's role in Kosovo, and to send a clear signal to both Milosevic and the Kosovar Albanians that Kosovo was definitely *off* the current international agenda.

This message had three serious conflict-escalating effects: it gave the FRY a free hand in Kosovo; it demoralized and weakened the non-violent movement in Kosovo, which felt betrayed by the international community and began to doubt the effectiveness of its own tactics; and it led directly to a decisive surge of support among Kosovars for the path of violent resistance as the only politically realistic path to independence.

After Dayton, the EU formally recognized the Federal Republic of Yugoslavia (FRY) as including Kosovo, and Germany even repatriated 130,000 Kosovar Albanians. According to Bukoshi, "It was a shock. We weren't expecting it and it was a fatal mistake."[44]

Attempts were made to soften the blow of Dayton. The United States, while recognizing the FRY, insisted on maintaining the outer wall of sanctions against the FRY because of the situation in Kosovo. Also in 1996, a US Information Service (USIS) office was established and this had considerable symbolic value. In fact, the USIS presence was in part a result of pressure brought to bear at Dayton. Nevertheless, the Dayton process did aggravate the Kosovo problem. Although it was highly unlikely that Dayton would have been able to devise a solution for the Kosovo crisis, it would have been helpful if the process had at least included a discussion of the situation in Kosovo. For example, despite Milosevic's supposedly constructive role in negotiations around Bosnia, the earlier "hands off Kosovo" message of President Bush could have been reiterated in some fashion; or Dayton could have been used as a forum to encourage FRY acceptance of an NGO presence in Kosovo — and even in the rest of Serbia.

Indeed, the only significant actors during the period 1993-7 were NGOs. Human Rights Watch, Mercy Corps, and Amnesty International, as well as human rights groups in Kosovo and in Belgrade such as the Humanitarian Law Foundation and the Yugoslav Red Cross, were monitoring human rights violations.[45] A number of other organizations were making statements about Kosovo and calling for a UN protectorate or trusteeship, for example the United Nations Peoples Organization, the Transnational Foundation in Sweden, the Helsinki Citizens Assembly, and the Minnesota Advocates for Human Rights. But undoubtedly, the two most important NGOs were the Communita di Sant'Egidio, which negotiated the education agreement in 1996, and the Open Society Foundation of Belgrade (OSF), which played a unique role in supporting the parallel system and fostering dialogue among Albanians and Serbs. The OSF began its work at the end of 1992 with children's programs. The first English classes were established for both Albanian and Serbian children, and in 1994 an Open Club was established in Prishtina/

Pristina for both Albanian and Serbian young people (though they tended to come in separate groups). The OSF also supported the Mother Teresa Society, women and youth NGOs, the independent media, and various cultural activities — the first art gallery was opened in Prishtina/Pristina in the mid-1990s and an exhibition of Albanian painters was held in Belgrade in June 1997. Particularly successful was the educational enrichment program, which set up computer centers all over Kosovo and, in the first two years, attracted more than 15,000 participants.

The problem for OSF was that other donors were almost totally absent, and that it was almost impossible to get official international support and backing for these activities, which could have greatly increased their effectiveness. Norwegian Peoples Aid supported the Post-Pessimists, and the Swiss Disaster Relief and the American International Rescue Committee assisted in the physical rebuilding of schools, but these were exceptions rather than the rule. The parallel system was, in practice, rather limited and could not be sustained in the long run as an alternative to a functioning public sector. The difficulties of everyday life and the frustration, especially of young people denied a formal education, were bound to escalate tension. When, for example, in late 1997 the authorities finally agreed to open up the technical faculty of the university to Albanian students, it was discovered that everything had been packed up and taken away; the faculty was nothing but an empty building, and there were no donors available to invest in the necessary equipment.

The OSF lobbied governments and other donors but, according to the OSF Director Sonja Licht, it was like "kicking the Chinese Wall." In November 1997 a State Department official told her that the US government "cannot support civil society because it would lead to secession." She replied that "if civil society is not supported, then secession will be achieved through terrorism."

# CONCLUSION

From the 1980s onwards, Kosovo exhibited all the signs of a cata-strophe waiting to happen. Here was an authoritarian society ex-posed to pressures for liberalization and democratization. Un-employment was very high, especially among young, educated people and criminality was growing. Nationalist propaganda, es-pecially on the Serbian side, was being pumped out by the media and by intellectuals. An active Diaspora on the Albanian side was becoming increasingly radical. These are the conditions that typ-ically give rise to "new wars". [46]

Moreover, no one can claim that the international community was ignorant of developments in Kosovo. Quite apart from intel-ligence and media reports, a number of well-known NGOs as well as the UN Special Rapporteurs for Human Rights were regularly monitoring the situation. Yet the international community re-sponded with a series of mixed signals. The non-violent move-ment received international endorsements and praise, but no solid commitments. US officials courted Rugova, but then Dayton ignored Kosovo. The West continued to acknowledge Rugova post-Dayton, but there was no visible effort to encourage the LDK to develop a more accommodating political stance on the status of Kosovo, and there were no moves to put the issue back on the diplomatic table. Milosevic, meanwhile, who had been warned early about Kosovo, was later repeatedly assured that its status within the FRY was beyond challenge and that its administration was an internal matter.

Three general lessons can be drawn from the experience of this period. First of all, the failure to respond adequately at an early stage of the evolution of the conflict created difficulties in later stages. At each stage of the conflict, the diplomatic options nar-rowed. The decision not to deal seriously with the Kosovo issue in 1991 created obstacles to action in 1992–3. The decision not to confront the intransigence of Milosevic in 1993, and above all the neglect of Kosovo during the Dayton negotiations, contributed to the developments that were to escalate the conflict in 1996–7. The inadequacy of diplomatic efforts in the period 1997–8 was to culminate eventually with Rambouillet where the space for maneuver was extremely limited.

Second, during this period it was more important to establish an international presence on the ground and to support efforts to normalize the situation than to find a solution to status questions. Any compromise on status was bound to be very difficult since the Kosovars insisted on independence and the Belgrade authorities insisted on the integrity of Yugoslavia. Conflict prevention should have focused instead on establishing a presence on the ground to provide some protection against human rights violations, to support and facilitate the parallel institutions, and to encourage dialogue. The deterring impact of an international NGO or intergovernmental (UN or OSCE) civilian presence on human rights abuse has been amply demonstrated in many conflicts. Unless or until a situation escalates to the point where the international presence is itself in great peril, an unarmed presence can not only impact the daily life of the oppressed population, but often can also be reconciled with state concerns over infringement of sovereignty. The presence of the Mission of Long Duration does seem to have ameliorated the situation in 1992–3. Much more effort should have been directed towards ensuring a strong international presence within Kosovo, improving conditions of everyday life, and fostering communication among Serbs and Albanians inside Kosovo as well as with people in the rest of Serbia.

Third, much more could have been done by the international community to support the initiatives of the parallel society.[47] For example, universities in other nations did little to aid the alternative educational efforts developed as passive resistance after Serbian officials fired Kosovar faculty and removed Kosovar students from the University of Pristina. Year after year, the LDK appealed to the international community for support in dealing with the tensions and ongoing repression in Kosovo. The LDK offered itself as a legitimate and willing ally for diplomatic, political, or other levels of non-forceful pressure or intervention that might have been undertaken. The unarmed nature (at least on one side) of the conflict provided potential avenues of civilian international involvement that were less intrusive, and not as threatening to the sovereignty and security concerns of the FRY as an armed presence.

Although no one can answer the "what ifs" of retrospective assessment, international support for these parallel systems might have sustained peaceful resistance sufficiently to have carved a different path for Kosovo. Furthermore, the failure to take more seriously the demands of the non-violent movement at an early stage led to the conclusion that violence produces results and is a more effective political strategy. This had profound implications for the post-conflict political culture. The parallel structures that were created in this period still exist and command widespread loyalty, especially outside Prishtina/Pristina. However, this loyalty is undermined daily by the actions of those who have learned that violence is an effective way to achieve political objectives.

A KLA-soldier in action.
PHOTO: VISAR KRYWZIU/PRESSENS BILD

## 2

# INTERNAL ARMED CONFLICT

## FEBRUARY 1998–MARCH 1999

At the beginning of 1998, Kosovo was on the brink of open conflict. Student demonstrations in August 1997 had made it clear that the LDK was no longer in control of Kosovar Albanian political activity. More confrontational tactics were taking the initiative. In September student protesters took further steps away from the LDK, refusing Rugova's call to stop street protests and seeking contact with groups connected with the KLA.

On October 1, 1997, Serbian police had assaulted a peaceful protest of 20,000 students in Prishtina/Pristina, and started to detain known opponents throughout Kosovo. In October and November 1997 the KLA began, for the first time, to make public appearances at funerals of its soldiers and sympathizers. These events drew tens of thousands of people. During this time period, the KLA began to openly confront Serbian Police control in the areas of Drenice/Drenica and Peje/Pec, declaring them the first "liberated areas" in Kosovo. In response to these actions, the number of armed skirmishes in Kosovo increased dramatically, with 66 in January and February 1998, up from 55 in all of 1997, and 31 in 1996.[1]

Despite international calls for restraint and dialogue,[2] Serb forces accelerated their repressive and counterinsurgency actions.

At the beginning of January 1998, Serbian special police forces commenced exercises in the Drenice/Drenica region, near Peje/Pec and Lipjan/Lipljan, apparently aimed at intimidating the Kosovar Albanian population. At the same time, Serb civilians were armed and paramilitary groups entered Kosovo from Serbia.

On February 27, 1998, heavily armed Yugoslav forces attacked the Drenice/Drenica village of Liksoshan/Likosane, using armored units and helicopter gunships. Four Yugoslav policemen and an unknown number of Albanians were killed. The fighting continued for several days in the Drenice/Drenica area. In response, a street protest was organized in Prishtina/Pristina on March 2. Yugoslav forces violently broke up the protest with water canons, tear gas, and batons, injuring at least 289 people.[3]

A particularly critical series of actions was taken against the Jashari clan, key players in the local growth of the KLA in the Drenice/Drenica region. Police had tried to arrest Adem Jashari on January 22, but were resisted by the KLA and retreated. On March 5, after a week of fighting in Drenice/Drenica, a concerted and heavily armed police action converged on the houses of the Jashari clan in Prekazi/Prekaze. Using artillery against the houses and sharpshooters against those who fled, the massacre left 58 dead, including Adem Jashari, and created a martyr for the KLA cause.[4]

Human Rights Watch (HRW) conducted an extensive investigation into the events surrounding the Drenice/Drenica violence and concluded that these events constituted a "turning point in the Kosovo crisis."[5] After reviewing Serb actions in both Likoshan/Likosane and the neighboring village of Qirez/Cirez, it concluded:

> Regardless of what triggered the incident, there is no question that the special police forces acted in a quick and well-organized manner, which suggests that the police may have been planning to attack. There is also no doubt that the police used arbitrary and excessive force against the villagers long after resistance had ceased.[6]

The report goes on to look at actions in several other villages, and it concludes that a wide range of civilians, including dozens of women and children, died in the conflict. In addition to killings, the report chronicles a range of other human rights violations committed by Serb forces and authorities, including attacks and restrictions on humanitarian workers, arbitrary arrests and detentions, restrictions on the media, and forced disappearances.[7] Some KLA abuses are also detailed, focusing predominantly on abductions. Reported KLA abuses concentrated on Serbs, but also on occasion included Albanians who were deemed to be "collaborators."[8]

The Yugoslav government continued to characterize the situation as an internal conflict that was under control. Following the four-day clear and sweep operation in Drenice/Drenica, the Serb deputy chief of the Kosovo province, Veljko/Odalevic, announced: "The operation to liquidate the heart of Kosovo terrorism has ended." Thereafter, Yugoslav officials bused reporters and officials into Kosovo to tour the villages where the operations had been conducted.[9] Meanwhile, the region remained sealed off and the estimated 5000 internally displaced people remained without food or medical deliveries.[10] Simultaneously, *Tanjug*, the Yugoslav news agency, quoted Milosevic as saying, "[T]he Federal Republic of Yugoslavia is resolutely opposed to all the attempts to internationalize internal problems of another country."

Nevertheless, the problem was now undeniably internationalized.[11] The United States withdrew certain diplomatic concessions. The American press reported CIA warnings that the Yugoslav army was mobilizing on the Kosovo border. On March 9, the Contact Group called for an arms embargo. On March 10, Louise Arbour, chief prosecutor of the International Criminal Tribunal for the Former Yugoslavia (ICTY), publicly asserted the Tribunal's jurisdiction over violations of international humanitarian law in Kosovo.[12] On March 31 the UN Security Council passed Resolution 1160 by a vote of 14–0, with China abstaining, imposing an arms embargo on Yugoslavia and calling for autonomy and "meaningful self-administration" for Kosovo.[13] The Council warned that "additional measures" were possible if no progress was made toward a peaceful solution. Yugoslavia's ambassador to the UN, Vladislav Jovanovic, decried the move stating: "There is not, nor has there been, any armed conflict in Kosovo. Hence, there is no danger of a spillover, there is no threat to peace and security."[14]

The Drenice/Drenica violence and the police brutality against the peaceful student protests in Prishtina/Pristina had internal consequences as well. The KLA at this point had no political program, no accepted representation, no international recognition, and no control over military forces of any significance. But reports of massacres and myths of national martyrs suddenly made the KLA the driving force of national liberation in the eyes of a growing number of Kosovar Albanians. For the first time, the KLA could claim significant political power. As the number of Kosovar Albanians who looked to the KLA for liberation or affiliated themselves with the KLA increased, support for the LDK party's non-violent parallel state strategy diminished.

Self-defense militias formed independently and seemingly overnight in many rural Kosovo villages. This formation process was not affiliated with a national KLA organization, but rather was the product of Kosovar Albanians taking up arms to defend themselves. These militias, although pervasive, lacked coordination and logistical structure. Meanwhile, Rugova called for elections to be held on March 22, and received an overwhelming majority of votes. Thus, it appeared that Kosovar Albanians still looked to the LDK and Rugova for political leadership, but looked to the KLA to defend them from Serbian aggression.

## ESCALATION OF THE CONFLICT

In the aftermath of the events in Drenice/Drenica, both sides in the conflict increased the depth and scope of their activities.

Several hundred expatriates Kosovar Albanians began arriving in the northern Albanian town of Kukes to train and organize. The KLA was reportedly unprepared to accommodate the swelling numbers of volunteers crossing the border to northern Albania or trying to join the local groups inside Kosovo. Supply routes were organized from northern Albania to bring arms and ammunition into the province. Spring 1998 brought a widespread wave of small or non-coordinated attacks on Serbian police installations, as well as fighting between armed Serbian and Albanian villages in some areas. The KLA claimed to have spread its control over the countryside with Serbian forces controlling the towns and the main roads. During this time several independent regional KLA groups competed for influence and often refused to share information or resources. Disunity among KLA factions remained a factor until the international armed intervention began.[15] Simultaneously, FRY forces expanded their campaign of repression. Yugoslav army officials announced the killing of Kosovar Albanians trying to cross into Kosovo from Albania.[16] The conflict was now escalating province-wide, engulfing the border regions as well as the interior.

The spreading of violence in Kosovo in the spring of 1998 and the growing international pressure on his regime may well have served to legitimize Milosevic among his domestic audience. Only one year before, three months of opposition street protests had placed him on the brink of being overthrown. Now he could use the Kosovo crisis to drum up domestic support. On April 24, 1998, Milosevic called for a national referendum on whether or not to accept international mediation in the Kosovo crisis. His increasingly chauvinistic policies toward the Albanian majority population in Kosovo received support at the polls, gathering 95% of votes cast. The turnout was however low.

Facing a rapidly expanding KLA presence, the Yugoslav army entered Kosovo with massive reinforcements and started a large-scale operation coordinated with police and paramilitary units.

This campaign was aimed not only at stopping the spread of KLA activities, but intended to achieve this by directly targeting the Albanian majority civilian population in rural areas.

Starting in April and continuing into the summer of 1999, increases in attacks on civilians were reported against all parties involved in the widening conflict. The Humanitarian Law Center (HLC) began registering an increased variety of abuses committed against Serbs, and in some cases Roma, including disappearances, abduction, and arbitrary detentions. In a number of cases, KLA activities were directly linked to abuses, causing Serb residents to flee their homes and villages. For example, on April 21, 1998, the KLA took over Ratishi i Eperme/Gornji Ratis, and on April 22, 1998, the KLA took over Dashinovc/Dasinovac. In both cases, the majority of local Serbs fled amid reports of associated unexplained disappearances.[17]

This increase in KLA abuses, while notable, was far outstripped by the rise in abuses perpetrated by FRY security and paramilitary forces. Extra-judicial executions, excessive use of force, and disappearances were frequent, and were described by Amnesty International as an established pattern.[18] Specific, detailed reports of this type of abuse were collected, such as the Serbian police actions against Lubeniq/Ljubenic on May 25, 1998, and against Poklek i Ri/Novi Poklek on May 31, 1998. In the former, armored police forces summarily executed eight men and set fire to homes, and in the latter, eight men "disappeared" after being detained by police.[19] The escalation continued throughout the month. By the end of May, 300 people were estimated to have been killed since the start of the Yugoslav operation in February. In addition, approximately 12,000 refugees had spilled over into Albania.[20]

These increases in military activity and violence against civilians led to the first public consideration by the NATO Alliance of military intervention in June 1998. One senior NATO official is quoted as saying: "There is a new sense of urgency, and the focus of the debate is on air strikes."[21] On June 10, 1998, British Prime

Minister Tony Blair stated the need for military action if diplomacy were unable to end the crisis.[22] According to the ICTY Deputy Prosecutor, Graham Blewitt, "There is an armed conflict taking place here."[23] The Permanent Council of the OSCE issued Decision 218, authorizing the establishment of border monitoring stations along the Kosovo–Albania border.[24] These stations became fully operational at the end of June 1998. Immediately upon their establishment, OSCE border monitors began reporting a substantial level of military activity and fighting along the border. These reports caught the attention of high-level Western diplomats. In the second week of July, German Minister of Foreign Affairs, Klaus Kinkel, made a visit to the area to get a first-hand briefing from the OSCE border monitors regarding the state of the conflict.[25] From that point forward, the OSCE maintained an active presence on the border.

In another important monitoring development, the Yeltsin–Milosevic meeting in June opened the way for the installation in July of the US Kosovo Diplomatic Observer Mission (KDOM), which attempted to unite the disparate fragments of the KLA.[26] The KDOM office filled a vacuum: as one journalist put it, "finally there was a place where the KLA leadership could be contacted."[27] Several European countries and Russia also participated in the KDOM operation, and their respective embassies began a series of regular monitoring meetings in Belgrade.

Throughout July and August, Serb incursions into Albanian territory and air space were commonplace, as was the bombing and burning of villages in the Prizren/Prizren–Gjakove/Djakovica area. KLA incursions into Kosovo were also frequent, and Serb forces responded with a variety of tactics, including the use of landmines and ambushes. KLA casualties were sometimes substantial.[28] The HRW interviewed refugees from the conflict in both Montenegro and Albania who consistently reported the indiscriminate Serb shelling of villages and attacks on fleeing civilians.[29]

The conflict was not limited to the border region. Reports in July from the interior also detailed intense points of conflict inside Kosovo. Two examples are the battle for Rrahovec/Orahovac and the Serb actions in Vushtrri/Vucitrn. As with the border region, the civilian population suffered substantially in the conflicts.

On July 17, 1998, KLA forces overran Rrahovec/Orahovac. Fierce fighting ensued, and by July 21, Serb forces had expelled the KLA and reasserted control. Serbs destroyed numerous houses, and some reports indicated that they might have killed fleeing civilians. The KLA also took about 55 Serbs into custody, including medical personnel, which resulted in "disappearances." Later, at least 35 Serbs were released.[30] Violence was also reported in the area of Vushtrri/Vucitrn, close to Mitrovice/Kosovska Mitrovica.[31]

While precise details were not available, as of the beginning of August, reports estimated that between 200,000 and 300,000 Kosovar Albanians had been displaced from their homes as a result of sustained Yugoslav attacks, which included shelling of cities and villages.[32] These figures include internal displacement as well as large numbers fleeing into refuge in Montenegro, Albania, and Macedonia. Property damage resulting from these attacks was also extensive.

During this period, European diplomats referred to the destruction as an excessive use of military force. Responding to this summer long escalation, the president of the UN Security Council issued a statement at the end of August calling for an immediate cease-fire.[33]

UNHCR displacement figures for August 1998 state that there were 260,000 internally displaced people (IDP), and 200,000 refugees outside of Kosovo. Whether all of the refugees and internally displaced people left their homes to avoid combat, or as a result of a campaign of expulsion remains a debated topic.

On July 7, 1998, the ICTY Office of the Prosecutor had announced its preliminary determination as to the existence of an "armed conflict."[34] Furthermore, the same press release stated ICTY's intent to devote additional resources to the investigations.[35] With its team of trained and experienced investigators, the precise details of alleged abuses of human rights and humanitarian law could be documented, catalogued, and prosecuted. However, in mid-September criticism of the scope of ICTY efforts emerged, along with a public critique of the fact that Chief Prosecutor Arbour had not taken a more visible role, including a trip to Kosovo.[36] The Chief Prosecutor, in a published rebuttal, called the suggestion of a "highly political role" for the chief prosecutor of the ICTY "unfounded."[37]

Meanwhile, throughout the month of September 1998, OSCE border monitors in Albania reported shelling of villages in the Prizren/Prizren and Gjakove/Djakovica areas. Burning houses were commonplace occurrences. The refugee flows into the northern Albania area remained relatively constant — sometimes exceeding 100 a day — and during the last week of the month 3500 refugees were expelled from Montenegro.[38]

On September 23, 1998, the UN Security Council passed Resolution 1199, which cited Chapter VII of the UN Charter and demanded a ceasefire and the withdrawal of Yugoslav forces "used for civilian repression."[39] Three days later, on September 26, 1998, Yugoslav forces reportedly mortared the village of Obri e Eperme/ Gornje Obrinje, killing at least 18 women, children, and elderly persons.[40]

## AN UNSTABLE CEASEFIRE

The FRY military campaign of the summer of 1998 in Kosovo was in many ways a success. The KLA had been effectively uprooted as a military force and proven unable to protect civilians in all contested areas. Yugoslav army units and officer corps conducted what at the beginning some believed to be an unconstitutional military campaign against its civilian population. The international response, in military terms, had been limited to air maneuvers over Albania and Macedonia.

On October 13, 1998, however, NATO authorities voted to authorize air strikes if security forces were not withdrawn from Kosovo within 96 hours. After a period of intense negotiations, US Special Envoy Richard Holbrooke, representing the Contact Group, and Serbian President Slobodan Milosevic reached an agreement, based on the demands in Resolution 1199, and obviously under the threat of the NATO activation order. While the agreement was never published, its major points addressed the reduction in forces and deployment of monitors.[41] This agreement was submitted to the UN Security Council for approval. Milosevic agreed with negotiators to pull back security forces, allow access to aid groups, and accept the OSCE Kosovo Verification Mission (OSCE-KVM), a team of 2000 civilian observers who would monitor the enforcement of the agreement. This monitoring effort would be complemented by NATO overflights. Despite these positive developments, NATO authorities kept the activation order in place, permitting the NATO Supreme Allied Commander in Europe, US Army General Wesley Clark, to launch air strikes in the event of FRY non-compliance.[42]

On October 24, 1998, the UN Security Council passed Resolution 1203, which affirmed the agreement between Contact Group negotiators and the Yugoslav government, providing for OSCE-KVM deployment and Yugoslav troop withdrawals.[43] By the end of October, large numbers of Yugoslav forces had been withdrawn and KVM monitors deployed. Holbrooke announced: "Anyone who's alive is not, in my view, in danger any more, and that couldn't have been said a few weeks ago." The Yugoslav troop strength was set to be reduced from 18,000 to 12,500 men and special police limited to 6500. Also, a series of steps toward autonomy were to be initiated, including elections within nine months and the development of Kosovar Albanian police forces.[44]

Also on October 24, the Security Council passed Resolution

1207, which called upon Yugoslav authorities to comply with the requests of the ICTY, including the arrest of certain individuals.[45] At the beginning of October, the Yugoslav Foreign Ministry had refused to acknowledge the ICTY's jurisdiction in Kosovo, claiming it to be an infringement of national sovereignty. Pursuant to this position, Yugoslav authorities had denied visas to ICTY investigators and threatened to cease cooperation with the ICTY Liaison Office in Belgrade. The Chief Prosecutor declared the Yugoslav actions to be "totally unacceptable."[46] With Resolution 1207, the Security Council rejected the Yugoslav sovereignty argument and firmly established ICTY's investigative authority.

The violence against the civilian population in Kosovo throughout 1998 was accompanied by a series of other systematic and institutional violations of civil rights by Serbian and FRY authorities, further establishing a hostile environment for the civilian population. The two most notable violations were political trials that lacked due process, and efforts to suppress any free and independent media.

Human Rights Watch reported that, as of October 3, 1998, 1242 ethnic Albanians had been charged with "terrorist acts" against the state.[47] Throughout October and November arrests were commonplace. By the end of the year, an estimated 1500 people were in custody by the end of the year. The International Committee of the Red Cross (ICRC) was denied access to many of the detainees. Reports of abuses, ranging from violence to shortcomings in due process, were numerous, and additional judges were transferred from Kosovo to Serbia to handle the heavy caseload.[48]

The HLC issued a report on the infringement of media freedoms during 1998. Measures ranged from censorship to police violence against journalists. The Serb government took a particularly active role at certain points. For example, in October, once concrete threats of NATO actions materialized, the Serbian Ministry of Information ordered all stations re-broadcasting Voice of

America, BBC, and Deutsche Welle to discontinue such broad-casts.[49]

## AFTER THE MILOSEVIC–HOLBROOKE AGREEMENT

Serbia initially implemented the agreement and withdrew its forces accordingly.[50] The KLA, by contrast, took advantage of the new situation and renewed military action. In fact, KLA forces moved in to take up positions vacated by the redeployed Serbian forces. The UN as well as NATO and the OSCE were alarmed by the KLA's actions. According to the UN Secretary-General,

> Recent attacks by Kosovo Albanian paramilitary units have indicated their readiness, capability and intention to actively pursue the advantage gained by the partial withdrawal of the police and military formations (...) Reports of new weapons, ammunition and equipment indicate that the capacity of those units to crisply defend themselves is still fairly good." This development is "disturbing.[51]

NATO noted in a statement of December 8, that "both Belgrade authorities and the armed Kosovar elements have failed to comply fully with the requirements set out in SCR 1160, 1199 and 1203. We call upon the armed Kosovar elements to cease and desist from provocative actions and we call upon the FRY and Serbian authorities to reduce the number and visibility of MUP special police in Kosovo and abstain from intimidating behavior."[52] At the same time, the KLA was trying to strengthen its political influence by threatening LDK political representation in rural areas. The organization kidnapped, and in some cases executed, both Serbs and Albanian civilians.

The situation got worse in December. On December 14, around 100 KLA soldiers transporting weapons were caught in a regular Serbian army ambush at the border of Albania: 36 were killed. That same evening two masked men stormed a bar in Peje/Pec and killed six young Serbs. This event was never investigated by KVM. On December 17, the Serbian deputy major in

Fushe Kosove/Kosovo Polje was abducted and later found murdered. A Serbian military response came a few days later. In December, OSCE border monitors began to report increased tensions on the border. FRY attacks on villages and border incursions were again commonplace.[53] The ongoing conflict and the onset of winter left displaced villagers in very difficult conditions.[54]

According to the UN Secretary-General's December 24 report,

> Kosovo Albanian paramilitary units have taken advantage of the lull on the fighting to re-establish their control over many villages in Kosovo as well as over some areas near urban center and highways. These actions (…) have only served to provoke the Serbian authorities, leading to statements that if the Kosovo Verification mission cannot control these units the Government would.

There is now

> a new cycle of major hostilities and there are reports that suggest that the number of Yugoslav forces deployed in Kosovo may exceed agreed figures.[55]

The UN also reported that between 1500 and 2000 Albanians had been detained by the authorities since the October agreement and that an estimated 150 civilians had been kidnapped by the KLA.[56] In clear violation of the October agreement, the Yugoslav army positioned 24 battalion size units with more than 12,000 men around the Kosovo borders. At the end of the month, the army moved them inside the province on the Podujevo/Podujevo road, once again using tanks and armored personnel carriers to fire on villages. Serbian authorities were also challenging the international community's push for independent investigations and were interfering with forensic specialists' access to specific sites[57]

While the reliability of Milosevic's commitments to this October arrangement can certainly be questioned, the evident contradiction between Holbrooke's supposed assurances and KLA actions nevertheless provided the FRY with substantial grounds to doubt the sincerity of "the West." KLA actions undoubtedly exerted strong internal security pressure in Belgrade to renew its counter-insurgency efforts on an all-out basis .[58]

It was becoming clear that, despite the initial success of the Milosevic–Holbrooke agreement and the KVM presence in protecting civilians, Kosovo Verification Mission was no longer in a position to address necessary peacekeeping issues. From aerial monitoring over the region, NATO was aware of violations of the cease-fire agreement during this period.

In the first 11 days of January 1999, 21 people died as a result of clashes between KLA and Serb forces. The Serb army moved into Kosovo in large numbers. With the help of special police units, the army created at least three sealed areas along the main north–south road, using artillery and tank shelling to push the civilian residents to leave the villages. However, unlike the summer of 1998, displaced people, including women, children, and the elderly, were prevented from leaving the sealed areas. In the sealed area west of Vushtrri/Vucitrn, there had been no armed clashes or reports of KLA activity. This "sealed area" tactic is cited by some analysts as evidence suggesting an advance plan for ethnic cleansing. Yugoslav army activities, the argument goes, were part of a strategy to secure each area and subsequently to empty each of sealed areas of Albanian civilian population at a chosen time, thus preventing the KLA from forming interconnected "liberated areas" in the province.

By late January 1999, Serb forces with tanks and heavy armor established permanent positions along the Macedonian border with Kosovo. Their main strategic goal was to block the borders with Macedonia, and shortly thereafter with Albania, so as to deter a possible NATO ground attack.[59] In addition, the units along the Albanian border assisted the special police units to cut the KLA supply routes. Paramilitary groups from Serbia infiltrated Kosovo and assembled in the Interior Ministry barracks near Peje/Pec, Podujeve/Podujevo, and Shterpce/Strpce. There were also reports of additional light arms flowing into Serb villages in those regions to bolster their defense capacity under Yugoslav Territorial Defense law.[60]Each of these actions clearly violated the October Agreement.[61]

From January 12, to January 15, 1999, Serb forces brought heavy military equipment into the municipality of Shtime/Stimlje, establishing permanent positions.[62] On January 15, 1999, Yugoslav forces assaulted Recak/Racak village within the municipality; in the process, they executed 45 ethnic Albanians. On January 16, 1999, OSCE-KVM investigated the site of the massacre. The team found "evidence of arbitrary detentions, extra-judicial killings, and mutilation of unarmed civilians."[63] OSCE-KVM head of mission, Ambassador William Walker, joined the team at the site to observe the evidence first-hand. Directly thereafter, he publicly condemned the massacre, called upon the ICTY to investigate the atrocity, and requested that Serb authorities supply the names of the officers commanding the action. Serb authorities denied that any civilians had been killed, stating that it was simply an action against the KLA.[64] A notable factor encouraging a rapid international response to this incident was the speed with which the KVM monitoring team was able to document the event.

On January 18, 1999, the ICTY Chief Prosecutor was refused entry into Kosovo at the border with Macedonia. The NATO Commander, General Clark, immediately engaged Serb authorities in an effort to secure the Chief Prosecutor's access to Kosovo. Simultaneously, the Chief Prosecutor communicated her assurances to the Serbian Minister of Justice that her office would not construe access as "an admission by the FRY that the ICTY has any jurisdiction in this matter."[65] Despite these efforts, access was not granted, and the Chief Prosecutor returned to The Hague.[66]

Shortly thereafter, the FRY government declared Ambassador Walker persona non grata. The President of the Security Council and the OSCE Ministerial Troika protested this move immediately, unequivocally condemning both the massacre at Recak/Racak and the subsequent Serb refusal to permit ICTY access.[67] Both organizations called for an immediate cessation of hostilities and dialogue.[68] As a result of this intervention, the persona non grata declaration was frozen.[69]

Following up on calls for dialogue, Contact Group members organized peace negotiations to be held in Rambouillet, France, commencing February 6. Serb and Kosovar Albanian leaders (including both the KLA and the LDK) were invited to attend, as were representatives of the FRY. The core of the Contact Group plan included the disarming of the KLA and the withdrawal of Serb forces with supervision from an "enabling force" of 30,000 NATO troops.[70] The plan provided for a restoration of Kosovo's autonomy and its independent institutions, but left the issue of future status (i.e. independence) for reconsideration after three years. In a process that will be more fully discussed in the subsequent chapter, the Contact Group was, in the end, unable to formulate a plan to which both FRY and Kosovar negotiators could agree. A second round of talks took place in Paris March 15–19. On March 18 the Kosovar Albanian delegation signed the proposal then on the table; the FRY/Serb delegation did not. The negotiations failed.

On March 19, 1999, the OSCE chairman-in-office, Norwegian Foreign Minister Knut Vollebæk, decided to remove OSCE-KVM personnel from Kosovo. Citing the deteriorating security situation, Foreign Minister Vollebæk stated, "[A]s OSCE Chairman-in-Office, responsible for the safety of approximately 1400 verifiers from many different countries in Kosovo, I have no other choice in the present situation than to withdraw the OSCE personnel." The FRY authorities escorted the monitors to the frontier.

UNHCR estimated that from 150,000 to over 200,000 new refugees were driven from their homes in Kosovo between January and mid-March 1999. On March 15, in the midst of ongoing Paris talks, the Serb army moved into the Podujeve/ Podujevo region with large armored units. This action resulted in 25,000 to 40,000 new refugees.

It is important to note that for the entire period of internal war, between February 1998 and March 1999, preceding the bombing campaign, the Commission has had considerable difficulty pinpointing statistics on the levels of lethal violence committed against civilians in Kosovo. A precise quantification of abuses, particularly killings, was difficult if not impossible to determine because detailed, verified data was not readily available. Major human rights groups have consistently expressed the need for greater rigor in the collection and presentation of Kosovo data. As mentioned earlier, the UNHCR reported that 300 people were killed between February and May 1998, and the Council for Defense of Human Rights and Freedoms asserts that 750 people were killed between May and August 1998. But neither set of numbers indicates how many of the victims were KLA members and how many were civilians. The Commission has been unable to identify any dependable figure on killings between September 1998 and March 1999, despite the substantial OSCE monitoring presence during most of these months. Therefore the Commission cannot make a reliable estimate of the number of deaths in this period. However, apart from the shocking exception of the Recak/Racak massacre, it is reasonable to assume that the number of civilian killings was significantly lower during the presence of KVM monitors than during the earlier months.

The crisis had been building for a long time. It seemed almost inevitable that the abolition of Kosovo's autonomy in 1990, the resulting fatal spiral of action and reaction, repression and resistance, hardening Serb intransigence and growing Kosovar Albanian armament would lead to war — a war which was bound to involve the international community. In the face of Milosevic's ruthless strategy of oppression, the Kosovar moderates around Ibrahim Rugova had no chance of prevailing. More militant elements then took the initiative through armed resistance, and the FRY's repression against civilians escalated. Western diplomacy failed to defuse the conflict, which by early 1999 had become an outright civil war. This civil war would continue on the ground, and even intensify, but superimposed upon it was now a fully fledged international war between the NATO Alliance and Yugoslavia.

The Sloboda (Freedom) bridge connecting Novi Sad and
Sremska Kamenica, Serbia, was hit during NATO air strikes
on April 3, 1999.

# 3

# INTERNATIONAL WAR SUPERVENES

## MARCH 1998–JUNE 1999

As late as March 22 and 23, UN Secretary-General Annan demanded that the Yugoslav armed forces immediately cease their offensive in Kosovo. On March 23, 1999, the NATO Secretary-General, Dr. Javier Solana, in a letter to the UN Secretary-General, outlined a series of incidents demonstrating a rapid decay of the situation in Kosovo. In particular, he noted the dramatic increase in FRY military activities following the pullout of OSCE-KVM. The NATO Secretary-General also warned of a humanitarian catastrophe resulting from the excessive force used by the FRY. On the same day, the Yugoslav government declared a state of emergency. On March 24, at 8pm local time, NATO aircraft started the bombing campaign against Yugoslavia.

President Clinton articulated the goals of the NATO campaign in his TV speech on March 24: to demonstrate the seriousness of NATO's response to aggression, to deter Milosevic's escalating attacks in Kosovo, and seriously to damage Yugoslavia's military capacity to wage war in the future.[1] The European leaders said about the same but stressed more strongly that the NATO intervention was necessary to prevent a humanitarian catastrophe. Clinton also clarified that the US government had no intention of deploying ground troops to fight a war. The other NATO govern-

ments took the same position. A British House of Commons select committee has since pointed out that "the question as to
whether NATO was acting primarily to preserve its credibility, or
primarily to avert a humanitarian catastrophe (...) did not help to
explain NATO's action to the public and rather suggests that NATO
was not itself clear about what it was trying to do."[2] More specific goals were outlined by NATO of April 12th and reaffirmed by
NATO Heads of State in the Washington meeting April 23rd.

The underlying NATO assumption was that a relatively short
bombing campaign would persuade Milosevic to come back to
sign the Rambouillet agreement.[3] NATO also underestimated the
obvious risk that the Belgrade government in one way or another
would reciprocate by attacking Kosovar Albanians. In spite of all
the western intelligence, there was no contingency planning for
refugees.

The Commission has not had access to the considerations of
the Belgrade government regarding its war goals, but can guess
that they included: keeping NATO out of the FRY; keeping control
of Kosovo; crushing the KLA and, finally, using the war as a pretext to expel the Kosovar Albanian population, hopefully for
good but at least as a card in future negotiations. Milosevic clearly seemed also to be counting on the NATO alliance splitting, and
may also have expected more support from Russia.

NATO's military superiority was of course extraordinary, with
the most sophisticated military capabilities in the world. The
Yugoslav military, however, was well organized and trained to
deter a military superpower. Air defense was crucial, and the FRY
military had carefully studied the Iraqi experience from the 1991
war. Although FRY air defense capability was outdated and inefficient, it was sufficient to keep the NATO air force above 15,000
feet, thereby reducing NATO's ability to hit FRY military forces.[4]

At the start of the NATO bombing campaign, the Yugoslav
armed forces (VJ) enjoyed a clear advantage over the KLA forces,
with 40,000 combat troops, a unified police and paramilitary task

force, 300 tanks, and anti-aircraft and ground artillery units available in Kosovo or at its borders. In contrast, before mid-March 1999, the KLA was not yet a centrally organized military force. The Albanian resistance consisted of 8000–10,000 lightly armed, poorly trained men in Kosovo, with an additional 5000–8000 men training in northern Albania. These men belonged to different armed resistance groups. Most of the groups had some connection to the KLA, but they also maintained their individual identity. Only at this time, in the face of a large-scale FRY offensive, did the KLA begin to build a unified command structure under the leadership of Agim Ceku, a former Croatian army officer.[5]

From a military standpoint, the KLA was still unprepared for, and did not expect, any large-scale confrontation. Its ideological and strategic thinking at the time was "to create Serbian Vietnam in Kosovo."[6] The KLA hoped that a prolonged war of attrition against FRY security forces would inflict politically unbearable losses for the Belgrade regime. The KLA's only real advantage over FRY forces was of course the support it got from NATO.

Even if the NATO member governments had been prepared to deploy ground troops, NATO was months away from being in a position to launch a ground assault in March 1999.[7] NATO forces in the region at that time included 8000 troops in Macedonia and 27,000 Stabilization Force, Bosnia, (SFOR) troops in Bosnia-Herzegovina. The troops in Macedonia were there to provide support and extraction capability for the OSCE-KVM force authorized by the October agreement. The SFOR troops were not authorized to serve outside Bosnia-Herzegovina.

The composition and placement of the Yugoslav army task force in Kosovo clearly suggests that it used the early months of 1999 to build up a territorial defense capacity in Kosovo sufficient to deter the threat of a NATO ground invasion. Time gained during the Rambouillet and Paris negotiations assisted the Yugoslav army in this effort.

## THE "CLEANSING" OF KOSOVO

The war quickly took a direction that surprised and shocked the world. The FRY military and paramilitary forces launched a vicious campaign against the Kosovar Albanian population. The FRY government maintained throughout the conflict that it was only conducting military activities against the KLA, and blamed all human rights violations, especially the forced displacement of Kosovar Albanians, on NATO and the KLA. However, virtually every other international, governmental and non-governmental organization that has studied the facts has reached the opposite conclusion. There is widespread agreement that FRY forces were engaged in a well-planned campaign of terror and expulsion of the Kosovar Albanians.[8] This campaign is most frequently described as one of "ethnic cleansing," intended to drive many, if not all, Kosovar Albanians from Kosovo, destroy the foundations of their society, and prevent them from returning.[9]

There are two important questions here that have been much discussed. The first is whether there was a FRY military plan ("Operation Horseshoe") to expel the Albanian population. There has been an intensive debate on whether such a plan did exist, and if so, what relevance it had. The issue is still open, but it is very clear that there was a deliberate organized effort to expel a huge part of the Kosovar Albanian population and such a massive operation cannot be implemented without planning and preparation. The second related issue is the allegation that the NATO bombing campaign in fact provoked this FRY campaign, and that NATO consequently created a humanitarian disaster instead of stopping it.

The latter allegation is difficult to assess. We cannot know what would have happened if NATO had not started the bombing. It is however certainly not true that NATO *provoked* the attacks on the civilian Kosovar population — the responsibility for that campaign rests entirely on the Belgrade government. It is nonetheless likely that the bombing campaign and the removal of the unarmed monitors created an internal environment that made such an operation feasible. The FRY forces could not hit NATO, but they could hit the Albanians who had asked for NATO's support and intervention. It was thus both revenge on the Albanians and a deliberate strategy at the same time.

But this campaign was also Milosevic's most crucial mistake. FRY leaders may have thought that the resulting huge flow of refugees would create a political crisis for neighboring countries, or that the European governments would be nervous in the face of hundreds of thousands of new refugees on their doorsteps. They may also have thought that they could create a kind of *fait accompli* — that a later negotiated agreement would allow that at least some part of the Kosovar Albanian population would stay outside Kosovo. Whatever they thought, it was an enormous miscalculation. The internationally isolated Yugoslav government misjudged the international reaction to this huge forced dislocation of people, evoking memories of the darkest days in European history. They provided the NATO side with the best argument for the war and made all the governments in the Alliance more committed to forcing the FRY government to yield. The NATO objective was also adjusted to the new situation: the promise to the refugees, which was repeated over and over again, was "we will bring you back". This was the kind of concrete promise that NATO could never abandon. The drama of the refugees made a huge impact on public opinion, not the least in Europe. Without these actions it cannot be taken for granted that the NATO campaign could have continued even for the 78 days.

At the same time, it was also a serious mistake by the NATO countries not to foresee that the bombing would lead to severe attacks on the Albanian population. The British House of Commons report talks about NATO's serious misjudgment, and the Commission concurs.[10]

The horror and devastation visited upon the Kosovar Albanian civilian population between March and June of 1999 has been documented in detail by numerous organizations. In Annex 1 to this report, there is an attempt to integrate all available data into a single analysis. Annex 1 also includes a number of methodological observations which we hope will facilitate the accurate compilation of such data in future crises.[11]

A brief summary is, however, essential. During the course of the NATO air campaign, approximately 863,000 civilians sought or were forced into refuge outside of Kosovo. An estimated additional 590,000 were internally displaced. Together, these figures imply that over 90% of the Kosovar Albanian population were displaced from their homes.

Many displaced Kosovar Albanians who were forced from their homes, were then loaded on busses and driven to the Macedonian border; in other cases, people were allowed to take cars and tractors and were ordered to follow a prescribed route to the border. Many residents of municipalities east of the main north–south railroad were forced to walk to railway stations and were taken by trains to the Macedonian border. The substantial planning and coordination of these mass deportations is illustrated by the fact that before March there were two regular daily trains between Prishtina/Pristina and the Macedonian border, usually with three carriages each. During deportations, three to four extra trains were added each day, each with between 13 and 20 carriages. One report recounts a train with 28 carriages crammed full of people leaving Prishtina/Pristina for Macedonia.[12]

Narrative information from refugees suggests that virtually all of those displaced were forced from their homes by members of the Yugoslav armed forces, Serbian police or paramilitary units, in a process routinely preceded by shelling, and subsequently accompanied by abuse, extortion, and killings. In addition, an American Association for the Advancement of Science (AAAS) study correlating refugee departure information with NATO bombing reports clearly demonstrates that refugee flow patterns do not correlate positively with either NATO bombings or mass killing patterns; the AAAS study concludes that the data does not support the analysis that the refugees "fled," but is more consistent with an organized expulsion.

There is an ongoing debate as to the exact number of killings during this period. For instance, to date, exhumations by the ICTY have located 2788 bodies from 345 mass gravesites in Kosovo.[13] However, instances of individual murder were not included in this forensic assessment. The findings, which are set out in the Annex 1, place the number of killings in the neighborhood of 10,000, with the vast majority of the victims being Kosovar Albanians killed by FRY forces. There are around 3000 missing people. The International Committee of the Red Cross (ICRC) estimated in November 1999 that approximately 1700 were in Serbian prisons. Others missing are presumed dead. The Humanitarian Law Center estimates the missing at 2000 to 2150 most of whom are dead.[14]

Looting, pillaging and extortion were also widespread. The OSCE documented some instances of torture as well. These attacks against people were accompanied by massive physical destruction.

An important achievement for victims of armed conflict has been the wider recognition of the different destructive impacts of conflict on women and men. The Rome Statute of the International Criminal Court provides that rape, sexual slavery, enforced prostitution, forced pregnancy, enforced sterilization and other forms of sexual violence are war crimes when committed in the context of armed conflict. During these devastating three months in Kosovo, rape was a prevalent tool of political terror. Rape, however, is notoriously difficult to quantify statistically, due to societal inhibitions against reporting. Nevertheless, in addition to data cited in Annex 1, the Commission has received numerous reports of substantial levels of rapes of Kosovar Albanian women by FRY forces during the crisis. These rapes resulted in dramatic demand for abortion services after the war ended, and a severe problem of unwanted children in the ensuing year.

## CONDUCT OF THE NATO AIR CAMPAIGN

The NATO air campaign against Yugoslavia was conducted between March 24, 1999 and June 10, 1999. NATO aircraft from 13 countries flew 38,400 sorties in the campaign, including 10,484 strike sorties in which 26,614 air munitions were released.[15]

The campaign was a complex, constantly evolving military operation. Decision-making throughout the campaign was influenced by micro-management and political judgment calls from several key NATO member governments. The need for consensus among all 19 members of the Alliance, including three new member states—Poland, Czech Republic, and Hungary—and those, like Greece, with close historical ties to Serbia, put additional constraints on the military decision-making process.

The political cohesion of the Alliance held throughout the campaign, despite serious debates and disagreements between members. The United States flew over 60% of all sorties, and over 80% of the strike sorties. It played an even more dominant role in carrying out high-tech aspects of the campaign.

NATO began the bombing campaign, as has been pointed out, with the expectation that the Yugoslav government would propose a cease-fire and wish to renew negotiations after only a few days. Two other mistaken assumptions followed unavoidably from this erroneous starting point.

1 Since the bombing campaign was originally planned to last only several days and to include a limited number of military targets, NATO governments did not prepare their constituencies for the consequences of what was to become 78 days of intense conflict.

2 NATO erroneously assumed that a short bombing campaign would not lead to dramatic escalation in the displacement and

expulsion of the Kosovar Albanian population.

In its first days, the bombing campaign struck military targets including air defense and communications installations. Though the bombing succeeded in completely grounding the Yugoslav air force it did not succeed in destroying its air defense, even though this was seriously damaged by the end of the war. NATO pilots were ordered to fly at altitudes above 15,000 feet to avoid the continuing threat of Yugoslav air defense systems. This decision has been criticized by opponents of the NATO campaign as limiting pilots' ability to positively establish the military nature of targets. The large number of decoy targets hit suggests that pilots were not able to make positive visual identification before attacking.

According to a number of reports, the NATO attacks in Kosovo did relatively little damage to FRY ground forces.[16] In spite of the bombing, the FRY military forces attacked the KLA rather successfully throughout Kosovo. It was also impossible for the NATO forces to stop the expulsion and killings of civilian Albanians.

After four weeks of bombing, the Yugoslav leadership still would not respond to negotiation proposals. At a NATO summit in Washington on April 23, 1999, Alliance leaders decided to further intensify the air campaign by expanding the target set to include military-industrial infrastructure, media, and other targets in Serbia itself. 59 bridges (seven on the Danube), nine major highways (including Belgrade–Nis or Belgrade–Zagreb), and seven airports were destroyed. Most of the main telecommunications transmitters were damaged, two thirds of the main industrial plants were nearly destroyed. According to NATO, 70% of the electricity production capacity and 80% of the oil refinery capacity was knocked out.[17] Hitting these targets, however, had significant political fallout: the consequent suffering of the Serbian civilian population contradicted initial NATO assurances that the war was not aimed at the Serbian people. An extended campaign with increasing destruction of Serbia would certainly have been heavily criticized in many NATO countries.

There were very few military casualties in this war. There were no casualties at all on the NATO side, unique in any war. According to FRY sources, at least 600 FRY soldiers were killed in action; with about 300 of these killed in action with KLA. How many KLA soldiers who were killed is unknown.

## CIVILIAN CASUALTIES
## OF THE NATO BOMBING CAMPAIGN

NATO made substantial efforts to avoid civilian casualties. In spite of these efforts there were some serious mistakes. The bombing of the Chinese embassy on May 7, had a significant political impact and most likely encouraged Milosevic to wait and see if he could profit from the error. Another catastrophic mistake was the bombing of Korishe/Korisa, with more than 80 Kosovars killed: There were a number of other instances during the NATO air campaign in which civilians were killed or injured by NATO bombs. These included two incidents on one day when many IDP convoys of internally displaced Kosovars were struck by NATO bombs, and another in which a passenger train was bombed.

In its report, Civilian Deaths in the NATO Air Campaign, Human Rights Watch (HRW) documented some 500 civilian deaths in 90 separate incidents. It concluded: "as few as 488 and as many as 527 Yugoslav civilians were killed as a result of NATO bombing. Between 62 and 66 percent of the total registered civilian deaths occurred in just twelve incidents." HRW also found the FRY Ministry of Foreign Affairs publication, NATO Crimes in Yugoslavia, to be largely credible on the basis of its own research and correlation with other sources. This publication provides an estimated total of approximately 495 civilians killed and 820 civilians wounded in specific documented instances.

## BRINGING THE WAR TO A CLOSE

When the bombing campaign failed to bring Milosevic back to the table, NATO member states realized they had made some erroneous assumptions. At the end of April, the question floating nervously around many NATO capitals was "How are we going to end this war?" As uncertainty mounted as to whether the bombing campaign could achieve the desired result, the German government promoted the first main diplomatic initiative in April. This plan insisted that the UN should be brought into the process and should have some role in the administration of Kosovo. Russia was a key factor. The Russians were adamantly opposed to the war, but were also very interested in finding a diplomatic solution to end it. At the G8 [18] meeting in Cologne there was an agreement between Russia and the G7 countries on a seven-point peace plan that closely followed the original German initiative. This became the framework for subsequent diplomatic efforts and discussion between Russian envoy Viktor Chernomyrdin and Slobodan Milosevic in Belgrade on May 19.

In April, planning for a ground invasion began at NATO headquarters. Military planners, led by General Wesley Clark, warned politicians that for an invasion to begin in the first week of September, before the onset of winter, the orders to begin preparing would have to have been given in the first week of June. [19] There was, however, strong political resistance against ground troops in several of the NATO countries, and certainly in United States. The discussion about ground troops was also aimed at increasing the pressure on Milosevic; it was understood from the start that ground troops were only a distant possibility, and that the necessary political consensus would be difficult to achieve.

A final round of negotiations completed in early June averted the need for a ground invasion. EU envoy Martti Ahtisaari and Russian envoy Viktor Chernomyrdin brought a proposal to Belgrade that was based G8 principles. These principles called for an immediate and verifiable end to the repression and violence in Kosovo; the withdrawal of FRY military, police, and paramilitary forces; the deployment of effective international civil and security presences; and the return of all refugees. While the plan stated that "the people of Kosovo will enjoy substantial autonomy within the Federal Republic of Yugoslavia," no timeline or mechanism for resolving Kosovo's long-term status was included in the agreement.[20] On June 1, 1999, the Yugoslav government advised the government of Germany that it would accept the G8 principles.

On June 3, the Serb Parliament formally approved a peace plan based on the G8 principles. After delays caused by difficulties working out a technical agreement, NATO suspended its air attacks on June 10. That same day, after confirming that FRY forces were withdrawing pursuant to the peace plan, the UN Security Council passed Resolution 1244, which established the framework for UN civil administration of the province and the establishment of an international security presence.[21]

We cannot know for sure why Milosevic eventually yielded to an agreement to pull FRY forces out of Kosovo. It is likely that the increasingly intensive bombing of Serbian infrastructure had a profound impact on Belgrade decision–makers. They faced the possibility of the total destruction of the Serbian economy together with resulting internal criticism. They may have had fears about their own power, as well as their private economy. The political prospects were bleak. The NATO alliance had maintained unity. The Russian government had made it clear that its support for the FRY had reached a limit. At the same time, the final agreement did contain some gains from the FRY point of view: the UN rather than NATO would take over Kosovo, and unlike in the Rambouillet proposal, international troops would not have access to Yugoslavian territory outside of Kosovo. Kosovo would still formally be a part of the FRY; and Russian troops would participate in the international force in Kosovo.

Was NATO's campaign a success or a failure? That question cannot be answered easily, since it was, in fact, both. It forced the FRY government to withdraw its army and police from Kosovo and to sign an agreement closely modeled on the aborted Rambouillet accord. It stopped the systematic oppression of the Kosovar Albanians. NATO had demonstrated its military clout as well as the ability to maintain its political cohesion in the face of a challenge that could have torn the Alliance apart.

But, the intervention failed to achieve its avowed aim of preventing massive ethnic cleansing. More than a million Kosovar Albanians became refugees, around 10,000 lost their lives; many were wounded, raped or assaulted in other ways. There was widespread destruction. The Kosovar Albanian population had to endure tremendous suffering before finally achieving their freedom. Milosevic remained in power, however, as an indicted war criminal.

NATO had prevailed in its 78-day campaign. It is a moot question whether the Alliance could have maintained its cohesion if Milosevic had held out for very much longer. A ground war, which some Western politicians and many military analysts advocated in the event that the FRY refused to surrender, enjoyed little public support except perhaps in Britain and France, as the high-intensity and low-casualty air war might well have been replaced by one with significant military casualties. Nor would an intensification of the bombing campaign have found favor with the Western public. Any "countervalue strategy" of full-scale retaliation against Serbia as a whole would rightly have been considered to be repugnant terror bombing—as unacceptable as the pulverization of Grozny by Russia.

Unfortunately, many of the basic problems that precipitated the conflict still plague the region. NATO won the war. Now the United Nations has to win the peace.

UN Secretary General Kofi Annan (right)
and his Special Representative in Kosovo,
Dr. Bernard Kouchner.
PHOTO: UN PHOTO

# 4

# KOSOVO UNDER
# UNITED NATIONS RULE

On the same day that NATO ceased its air campaign against Yugoslavia, June 10, 1999, the UN Security Council (UNSC) passed Resolution 1244.[1] The resolution set out the basic guidelines that would regulate the international community's response to the postwar situation in Kosovo.

Resolution 1244 provided for "the deployment in Kosovo, under United Nations auspices, of international civil and security presences" and requested the Secretary-General to appoint a Special Representative to supervise the international civil presence and coordinate its activities with the operations of the military security presence under the overall command of NATO. It endorsed the establishment of an interim administration for Kosovo, directed the international civil presence to facilitate a political process designed to determine Kosovo's future status, called for the safe and free return home of all refugees and displaced persons, and demanded the demilitarization of the KLA. In addition, it welcomed "the work in hand in the European Union" aimed at:

> the economic development and stabilization of the region affected by the Kosovo crisis, including the implementation of a Stability Pact for South Eastern Europe.

Resolution 1244 has, however, contributed to the uncertainty that surrounds a number of contentious issues. The text makes reference to the commitment of all member states to the sovereignty and territorial integrity of the Federal Republic of Yugoslavia, and yet also calls for "substantial autonomy and meaningful self-administration for Kosovo." Present conditions belie the territorial integrity of Yugoslavia—there is a physical, political, and economic separation between Kosovo and the rest of the country. For the moment, at any rate, Kosovo—legally still part of the FRY —is unmistakably a protectorate. The question is whose protectorate? The United Nations' or NATO's? The nations' contributing to KFOR or the European Union's? Is it the ward of the "international community," whatever that may be, or an orphan of war?[2]

Uncertainty also surrounds the eventual distribution of authority between the UN and the emerging institutions of Kosovo self-government. Resolution 1244 authorized the Special Representative of the Secretary-General (SRSG) to oversee the development of "provisional democratic self-government institutions" pending a political settlement. Municipal elections have been scheduled for the fall of 2000 and provincial ones will follow sometime in 2001. SRSG will continue to exercise final authority in Kosovo, but some power will begin to flow to locally elected municipal and provincial bodies in the next few years. A provisional constitution is being drafted by officials from the Contact Group governments. While it has transpired that its terms borrow from the draft Rambouillet Accords, the exact nature of the transitional constitution is still undisclosed.

The text of Resolution 1244 foreshadowed the "four pillars" on which the United Nations Interim Mission in Kosovo (UNMIK) later came to rest its activities:

Pillar I:    humanitarian affairs, led by the UNHCR;
Pillar II:   civil administration under UNMIK itself;
Pillar III:  democratization and institution-building, led by the
             Organization for Security and Cooperation in Europe
             (OSCE); and
Pillar IV:   economic development, managed by the European
             Union:

These four areas of responsibility are not always easily distinguished from each other. Overlap, duplication and bureaucratic friction inevitably arise. The difficulty is compounded by the presence of a vast and confusing array of approximately 500 non-governmental organizations with competing and sometimes conflicting ambitions. From the very beginning, this has made the civilian effort in Kosovo look somewhat less impressive than the operations of KFOR (although this force, composed of soldiers from many different countries, has not been free from friction either). The military's mandate was, however, more narrowly defined: to deter renewed hostilities, maintain and, where necessary, enforce the cease-fire; to demilitarize the KLA; and to establish a secure environment in Kosovo. And the soldiers had the advantage: they got there first.

## KFOR TAKES OVER

The terms and objectives of the deployment of an international military presence were set out in the Military–Technical Agreement (MTA) between the Kosovo International Security Force (KFOR) and the governments of the Federal Republic of Yugoslavia and the Republic of Serbia, signed on June 9. On June 10, 1999, following the adoption of Resolution 1244, the North Atlantic Council authorized the deployment of KFOR troops, designating the action "Operation Joint Guardian." Actual deployment of troops was initiated on June 12.

The MTA, which took immediate effect upon signing, contains

two annexes. The first delineated the gradual withdrawal of the Yugoslav military, paramilitary, and security forces. Yugoslav forces were given 11 days to withdraw completely from Kosovo's three zones demarcated in the first annex, though only three days were afforded to secure the withdrawal of Yugoslav air and air defense forces.

The second annex defined the mandate for KFOR operations in Kosovo. This mandate was then slightly amended in UNSC Resolution 1244, which called on KFOR to:

- establish and maintain a secure environment for all citizens of Kosovo and otherwise carry out its mission;
- contribute to a secure environment for the international civil implementation presence, and other international organizations, agencies, and non-governmental organizations;
- provide appropriate control of the borders of FRY in Kosovo with Albania and FYROM [Macedonia] until the arrival of the civilian mission of the UN.[3]

Although in theory Resolution 1244 allows any UN member state to station troops in Kosovo, in practice it was assumed that KFOR would be the only international force present. Russian forces stationed in Bosnia dramatically challenged this assumption, moving in quickly to take possession of the Prishtina/Pristina airport before KFOR's arrival. This potential confrontation was resolved, however, with an accord signed in Helsinki on June 18, which set out agreed principles for Russian participation in KFOR operations. The accord limited the Russian contingent to 2850 troops plus an additional 750 troops for airfield and logistic base operation; these units were assigned to the German, American, and French sectors. On this understanding, Russian participation in KFOR has proceeded with relatively little friction.

The same cannot be said of diplomatic relations between Russia and the Western powers. Moscow complains that the security situation subsequent to NATO's intervention is far worse, has criticized the International Tribunal for the former Yugoslavia for

not investigating KLA crimes against the non-Albanian population, and accuses UN authorities in Kosovo, and Bernard Kouchner
in particular, of constantly and conscientiously violating Resolution 1244. The Russians further claim that the economic recovery of Kosovo is far slower than that in the rest of Yugoslavia;
that aid promised by the EU and the US has not been forthcoming; and that sanctions against the FRY have become counterpro-
ductive and should be ended. They pointedly demand that UN
Secretary-General's Special Representative, Kouchner, be replaced and that UNMIK establish official relations with Belgrade.
More specific complaints relate to the issue of identity papers and
license plates that bear no Yugoslav state symbols, the privatization schemes that dispose of FRY state property without Belgrade's consent, the introduction of the Deutschmark as legal
tender, and the fact that provisions for the return of an agreed
number of Yugoslav and Serbian military personnel to Kosovo
are not being implemented. Finally, the Russians insist that negotiations over Kosovo's final status be initiated — a subject so far
eschewed by Western powers.[4]

During the first phase of *Operation Joint Guardian*, NATO troops
moved into Kosovo and set up KFOR headquarters in Prish-
tina/Pristina. To facilitate peacekeeping, KFOR divided the area
into five zones, each under the control of a different NATO member
state. The north, in the region of Mitrovice/Kosovska Mitrovica,
was placed under the control of France, which contributed 7000
troops to the operation. The south, in the region of Prizren/Priz-
ren, was to be Germany's responsibility (8000 troops). The region
of Peje/Pec, in the west, was placed under control of Italy (6000).
Finally, the central area around Prishtina/Pristina and the eastern
region around Gjilan/Gnjilane were to be the responsibility of the
United Kingdom (8000) and the United States (6000), respectively.[5]

KFOR peacekeeping units advancing into Kosovo from Macedonia and Albania met with negligible Serb resistance, consisting
of only a few isolated encounters with Serb security units. Yugo-

slav military and paramilitary forces withdrew from Kosovo within the time period stipulated in the MTA. But while KFOR was militarily in control of the territory, the situation was acutely unstable.

Yugoslav forces did not present the real challenge. NATO and the United Nations were presented with a situation quite unlike any they had experienced before. The UN had overseen transitions, but had done so in respect of states in their entirety, in Namibia, Cambodia, and Mozambique, and had operated under a mandate limited in its duration. The closest the UN had come to a situation like Kosovo was Bosnia-Herzegovina. But even Bosnia was significantly different: it was a state, according to the Dayton agreements, and it had an administrative infrastructure, even if it was divided along ethnic lines.

In Kosovo the administration had collapsed. Serbs who had been part of the ruling administration were fleeing. Two different Albanian polities were vying to fill the vacuum while the KFOR units were still pitching their tents. *The Government of the Republic of Kosova* — the "parallel government" headed by "President" Ibrahim Rugova of the LDK — could claim legitimacy on the basis of unofficial elections held in the early 1990s, and it maintained a residual, but still substantial, grassroots network developed over a decade. *The Provisional Government of Kosova* under "Prime Minister" and KLA commander Hashim Thaci, had authority derived from the Albanian delegation at Rambouillet, where it was constituted in March 1999, as well as the popular authority accorded it for its role in the hostilities. At times these structures, as well as rival factions of the KLA, seemed on the verge of an intra-Albanian armed conflict.

Meanwhile, and even more troubling, Serbian Kosovars and suspected Roma collaborators became the targets of revenge attacks. A disturbing spate of cold-blooded killings followed the cessation of formal hostilities. Many Serbs who had not fled with the departing Yugoslav troops were now forcibly evicted from their homes.

KFOR was evidently unable, during the early days of its deployment, to avert Albanian acts of revenge. The killings of Serbs and other minorities, as well as the destruction of their homes, under the very noses of armed international soldiers represented a profound failure of the international community to uphold the principles that had been hailed as the driving force behind the war effort. The principle of maintaining a secure environment for all citizens was part of Resolution 1244. Given the Bosnian experience, however, KFOR should have prepared itself for this type of violence. More should have been done to stop the rampage. The KFOR troops should had been alerted and told what to do before they entered Kosovo, and they should have been mandated and instructed to use military force against those who were aggressively threatening other people's lives. But during the early days of attacks KFOR troops and infrastructure were not yet fully in place, and KFOR's own security was its chief concern.

As it was, KFOR discovered early on that its mission involved far more than just the military occupation of a liberated province. For the first two months there was not much civilian support from either the United Nations or the OSCE. Thus, the task of maintaining law and order, repairing local infrastructure and administering the region fell to the soldiers. They acted as policemen, repaired roads, bridges, and houses, ran prisons and hospitals, and performed de-mining operations along major roads. At the same time, they began the task of demilitarizing the KLA and disbanding its military structures.

Overall, much of KFOR's mission appears to have been successful, but its operations were by no means trouble-free. Differing national interests and practices caused friction — on several occasions endangering the unity of action. A tightening of procedures seems overdue. German General Klaus Reinhardt, KFOR commander from October 1999 until April 2000, complained bitterly that, contrary to appearances, the KFOR commander "has nothing to command." His proposals to the military leaders of the various national contingents stationed in Kosovo were constantly referred back to their governments for approval. It took him four months of negotiations to get agreement, in principle at least, to deploy other than French forces in Mitrovice/Kosovska Mitrovica. Frequently, units reported for duty at below their full strength, and NATO member states have sometimes withdrawn their contingents without any attempt at coordination. NATO plans to replace the permanent KFOR staff in Kosovo by officers seconded, post for post, for duty in the province, rather than having entire staffs exchanged, would seem to further undermine the efficacy of the military operation.[6] Added to this list of difficulties is KFOR's inadequate intelligence gathering capacity.

## NATION-BUILDING FOR A NON-NATION

**THE MANDATE** * Resolution 1244, the UN blueprint for Kosovo's peace, has both immediate and long-term objectives. For Kosovo's administration, it mandates a three-phased process:

1   performance of basic civilian administration by an international presence where and for as long as this is necessary;
2   administration by provisional self-governing institutions, pending a political settlement; and
3   administration by institutions established under a political settlement.

Civil law and order is to be maintained initially by international police personnel but ultimately through the establishment of a local police force. Refugees and displaced persons are assured safe and unimpeded return to their homes. Initiatives mandated by the Resolution that require sustained, long-term efforts include the protection and promotion of human rights, and support for the reconstruction of key infrastructure and the economy.[7]

## UNMIK'S ARRIVAL

The United Nations Interim Administration Mission in Kosovo (UNMIK) was slow to arrive and make its presence felt. Facing the massive task of recruiting and deploying an entire civil administration, it was frequently criticized for its initial inactivity. Bernard Kouchner was appointed UN Special Representative on July 2, 1999,[8] and assumed his duties on July 15. By June 2000, the international civil administration had grown to 292 professional personnel out of an authorized total of 435. Staffing levels reached 86% of authorized levels at headquarters, 42% in the regions and 60% in the municipalities. The institution-building pillar of OSCE, with an authorized total of 751 staff, had 564 international staff members in place, UNHCR had 78, and the economic reconstruction pillar, 63. In addition, there were 547 UN volunteers from 83 countries.[9]

Secretary-General Annan has pointed to a long list of UNMIK's achievements:

> Within the first months, more than 700,000 refugees returned to their homes, reconstruction had started and preparations for winter were well underway. As a result, despite widespread fears, there were no fatalities as a result of the cold. The Kosovo Liberation Army (KLA) was demilitarized, and the long process of transforming soldiers into civilians began with the formation of the Kosovo Protection Corps (KPC). UNMIK police have made significant progress towards bringing order to the streets of Kosovo, and the training and development of the locally recruited Kosovo Police Service (KPS) is now well underway. The economy is showing signs of a vibrant recovery, and preparations are continuing to revitalize and reform the private sector and to continue the development of a market economy. Local political leaders now share some of the responsibility for guiding Kosovo, and a joint interim administration has been established to allow local residents to share in the administration of the area ...

Many commentators on the Kosovo scene find this assessment far too rosy. There has indeed been progress since June 1999, yet it seems vulnerable to reversal. Dr. Kouchner complains that "the press is silent because there is no big crisis, because children attend school, because the houses have roofs again and the number of murders has gone down from 50 a week to six";[10] but many serious concerns persist.

## THE SECURITY SITUATION

Preventing inter-ethnic violence has proved exceptionally difficult. Over 90% of the population are Kosovar Albanians. Before and during the war they suffered persecution, displacement, and heinous criminal acts at the hand of the Serbs. With the cessation of hostilities and withdrawal from Kosovo of Serb military, many Albanians sought to engage in retribution. Some radical Albanian nationalists wish to "cleanse" Kosovo of all other groups. In his report of June 6, 2000, Secretary-General Annan noted that:

> [t]he general security situation in Kosovo has not changed significantly. Members of minority communities continued to be victims of intimidation, assaults and threats throughout Kosovo.[11]

Recent crime statistics, released by UNMIK, suggest that the general incidence of crime has decreased, but the extent of ethnically motivated crimes, continues to be cause for concern. Serbs, in particular, are disproportionately victimized. (See Table 2)

Approximately 200,000 Serbs lived in Kosovo before the war. While some left voluntarily, many left in fear or were directly forced out by retaliatory attacks. After the summer of 1999 only half were left. The 100,000 remaining Serbs are concentrated in several enclaves (for instance, northern Mitrovice/Kosovska Mitro-

|  | June 1999–Dec 1999 | 2 Jan 2000–30 June 2000 |
| --- | --- | --- |
| Murders | 454 | 146 |
| Kidnappings | 190 | 94 |
| Arson | 1327 | 362 |

Table 2: UNMIK CIVPOL, "Crime Statistics" www.civpol.org/unmik/statistics.htm, August 7, 2000.

vica, Ulpiana/Gracanica, Rrahovec/Orahovac). Elsewhere, KFOR finds itself providing escorts and physical protection for the Serb, Roma, and other minorities who face unrelenting ethnic animosity. Orthodox churches are guarded around the clock. So are some isolated old women in remote villages. A large proportion of KFOR soldiers is, at present, doing their duty by protecting minority members.

The city of Mitrovice/Kosovska Mitrovica has become the focal point for inter-ethnic conflict. The town is divided into a Serb Northern part, which has provided a haven for Serbs from all over Kosovo and an Albanian Southern part. The migration of Albanians from the North to the South and Serbs from the South to the North is still continuing. The Northern part contains the Trepce/Trepca mine complex and the technical faculty of Pristina University, which has been transformed into a Serb university. Kosovar Albanians will never accept the loss of Northern Mitrovice/Kosovska Mitrovica and the continued partition of Mitrovice/Kosovska Mitrovica poses a permanent risk of renewed violence.

A major mistake, at an early stage, was the failure of the French KFOR to insist on an undivided city. Based on past peacekeeping experience, especially in Bosnia, the strategy adopted was to separate Serbs and Albanians in the belief that this was the best way to maintain security. Now it is much more difficult to reverse that strategy. The future of Mitrovice/Kosovska Mitrovica depends on the future of Kosovo and of Resolution 1244. Until the Serbs of Northern Mitrovice/Kosovska Mitrovica accept that they are part of Kosovo, and not Serbia, it will be very difficult to resolve the problem.

Restriction of minorities' freedom of movement affects their access to health care, education, and social welfare. In the face of the deteriorating security situation, the Secretary-General sternly warned both leaders and residents of the province that: "[t]he international community did not intervene in Kosovo to make it a haven for revenge and crime."[12] Its continued support and involvement, he cautioned, was conditional on the full cooperation of all political parties and communities. NATO's Secretary-General similarly admonished the Kosovar Albanians to cooperate with KFOR and UNMIK.[13]

Although violence in Kosovo has abated, the situation of the minorities is still very insecure. Only a small number of Albanians are directly responsible for the violence, but there is very little public condemnation of the violence. There are a few courageous voices — Veton Surroi in the Albanian daily newspaper *Koha Ditore*, for example, or the young people in Prishtina/Pristina who took part in a candlelight demonstration for tolerance in December 1999. But it is difficult to be hopeful about a multi-ethnic society; at present the only way for Serbs to survive is to accept armed protection, with the resulting severe restrictions on movement, in itself a loss of freedom.

## SLOW IN SHOWING UP:
## THE INTERNATIONAL POLICE FORCE

The June 1999 plans had envisaged the speedy deployment of 3000 international policemen in Kosovo. Yet for two months, KFOR was left to enforce law, and order on its own. It was only on August 8 that the first international police units arrived, and started their patrols, chiefly in Prishtina/Pristina. It took three months for the first 1400 to be installed. "Why can NATO bring in 30,000 troops while the UN cannot bring 1000 policemen?" was the plaintive question posed by Agrom Bajrami, an editor at *Koha Ditore*. By mid-September, 500 international policemen were stationed in Prishtina/Pristina (20,000 Serbs), 49 in Mitrovice/Kosovska Mitrovica (12,000 Serbs), 35 in Prizren/ Prizren (150 Serbs), 35 in Gjilan/Gnjilane (3500 Serbs), 26 in Peje/ Pec (450 Serbs), and another 78 were involved in border policing duties. Nine months later 3626 international police were deployed in the province, including 207 border police, out of an authorized strength of 4718. Included in the total number were a Pakistani unit (115 special police officers), two Jordanian units (240 police officers) and two Indian units (214 police officers). By June 2000, the international police force had reached barely 77% of its authorized strength.[14]

The UN police officers were not only slow to arrive, but frequently were unprepared for the tasks that awaited them. Several detachments had to be sent home because of inadequate training. A considerable number did not return from furlough or returned home prematurely. Nevertheless, over time UNMIK's police have assumed more and more of their responsibilities. They enforce the law in the Prishtina/Pristina and Prizren/Prizren regions as well as in Prishtina/Pristina airport; they have investigative authority in Gjilan/Gnjilane, Mitrovice/Kosovska Mitrovica, Peje/Pec, and at the border crossings, Blace and Globovica. They also run the detention facilities in Prishtina/Pristina and Prizren/Prizren. In other regions, however, non-investigative tasks are still being carried out by KFOR. Operations conducted jointly by UNMIK police and KFOR soldiers—especially in Mitrovice/Kosovska Mitrovica — give clout to the UN effort.[15]

UNMIK is responsible for the establishment of the future local police, the Kosovo Police Service (KPS). Training in the OSCE-run KPS school is coordinated with the UNMIK police field training. By January 2001, more than 3500 trained KPS officers will be able to serve as an integral part of UNMIK's police force. KPS is, at present, the only functioning multi-ethnic public service institution in Kosovo.

The international community has conspicuously failed to build up the UNMIK force to the strength of 4718 requested by the UN Secretary-General. In some countries, the constitution prevents the central government from deploying police. In others, policemen are not trained to use firearms, which they might well be required to use in an environment like Kosovo with its ethnic divisions and its gangland criminality. Ideally, UN police should have some specialized training preparing them for UN service in cultures distinctly different from their own.

The police force faces some of the most severe challenges of post-conflict Kosovo. Local communities are caught in the grip of spiraling crime. Albanian mafia structures are increasingly common: their reach extends to Italy and even northern Europe. Drug-running and enforced prostitution are their most characteristic criminal activities. This issue needs to be pushed to the top of the UN, and particularly the EU's, agenda. It is evident that UNMIK and KFOR need far better intelligence on the ground.

The experience in Kosovo, particularly the excruciatingly slow buildup of police, has demonstrated the need for the establishment of stand-by UN police units, earmarked by national governments for assignment to the Secretary-General. This is not a new idea. The Commission considers it extremely urgent to add its voice to the appeal to member states to provide UNMIK with the number of police officers and special police units necessary to implement its mandate.

## STILL MISSING: AN EFFECTIVE JUDICIAL SYSTEM

Establishing a proper judicial administration for Kosovo is one of UNMIK's chief objectives. More than 400 judges, prosecutors, and lay judges were sworn in during January and February 2000, but the judicial process continues to be snail-like. This is true of both ordinary criminal cases, which have dramatically increased in number, and war crimes and ethnically motivated crimes.

A Supreme Court, five district courts, 17 municipal courts, one commercial court and 13 Offices of the Public Prosecutor have been established. They have been provided with cars, desks, chairs, bookcases, filing cabinets, and generators as well as registers, court stamps, stationery, and legal forms. By June 2000, Kosovo's judicial system comprised 274 judges, 40 prosecutors, and 238 lay judges, all of whom had been screened by an Advisory Judicial Commission. However, owing to the continuing ethnic conflict, the shortage of international prosecutors and judges, and the uncertainty about which laws to apply, the judicial system can hardly be described as working fairly and effectively. Low salaries have also predisposed some legal professionals to bribery and corruption.

Establishment of a multi-ethnic criminal justice system has been hampered by the reluctance of members of minorities to serve on the bench as well as by the pronounced bias of many Albanian judges. Fair trials for inter-ethnic conflicts are all but impossible. Detainees frequently have to be released after a few days —often because of space or staffing constraints. Almost 40% are immediately released, significantly undermining efforts to restore public order. The number of persons actually tried rose from 24 in February 2000 to 367 in May. But many obstacles remain: dilapidated judicial buildings, the absence of a forensic laboratory, and a shortage of detention spaces. There is growing concern that criminals and human rights violators go unpunished.[16]

These difficulties are compounded by the fact that Resolution 1244 did not specify which law should be applied in occupied Kosovo. Initially UNMIK decided to apply Serbian and FRY law because of 1244's commitment to respect Yugoslav sovereignty. The Kosovar Albanians protested, demanding the restoration of laws operative pre-1989 which had been passed by the largely Albanian legislature in that era. Thereupon UNMIK reversed its course, deciding to apply Kosovo law as it existed in 1989. Serb judges were even less inclined to serve. Many of the old laws were based on socialist agendas, and there were several types of law in force on March 22, 1989, including FRY laws.

In order to restore confidence in the Kosovo courts, UNMIK called in February 2000 for the appointment of foreign judges and prosecutors. By September 2000, six of the foreign judges and two of the foreign prosecutors had been appointed. It was hoped that this would help overcome the slowness and partiality of the judicial system, but the effects of international recruitment have yet to be demonstrated. There is also a serious shortage of qualified defense lawyers—no more than 150 attorneys in Kosovo are available to defend suspects. Any NGO efforts to extend legal aid to indigent criminal defendants would be highly valued.

Dr Kouchner's plan to establish a special court to deal with war crimes will not be realized until the United Nations approves the $5 million budget plus $10 million operational costs.

## IMPOSING LAW AND ORDER

UNMIK has succeeded in replacing the chaos it first met in Kosovo with some semblance of order. The first regulation passed by the UN Administration, in July 1999, vested "all legislative and executive authority, including the administration of the judiciary," in the hands of the Special Representative of the Secretary-General, (SRSG). Using these powers, Kouchner secured the demobilization of the KLA and the dismantling of the parallel and provisional structures of self-government established by the KLA and its political leadership following the entry of NATO's forces.

UNMIK is an unprecedented experiment in international affairs. It has more extensive authority than any previous UN mission, and far more than that delegated to the High Representative in Bosnia-Herzegovina. Kouchner and his officials can wield this authority at their discretion, appoint and dismiss Albanian officials, determine which laws are to be applied and which are not, or override, should they feel compelled to do so, the decisions taken by the elected bodies of the future. Yet given the complexity of contemporary society, it is almost impossible to implement policy and to sustain legitimacy without cooperation with, and indeed reliance on, local experts and persons of influence.

Local political leaders have been included in the administrative process, but it has been a precarious process. UNMIK, under-staffed on its arrival, was faced with strong KLA structures. Pro-visional mayors resented being subordinated to foreigners. As late as October 1999, UNMIK had only one UN official in each municipality. Where UN officials took a cautious and consultative approach, cooperation gradually emerged; where they behaved more assertively, confrontation tended to be the result. At times the suitability of some UN personnel's qualifications for adminis-tering a town was questioned, causing conflict beyond the in-evitable political or personal friction. The UN had powerful lever-age derived from the fact that it offered a route to funding from and contacts with the outside world. This leverage was often de-cisive when conflicts over administrative power emerged.

In order to fulfill the UNMIK mandate to develop "provisional democratic self-government institutions." Dr. Kouchner created the Kosovo Transition Council (KTC), an executive committee of leading political figures in the province. While all authority re-mains in the hands of the UNMIK head, the Council has both consultative and advisory functions, involving the political lead-ership of the province in a process of dialogue and peace making. The enlarged 36-member KTC meets each week under the chair-manship of the SRSG. The Serbian community has been reluctant to participate, although Serbs represented by Bishop Artemije at Ulpiana/Gracanica have cooperated and attended meetings. The "Gracanica Serbs", however, have from time to time withdrawn in protest against continuing attacks on members of their ethnic group. Serbs from north Mitrovice/Kosovska Mitrovica have re-fused to join the Council, though their leadership meets sepa-rately with regional UNMIK representatives and with representa-tives of the Kosovar community in the south of the city.

On December 15, 1999, the UNMIK established the Joint Interim Administrative Structure (JIAS). The JIAS provided the framework for sharing responsibilities for provisional administration with representatives of a broad cross-section of Kosovar society. From this body evolved the Joint Interim Administrative Council (JIAC), which functions as an executive board. The JIAC endorsed the establishment of 20 departments, each of which is controlled by two heads, one international, and one local. Under the December Agreement, all parallel structures, whether executive, legislative, or judicial, were to be dissolved by January 31, 2000. This demand had largely been met by February. The JIAC subsequently created the Central Election Commission, the Civil Registry, and the Victim Recovery and Identification Commission.

An important feature of any local empowerment and democratization initiative must be the active involvement of women in the decision-making and management process during a post-conflict period. This is, in fact, an explicit part of the current UN mandate. The "Recommendations for Further Implementation of the Beijing Platform of Action," the outcome document of the United Nations Beijing+5 Women 2000 Conference held in New York in June 2000, urges the UN and its members, as well as other international organizations, to "provide support to and empower women who play an important role within their families as stabilizing factors in conflict and post-conflict situations." In addition, it asks that the UN encourage its member nations and the rest of the international community to "improve and strengthen the capacity of women affected by situations of armed conflict including refugees and displaced women by, inter alia, involving them in the design and management of humanitarian activities so that they benefit from these activities on an equal basis with men." The Commission believes that this policy should be reflected in UNMIK's work and in any UN response to armed conflict in the future.

Considerable progress has also been made in the establishment of administrative bodies. By the end of May 2000, 27 out of 30 municipal councils had been established, and the same number of municipal administrative boards. In this process, as elsewhere, the limited participation of minority communities continues to be a matter of concern. Serb, Turkish, Roma and Bosniak

Kosovars are all reluctant to assume municipal positions. The creation of representative municipal structures has proven particularly difficult in Mitrovice/Kosovska Mitrovica.

An Institute for Civil Administration has been established as the training institution for the public sector. Five party centers provide access to basic infrastructure and communication facilities to all political parties. Since April 2000, preparations have been under way for municipal elections to be held in the autumn. By July 1, 28 political parties had registered for the elections, highlighting a trend towards increasing intra-ethnic pluralism in the Kosovar Albanian political landscape. Approximately 1.2 million Kosovars are eligible for registration. Again, however, Serb distrust of the political process has made Serbs reluctant to register. UN and OSCE officials continue to press for the registration of both the "Gracanica Serbs" and the "Mitrovica Serbs," but their participation is uncertain. Serb reluctance bodes ill for elections at the wider provincial level in 2001. Some UN officials fear that elections may cement ethnic divisions, as occurred in Bosnia-Herzegovina, rather than bridging them.

Although Kosovo has never formally held free elections, Kosovar Albanians have ten years of experience of organizing elections and referenda for their parallel institutions. Today, as a protectorate, Kosovo is subjected to a fairly non-democratic form of governance: although people are supposed to elect municipal and provincial authorities, they have no final say when it comes to determining their future status. When the international community arrived in Kosovo, there was enormous enthusiasm and excitement about the prospect of rebuilding Kosovo. Now there is growing frustration among large sections of the population about the constraints on self-rule. This frustration is not likely to ease unless there is much greater involvement of Kosovars (both Albanians and others) at all levels of governance.

UNMIK has met with much greater success in its demilitarization of the KLA. On June 21, 1999, KFOR and the KLA signed an

Undertaking on Demilitarization of the Kosovar Albanian force, then approximately 20,000 strong. The KLA was to be transformed into a civilian agency, the Kosovo Protection Corps (KPC), charged with providing emergency response and reconstruction services. The demobilization initiative offered individual KLA members the opportunity to join the KPC.

Demilitarization was completed by September 20, 1999. On the same day, the Kosovo Protection Corps was established. Modeled on the French Securité Civile, the KPC is intended to have 3000 members and an auxiliary branch of 2000. Ten percent of its members are required to be members of minority communities. Only 200 members will be authorized to carry weapons. The Corps is not to be used for riot control, counter-terror operations, or tasks related to the maintenance of law and order.

Screening by the International Organization for Migration (IOM) for positions within the KPC began in the fall of 1999. The IOM interviewed more than 18,500 KLA soldiers. No Serbs applied, and most of the 500 positions for minorities remain empty. All candidates were tested for a variety of skills and screened for criminal records. The IOM subsequently coordinated KPC training. The former guerilla fighters took courses in construction, electrical work, transportation, supply and maintenance, and general management. At the same time, they received advanced training in rescue missions and disaster relief, mine-awareness training, and training in civilian protection, human rights, and first aid.

On January 21, 2000, the KPC was officially inaugurated. By the end of May, KPC strength stood at 4542. Only 53 were from minority groups. All members have been placed on probationary status for one year. The KPC established five fixed Regional Emergency Response Units, one in each KFOR/UNMIK sector, as well as a mobile Rapid Response Unit. More than 2000 KPC members were engaged in various work projects like garbage cleanup, road repair, school reconstruction, and the building of bakeries or green-houses. The KPC was scheduled to be fully trained, equipped, and operational by September 2000.

It would be naïve to expect the KLA to easily relinquish its ambition to become the future army of an independent Kosovo. On the other hand, KFOR —under whose daily supervision KPC operates—has a keen interest in preventing the former KLA from evolving into a kind of Kosovar Taliban, turning against its former mentors. The discovery in mid-June of a huge arms cache near the headquarters of former KLA General Ceku, now the KPC sector chief in Klecke/Klecka, was the clearest indication yet of a perilous potential for future conflict.

## THE RETURN OF THE REFUGEES

The return of the refugees was one of the chief objectives and accomplishments of the UN mission. Of some 848,000 people who had fled or been expelled from the province, most returned on their own, following hard on their heels of the KFOR units. Despite early fears that some of the returning refugees might die of exposure to the cold, these efforts succeeded in averting this risk entirely.

The victims of reverse ethnic cleansing — some 100,000 Serbs who left the territory or were driven out after the arrival of KFOR — are still in Serbia or Montenegro. The safe and secure environment that would allow their return seems unlikely to be created in the near future. Likewise, conditions are not yet adequate for the forced return of the refugees from Western Europe.

Once the emergency relief needs were successfully met, the humanitarian affairs pillar ceased to exist at the end of June 2000 as a formal component of the UNMIK structure. UNHCR will, however, remain deeply engaged in the province. A Humanitarian Coordinator will help facilitate the transition from the relief program to longer-term reconstruction and development. In the light of the Kosovo experience, the international community should urgently raise the level of its support for UNHCR activities.

Many refugees remain missing or are detained in Serbia. The complete disregard for their plight was a glaring omission in Resolution 1244. According to the International Committee of the Red Cross (ICRC), as of March 21, 2000 there were 1571 Kosovo-Albanian prisoners in Serb prisons, held for "sedition" or similar offences. Some have been tried and sentenced, some still await trial, and some have been freed after their families paid ransom. The ICRC estimates that there are 3000 missing persons, most of whom are Kosovar Albanians. Other observers claim that the figure for missing people is much higher. UNMIK's Victim Recovery Identification Commission may, as its work progresses, shed some light on their fate.[17]

## REBUILDING THE ECONOMY

The world still remembers what KFOR and UNMIK found when they first moved into Kosovo:

> Empty streets. Shattered shops. No water. No work. Smoking ruins. Murders in the open streets. Dead bodies and piles of garbage. Not a newspaper to buy, not even a loaf of bread. Not a child in school. No fields safe to plough. Most of the livestock lost. No one in charge.[18]

Kosovo was one of the poorest provinces in one of the poorest countries in Europe. Like the rest of post-Tito Yugoslavia, it suffered from the inefficiencies of a rigidified communist system that proved incapable of reforming itself even after the fall of the Berlin Wall. Then the province was further devastated by the war.

As the UNMIK and Civilian Military Cooperation (CIMIC) teams assembled by various KFOR contingents, as well as the EC Task Force,[19] surveyed the province, they registered 120,000 houses damaged or destroyed by war; 250 schoolhouses were in need of repair; the health care system and the banking system had collapsed; roads were in ruins, bridges destroyed; there was no electricity; no mail service, and telephone lines were down.

The situation has vastly improved since June 1999. A massive effort was quickly mounted to re-roof houses and rebuild them, and to repair schools and hospitals. A broad range of governments, international agencies, and NGOs is funding the reconstruction effort and it has made an impressive start:

- Eighty-six percent of school-age children attend schools now furnished with tens of thousands of desks, chairs, and schoolbags. New textbooks were published in Albanian, Serbian, Bosnian, and Turkish. A project for formulating a blueprint for Kosovo's educational system has been initiated. Universities and colleges have been reopened.

- Physical infrastructure has been repaired to some extent. Over DM150 million has been invested in the electrical sector, and water services have been maintained. Nevertheless, electricity is available for only three hours a day in Prishtina/Pristina, and water for only four hours. A mobile telephone system covers four cities and Prishtina/Pristina airport; the old land-line system is being repaired. Television and radio are back on the air.

- Postal services have been restored with the assistance of the EU. The European Agency for Reconstruction supplied delivery vehicles and equipment like workstations, copy and fax machines, furniture, scales, and trolleys. The sale of UNMIK postage stamps began on March 15, 2000. International letter service resumed in June 2000.

- UNMIK, FAO, and the World Bank started a major effort to revitalize agricultural activity. Fertilizers, seed, potatoes, maize, and vegetable kits were distributed to farmers for the spring sowing season. The wheat harvest in July was expected to meet the needs of 65% of the population.

- There is a Central Fiscal Authority and the Banking and Payments Bureau (the equivalent of a central bank). A number of commercial banks and micro-credit institutions have been licensed. The Deutschmark has been legalized as official currency.

The term "vibrant," however, describes neither the economic situation nor the mood in any adequate way. Against the UN claim that roughly 70% of private enterprises have restarted, producing more and employing more than in 1998, one has to hold the fact that the size of this sector remains comparatively modest. The only truly vibrant economic sector is the flourishing black market. Privatization has made slow progress — perhaps fortuitously, as only the existing mafia structures are likely to have benefited. An efficient tax system remains to be developed, and UNMIK will have to wait some time before internal revenues can meet a significant portion of its costs.

The continuing job crisis presents the greatest challenge to the Kosovo economy. The province has the highest unemployment rate in Europe: over 50% according to most estimates. As more refugees return from abroad, this rate is likely to increase. The population shift from the rural areas to the cities has further compounded the problem of urban unemployment. Strategies to combat joblessness in Kosovo have to be developed urgently. A public works project for clearing the rubble left behind by the war and cleaning away the garbage could provide a substantial number of jobs to unemployed Kosovars.

More speedy recovery presupposes, of course, a much more focused—and more generous—effort on the part of the international donor community, especially the European Union. UNMIK, at present, is desperately short of funds.

## EXTERNAL FINANCIAL SUPPORT

The Kosovo consolidated budget for the 2000 fiscal year provides for expenditures of DM562 million. Donor pledges have been only partially fulfilled, with DM200 million pledged but only DM149 million actually received by early June 2000.[20] Domestically generated revenue was expected to reach DM49 million. Thus, there was a significant shortfall. Kosovo's cash requirements could be met only through September 2000.

The balance with regard to general reconstruction needs is similarly sobering. A comprehensive reconstruction program is estimated to cost DM2 billion, not considering other investments deemed necessary. Funds pledged by donors total DM2.6 billion, and known commitments DM1.2 billion. The shortfall explains Secretary-General Annan's remark:

> A number of high-priority needs remain without funding, including the rehabilitation of courts, schools, hospitals and other public buildings; the development of multiple solid waste disposal facilities and environmental clean-up; and the development of the local human resources.

Lasting peace in the Kosovo region rests on its future prosperity. Economic recovery is a precondition of societal tranquility and communal coexistence. It requires, however, the continual provision of international funds, both for the UN mission and for the reconstruction of the province.

UN member states, unfortunately, have been slow to pay their share of the initial $125 million assessed for the operation. This has helped foster UNMIK's reputation as a near-insolvent operation barely able to pay its bills, and has undermined its leverage with local parties.

The United States has preferred to direct its additional aid bilaterally, focusing on Washington's priorities, such as the transformation of the KLA into the Kosovo Protection Force. The European Union, for its part, has pledged substantial resources — the grand total for 1999 and 2000 amounts to €825 million. To this sum, the bilateral aid extended by individual EU states has to be added. In fact, the EU and its member states have been the main providers of financial support. As Javier Solana, Secretary-General of the Council and High Representative for the EU Common Foreign and Security Policy, pointed out to the Security Council, they have contributed over €17 billion to the Balkans as a whole since 1991. In Kosovo alone they have spent more than €3 billion on non-military programs, in addition to their substantial military commitment, which includes the provision of 28,000 troops to KFOR and 1700 policemen.

However, the lengthy approval processes of the EU apparatus have severely inhibited the speedy allocation of urgently needed sums. Millions of euros were committed but not disbursed. Delays were caused partly by the fact that EU finance ministers objected to making budgetary contributions to an entity that could not in the ordinary sense be understood as a country. This refusal directly contributed to UNMIK's inability to meet its financial obligations at the end of 1999. EU procedures have now been streamlined and the approval process made more efficient, but obstacles remain. For one thing, the EU Commission has assessed the Kosovo alimentation requirement until 2006 at €6 billion; this figure is at odds with that put forward by EU finance ministers. For another, the European Agency for Reconstruction is controlled by two administrative committees, one in Prishtina/Pristina and the other one in Brussels. This creates unnecessary duplication in every single decision. They have to base their deliberations on 80 different EU regulations. The various committees do not meet more than once a month, which causes additional delay. New guidelines which limit the administrative committees to strategic orientation rather than to micro management are desperately needed. The European Agency for Reconstruction in Prishtina/Pristina is controlled by an Administrative Committee that consists of representatives from all of the 15 member states. Thus, Brussels red tape impedes not only the reconstruction of Kosovo, but the recovery of the wider Balkan region. The Stability Pact[21] has made some progress, but is far from meeting the expectations of the Balkan peoples.

The World Bank convened several Kosovo donor conferences. At the first (July 28, 1999), $2.1 billion was pledged; a further $1 billion was pledged at the second (November 17, 1999). In March 2000 the donors agreed to provide €2,4 billion for the most urgent projects. But here, too, crippling bureaucracy continues to undercut the potential of the reconstruction programs. As the World Bank's Balkan representative Rory O'Sullivan put it, there are sufficient financial resources: "from now on it is a matter of implementation."

The challenges to the economy are immense. If funds promised are not allocated fast, Kosovar teachers, local civil servants, and health workers will go unpaid. New enterprise is needed to galvanize the economy or it will never get off the ground. Clumsy bureaucracy has afflicted nearly every internationally backed economic initiative. The EU in particular must look to its grant approval process and move more quickly towards its Stability Pact goals. Economic initiatives must heed the fact that the Kosovo problem can only be resolved in a wider regional framework of intra-Balkan cooperation, facilitating both stronger political and economic linkages.

The most severe economic challenges for Kosovo do not stem from war damage, inflicted by either Yugoslav and Serbian forces or from NATO bombs, but from decades of underdevelopment. Given that the policies of the World Bank program designed for Kosovo reflect the same economic reforms and policies required of Yugoslavia in the 1980s, new problems of "underdevelopment" and new grievances may well be generated. Many of the political objectives of the international program do require a more diversified economy, workforce, and managerial class than currently exists. The distortions introduced into a local economy by an international operation of this sort — well known from peacekeeping missions elsewhere — make these reforms more urgent.

A major concern is the criminalization of the economy and the growth of the power of the mafia. Smuggling, drug trade and trafficking in human beings is accelerating. These developments distort the economic reconstruction in Kosovo, and will be difficult to rectify.

Moreover, liberation from Yugoslav security forces has not changed the logic of political behavior: that power begins with control over economic assets, including opportunities for patronage through allocation of jobs. This form of competition is likely to intensify, not abate.

Relations between Kosovo and Serbia proper, whatever the final status of Kosovo, will have to include economic relations. Both are landlocked. Both are impoverished by the policies of the 1980s and the wars and sanctions of the 1990s. Despite Serbia's current economic weakness, it will remain the richer neighbor. This suggests that positive relations between the two populations will be necessary for genuine Kosovo autonomy or independence. Aid dependency on the international community rather than Yugoslavia will not improve Kosovar prospects. Above all, a fundamentally new economic policy for Kosovo will be necessary to induce the changes in social structure and political behavior necessary for a tolerant, democratic regime in Kosovo.

## CONCLUSION

Kosovo—along with Bosnia—remains the most acute fracture zone in Europe. UNMIK has done a commendable job, but much remains to be done.[22] According to Carl Bildt, Special Envoy of the UN Secretary-General for the Balkans, "There is still far more of the rule of thugs than the rule of law."[23] The prevailing political and economic uncertainty about the future of both Kosovo and Serbia is a huge obstacle. Moreover, peace will be very difficult so long as there are protected enclaves and divided cities within Kosovo.

Several lessons of the UNMIK experience bear repeating. In the context of a humanitarian intervention, the failure of UN/KFOR to foresee and reduce revenge killings was the most critical weakness of the operation. It was not helped by the lack of coordination between NATO forces. Over the longer term, the lack of a qualified police force makes the establishment of law and order nearly impossible. Clearly, the UN needs a more capable and ready standby police force if it is to engage in such an ambitious operation. The necessary policing demands experience in anti-terrorist operations and dealing with organized crime, and access to effective intelligence gathering. Addressing these and other weaknesses in the current administration requires a substantial improvement and expansion in the funding available for both UN and UNHCR operations.

# PART 2:

# ANALYSIS

*

Peace talks were held at Rambouillet Castle,
southeast of Paris.

# 5

# THE DIPLOMATIC DIMENSION

In 1998 and early 1999, the international community faced a deep moral and legal dilemma: the responsibility to avoid force if at all possible, and the demand to protect a victimized population against severe abuse of human rights and gross violations of international humanitarian law. The assessment after the fact of the choices made is inherently difficult, since it necessarily involves speculation on alternative paths that might have been attempted. This will not be the last time such a dilemma arises. We can best prepare for the future by taking an honest and critical look at the past.

Such speculation and critique, however, must be anchored in an awareness of crucial factors over which the international community had very limited influence. For instance:

- FRY policies and actions were clearly the fundamental cause of violence and unrest in Kosovo during the whole decade of the 1990s, and especially in the period between 1997 and 99. The Milosevic regime by its oppressive policies and misrule in Kosovo bears full responsibility for provoking a crisis of decision among concerned governments and within international institutions, especially the United Nations and NATO. It is also accountable for the criminality of Serb official behavior in Kosovo itself.

- The FRY's approach to Kosovo was dominated by the play of domestic political forces. Arguably, by playing the nationalist and ethnic card in Kosovo as his path to power, Milosevic had made himself captive of internal ideological forces that were unwilling to compromise on Kosovo. In domestic terms, he may have had little possibility of accepting a pragmatic compromise, no matter which diplomatic strategy had been chosen by the international community.

- The Kosovar leadership did not offer much room for accommodation, either. The uncompromising and maximalist LDK and KLA demands for independence, and the subsequent violent and deliberately provocative insurgency of the KLA, confronted Belgrade with an escalating challenge whose demands went beyond what was acceptable even to the anti-Milosevic democratic opposition. The international community, in fact, was virtually unanimous in its opposition to the notion of Kosovo as an independent state. Nevertheless, the KLA "internationalization" strategy became that of inducing NATO-based military intervention rather than a diplomatic compromise, as only the former would likely lead toward independence rather than some form of autonomy of the pre-1989 variety.

Combining these factors with the previous chapter's striking portrait of the human rights abuse and violations of international humanitarian law in Kosovo, it is clear that criticism of the international response should not undermine the clarity of the moral imperative to act in the face of massive human rights abuse, even in the face of an ongoing insurgency that had been characterized by some as a "non-international armed conflict." The need for action was obvious. The constraints were enormous. The choices of actions taken are nevertheless always important to assess.

The international community's response was also plagued by factors not specific to Kosovo, but endemic to the current functioning of international politics. The weaknesses resulting from this functioning need not be fatalistically accepted. Indeed, a crisis such as we are assessing here points to the urgent need for broader institutional reforms within the UN and elsewhere and changes in attitude. Such changes, however important for future implementation, were supremely unlikely to occur prior to the Kosovo war. Thus, the following factors must also form a backdrop for the discussion:

The international response was formulated by a dozen or more key states, each with its own perceptions of national interest, its own particular set of domestic constraints and forces, including different perspectives of political and military leadership, and its own analysis of the past and possible future in the Balkans. In addition, these states were collaborating to reach joint policies simultaneously in several distinctly different groupings, including the UN, NATO, the OSCE, and the EU. The logical result was a lack of consistency in the diplomatic response.

These individual member states, as well as intergovernmental entities, are still deeply entrenched in perceiving all international problems solely in terms of short-term national self-interest. If a case can be made that the problem is someone else's responsibility, tough decisions will be avoided as long as possible. If the problem can be ignored, it will be. If national self-interest is not deemed to be crucially affected, states will not get involved until public international pressure mounts sufficiently to pressure them to do so. In cases of internal war and human rights abuse, the resulting engagement is inevitably late.

## CONFRONTING AN ESCALATING INTERNAL WAR:
## FEBRUARY–SEPTEMBER 1998

Before 1998, a pattern of mixed messages from the international community to the key players in the Kosovo drama was already well entrenched. The international community's early failure to respond, lack of consistency, and at times complete lack of engagement all contributed to the diplomatic difficulties that would arise later. Support for the "parallel society" and a greater attempt to establish and maintain an international presence on the ground would have strengthened the more moderate factions, while giving the international community more leverage to influence the local situation. A more consistent pattern of diplomatic effort was needed in this period to keep Kosovo on the international political agenda and maintain pressure on Serbia. Clearly, the most promising window of diplomatic opportunity to resolve the Kosovo crisis without war existed in this pre-1998 period. [1]

Paradoxically, the political will to mount such a diplomatic effort could be mobilized only after the conflict escalated into full-scale violence, while this violence in turn severely constrained the responsiveness of local players to diplomatic initiatives. Thus, once the KLA burst on the scene publicly with its attacks against Serbian police and other civilians, the FRY faced an armed uprising using arguably terrorist tactics. The FRY would have had little trouble arguing to the international community that such an uprising demanded a state response, even a forceful one. But in an era when public opinion plays a steadily increasing role in determining the stance of the international community, the extent to which the FRY response directly targeted civilians undermined the legitimacy of its claims of a statist justification of counter-insurgency. As casualties and displacement of Kosovar civilians mounted, the political will of the international community slowly coalesced.

The international community already had considerable experience of dealing with Milosevic and Serbia. The Bosnian experience conditioned everyone's attitudes and calculations of the possibilities. Distrust and skepticism were high, and deservedly so, but to a certain extent Milosevic was beginning to be seen as a known quantity. This conditioning both helped and hindered the diplomacy. The pitfalls of "fighting the previous war" proved very relevant.

The Kosovo leadership, on the other hand, presented the international community with a diplomatic conundrum. On the course of 1998, it was difficult to know whom to deal with. The LDK had a certain informal legitimacy in international circles, but it became increasingly evident that it had no sway over the insurgency and was losing its pre-eminence among the Albanian Kosovar population. The KLA, virtually unknown and very small prior to 1998, was a headless coagulation of factions, growing chaotically at a breakneck pace. Without centralized leadership, it could not be integrated into any rational diplomatic process.

The formulation of a coherent diplomatic response seeking resolution of an internal war requires an attempt to understand the motivations and interests of both parties to the conflict. Solutions must respond to those interests, or they will not be sustainable. The LDK and KLA were transparent in their goal: they insisted on independence. But without direct communication, the international community could not ascertain the extent of negotiability of this goal. Nor was the KLA strategy of internationalizing conflict clear until much later.

The underlying motivations of FRY behavior are still open to debate. There can be no question that the FRY behaved illegally and immorally, targeting massive human rights violations against civilians and using violence far disproportionate to the level of insurgency threat that it faced. But uncertainty over the mixture of motivations behind this violence dogged the international response, and remains unresolved. Fundamentally, there were two ways to interpret FRY actions: either as counter-insurgency operations designed to eliminate both the KLA threat and the popular support for it, or as a long-term strategy of ethnic cleansing to permanently alter the demographics and ethnic power balance in Kosovo.

These two motivations are by no means mutually exclusive, and either one could explain most of the violence. Forced displacement and killing of civilians is a cruel tactic often relied upon by the counter-insurgency side in such a civil war. The levels of abuse in Kosovo were comparable with those of numerous other recent counter-insurgency wars, for example Colombia or Turkey. Some analysts argue that the military and repressive strategy of the FRY can be entirely explained as a counter-insurgency strategy, albeit one that went well beyond the bounds of morality and humanitarian law.[2] At the same time, the history of FRY behavior in the 1990s gave rise to a reasonable suspicion of a longer-term ethnic cleansing goal in Kosovo. This suspicion was sustained not only by Milosevic's actions with respect to Croatia and Bosnia, but also by explicit statements of other key Serbian players who openly espoused the cleansing of Kosovo.[3] It is possible that there was a range of views on the goals of force among Serb officials and their counter-insurgency operatives, some recognizing the opportunity for ethnic cleansing under the label of counter-insurgency, others focusing only on the defeat of the KLA challenge to Serb rule. This type of war, especially given the demographic balance in Kosovo, tends to rely on tactics that displace those sectors of the population that are deemed hostile to the established order, which in Kosovo meant virtually the entire populace.

Evidence of an ethnic cleansing motive logically justifies pre-emptive international action to protect the targeted population, and to a certain extent this explains the greater constraints the international community was willing to apply to Serbia, as compared with other counter-insurgency situations. An apparent double standard, however, must be recognized, with many cruel counter-insurgency campaigns around the world generating no formal international response. This contrast feeds the belief widespread in Belgrade that the international responses to their counter-insurgency efforts were hypocritical expressions of an anti-Serbian global conspiracy.

At the same time, given the insurgency/counter-insurgency dynamic, the process of escalating provocation and reaction by

the two armed groups (KLA and FRY) in Kosovo, both using terrorist tactics (though on very different scales), should have conditioned the international community's attitude and approach toward the KLA. A resolution of the problem necessarily had to involve a cessation of hostilities on both sides. Despite Contact
Group calls for collaboration to constrain the KLA, no discernable
action was taken along such a line.[4]

## EARLY RESPONSES

The key intergovernmental players developing an international
response to the growing crisis were the UN, the Contact Group,
the OSCE, and, subsequently, NATO. Member states were meanwhile developing their individual foreign policy responses independently.

The Contact Group, initially constituted to deal with Bosnia,
comprised representatives of the Russian Federation, the USA,
the UK, Germany, France, and Italy. It assumed a dominant role
as diplomatic agent of the international community with respect
to the deepening Kosovo crisis. The Group began calling for dialogue between the Kosovo resistance and Belgrade as early as
September 1997, stressing in each communication that "we support neither independence nor the status quo."[5] On January 28,
1998, the Parliamentary Assembly of the Council of Europe (COE)
approved a resolution calling for an end to the repression of ethnic Albanians and immediate dialogue between the parties, and
highlighting the fact that the province was on the brink of civil
war.[6] On February 28, 1998, the Contact Group stated, "Our commitment to human rights values means that we cannot ignore
such disproportionate methods of control. Government authorities have a special responsibility to protect the human and civil
rights of all citizens and to ensure that public security forces act
judiciously and with restraint."[7]

In response to the events in Drenice/Drenica, the United

States unilaterally withdrew certain diplomatic concessions, including the resumption of civil aviation with Yugoslavia. These concessions had been offered in exchange for the Yugoslav government's support for moderate political forces in the Republic of Srpska in Bosnia–Herzegovina. Some of Milosevic's aides dismissed these actions as insignificant.[8]

On March 9, 1998, the Contact Group met to review these developments and unanimously decided to impose an arms embargo and a ban on transfers of equipment that could be used for repression. However, France, Italy, and Russia refused to agree to the full panoply of sanctions. On the American side, US Secretary of State Madeleine Albright called the measures merely "satisfactory" and stated that the threat of force was "essential to move forward."[9] British Foreign Secretary Robin Cook stated that "We do not accept that this is merely an internal matter." The German government proposed that the issue be raised before the UN Security Council, and the Russians sent clear signals that a resolution would be blocked.[10]

The Contact Group's March 1998 statements formed the basis for UNSC Resolution 1160 (discussed below) but also included proposals that did not make it into the Resolution. The Group's early recommendations were consistently aimed at getting a more visible multi-functional international presence into the province, including a proposed UNHCR mission to Kosovo, the return of OSCE long-term missions to Kosovo, and the establishment of an international consortium including NGOs to promote the building of a civil society in Kosovo. Finally, though without the agreement of Russia, the Contact Group called for the denial of visas to specific FRY representatives and a moratorium on export credit for Belgrade, pointing out that, if progress was not made on the other demands, Russia would agree to these as well. In April 1998, again without Russian support, the Contact Group put into effect a freeze on FRY funds held abroad, and threatened to block all new investment in Serbia.[11]

Prior to NATO's active involvement, the Contact Group was the primary forum for building coherence among the various responses of the US and the European states. Significant differences in diplomatic approach to Kosovo complicated diplomacy in the period leading up to the war. These differences concerned means rather than goals or values, and reflected different views about how to exert influence on Milosevic, how to pursue a diplomacy of force, and the degree to which a diplomatic solution was seen as a real option.

The US position, as expressed by its Secretary of State, Madeleine Albright, appeared to assume that the only effective means to influence Milosevic was to back up one's negotiating demands at all stages with a credible and serious commitment to the use of force.[12] Anything less would not seem to have heeded "the lessons of Bosnia," and, significantly, would be subject to scornful domestic right-wing criticism in the United States. The NATO bombing of Bosnia in 1995 was interpreted as having quickly forced Milosevic to the bargaining table at Dayton.[13] Such a strategy required a credible threat to inflict serious damage, depending upon convincing a wily opponent that it was not just a bluff, and putting in place an arrangement that was self-implementing because it was enforced by an adequate armed presence.

Given the experience of the Bosnian War, Western powers believed that the only effective way to protect the Kosovar Albanians without recourse to actual force was to threaten its use, even though such threat diplomacy runs counter to the UN Charter. They also wanted to put in place an arrangement that did not rely on Belgrade's good will. It seemed reasonable in this same spirit to distrust any commitment by Milosevic that was not based on coercion, and further, to assume it likely that he would back down at the last minute or, at worst, after the first days of any attack. In this regard, it is crucial to appreciate the perception of Milosevic as a pragmatist rather than a fanatic.

In Europe there was also general support for the idea of conveying a message to Belgrade that a continuing pattern of abuse in Kosovo would be disastrous for the FRY. Rather than threats of air power, the preferred approach promoted by the UK and France rested on a major preventive deployment of ground troops in neighboring countries, posing the implicit threat of a combined ground/air war. Such a deployment is more diplomatically ambiguous as it does not rest as directly on an explicit threat to use force, and at the same time might have conveyed more clearly a firmness of resolve to go beyond a bluff.

## UN SECURITY COUNCIL

The UNSC did not start to pay attention to Kosovo until violence increased rapidly in 1998. UNSC Resolution 1160 (March 31, 1998) drew directly on earlier formal recommendations and decisions of the Contact Group. It condemned both Serbian counter-insurgency and KLA terrorism and called for dialogue between the adversaries. Its text affirmed FRY territorial integrity and expressed support for "an enhanced status for Kosovo, which would include a substantially greater degree of autonomy and meaningful self-administration." Most importantly, the resolution called for an arms embargo to be imposed on the FRY and the KLA, and for the prevention of "arming and training for terrorist activities" by all states. As an added indication of engagement, it urged the Prosecutor of the International Criminal Tribunal in The Hague to begin gathering information related to possible prosecutions arising from the political violence in Kosovo.

The resolution also set out the conditions under which the prohibitions against the FRY would be lifted, including the commencement of a substantive dialogue, withdrawal of special police units, unimpeded access to Kosovo by humanitarian organizations, facilitation of a mission to Kosovo by the UNHCR, and permission for the return of a long-term OSCE mission.

Although this was a UNSC resolution under Chapter VII, it was evident from the surrounding circumstances that the UN itself would not be the primary implementing party.[14] Due at least in part to the dwindling enthusiasm of key member state contributors for peacekeeping operations, it lacked both the resources and the political will to take on a primary monitoring role. The work of monitoring was instead taken on by a range of regional organizations, each with differing membership, mandates, and strategic agendas, inherently lacking in coherence. Especially relevant are the differences between the OSCE and NATO approaches, as well as the ambivalent and inconsistent role of Russia. Throughout 1998, Kofi Annan's monthly reports to the UNSC on the situation started with a careful disclaimer that, since the UN has no active presence in the region, he was entirely dependent on secondhand information. In August, he again pointed out that resources pledged for the monitoring of Resolution 1160 were insufficient to allow for the establishment of a comprehensive monitoring regime as established by the resolution. It was evident that the Euro-American coalition that was the core of the later NATO undertaking was not seriously mobilized behind the effort to rely on an international unarmed presence under UN auspices.

After a summer of official FRY violence in Kosovo, on September 23, 1998, the UNSC adopted Resolution 1199, expressing concern over the displacement of 230,000 Kosovars from their homes. Significantly, the resolution frequently alluded to an "impending humanitarian catastrophe" drawing from the most recent report of the Secretary-General.[15] A key factor in this feared catastrophe was the imminent arrival of winter and the projections of starvation and freezing conditions that were likely to be experienced by the displaced Kosovars. Resolution 1199 also identified the deterioration of the situation in Kosovo as "a threat to peace and security in the region," arguably setting the stage for a possible future enforcement action. The resolution otherwise reaffirmed the main elements of Resolution 1160, demanding an end to Serb repression, the enabling of effective and continuous international monitoring, and the facilitation of the return of refugees and displaced persons in coordination with the UNHCR and ICRC. It also called on all states to prevent funds from being collected on behalf of the KLA, thereby re-confirming Serbian sovereignty over Kosovo. Finally, on October 24, UNSC Resolution 1203 endorsed the agreements that resulted from the Holbrooke mission, including the OSCE–FRY agreement to establish the Kosovo Verification Mission and the NATO–FRY agreement to allow overflights to confirm verification of its implementation.[16]

In summary, a certain degree of consensus existed in the UNSC. UNSC members shared the view that the FRY was primarily responsible for an imminent humanitarian catastrophe in Kosovo; that this catastrophe involved severe denials of internationally protected human rights; that it posed a threat to international peace and security; and that it was not regarded as a matter "essentially within the domestic jurisdiction" of the FRY. To address this unacceptable situation in Kosovo, support was given to the idea of establishing an unarmed international monitoring presence, even if it was not under the direct authority of the United Nations. Furthermore, the UN gave no encouragement to the KLA as a liberation movement or to the broader quest for Kosovo independence, but nor did it implement any steps to restrict international support for insurgency.

At the same time, there was no consensus regarding the threat or use of force. The UNSC never explicitly authorized its use. Russian and Chinese positions clearly emphasized that any attempt at such authorization would be vetoed.[17] Simultaneously, subsequent Resolution 1203 endorsed the Holbrooke–Milosevic agreement, which is generally believed to have been secured only as a result of the NATO threat.

## THE DILEMMA OF RUSSIAN PARTICIPATION

Russia's consistent reluctance to take measures as harsh as those being called for by other members was frustrating to the rest of the Contact Group, and provided part of the background for the later decision to act independently of both the UN and of Russia. The USA and Britain were especially critical, seeing Russia as spoiling the potential for unified and effective international action. But Russia also represented a potential negotiating bridge between the Contact Group and the FRY. Within Russia, both pan-Slavic and anti-NATO constituencies tended to support Serbia, seemingly for reasons mainly connected with Russian domestic politics. Russia had its own ethnic secessionist problems and agreed with the Serbian contention that Kosovo should be treated as an "internal" matter. Milosevic clearly regarded Russia as his only source of partial support in the Contact Group.

But this is only half the story. Russia was extremely ambivalent about Serbian excesses during the 1990s and about Milosevic in particular. Russia had cooperated with the West repeatedly on sanctioning Yugoslavia, and had supported UN expressions of concern and censure short of authorizations to threaten or use force. Foreign Minister Primakov seemed dedicated to improving relations with the West, rather than focusing on possible confrontations with NATO, and he was aware that Kosovo was a volatile issue that could blow up at any time. And there was little disagreement between Russia and the West regarding the desired final status for Kosovo as an autonomous unit inside Yugoslavia. This combination of sympathy with and ambivalence toward the Belgrade approach gave Russia a potentially crucial negotiating role: Russia had Milosevic's ear, and Milosevic needed Russia, while at the same time Russia was in general agreement with Western goals.

In some instances, Moscow appears to have used its intermediate outlook productively, cautioning Milosevic to moderate his responses, to take NATO threats seriously, and not to count on Russia as an ally in the event of overt conflict. But, for reasons of Russian internal politics, bureaucratic inertia, and lack of policy coherence, Russia, like the rest of the international community, was sending a variety of mixed signals, no doubt exasperating and confusing Milosevic as much as frustrating the governments of the United States and Britain.[18] Russia's failure to achieve policy coherence in the face of rising Serb violence may well have contributed to the deteriorating diplomatic process.

In one of Russia's most visible and important moves, in June 1998 President Yeltsin personally met Milosevic in Moscow, securing Belgrade's commitment to allow unrestricted access to Kosovo for international observers and humanitarian organizations, as well as a promise by Belgrade to end attacks upon Kosovar civilians.[19] It has been reported that Yeltsin and other Russian leaders were quite firm with Milosevic, expressing their displeasure at Serb excesses.[20] After this meeting, on July 16, 1998, the Contact Group reiterated its concerns and its offer to assist in a negotiating process, and even included an additional carrot of assuring "a clear and achievable path toward Belgrade's full integration in the international community including participation in the OSCE."[21]

Despite the Moscow agreement and the resulting small-scale observer presence, July and August 1998 brought stepped-up attacks by FRY forces on civilians in Kosovo. Between June and October, when NATO first threatened air attacks, some analysts assert that Russia was sidelined and eventually excluded by the United States from taking any significant role in the negotiating process. The Russian position was frequently attacked by American and British high officials in this period as pro-Serbian, and not helpful, while US and NATO rhetoric and action began to suggest the inevitability of military action, which needs to be understood as an integral part of the threat strategy being relied upon to compel Belgrade's compliance, and the interpretation of Belgrade unreliability as a negotiating partner except when coerced.[22]

The later NATO activation order worked to ensure overt Russian opposition. Behind the scenes, though, the USA was continuing to communicate regularly with Moscow, and seemed still to be trying to build a "common front" in support of the use of force, perhaps insisting that a common front on the threat would be persuasive with Milosevic, and actually in the end might obviate the need for force.

Russian diplomats went to Milosevic in October to urge him to accept the Holbrooke agreement, thereby strengthening the threat diplomacy, but at the same time encouraging Belgrade to pursue a path of negotiation. Russia continued to work with the Contact Group through the Rambouillet process, and served as co-chair. The Russian position could be seen as somewhat self-defeating, since Russia understood that NATO was serious and was likely eventually to go ahead with or without UN authorization. By promising a UNSC veto without proposing any productive alternative, Russia was encouraging an outcome that would inevitably weaken the role of the UNSC and contribute to NATO's "unilateralism" so far as Kosovo was concerned.

It must be noted, however, that, even if Russia had been persuaded to authorize the use of force in the UNSC, it was still unlikely that China would go along. The Chinese had also cooperated with various sanctions against Belgrade during the 1990's. When it came to the use of force, however, their view was not so much related to the specific controversy over Kosovo as it was an expression of their support for the sovereign rights of states to address internal challenges without external interference. China was also concerned that the UNSC was subject to manipulation by the United States and its allies, and thus should not be given any role in extending the Charter limits on the use of force.

The dilemma for the Contact Group, then, was that, while Russia provided the most effective negotiating bridge to the FRY in terms of open channels of communication and willingness to consider the FRY's sovereign interests, Russian officials were voicing their vehement opposition to military intervention under any circumstances, thereby seeming to weaken the threat of force. Thus, an either/or choice existed for NATO with respect to negotiating with Milosevic. A process of negotiating through effective communication over the real interests of all parties demanded Russian participation as the essential diplomatic link to the FRY. Negotiation premised principally on ultimate and credible threats of military force depended either on Russia's approval (which the USA pushed for behind the scenes) or its exclusion (by relying on NATO over the UN), since such threats could not be credible as long as the FRY could count on a Russian veto.

## THE USA, NATO
## AND THE HOLBROOKE–MILOSEVIC AGREEMENTS

Despite its 1992–3 warnings on Kosovo to Milosevic, the United States pursued a shifting line of policy that was no more coherent than that of other key players up until 1998, when the escalating violence prompted a more consistent response. It had paid little attention to the non-violent movement in the 1990s, and was largely responsible for the Dayton process that so thoroughly pushed Kosovo off the agenda. Although it had played an active role in the Contact Group since its inception, it moved towards a leadership role with respect to Kosovo only in 1998. Thereafter, the transmission of mixed signals continued, and was in certain respects, magnified.

At a Press Conference in Belgrade on February 23, 1998, the US Special Representative ambassador Gelbard, strongly praised Milosevic for his support of the Dayton process but also expressed the US concern about the escalating violence in Kosovo and the need for serious dialogue. He condemned "very strongly" the unacceptable violence done by terrorist groups in Kosovo and particularly the KLA. "That is without any question a terrorist group. I refuse to accept any kind of excuses. Having worked for years on counter terrorist activity I know very well that to look at a terrorist group, to define it; you strip away the rhetoric and just look at actions. And actions of this group speak for themselves"[23] The significance of high US officials associating the KLA explicitly with terrorism in such a context should not be underestimated in terms of US foreign policy in recent decades. It was most probably perceived by Belgrade as a signal that the FRY could act ruthlessly in Kosovo without arousing any strong critical response from the West, so long as its primary target appeared to be the KLA challenge rather than the Kosovar civilian population. Within a week of Gelbard's statement, Serb forces attacked and then massacred the leaders and other members of the famed Adem Jashari clan in Prekazi/Prekaze.

In May 1998, with a civil war now in full swing, the United States dispatched Richard Holbrooke to promote a negotiating process between the LDK and Belgrade. Holbrooke talked to Milosevic and then arranged for Rugova and a few other Albanian leaders to meet with Milosevic — an extremely controversial move within the LDK, which had previously as a matter of principle avoided formal contact with Belgrade without foreign mediation.[24] The LDK delegation also went to Washington and met with Clinton, providing an important but too belated show of high-level support for the alternative opposition in Kosovo to that being mounted by the KLA. However, with mounting Serb attacks against civilians in Kosovo and growing KLA strength, it was clearly too late to resolve the conflict without giving the KLA a key role in the process.

What went on during the summer of 1998 with respect to the USA, Milosevic and the KLA remains controversial. The KDOM was focusing on uniting the KLA. It is quite plausible that the Serbs and Milosevic would have received reports of this growing connection and would have been deeply suspicious of its intentions. The encouragement of KLA unity, even in the interest of clearer diplomacy, would logically be seen by Belgrade to have military implications damaging to its efforts to stabilize FRY control over Kosovo.

At the same time, surprisingly, the escalating Serb counteroffensive was not heavily criticized by the USA or the EU, despite causing a massive civilian upheaval, with hundreds of thousands of Kosovar Albanians being displaced, and lacking adequate shelter. This sparked allegations that the West was deliberately looking the other way in order to allow Milosevic to dispose of the troublesome KLA problem — a brutal contradiction of the June Moscow agreement in which Milosevic had pledged to terminate Serb violence directed at Kosovar civilians.

By September, as the scale of civilian suffering mounted, the momentum of diplomatic initiatives grew rapidly. UNSC Resolution 1199 condemning the Serb attacks was passed on September 23, 1998. Immediately thereafter, the United States orchestrated a concentrated diplomatic effort to convince European states that in fact the threat of NATO force, and the accompanying demands for an armed peacekeeping presence in Kosovo, was the only possible means to get Milosevic to observe the minimal human rights of the Kosovars. Despite many legal and political misgivings, every NATO country eventually went along with this policy.[25] This consensus led to the NATO activation order on October 13, 1998, which was designed to prepare for aerial bombardments of the FRY in the event of its non-compliance with Resolution 1199. The USA was by now unwilling to allow the issue of using force to come before the UNSC, anticipating a veto which would put NATO in the more difficult position of using force in defiance. The USA evidently wanted to avoid such clarity, which was seen as potentially reducing the credibility of the threat, as well as requiring an explicit circumvention of UN authority, which might have also weakened alliance coherence among NATO members.

The penultimate attempt to reach a diplomatic solution was the Holbrooke–Milosevic agreement of October 1998. Holbrooke managed to secure an agreement from Milosevic to curtail his counter-insurgency campaign in Kosovo, but only with both a re-articulation of the threat of NATO bombings, and the ill-founded assurance that the KLA would cease its attacks.[26] Perhaps more importantly on this occasion, given the generalized mistrust in the West of Milosevic's "word," Holbrooke secured permission for a monitoring arrangement in Kosovo, involving both a 2000-strong OSCE presence and NATO overflights.

UNSC Resolution 1203 and the bombing threat of October continued the long series of mixed messages. The KLA took it as a promise of a forthcoming NATO intervention, and stepped up their reliance on violence directed against Serbs, in order to internationalize the conflict in a definitive manner. The KLA leadership understandably believed that only a major interventionary initiative involving NATO could bring their movement for Kosovo independence closer to realization. Without military intervention the KLA could not hope to challenge FRY supremacy in Kosovo on its own, and at most could mount only a sporadic insurgent challenge, keeping the tension level high at the cost of great suffering for Kosovar Albanians. The NATO activation order seemed to bring KLA closer to their goal.

Milosevic, on the other hand, was confronted by a more bewildering set of images. Holbrooke had previously held a secret meeting with the KLA. During the meeting he was, without warning, joined by a uniformed and armed KLA leader who sat next to him. Photographers took advantage of the opportunity, and Holbrooke was shown to the world as being an apparent KLA confidant, seeming even to promise cooperation with the KLA. At the same time, the UN was reassuring Belgrade that Kosovo's status as part of the FRY would remain unchanged. The UN and Contact Group's resolutions constantly called attention to supporting civilian over "terrorist" strategies, yet no one was interdicting the KLA's foreign support, and Holbrooke never even consulted with the LDK civilian leadership before meeting with Milosevic.

Not surprisingly, then, the KLA, despite Holbrooke's apparent assurances to the contrary, took advantage of this lull to rearm and renew military action. In fact, KLA forces moved in to take up positions vacated by the redeployed Serbian forces. Despite Contact Group rhetoric about not condoning KLA terrorist attacks, no attempt was made by the West to interdict the flow of arms and money to the KLA or to challenge seriously its provocative tactics. The actual US capacity to restrain the KLA may have been quite limited at this stage, but there is no evidence that even an attempt was made.

Thus there is confusion, and likely contradiction, in the Western relationship to the KLA. It is plausible on the one hand to view the KLA as a source of pressure on Milosevic to reach an accommodation or face an escalating insurgent challenge to FRY sovereignty. On the other hand, a reliance on the KLA probably strengthened the impression in Belgrade that the West was supporting a secessionist outcome in Kosovo, and that any agreement allowing a NATO force to enter Kosovo would be used to promote KLA goals. At the same time, Milosevic evidently miscalculated the effects of the Serb anti-KLA campaign in earlier months, assuming that the KLA threat had been basically removed. This is a characteristic error in a counter-insurgency war: the dormancy of the insurgent challenge is misinterpreted as a defeat, and the resumption of armed resistance comes as a surprise.

Even though neither armed party respected the Holbrooke agreement for long, both the brief pause in hostilities and the KVM presence had a noticeable impact on the plight of Kosovar civilians. Although the FRY redeployed, the level of violence against civilians decreased significantly during the presence of KVM monitors, and a great many displaced Kosovars began returning to their homes in this period. The humanitarian catastrophe that had been envisaged for the cold winter was successfully averted, albeit only temporarily. Neither the Holbrooke agreement nor the KVM presence challenged the basic structure of oppression or the loss of Kosovo autonomy. Nor could it satisfy the self-determination claims of the people of Kosovo. Nor could the monitoring presence by itself stop a war from erupting, especially given the irreconcilable demands of independence and sovereignty of the two armed parties. But it did reduce civilian suffering, and that is not inconsequential. There may be important lessons to be taken from this experience regarding the effectiveness of unarmed monitoring missions in deterring human rights abuse and forestalling, if not preventing, humanitarian catastrophe, even under extremely adverse conditions.

## RAMBOUILLET

As the previous discussion shows, the KLA had no interest in a ceasefire. It had used the partial withdrawal of the Serbian forces to strengthen its own position, presumably expecting, quite correctly, that a violent counteraction by Serb forces would be the result. Unarmed verifiers could not prevent this from happening. Both the LDK and the KLA wanted an armed NATO presence on the ground, and neither had any intention whatsoever of pulling back from their political objective: independence. Shortly after the Holbrooke-Dayton agreement the so called Headquarters of KLA made a strong and threatening statement, saying the KLA "will punish anyone who dare to sign any agreement that means less than the decision made by the people of Kosova in the 1991 Referendum", that is independence.[27] The KLA had consequently heavily criticized the various outlines for a political agreement with the Belgrade government, which had been worked out by Ambassador Hill on behalf of the Contact Group. Hill had reported that it was impossible to reach an agreement on the future status of Kosovo but there was, he hoped, an informal understanding of a three-year stabilization and normalization period and after this period new efforts should be envisaged. Each of Hill's drafts were criticized by both the KLA and the FRY. The peace process seemed to have reached a dead end. None of the parties had evidenced any interest in a negotiated peace settlement. Rambouillet represented the last attempt to make progress.

The NATO threat of force had certainly played a role in getting Milosevic to discuss the issue at all. At the same time, it made the KLA less and less interested in negotiations and compromises. The stronger the threat was, the less inclined was KLA to yield. That was the real dilemma of enforced negotiations.

Many observers doubt that Serbia participated at Rambouillet with either an expectation or an intention of reaching agreement on the future of Kosovo. Milosevic, it is argued, was using the negotiating process to buy time to prepare for the next round of Serb military attacks in Kosovo. He did not send a high-level delegation to Rambouillet, and those he did send seemed to engage half-heartedly in the process. On the other hand, at various moments when European or US negotiators became frustrated by Belgrade's posture, they were able to obtain more serious negotiating responses by contacting FRY leaders by phone in Belgrade. At a later stage, Serb President Milan Milutinovic was dispatched to Paris to negotiate directly.

The Kosovar Albanian delegation, by contrast, was comprised of legitimate and high-level representation of both the KLA and the civilian movement. This legitimacy, however, was accompanied by serious internal power struggles and a thorough lack of unity in terms of objectives or negotiating strategy. The public perception of the Kosovar diplomacy reinforced the image that it was the KLA leadership, and not the LDK, which was the crucial voice of opposition.

The Contact Group, despite unity on certain key principles, was still an alliance of players from independent states with multiple and sometimes conflicting agendas and priorities. For many Europeans, the Rambouillet meetings were expected to be "Europe's Dayton," culminating in a diplomatic solution to avert the prospect that would provide a solution without recourse to war. Within US policy-making circles, some officials apparently shared this optimism. But there were clearly other key American players who saw the Rambouillet process quite differently. One objective was to help reticent European NATO members justify an armed intervention to their domestic constituencies, and thus build a tighter coalition in favor of what was by then being viewed as an almost certain recourse to force. Others on the US side wanted primarily to unite the various disparate Kosovar Albanian positions, thereby strengthening the normative case for intervention, which would take place regardless of Serbia's stance. At various points during the process, Madeleine Albright and James Rubin made statements confirming this one-sided view of the process. Rubin told the press on February 21, for instance, that, "in order to move towards military action, it has to be clear that the Serbs were responsible." And along the same lines, Albright stated: "it is now up to the Kosovar Albanians to create this black or white situation (...) to make clear that a NATO implementation force is something that they want."[28]

The Rambouillet discussions began with two key documents: a "non-negotiable" set of basic principles set forth by the Contact Group, and a draft Interim Agreement for Peace and Self-government in Kosovo. The Serbs accepted the Basic Principles, the Kosovar Albanians did not, fundamentally because of their refusal to accept the non-negotiability of the "territorial integrity of the Federal Republic of Yugoslavia." Without drawing FRY territorial integrity into question, it was impossible to maintain the goal of independence. The draft Interim Agreement was the result of months of shuttling back and forth by Contact Group members and the American diplomat, Ambassador Chris Hill, in particular. In the ensuing discussions, despite their opposition to the Basic Principles, the Kosovar Albanians appeared to be somewhat flexible and facilitated the forward momentum of the discussion of the Interim Agreement, but they never indicated a willingness to entertain the idea of autonomy as an alternative to independence.[29] Contact Group negotiators, meanwhile, were having what seemed to be productive "negotiations" with Belgrade over the phone. Perhaps misreading Albanian cooperativeness as a sign of weakness, the Contact Group came back to the table with a revised proposal, which Albanian negotiators rejected as much more "pro-Belgrade." [30]

As could be expected, the most difficult aspect of reaching a political agreement concerned the question of future status, which hinged on the question of what mechanism would be implemented after three years to move to the next stage of governance for Kosovo. The idea of a binding referendum was acceptable to the Kosovars but not to Serbia, and probably not to NATO either. Neither NATO nor the countries in the south Balkans looked with favor on the prospect of an independent Kosovo, and the Contact Group had thus far been unswervingly firm about not changing the borders. On the other hand, discussions of more vague international meetings or other processes that did not on the face of it leave a decision about the province solely in the hands of the Kosovar population might have been acceptable to Serbia. Both sides realized that the Contact Group was not advocating independence, so it seems likely that agreement could have been reached only on a proposal that left the status issue unresolved and ambiguous, providing room open for ongoing developments during the ensuing three years. Also, since Serbian and Contact Group goals substantially coincided on the final status question, any negotiable proposal would undoubtedly require pressure to be applied to the Kosovar Albanian side.

There had already been strong US pressure on the KLA to accept an agreement as a kind of precondition for further NATO involvement. To get the KLA on board, Ambassador Hill's January proposal had made clear steps in the direction of independence.[31] At Rambouillet the Kosovar Albanians were being advised that, if they did not cooperate with the NATO diplomacy, Western countries would take vigorous action to choke off Diaspora fund-ing for the KLA, troops from NATO countries might be deployed on the Albanian border with Kosovo to cut arms supplies, and the USA and other Western countries might revert to declaring the KLA a terrorist group.[32] Of course, the Contact Group had been talking about constraining the KLA for over a year without any of its members following through on the commitment, so it seems unlikely that such threats were taken seriously.

The Commission's research leads it to conclude that the ma-jority of the "Western group" (perhaps with the exception of the USA) expected Milosevic to accept an agreement under the pres-sure of the bomb threat. The Kosovo group or KLA was not sup-posed to be a problem; it was assumed that they would sign in the end if they could get armed NATO troops on the ground. A seri-ous effort to get Milosevic to accept an agreement was made by Ambassador Hill in direct negotiation with him in Belgrade. The KLA protested against this procedure and it protested even more vigorously when it got the proposal that resulted from this dis-cussion. The new draft had, in the KLA view, been changed in ac-cordance with Belgrade demands; in essence, this was true.

After many and complicated deliberations, the Kosovo delega-tion accepted the version of February 23. The crucial paragraph on the future of Kosovo now stated that there would be an inter-national conference after three years to determine the "final set-tlement of Kosovo," taking into account "the will of the people" but also the "opinions of relevant authorities." As Weller points out, there is a lot of ambiguity in this wording.[33] The United States made a last and, as it turned out, successful effort to get the Kosovars to sign by a side-letter which confirmed that Kosovo could hold a referendum on independence after three years, but not however saying that that referendum would decide the issue. The KLA statements at the end of February confirmed its "inde-pendence position." The international community still lives with this ambiguity.

As these discussions progressed, at a late stage at Rambouillet another crucial document, known as "Annex B," was introduced which dealt with the implementation provisions of the agreement, in particular the military provisions. Although Annex B was never fully discussed by the parties at Rambouillet proper, the implications of its provisions had a definite political impact on the process, and are widely viewed in retrospect as a blunder.[34] These included stipulations that NATO rather than the UN would maintain troops on FRY territory, and that these forces would be given free rein to traverse all parts of FRY territory with the costs of their presence borne by Belgrade. Although these provisions were lifted from fairly standard UN peacekeeping procedures, the intrusive power they delegated to NATO in this case, outside of any UN context, was bound to reinforce Serbian suspicions and resistance, especially considering that NATO was already threatening to attack Serbia without the benefit of a UN authorization. Milosevic also used this unwelcome claim of authority by the NATO peacekeeping forces to explain and legitimize his actions. He used it to feed Serb paranoid fears that there was a hidden plan to overthrow his regime and interfere fundamentally with the territorial integrity and political independence of the FRY as a sovereign country

Despite such concerns, during the final days of Rambouillet Serb participation increased, with Serb President Milan Milutinovic working out of the Yugoslav embassy in Paris. After a meeting with Milutinovic on February 20, Madeleine Albright said that he had told her that the Serbs could accept the political deal, but she added, "the Serb refusal to even consider the presence of a NATO-led military implementation force (...) is largely responsible for the failure to reach agreement."[35]

Some observers doubt that Serbia would have agreed to the political principles even if the implementation provisions had been changed. Others doubt that any Serbian agreement would have held without a strong NATO-led presence of indefinite duration. And the KLA was by this time overtly blocking any moves toward agreement, fearing an outcome that would have stabilized a Kosovo solution that left sovereignty in Belgrade. Despite these caveats, if Albright's statement is correct, it suggests an obvious negotiating opening that might have broken the impasse of the final days of Rambouillet. If NATO had initiated an offer to relent on the implementation provisions, Serbia would have lost a fundamental excuse for not signing on.

Chris Hill has said subsequently that there were deals possible on implementation, "but the Serbs would not engage."[36] There is no evidence available, however, that NATO offered to engage on this issue. In fact, Albright and others had been so firm about the supremacy of NATO over any other institutional actor in this context, and so many aspects of the Rambouillet process had been presented as explicitly non-negotiable, that there was little reason for Serbia to have expected flexibility from NATO. If a deal were possible, it would have had to have been initiated by NATO powers.

Chris Hill also says that Milosevic was open to the Rambouillet political deal but wanted to avoid the military element that came with it because "he felt that the true intention of the force was to eliminate him—and/or detach Kosovo from Serbia. In fact there was nothing in the political agreement that was unsellable to the Serbs."[37] The United States, then, was fully aware of these serious personal power concerns on Milosevic's part. The use of the UN, and especially the participation of Russia in the military implementation, might have assuaged these concerns. So far as is known, no such offer was made.

The reasons behind US and NATO inflexibility extended beyond the issue of Kosovo. NATO was seeking to clarify its longer-term mandate after the end of the Cold War, and the upcoming fiftieth anniversary scheduled for April 1999 was to be a key step in this process. Closely related, the reliance on threat diplomacy was at odds with any wavering on the part of NATO. In other words, a threat to use force so as to achieve an outcome that is non-negotiable, i.e. NATO peacekeeping force in Kosovo, is inconsistent with any indication that some alternative compromise is possible. Negotiations in the sense of actual bargaining would seem inconsistent and costly to the credibility of NATO as a political actor. Once NATO was seriously engaged in the diplomacy, this issue of credibility became important.

Given the confusion and severe differences among the Kosovar Albanians, it should have been possible for the Serbian side to sign a deal that could have been relatively good from their point of view — if they had been sufficiently interested in a deal and, above all, been prepared to accept an *armed* international force in Kosovo. The FRY delegation said in several statements at the end of the negotiations that they were prepared to discuss an international implementation force in Kosovo, but whether or not that included an armed force is still unknown. In the end. Milosevic miscalculated the effect of not to signing the agreement. As a result, Serbia was partly destroyed, and it lost more or less all influence on the future development of Kosovo or the ability to protect Serbs in Kosovo (if that was a true concern).

## DEADLINES

A defining feature of the Rambouillet process was the fixed timeline combined with the bombing ultimatum. Arguably, this was a no-nonsense approach designed to convince Serbia that it could no longer get away with stalling or backtracking, or making concessions on paper that would then be withdrawn by action. Facing a fundamentally duplicitous negotiating partner like Milosevic, Albright and others evidently saw the deadline/ultimatum/ armed peacekeeping force tactics as the only ones that could bring about a change in Serb policy in Kosovo. It was, however, a problematic strategy. International law formally outlaws the use of threat of force in international negotiations. The inherent brinkmanship of the strategy is not an approach designed to resolve underlying problems or to make war a matter of last resort. Unfortunately, in Bosnia and in the case of Kosovo, it turned out that only threat of force and deadlines could make negotiations possible.

## MOTIVATION FOR INTERVENTIONS

The overall levels of violent repression in late 1998 and early 1999 prior to the NATO decision to launch the air attacks appear to have been considerably lower than the violence of the summer and fall of 1998, but the Recak/Racak massacre made a major impact on public opinion and on the diplomatic climate. It served as a powerful symbolic "warning bell," placing NATO in a serious credibility dilemma, given the October bombing ultimatum. Aside from undercutting diplomatic options, threat diplomacy puts the threatener under pressure to demonstrate that the commitment is not just a bluff. Given the Bosnian failures of nerve and the post-cold war crisis of confidence surrounding the future of NATO, these background factors relating to credibility assumed great importance.

The rationale for military intervention by NATO thus rested not on the immediate scale of humanitarian catastrophe in early 1999, but rather on a weaving together of past experiences and future concerns:

- the resolve not to allow a repetition of the 1998 scale of violence and displacement in Kosovo;
- the related resolve to avert "another Bosnia," giving a crucial political and symbolic influence to reports of the Recak/Racak massacre;
- a post-Bosnia, post-Rwanda desire to demonstrate that the international community under US leadership was generally sincere about its resolve to prevent and punish severe patterns of human abuse;
- NATO's need to maintain credibility by following through on

its threats, and to show an altered relevance of the alliance for the security and well-being of Europe after the cold war, especially in view of its upcoming fiftieth anniversary agenda;

- concern among European states to avert the potential mass migrations that could result from an extended civil war in the region.
- the underlying conviction, based on extensive experience throughout the 1990s, that Milosevic could not be trusted,
- the belief that only an armed presence in Kosovo that was not subject to vetoes in the UNSC could ensure a transition to restore substantial autonomy for Kosovo.

## CONCLUSIONS

The central issue posed by this chapter is whether war could have been avoided while effectively protecting the Kosovar Albanians. A series of tensions made the diplomatic response confused and confusing. All parties miscalculated in a variety of ways. The overall narrative of the international response is inherently inconclusive, and hence without clear "lessons" beyond the prudential observations in favor of early engagement and greater attentiveness to nonviolent options. Certain key conclusions are worth emphasizing.

- Multiple and divergent agendas and expectations and mixed signals from the US and the international community impeded effective diplomacy.
- The international community's experience with Milosevic as not amenable to usual negotiations created a dilemma. The only language of diplomacy believed open to negotiators was that of coercion and threat. This lead to legal and diplomatic problems—such threat diplomacy is against the Charter, and is hard to reconcile with seeking peaceful settlement. The credibility of the threat must in the final analysis be upheld by the actual use of force.

- It is impossible to conclude, however, despite these weaknesses, that a diplomatic solution could have ended the internal struggle over the future of Kosovo. The minimum goals of the Kosovar Albanians and of Belgrade were irreconcilable.
- The impact of the war has been to resolve the contradiction largely in favor of the Kosovar Albanians by accepting an evolving structure of governance based on de facto independence.
- Russia's contribution to the process was ambiguous. Its particular relationship with Serbia enabled crucial diplomatic steps, but its rigid commitment to veto any enforcement action was the major factor forcing NATO into an unmandated action.
- The KLA goal of internationalizing the conflict was consistent with the Belgrade objective of ruthlessly suppressing the challenge to its authority in Kosovo. This enabled the KLA to pressure the international community to intervene.

A NATO EA-6B Prowler takes off from
the Aviano air base, Italy.
PHOTO: FRANCO DEBERNARDI/PRESSENS BILD

# 6

# INTERNATIONAL LAW
# AND HUMANITARIAN INTERVENTION

Any assessment of the legality of recourse to force in Kosovo and Serbia under NATO auspices should not lose sight of several elements of the surrounding circumstances. There was an impending and unfolding humanitarian catastrophe for the civilian Kosovar Albanian population against a background of events in Bosnia (i.e. a recent diplomatic failure to act decisively enough to avoid tragic consequences). Milosevic was an adversary with a track record of manipulation and criminality, and one whom few trusted to implement negotiated agreements. After the autumn of 1998, authorization for coercive action appeared politically impossible to secure under UN auspices, because of the expected Russian and Chinese vetoes.

In addition to these prior conditions, the results of the NATO action have an important bearing. Although the intervention produced a temporary and severe worsening of the ordeal faced by the Kosovar Albanians, over time it averted their worst fears of ethnic cleansing, and had the emancipatory effect for them of dismantling the oppressive Serb police and paramilitary structure. Participation after the intervention by the United Nations in the arrangements negotiated to end NATO's use of force (Security Council Resolution 1244) added a sense of ex-post UN legitimacy to the operation. Additionally, the postwar dynamic of "reverse ethnic cleansing" in which the Serb and Roma minorities in Kosovo were the principal victims is an important consideration.

It should also be kept in mind that the crisis was essentially provoked by a pattern of Serb violations of human rights in Kosovo during the decade of the 1990s, although the turn to armed struggle with unwavering secessionist aims by the Albanian opposition in Kosovo exacerbated the Serbian response. This pattern of Serb oppression included numerous atrocities that appeared to have the character of crimes against humanity in the sense that this term has been understood since the Nuremberg Judgment in 1945. These atrocities were greatly intensified in the period of the NATO military campaign in a manner that can find no justification in the law of war—or for that matter, in international morality. Also relevant is the fact that Slobodan Milosevic was indicted as a war criminal by the ICTY during the 1999 bombing campaign for his role in the crimes committed in the former Yugoslavia.

This complex of circumstances raises a central question—are the constraints imposed by international law on the non-defensive use of force adequate for the maintenance of peace and security in the contemporary world? The question is particularly relevant where force is used for the protection of a vulnerable people threatened with catastrophe. If international law no longer provides acceptable guidelines in such a situation, what are the alternatives? In responding to these challenges, the Commission considers the international law controversy provoked by the NATO campaign. It also puts forward an interpretation of the emerging doctrine of humanitarian intervention. This interpretation is situated in a gray zone of ambiguity between an extension of international law and a proposal for an international moral consensus. In essence, this gray zone goes beyond strict ideas of *legality* to incorporate more flexible views of *legitimacy*.

This chapter has two main parts:

- a consideration of the legality of forceful humanitarian intervention by reference to both *jus ad bellum* (recourse to war)
  and *jus in bellum* (lawfulness of conduct in war);
- an argument on behalf of legitimacy by way of an emergent
  framework of principled humanitarian intervention.

The FRY alleged that the NATO attack and the subsequent bombing were violations of international law, and appealed to the ICTY
and the International Court of Justice (ICJ) for formal legal action against the responsible NATO governments. The ICJ has not
yet reached a determination as to whether it has jurisdiction to
hear the matter, although it has refused a FRY request for Preliminary Measures and it has, on prima facie grounds, excluded
the USA and Spain from the case, leaving ten NATO members as
potential defendants. The Final Report of the ICTY Prosecutor
by the committee established to review the NATO bombing exerted some influence on the Commission's approach to the issues
posed.[1] The Report concluded that the principal allegation of the
illegality of the initial NATO recourse to force was currently under
consideration by the ICJ, and in any event was not within the purview of the Tribunal's authority. This foundational issue of international law will, however, be addressed by the Commission.

The main body of the ICTY Final Report examines in some
detail whether the main specific complaints about NATO tactics
and methods of warfare amounted to violations of the law of war,
and concludes that the allegations were not of sufficient weight
even to be worthy of investigation. The Commission defers to
this Report, although it does supply some independent analysis
of its own that reaches less confident conclusions on some points.
Furthermore, the Commission suggests that an assessment of
NATO tactics and methods in an undertaking justified as "a humanitarian war" should be subject to more demanding standards
than those required under current international humanitarian law
in wartime. In effect, the Commission believes that a greater ob-

ligation is imposed on the intervening side to take care of the civilian population in a humanitarian campaign. The specific modalities of this higher standard of "military necessity" do not yet exist in any international agreement or United Nations declaration, but the Commission envisages this standard to be a flexible notion that complements the adaptation of legal constraints on the use of force to the realities of the early twenty-first century. The Commission believes that this proposal should be formalized in international law, perhaps in the form of a "Protocol III" to the Geneva Conventions.

## MILITARY INTERVENTION AND INTERNATIONAL LAW

The analysis of the previous chapter concludes that the negotiations conducted before March 24, 1999, although extensive, were enmeshed in threat diplomacy and ambiguous offers of negotiation, and thus failed to satisfy fully the legal requirements associated with the obligation to pursue the peaceful settlement of all international disputes. Such an assessment of the Kosovo negotiations is particularly important since NATO actions were, in any event, on shaky legal ground, given the decision to proceed with an armed intervention without obtaining, or even seeking, a clear UN Security Council (UNSC) authorization, and without making any sort of secondary appeal to the General Assembly. Under the Uniting for Peace Resolution,[2] the General Assembly is authorized to act in the event that the UNSC cannot meet its obligations to address threats to international peace and security). NATO's own constituting treaty[3] does not provide any convincing legal grounds for recourse to force aside from meeting an external use of force directed at the territorial integrity and political independence of its member countries.

International law as embodied textually in the UN Charter is on the surface clear with respect to the permissible scope for the use of force in international life.[4] The threat or use of force by states is categorically prohibited by Article 2(4). The sole exception set forth in Article 51 is a right of self-defense, but only if exercised in response to a prior armed attack across an international frontier, and then only provisionally. A claim to act in self-defense must be promptly communicated to the UNSC, which is empowered to pass final judgment. The UNSC, in discharging its responsibility for international peace and security under Chapter VII is empowered to authorize the use of force. This narrow interpretation of the legal framework governing the use of force was strongly endorsed by a commanding majority within the International Court of Justice in the Nicaragua Case decided in 1986.[5] The only other relevant directive as to the use of force is contained in Article 53, which allows regional organizations to engage in enforcement actions provided that they do so on the basis of UNSC authorization. Although there is a subsidiary argument about implied authorization to use force once a conflict has been formally treated by the UNSC as a threat to international peace and security under Chapter VII of the Charter,[6] it remains difficult to reconcile NATO's recourse to armed intervention on behalf of Kosovo with the general framework of legal rights and duties which determines the legality of the use of force.

It is, however, possible to argue that, running parallel to the Charter's limitations on the use of force, is Charter support for the international promotion and protection of human rights.[7] In this vein it has been asserted that, given the unfolding humanitarian catastrophe precipitated by the Serb pattern of oppressive criminality toward the civilian Albanian population in Kosovo, the use of force by NATO was legitimate, as it was the only practical means available to protect the Albanian Kosovars from further violent abuse. The main difficulty with such a line of argument is that Charter restrictions on the use of force represented a core commitment when the United Nations was established in 1945 — a commitment which has reshaped general international law. In contrast, the Charter provisions relating to human rights were left deliberately vague, and were clearly not intended when written to provide a legal rationale for any kind of enforcement, much less a free-standing mandate for military intervention without UNSC approval. Human rights were given a subordinate and marginal role in the UN system in 1945, a role that was understood to be, at most, aspirational.

Any interventionary claim based on human rights would face the additional legal obstacle posed by Article 2(7) which forbids intervention, even by the United Nations, in matters that fall essentially within the "domestic jurisdiction" of states. Even serious infractions of human rights were considered to be matters of domestic jurisdiction when the Charter was drafted, and were not thought to provide any grounds for an external use of force. The more sovereignty-oriented members of the United Nations, including notably China and Russia, continue to support such a view of human rights. Additionally, there has been as yet no clarification by the ICJ or other authoritative body as to the extent to which the evolution of law in relation to international human rights erodes the prohibition on non-defensive uses of force.

However, the Commission recognizes that, in the more than fifty years of UN existence, the status of human rights has changed dramatically. International legal standards have been agreed upon. Numerous NGOs have devoted great energy to their implementation. During the anti-apartheid campaigns of the 1980s, the UN committed itself to the implementation of human rights with respect to South Africa, and even went so far as to reject claims of sovereign rights. European states have shown a willingness to accept external accountability for upholding human rights, including giving their citizens the right to petition for relief to the European Commission on Human Rights. If the claim is viewed as substantial, citizens then have the right of access to the European Court of Human Rights. Also, the Helsinki Accords of 1975 led to an important process, as the countries of East Europe accepted both an obligation to uphold human rights and a procedure of regional assessment. Such an experience is widely credited with undermining the legitimacy of authoritarian rule in East Europe and precipitating the non-violent transitions (except in Romania) to market constitutionalism at the end of the 1980s.

Such developments have led Secretary General Kofi Annan and his two predecessors, Javier Perez de Cuellar and Boutros Boutros Ghali, to insist that the evolution of international human rights standards and support for their implementation has now reached the stage where norms of non-intervention, and the related deference to sovereign rights, no longer apply to the same extent in the face of severe human rights or humanitarian abuses.[8] The organized international community, according to this view, now enjoys a permissible option of humanitarian intervention as one way to protect vulnerable people against severe abuses of human rights, crimes against humanity, and genocide. Nevertheless, prudential considerations still inhibit humanitarian intervention, especially when the effort is likely to require a serious military commitment or involves the risk of provoking a major war. Still, this process of evolution could suggest that interventionary force to uphold human rights in extreme situations of abuse is less inconsistent with the spirit of the UN Charter and general international law than has been suggested by some.[9]

Even against this background, it remains open to question whether, under the circumstances of political blockage in the UNSC, NATO was a suitable agent for carrying out the intervention into Kosovo. At the time, the prevailing view in support of the approach adopted was that there was no realistic alternative to NATO available in 1999. Indeed, advocates of NATO's action argue that its performance as compared to the inadequacy of the protective response of the UN to the ethnic cleansing in Bosnia a few years earlier,[10] vindicates the bypassing of the UNSC. In this regard, not only is the validity of the interventionary claim important, but also the question of political will, perseverance, and capabilities.

This argumentation is, however, somewhat self-serving, as the earlier UN failure was partly a result of the refusal by the NATO countries to support the Bosnian effort in a more vigorous and effective manner. The mandating powers viewed damage to the UN's credibility as a result of its failure in Bosnia unfortunate, but not an occasion for greatly expanded commitment. In contrast, in relation to Kosovo, the central involvement of NATO assumed a different form, and the major states were unwilling to accept an outcome that could not be presented as "a success" because damage to the credibility of NATO was unacceptable

International law on these matters is not yet settled, and the fluidity caused by competing doctrines generates controversy and uncertainty. In these settings "coalitions of the willing" provide a subsidiary source of protection for a beleaguered people that cannot summon a response from the UN System, but this in turn creates a concern about the loosening of legal restraints on war and intervention. The Rwanda genocide in 1994 reinforced a perception that effective action to prevent such a tragedy should not be inhibited by deference to the UN or to outmoded or overly rigid restrictions governing use of force. But much of the non-Western world remains unconvinced, and is suspicious of validating use of force that endow the powerful countries of the North with such a discretionary option in this regard.[11] This suspicion is associated not only with NATO action in Bosnia and Kosovo, but with the sort of open-ended mandate provided by the UNSC regarding the use force against Iraq to recover the sovereignty of Kuwait in 1990–91, and the indefinite prolongation of this use of force without a subsequent renewal of the mandate.[12]

It is also suggested by advocates of intervention that UN practice has created greater flexibility and permissiveness with respect to the use of force than can be derived from the most relevant international law texts, including the Charter.[13] On this reading of international law, the Charter is overly restrictive.[14] This conclusion is arguably reinforced by the failure of UN membership, even after the end of the cold war, to implement the collective security provisions of Chapter VII (including the designation of standby forces and the active operation of the Military Staff Committee). As a result, all claims to use force must be considered in each context, and evaluated as reasonable or not, based on their specific merit.[15] Such a view is usually coupled with the argument that states have often acted in apparent opposition to these Charter restrictions, and have not encountered legal censure. In part, this more flexible approach to the interpretation of international law governing the use of force acknowledges the reasonableness of taking transnational action to respond to either international terrorism or genocidal behavior. It also accepts the necessity of acting in some circumstances without a UN authorization, when such authorization might be unavailable due to a veto being cast or anticipated by a Permanent Member of the UNSC.

In the case of NATO's recourse to force, some clarification of its claims can be made, but the controversy as to their legal propriety cannot be put to rest. There was no factual basis upon which NATO could claim a defensive use of force that could qualify as self-defense under international law. Not even an authorization by the United Nations could have persuasively converted the NATO use of force into an instance of self-defense. NATO's action could more plausibly have been treated as an instance of enforcement of peace and security by a regional organization, an option embodied in Article 53 of the Charter.[16]

The most convincing legal ground for the NATO military campaign relates to the UNSC's authority to regard any set of circumstances as posing a threat to international peace and security as understood by Chapter VII of the Charter, and thereby opening up the possibility of authorizing the use of force to "maintain or restore" peace and security.[17] The Gulf War proceeded on this logic, although in that instance there also existed a clear factual foundation for the more accepted claim of collective self-defense of territorial integrity and political independence under Article 51 of the Charter.[18] It is certainly legally relevant that the deteriorating situation in Kosovo in the year prior to the NATO campaign was being treated as falling within Chapter VII.[19] The international dimension of Kosovo was explicitly associated with the wider danger of instability spreading to such neighboring countries as Macedonia, Albania, and Bulgaria and with the prospect of hundreds of thousands of refugees streaming across Europe.[20]

In considering the legality of NATO's campaign, an additional extra-legal complexity makes reliance on force more reasonable. There were strong grounds for believing that a political compromise, even if negotiable, would not work reliably to protect the Kosovar Albanians, given the nature of Milosevic's past record of war crimes and illusory reassurances, and especially considering the precariousness of the situation in Kosovo. This consideration was a further basis for the view that it was not feasible to act within the UN to achieve the goal of effective protection of the Kosovar civilian population. This analysis reverts to the difficulties of reconciling legality and legitimacy in the Kosovo setting, and also evokes the anguished memories of international complicity in the terrible events in Bosnia, particularly the massacre at Srebrenica.[21]

One way to analyze the international law status of the NATO campaign is to consider legality a matter of degree. This approach acknowledges the current fluidity of international law on humanitarian intervention, caught between strict Charter prohibitions of non-defensive uses of force and more permissive patterns of state practice with respect to humanitarian interventions and counter-terrorist use of force.[22] The Chapter VII resolutions prior to March 1999 usefully support this analysis, as does the one-sided rejection of the Russian-sponsored resolution of censure after the intervention.[23] Even more indicative of a quasi-ratification of the NATO action was the willingness of the UNSC in Resolution 1244 to accept a central role for restoring normality to

Kosovo on the basis of the NATO negotiating position at Rambouillet and elsewhere, including the imposition of an UNMIK regime that amounts to de facto independence for the former province. These factors supportive of "legality" are offset in part, though, by the negotiating ambiguities outlined in the previous chapter, the exclusive reliance on air warfare, and the ambivalent relationship to the KLA.

Another fundamental legal concern relates to the kind of precedent being established by forceful intervention in Kosovo and Serbia. To endow the NATO campaign with an aura of legality on the basis of "implicit" authorization to use force by the UNSC seems an undesirable precedent. This is likely to encourage an even greater reliance on the veto by those Permanent Members who fear expansive subsequent interpretations. Such states may well be concerned that their concurring vote on what seems like a preliminary resolution on a threat to peace might later be relied upon by some states to justify force and what they would regard as unwarranted intrusions on sovereign rights. There is little doubt that any move toward an implicit authorization for force tends to undermine "the bright red line" that the Charter has attempted to draw around permissible force, although this dilution, it must be admitted, may already be occurring in practice.

Several non-legal or quasi-legal justifications for the intervention have been put forward after the fact by supporters of the NATO undertaking. These include assertions that the Charter framework is obsolete in the current era of intrastate conflict, and that the moral priority of preventing genocide and severe crimes against humanity justifies action even when the UNSC cannot find a political consensus.[24] This geopolitically grounded argument suggests that a coalition of like-minded or "enlightened" states excluding the blocking Permanent Members can still wield sufficient moral authority for the international community to justify bypassing a paralyzed UNSC when the circumstances demand it. At the very least, such an argument demands that it be demon-

strable that what is at stake is indeed as morally extreme as genocide or severe criminality, and that no course of action within the
capacity of the UNSC could reasonably be expected to stop it.
Despite this high threshold and the ambiguities surrounding
whether Kosovo met such conditions, the recognition of such a
vaguely defined right to "coalition" action has disturbing implications for future world stability. If the Kosovo war is employed as a
precedent for allowing states, whether singly or in coalition, to
ignore or contradict the UNSC based on their own interpretation
of international morality, the stabilizing function of the UNSC
will be seriously imperiled, as will the effort to circumscribe the
conditions under which recourse to force by states is permissible.

In situations such as the Kosovo crisis, however, a decisive obstacle to recourse to the United Nations may have to do with the
general absence of a supportive consensus among states rather
than merely with the prospect of a veto. Indeed, the NATO states
chose not to utilize the residual role of the General Assembly
under the Uniting for Peace Resolution because, even though
there is no veto in the General Assembly, the sensitivity of non-
Western states to interventionary claims of any sort made it unlikely that an authorization of force would have been endorsed by
the required two-thirds majority. Arguably, Kosovo thus fell into
a special zone where neither approval nor censure was forthcoming, making a weak case for bypassing the United Nations.

NATO and its supporters have wisely avoided staking out any
doctrinal claims for its action either prior to or after the war.
Rather than defining the Kosovo intervention as a precedent,
most NATO supporters among international jurists presented the
intervention as an unfortunate but necessary and reasonable exception. Nevertheless, NATO cannot hope to preclude states, and
especially other regional organizations, from referring to its
claims of intervention in Kosovo as a precedent. NATO could in
theory formally commit itself not to repeat such an unauthorized
intervention in the event of similar circumstances arising in the

future, but such a step would be seen as amounting to the repudiation of its campaign on behalf of Kosovo, and is extremely unlikely.

The Kosovo "exception" now exists, for better and worse, as a contested precedent that must be assessed in relation to a wide range of international effects and undertakings. Chief among these is that NATO, as mentioned earlier, was widely viewed by many non-NATO countries as having independently waged a non-defensive war without having made sufficient effort to obtain proper authorization or to achieve a peaceful settlement. The ambiguities of these efforts, which support the judgment of "insufficiency", were discussed in the previous chapter. NATO was either engaging in threat diplomacy or treating the use of force as a foregone conclusion, and in any event seemed prepared to circumvent the UN because of anticipated Russian and Chinese opposition, reasons of military and political efficiency, and possibly because of an ancillary interest in constructing a new post-cold war security architecture in Europe based on a renovated NATO.

Even if the benefit of the doubt is given to the diplomacy conducted on behalf of NATO, there was a failure to make a maximal effort at the UN level, where it did no more than informally justify non-recourse to the UNSC on the grounds that a veto was anticipated. Such an anticipation is itself highly subjective and conjectural, and does not take into account the obligation to explore the grounds for agreement with potential objecting states so as to achieve a UNSC consensus. In evaluating claims by parties that there is no reasonable alternative to the use of force in a given set of circumstances, the international law approach gives primacy to the UNSC and to the related priority accorded the avoidance of war.

Finally, eventual assessment of the "Kosovo principle" will also be strongly influenced by the ultimate outcome in Kosovo — whether the international action is seen as producing stable and humane governance, or the opposite.

The above discussions of the ambiguities inherent in all facets of adjudicating NATO's intervention into Kosovo place before the Commission a central question — whether, in a post-Cold War setting, international law as conceived a half century earlier provides adequate guidelines, especially given the failure of states to endow the United Nations with sufficient authority and capabilities? In answering this question, the Commission feels strongly that the moral imperative of protecting vulnerable people in an increasingly globalized world should not be lightly cast aside by adopting a legalistic view of international responses to humanitarian catastrophes. The effectiveness of rescue initiatives would seem to take precedence over formal niceties.

In this regard, it must be acknowledged that even a negotiated outcome attained by NATO diplomacy would still have consigned over 90% of the Kosovo population to oppressive and discriminatory rule under the FRY. The NATO military campaign, despite its vulnerability to legal and moral criticism, did at least have the effect of liberating the majority population from a long period abuse, and has given them some hope for a secure and genuinely autonomous future based on a seemingly irreversible de facto independence. Such a favorable set of circumstances for Kosovar Albanians would not have been achieved even if the restoration of pre-1989 style autonomy had been agreed to by Belgrade. Autonomy would have left Kosovo with a continued Serb police presence, and an ongoing vulnerability to FRY armed interference. Consequently, it would have also been subject to the probable continuation of a KLA-led movement for an independent Kosovo. Of course, the beneficial aspects of the actual outcome for Kosovar Albanians need to be balanced against the failure to protect the non-Albanian minorities since June 1999, and the related unlikelihood of a future multiethnic, democratic Kosovo.[25]

## LAWS OF WAR: METHODS AND TACTICS

International law governing conduct in war is set forth in a series of international agreements that have the status of treaties.[26] The most pertinent treaty instrument is Additional Protocol I to the Geneva Conventions, which pertains to civil wars. More than 150 states have ratified Protocol I, but it has not been ratified by all members of NATO including France, Turkey, and the United States.[27] Nevertheless, most of its content is widely considered to be operative as "customary international law," that is, rules and standards that impose obligations on states as a result of their acceptance over time as norms which should be binding on states.[28] This is augmented by a series of customary law principles that have developed regarding the methods and tactics of warfare, including the principle of necessity (the use of force must be essential to achieve goals of war), the principle of proportionality (relation of means to ends; avoidance of excessive force), the principle of discrimination or distinction (methods and tactics must be directed at military targets), and the principle of humanity (methods and tactics must not inflict superfluous suffering on people; avoidance of cruelty).[29] Considerable latitude has been afforded to the interpretation of these principles.

In many respects, Article 48 of Protocol I formulates the basic rule relating to the protection of civilians, which is a treaty formulation of the customary rule of discrimination:

> In order to ensure respect for and protection of the civilian population and civilian objects, the Parties to the conflict shall at all times distinguish between the civilian population and combatants and between civilian objects and military objectives and accordingly direct their operations only against military objectives.

Article 52(2) elaborates on the nature of military objects as "those objects which by their nature, location, purpose or use make an effective contribution to military action and whose total or partial destruction, capture or neutralization, in the circumstances ruling at the time, offer a definite military advantage." Article 51(2) rules out the idea of weakening a military effort by attacking civilians: "(…) the civilian population as such, as well as individual civilians, shall not be the object of attack." Further, Articles 51(4) (5)(7) and (8) specify the facets of this underlying obligation.

In analyzing whether the NATO military campaign of 1999 complies with these treaty and customary rules of international law, the Commission has taken account of and given great weight to the Final Report of the Committee of the ICTY Established to Review the NATO Bombing Campaign Against the Federal Republic of Yugoslavia. On the basis of a detailed examination of the evidence presented to it by the FRY, and by its reliance on sources in the public domain, the ICTY concluded that the most serious allegations against NATO relating to the law of war were not of sufficient merit to warrant further investigation. It should be noted, however, that this conclusion goes directly against the recommendation of Amnesty International, which in its earlier report, "Violations of the Laws of War by NATO during Operation Allied Force," June 7, 2000, specifically enjoins the ICTY to conduct investigations of "all credible allegations of serious violations of international humanitarian law (…) with a view of bringing to trial anyone against whom there is sufficient admissible evidence."[30] The ICTY could argue that its inquiry was consistent with this recommendation to the extent that there was not sufficient admissible evidence available to justify an "investigation" of the sort being proposed by Amnesty International. The FRY's allegations against NATO either were found not "sufficiently well-established as violations of international law to form the basis of a prosecution" or were such that "the prospects for obtaining evidence sufficient to prove that the crime had been committed by an individual who merits prosecution in the international forum" were not available.[31]

It should be kept in mind that the ICTY was concerned only with the very specific question as to whether there was a basis to charge *particular* individuals with *crimes*. This type of criminal inquiry, while obviously appropriate for the ICTY, is an inappropriately narrow undertaking for an independent international commission. The Commission is concerned about whether there is a basis for believing that NATO committed *violations* of the applicable laws of war, and thus does not need to connect individuals with specific violations, but rather seeks to investigate the responsibility of the governments involved in possible violations. The focus of the Commission thus is more in accord with the sort of assessment made by the Amnesty International study. The ICTY also pointed out that "The Prosecutor may, in her discretion require a higher threshold be met before making a positive decision that there is sufficient basis to proceed."[32] Again, as the Commission is not responsible for prosecution, it is freer to inquire into allegations pertaining to the laws of war. When criminal responsibility is at stake, there is a stronger tendency to require a treaty basis for violations, but when the inquiry is more general and provisional, the principles of customary international law have greater relevance. Beyond this, where the claim is based on a rationale of "humanitarian intervention," adherence to the laws of war might properly be assessed in a particularly rigorous manner.

## TARGETS

After the first period of bombing, NATO expanded its target list and began destroying the civilian infrastructure of Serbia, bombing bridges, broadcasting stations, electricity supply, political party offices, and other facilities considered basic to civilian survival. Such targeting is questionable under the Geneva Conventions and Protocol I, but it must be acknowledged that state practice in wartime since World War II has consistently selected targets on the basis of an open-ended approach to "military necessity," rather than by observing the customary and conventional norm that disallows deliberate attacks on non-military targets. It must also be noted that the NATO campaign was more careful, in relation to its targeting, than was any previous occasion of major warfare conducted from the air. This care with targeting was partly an expression of declared policy, and it reflected the availability of "smart" technology that had the capacity to be precise. As the ICTY noted, several serious mistakes were made. Nevertheless, there is no evidence of deliberate targeting of civilians. There is, nevertheless, reason to question the selection of targets relating to the civilian infrastructure of the FRY in which the probability of civilians being present and killed was quite high. There are also allegations and evidence to suggest that NATO persisted with attacks after it realized that civilians were present at the target site, including Grdelica railroad bridge, the automobile bridge at Luan/Luan, and the Barbarin/Barbarin bridge.

## CLUSTER BOMBS

Human Rights Watch has carefully documented that at least 500 non-combatant civilians were killed by NATO bombs and missiles in Serbia and Kosovo. A significant number of these civilian deaths occurred during attacks on civilian infrastructure targets, and others as a result of the use of legally dubious cluster bombs against targets located in densely populated areas. Thousands of cluster bombs remain unexploded throughout Kosovo and Serb territory, posing a serious ongoing hazard somewhat analogous to "anti-personnel landmines" that have been outlawed since the 1998 Ottawa Treaty.[33] Although the legal force of this analogy can be questioned, especially with respect to those members of NATO that have so far not signed the treaty, the analogy is sound in that cluster bombs are often more destructive than mines, and have been responsible for over 500 civilian deaths. NATO has been slow to deploy its own expert teams to help in the locating and defusing of these unexploded bombs. In Kosovo, UN teams and NGOs are taking on the task, mostly with newly trained Albanian staff, but at a very slow pace due to limited resources. The ICTY view is that cluster bombs are not clearly prohibited by international humanitarian law, and thus are not suitable for an investigation as to individual responsibility for their use. The Commission does not dispute this conclusion, but nevertheless recommends that cluster bombs should never be used in any future undertaking under UN auspices or claiming to be a "humanitarian intervention."[34]

## TACTICS

The reliance by NATO on a high-altitude rule of engagement for its bombing sorties so as to minimize the risk of casualties to itself has been widely criticized. The fact that NATO endured zero casualties despite the magnitude of the war and the damage inflicted has underscored this critique. In the words of the Amnesty International report, "the requirement that NATO aircraft fly above 15,000 feet, made full adherence to international humanitarian law virtually impossible."[35] Nevertheless, it must be kept in mind that, despite a series of "mistakes," NATO's overall record was unprecedented to the extent that it avoided civilian damage through the accuracy of its targeting. The ICTY concluded that:

> there is nothing inherently unlawful about flying above the height which can be reached by enemy air defenses. However, NATO air commanders have a duty to take practicable measures to distinguish military objectives from civilians or civilian objectives. The 15,000 feet minimum altitude adopted for part of the campaign may have meant the target could not be verified with the naked eye. However, it appears that with the use of modern technology, the obligation to distinguish was effectively carried out in the vast majority of cases during the bombing campaign.[36]

The high-altitude tactic does not seem to have legal significance, although it does weaken the claim of humanitarianism to the extent that it appears to value the lives of the NATO combatants more than those of the civilian population in Kosovo and Serbia, and especially the lives of the Kosovar Albanians that it was acting to protect.

## ENVIRONMENTAL DAMAGE

The ecological/environmental effects of the bombing campaign also are alleged to have a long-term civilian consequences, both in Serbia and in Kosovo. A recent United Nations Environmental Program (UNEP) study conducted by the Balkan Task Force concludes that the environmental consequences it could document were in most cases either not substantial or not long-lasting,[37] in contrast to some of the NGO contentions that were made during and shortly after the war. However, UNEP does document several extremely serious toxic leaks caused by the bombing of industrial and petroleum complexes in several cities. These leaks created environmental and humanitarian emergencies posing uncertain long-term risks and demanding immediate clean-up. The UNEP report asserts that the FRY is responsible for its own environmental clean-up, but it does acknowledge that any such clean-up efforts might be hindered by the ongoing embargo. Some NGO reports and scholarly assessments suggest more extensive and serious environmental damage that seems to cross the threshold of accountability embodied in Articles 35(3) and 55 of Protocol I. The ICTY Final Report stresses the demanding character of this threshold, with the key words being that the damage sustained must be "widespread, long-term, and severe," taking special note of the word "and" that suggests that all three features must be cumulatively present for a violation to take place.[38]

Another disturbing environmental concern raised during the war was the widespread use of depleted-uranium (DU) tipped armor-piercing shells and missiles. Upon explosion, such shells and missiles release respirable uranium dioxide into the atmosphere, with potential serious long-term health consequences. NATO does not deny the use of such shells and missiles, as DU is considered a cost-effective material with valued armor-piercing properties. Disturbingly, though, as of this writing NATO has been slow to assist the UNEP investigation. The UNEP report called for a World Health Organization investigation of the long-term health implications of the use of DU armament. Five months after a special request to NATO from Kofi Annan for more precise information, NATO confirmed that 31,000 rounds of DU ammunition, equivalent to 10 tons, was used in the Kosovo conflict, but UNEP still lacks sufficient targeting detail to allow for additional investigation of whether a significant radiation hazard might exist. Other studies provide reassurance that the damage resulting from DU is not substantial and not dangerous for the civilian population. The ICTY conclusion is that at present there is no consensus supportive of the prohibition of such DU ordinance, although it raises the possibility of such a development in the future.[39] It reinforces its conclusion more questionably by suggesting that the ICJ was unable to agree that even nuclear weapons were unconditionally prohibited despite their undoubted character of doing severe and extensive environmental damage.[40] What makes this reasoning questionable is that the ICJ was considering the legality of a possible use of nuclear weapons without any real consideration of effects, and limited such use to extreme circumstances of self-defense, and then only as a legal possibility.

The Commission recommends that particular care be taken in the context of a humanitarian intervention to avoid targets that would cause serious environmental damage, adhering to standards of restraint greater than needed to comply with the current high threshold of Protocol I. It is noted that Iraq has been charged with tactics designed to inflict environmental damage in the course of the Gulf War, although its actions were connected with measures related to "military necessity" as seen from its perspective.

## DISCUSSION

The Commission is impressed by the relatively small scale of civilian damage considering the magnitude of the war and its duration. It is further of the view that NATO succeeded better than any air war in history in selective targeting that adhered to principles of discrimination, proportionality, and necessity, with only relatively minor breaches that were themselves reasonable interpretations of "military necessity" in the context. The Commission accepts the view of the Final Report of the ICTY that there is no basis in available evidence for charging specific individuals with criminal violations of the laws of war during the NATO campaign. Nevertheless, some practices do seem vulnerable to the allegation that violations might have occurred, and depend for final assessment upon the availability of further evidence.

The Commission does recommend that the ICRC or other appropriate expert body prepare a new legal convention for military operations that are either instances of UN peacekeeping or humanitarian intervention. This convention should impose more constraints on the use of force than are embodied in the law of war as now generally interpreted. A less ambitious alternative, recommended by Amnesty International, would be to accept stricter adherence to the existing standards of international law, particularly as already embodied in Protocol 1. Such an interpretation has been provided in competent form by the ICTY Final Report. While so recommending, the Commission is mindful of the importance of effectiveness in carrying out a humanitarian intervention under difficult conditions, and with a sense of urgency, and does not intend its emphasis on enhanced legal guidelines to undermine a reasonable view of "military necessity." There is a delicate balance here, as countries are being asked to take risks for humanitarian purposes, and may be reluctant to do so. Such reluctance points to the need for some form of global professional voluntary military, peace observation, and police force. Unfortunately, the current political obstacles to moving in such a desirable direction are formidable.

## ON THE DOCTRINE OF HUMANITARIAN INTERVENTION

With the ending of the Cold War, new conditions of world order have complicated earlier priorities with respect to the use of force in international relations. The post-1945 preoccupation was with the prevention of *international wars* between two or more states, and especially between major states. Nuclear weaponry and missile guidance systems lent a geopolitical urgency to this undertaking. Nevertheless, even before the Soviet collapse, many of the most serious challenges to international peace and security were arising in the course of *intra-national crises* of a wide variety. The UN Charter discouraged responses to such crises with its assurance that matters "essentially within the domestic jurisdiction" of states were beyond its purview unless defined by the UNSC as threats to international peace and security.[41] Although the UNSC has increasingly identified domestic crises as threats to international peace and security, the feeling persists that the Charter as originally written is not satisfactory for a world order that is increasingly called upon to respond to humanitarian challenges. This concern had already been clearly articulated before the Kosovo challenge, but it was accentuated by the NATO response.

The Commission's initial discussion above of the legality of the NATO campaign ended inconclusively with an appreciation of the difficulty of reconciling what was done to protect the people of Kosovo with the core prohibition on recourse to non-defensive force that has not been authorized by the United Nations. At the same time, the Commission takes the view that the pattern of Serb oppression in Kosovo, the experience of ethnic cleansing a few years earlier in Bosnia, and the lack of international response to genocide in Rwanda in 1994 combine to create a strong moral and political duty on the part of the international community to act effectively, and to express solidarity with civilian societies victimized by governments guilty of grave breaches of human rights.[42] This duty pertains both to the protection of the Kosovar

Albanians and to the reestablishment of autonomy for the province. Arguably, it extends to the realization of the right of self-determination for the people of Kosovo. As the previous has argued, diplomacy failed to produce these results in a reliable manner, leaving the options of doing nothing or mounting a military intervention under NATO auspices. This situation supports the general conclusion that the NATO campaign was illegal, yet legitimate. Such a conclusion is related to the controversial idea that a "right" of humanitarian intervention is not consistent with the UN Charter if conceived as a legal text, but that it may, depending on context, nevertheless, reflect the spirit of the Charter as it relates to the overall protection of people against gross abuse. Humanitarian intervention may also thus be legitimately authorized by the UN, but will often be challenged legally from the perspective of Charter obligations to respect the sovereignty of states.

Allowing this gap between legality and legitimacy to persist is not healthy, for several reasons. Acknowledging the tension with most interpretations of international law either inhibits solidarity with civilian victims of severe abuse by territorial governments, or seriously erodes the prohibition on the use of force that the World Court and other authorities have deemed valid. Closely related to this effect, recourse to force without proper UN authorization tends to weaken the authority of, and respect for, the United Nations, especially the UNSC, in the domain of international peace and security. It needs to be observed, at the same time, that a failure to act on behalf of the Kosovars, or a repetition of the Bosnian or Rwandan experience of an insufficient UN mandate and capabilities, would have also weakened the United Nations, probably to a greater degree.[43] Therefore, although the Commission's finding is that the use of force by NATO in intervening in Kosovo is validated from the perspective of the legitimacy of the undertaking and its overall societal effects, the Commission feels that it would be most beneficial to work diligently to close the gap between legality and legitimacy in a convincing manner for the future.

The Commission is of the opinion that the best way to do this is to conceive of an emergent doctrine of humanitarian intervention that consists of a process of three phases:

- a recommended framework of principles useful in a setting where humanitarian intervention is proposed as an international response and where it actually occurs;
- the formal adoption of such a framework by the General Assembly of the United Nations in the form of a Declaration on the Right and Responsibility of Humanitarian Intervention, accompanied by UNSC interpretations of the UN Charter that reconciles such practice with the balance between respect for sovereign rights, implementation of human rights, and prevention of humanitarian catastrophe;
- the amendment of the Charter to incorporate these changes in the role and responsibility of the United Nations and other collective actors in international society to implement the Declaration on the Right and Responsibility of Humanitarian Intervention.

The main problems relating to the protection of human rights and the prevention of humanitarian catastrophes are political rather than legal. In the face of serious abuses of human rights, even genocide, or the need to prevent or mitigate a humanitarian catastrophe, armed or unarmed intervention will not occur in an effective form unless such action conforms to the interests of potential intervening states; the action does not fly in the face of prudential concerns about sustaining the stability of world order; and, above all, the action does not risk the outbreak of a major war among states with nuclear capacity. For these reasons, it is unrealistic to expect humanitarian intervention to evolve according to the rule of law such that equal cases are treated equally. The only viable option is to prohibit such interventionary claims altogether, or to accept their selective implementation, ensuring only that in *appropriate* instances such intervention proceeds on a principled basis that is as consistent as possible with the humanitarian rationale.

During the cold war there was not the political will, nor the foundation in law, nor the practical conditions that would support a humanitarian diplomacy that might include the use of interventionary force. For different reasons, both superpowers were most reluctant to pursue goals in international society that did not relate to their rivalry, and both were acutely conscious of not taking action that would be likely to provoke its adversary to embark on warfare. The Soviet Union essentially appropriated the sovereignty of its client states in eastern Europe in an oppressive manner, but at the same time it dogmatically resisted any infringement of sovereignty by the West. The United States allied itself with many states that were guilty of extreme violations of human rights, so long as their governments adopted an anti-Communist orientation and supported the Western cause in international settings. The only important exception arose in relation to the apartheid regime in South Africa, where East and West, North and South, could, at least in the 1980s, agree on the illegality[44] of the racist practices, and on a gradually more coercive approach toward the official government that included the imposition of sanctions. The South African example generated an interventionary approach which, while falling well short of the threat or use of force, provided a sort of prelude to subsequent claims of humanitarian intervention.

There were additional inhibitions on any authorization of interventionary force by the United Nations. First of all, the normative standards associated with international human rights had not been accepted as internally binding in any serious sense. Second, the cold war era interventions were seen as extremely destructive exercises in geopolitics which had little bearing on the well-being of the societies in which the violence occurred, despite lofty ideals proclaimed by the intervenors. This legacy has result-

ed in continuing suspicion, especially by states that had been col-
onized or dominated by the West, that "humanitarian intervention" is a new name for Western domination. For the UN to give
such claims any sort of legitimacy would be to create a "Trojan
Horse" that could be used to undermine political independence
and even the territorial integrity of weaker sovereign states. As
such, the most that can be said regarding humanitarian intervention is that there is a disposition to approach imminent humanitarian catastrophes on an ad hoc or case-by-case basis. This reinforces an impression of double standards (taking action in Kosovo, but not in other places of equal or greater abuse), but it re-
tains the basic norm of unconditional non-intervention in
internal affairs. For opposite reasons—the desire to avoid pressures to act, as in sub-Saharan Africa or South Asia—those
states that mounted the intervention on behalf of the Kosovars
are also inclined to prefer an ad hoc approach at this point.

The Commission believes that the end of the Cold War has
brought about some dramatic changes in circumstances, which
make the case for a doctrine of humanitarian intervention much
more compelling than in the past. There has been an impressive
evolution of international standards governing human rights, and
some expectation of implementation both by the organized
international community (such as the anti-apartheid campaign)
and through the initiative of civil society organizations and concerned governments. Further, there is a growing trend toward an
insistence on accountability of leaders for crimes of states,
demonstrated by the controversy over the extradition case against
General Augusto Pinochet, and epitomized by the ICTY and by
the Rome Treaty of 1998, which sets the framework for the establishment of an International Criminal Court.

Meanwhile, the threat that interventions undertaken for humanitarian goals will provoke strategic warfare among leading
states has declined. In recent years the United Nations and other
powerful actors have been harshly criticized for taking insufficient

action in response to threatened or imminent humanitarian catastrophes. The Organization of African Unity (OAU) issued a report recently criticizing the UN, France, and the United States for their failure to take action to prevent genocide in Rwanda in 1994.[45] A similar pattern is associated with the UN role in Bosnia, culminating in its ineffectiveness in upholding "the safe havens" established under the authority of the UN, and not protecting them sufficiently.[46] In other words, the political, moral, and legal ground now exists to strike a new balance between the general duty of non-intervention in internal affairs of states and the ethos of humanitarian intervention on the basis of principled, collective decisions.

To advance discussion and to present recommendations for addressing these important issues, the Commission believes that the time is now ripe for the presentation of a principled framework, useful for evaluating past claims of humanitarian intervention, to guide future responses in the face of imminent or unfolding humanitarian catastrophe. It is important to understand that the scope of this framework extends beyond situations of governmental abuse to encompass acute human suffering associated with governmental collapse, as in Somalia in the early 1990s. It is our hope that this framework can be subsequently adopted in some modified form as a Declaration on Humanitarian Intervention by the UN General Assembly. On this basis, two lines of development can be projected. The preferred approach would be to have the Charter adapted to this Humanitarian Intervention Declaration by upgrading human rights and conditioning sovereign rights on respect for human rights and the maintenance of the capacity to govern. An alternative approach would be to encourage UNSC interpretations of the Charter that moved explicitly in this direction on a case-by-case basis, building up a new authoritative approach to this subject along the lines of the Humanitarian Intervention Declaration.

Such "innovations" in Charter interpretation have been part of the UN history all along, and were most notably associated with

Dag Hammarskjold's tenure as Secretary General, particularly in the context of UN peacekeeping activities. A good example of such "legislative" interpretation is the conversion of the Article 27(3) requirement that UNSC decisions be supported by the "concurring" votes of the five Permanent Members into a pattern of practice in which "abstentions" or absences are treated as equivalent to "concurring".

It might be unrealistic, however, to expect such an outcome in the near future. A large number of states continue to view humanitarian intervention outside the United Nations with great suspicion, and are not favorably disposed to such claims even within the UN. They distrust the assertion of "humanitarian" intentions and oppose intrusions on territorial sovereignty. The majority of states on the UNSC indicated a willingness to confirm the result of the Kosovo intervention as a practical reality. Similarly, many have given some indirect support to the intervention via UNMIK, by way of appropriations and through refusal to pass any kind of critical resolution. Nevertheless, there is no current disposition at the United Nations to provide a principled regime that would "legalize" such interventions in the future.

There is another source of resistance to any effort to put humanitarian intervention on a principled basis. Several important countries are extremely reluctant to remove humanitarian intervention from the realm of ad hoc diplomacy for fear of building expectations that, whenever a humanitarian catastrophe occurs, an interventionary duty to prevent or the ameliorate the crisis would arise. Here, their objective is to retain the diplomatic flexibility associated with treating such challenges selectively, responding where the political will is present, but not undertaking a more general commitment to act in a consistent fashion that might not accord with their interests or reflect the outlook of their domestic society. These states are not currently willing to accept a duty of humanitarian intervention except at times and places of their own choosing.

We acknowledge that a framework for intervention is thus a controversial step. One opposing position argues that it is not necessary, because of the possibility of loosening the interpretation of the prohibition on force to an extent that "international law" encompasses what is here called "legitimacy." The second position insists that positing such a principles regime would contribute further to a revival of geopolitical discretion with respect to force, weakening both international law and the United Nations in the process. This position was particularly firmly emphasized to the Commission by participants at its Johannesburg seminar.

However, the importance of agreeing upon a principled regime for humanitarian intervention or human rights enforcement has assumed prominence throughout the 1990s. Somalia, Bosnia, Haiti, Rwanda, and East Timor are only the most salient cases in which great moral pressure was exerted on the international community and the UN system to take forcible action to end a humanitarian catastrophe in the making—pressure exerted as a result of domestic circumstances. Kosovo underscored the challenge, and the NATO response is being treated by many commentators as the defining moment in the debate on humanitarian intervention.

## A FRAMEWORK FOR PRINCIPLED HUMANITARIAN INTERVENTION

The Danish Institute of International Affairs suggests five "possible criteria" for "legitimate humanitarian intervention." Although the Institute frowns on creating any basis for the use of force outside the framework of existing international law, these criteria nonetheless offer a useful background to the Commission's recommended informal regime applicable to humanitarian intervention. The Danish Institute's criteria are as follows:

- serious violations of human rights or international humanitarian law;
- a failure by the UNSC to act;
- multilateral bases for the action undertaken;
- only necessary and proportionate force used;
- "disinterestedness" of the intervening states.[47]

The Commission's recommended framework of principles is divided into two parts. The first suggests threshold principles that must be satisfied in order for any claim of humanitarian intervention to be legitimate. The second puts forward principles that enhance or diminish the *degree* of legitimacy possessed by forceful intervention. These "contextual principles" can be applied either before an intervention in order to determine whether force should be used, or to assess whether an intervention was justifiable. Unless it is apparent from the text that a principle is relevant only to instances of intervention without a UN mandate, these principles should be understood to be capable of application to coercive humanitarian intervention either by the UN, or by a coalition of the willing acting with or without the approval of the UN. It should further be kept in mind that the term "intervention" is not applicable to a situation where a government in power gives its consent to an international presence, given that, in such a situation, no legal problem arises regarding the legitimacy of the humanitarian participation.

## THRESHOLD PRINCIPLES

1 There are two valid triggers of humanitarian intervention. The first is severe violations of international human rights or humanitarian law on a sustained basis. The second is the subjection of a civilian society to great suffering and risk due to the "failure" of their state, which entails the breakdown of governance at the level of the territorial sovereign state.

2 The overriding aim of all phases of the intervention involving the threat and the use of force must be the direct protection of the victimized population.

3 The method of intervention must be reasonably calculated to end the humanitarian catastrophe as rapidly as possible, and must specifically take measures to protect all civilians, to avoid collateral damage to civilian society, and to preclude any secondary punitive or retaliatory action against the target government.

## CONTEXTUAL PRINCIPLES

4 There must be a serious attempt to find a peaceful solution to the conflict. This solution must ensure that the pattern of abuse is terminated in a reliable and sustainable fashion, or that a process of restoring adequate governance is undertaken.

5 Recourse to the United Nations UNSC, or the lack thereof, is not conclusive. This is so if approaching the Council fails because of the exercise of a veto by one or more of the permanent members; or if the failure to have recourse to the UNSC is due to the reasonable anticipation of such a veto, where subsequent further appeal to the General Assembly is not practical. Effectively, the latter case suggests that the veto right is superseded by a ⅔ or better majority determination by "a coalition of the willing" that a humanitarian catastrophe is present or imminent.

6 Before military action is taken, lesser measures of mediating and coercive action, including sanctions, embargoes and non-violent methods of peace observation, must have been attempted without success. Further delay must be reasonably deemed to significantly increase the prospect of a humanitarian catastrophe;

7 Any recourse to the threat or use of force should not be uni-

lateral, but enjoy some established collective support that is expressed both by a multilateral process of authorization and the participation of countries in the undertaking;

8 There should not be any formal act of censure or condemnation of the intervention by a principle organ of the United Nations, especially by the International Court of Justice or the UNSC.

9 There must be even stricter adherence to the laws of war and international humanitarian law than in standard military operations. This applies to all aspects of the military operation, including any post cease-fire occupation.

10 Territorial or economic goals are illegitimate as justification for intervention, and there should be a credible willingness on their part of intervening states to withdraw military forces and to end economic coercive measures at the earliest point in time consistent with the humanitarian objectives.

11 After the use of armed force has achieved its objectives, there should be energetic implementation of the humanitarian mission by a sufficient commitment of resources to sustain the population in the target society and to ensure speedy and humane reconstruction of that society in order for the whole population to return to normality. This implies a rejection of prolonged comprehensive or punitive sanctions.

## SUGGESTED REVISIONS OF THE UN CHARTER

The challenge for the future is certainly not that countries or groups of countries are too eager to intervene to stop serious abuse human rights, but rather the opposite. The pattern of the recent past suggests that states are eager to find excuses not to intervene. Optimistically, the Kosovo experience might make it somewhat more difficult for the UNSC and individual countries to avoid taking action against serious abuse of human rights in the future. However, it is extremely important that such actions should involve UNSC consideration and decision. It is consequently reasonable and necessary to give the protection of human rights a more important role in the UN Charter. At present, the Charter does not explicitly give the UNSC the power to take measures in cases of violations of human rights.

The distribution of powers between the different organs of the UN is part of a complex political and legal construction with the collective security system at its center. Under the collective security system, the role of the UNSC is, or has been until now, to ensure international peace and international order. The issue of human rights protection has been of only secondary importance to the UNSC within this framework. Ideally, the Charter must be amended to enhance the role of human rights in their own right within the system for collective security.

Such amendment would both put pressure on and make it possible for the UNSC to invoke violations of human rights and humanitarian law directly as a reason for taking a variety of types of measures. The Council would consequently no longer have to stretch reality to invoke the notion of "threat to the peace" in every case, and would also have greater difficulty standing by and doing nothing.

References to human rights could be inserted into a number of existing articles in the UN Charter. For example, in Article 1 of the Charter concerning the purposes of the UN a reference to human rights could be inserted in sub-paragraph 1 after "international peace and security" in the very first sentence. The first sentence of sub-paragraph 1 would then read "To maintain international peace and security and respect for human rights (...)"

In Article 24 sub-paragraph 1 on the functions and powers of the UNSC, the passage "and respect for fundamental human rights" could be inserted after "maintenance of international peace and security," so that Article 24(1) would read:

> "In order to ensure prompt and effective action by the United Nations, its Members confer on the UNSC primary responsibility for the maintenance

of international peace and security and respect for fundamental human rights, and agree that in carrying out its duties under this responsibility the UNSC acts on their behalf."

(Currently the General Assembly has the primary responsibility for the work for human rights within the UN organization. Rather than overturn this state of things the term "fundamental" is inserted before "human rights" in the proposed amendment in order to indicate that the UNSC would be involved only concerning serious human rights violations.)

At the end of Article 39, a reference to "respect for human rights" could also be inserted. This article would then read: "The UNSC shall determine the existence of any threat to the peace, breach of the peace, act of aggression or serious violation of human rights and shall make recommendations, or decide what measures shall be taken in accordance with Articles 41 and 42, to maintain or restore international peace and security and respect for human rights."

We are of course aware of the powerful political resistance to amending the UN Charter. In the meantime, there are also "softer" courses of action than formal changes of the Charter, such as adopting interpretative declarations concerning certain passages in the Charter, or resolutions in the General Assembly.

But there is a growing international momentum for UN reform, and the Commission would hope to provide some fuel for that process. The Commission feels that, in addition to the specific inclusion of human rights wording in the charter, other key ongoing debates related to UNSC reform have direct relevance to the topic of humanitarian intervention. Since the UN was formed, its structure has not changed with the changing post-Cold War political atmosphere. The Commission acknowledges that in order for the UNSC to maintain its functionality and global legitimacy, it should be reformed. Expanding the assignment of permanent and non-permanent seats on the UNSC should allow for more expedient and appropriate decision-making and more equitable representation of the UN membership. It is also our position, given the lessons of the Kosovo experience, as well as Rwanda and other cases, that the current system allowing any Permanent UNSC member to paralyze UN action through the use of the veto must be adjusted in a judicious manner to deal effectively with cases of extreme humanitarian crisis. The Commission wishes to emphasize that such change is urgent both for the sake of future victims of humanitarian crises and for the very legitimacy and credibility of the UN as the legally authorized guardian of global security.

## CONCLUSION

The application of this framework for humanitarian intervention to Kosovo is intended to structure debate rather than to resolve controversy. The relationship between the principles articulated and the facts is complex and subject to diverse lines of interpretation. Reasonable disagreement is to be expected. The benefit of such a framework is that it encourages a more comprehensive approach to the interventionary action, and discourages a one-sided view. It also provides a pre-legal proposal for initiatives by governments and international institutions to move in the direction of establishing a legal doctrine of humanitarian intervention that balances the claims to protect peoples against the importance of restricting discretion to use force in international relations.

Red Cross bus at the Stenkovec refugee camp outside
Skopje, Macedonia.
PHOTO: ROBBAN ANDERSSON/PRESSENS BILD

# 7

# HUMANITARIAN ORGANIZATIONS AND THE ROLE OF MEDIA

The Kosovo crisis produced the largest population displacement in Europe since the aftermath of World War II. Observers indicate that there were accurate estimates of internal displacement before the bombing.[1] Yet both governmental and non-governmental agencies were surprised by the scale of the refugee crisis. Two days after the bombing began, the United Nations High Commissioner for Refugees (UNHCR) representative's briefing in Tirana gave no indication that a massive refugee crisis was about to happen. Subsequent press accounts indicated that the German intelligence services had known of "Operation Horseshoe," a Serbian plan (the existence of which has been extensively debated) to force the immediate mass expulsion of ethnic Albanians from Kosovo. Nevertheless, even though the UNHCR would be expected to serve as the lead agency to coordinate responses to any refugee crisis, no government or other source gave the UNHCR advance information about such a plan.[2]

Neighboring countries had feared massive refugee flows for several years before the crisis erupted. Humanitarian groups, however, lacked specific information about the risks of the potential scale of the crisis, and they did not develop sufficient contingency planning for the possibility of mass expulsions. Preparing for an emergency requires anticipating the unanticipated. Humanitarian groups have learned the lesson that when there are large numbers of internally displaced peoples, a large outflow of refugees should be anticipated at least in contingency planning. Unfortunately, the perpetual underfunding of UNHCR constrains its capacities for such planning. UNHCR appeared even more underfunded relative to the unusually generous funding received by many other humanitarian agencies after the crisis emerged. As a result, UNHCR faced special challenges in trying to fulfill its role as lead agency when surrounded by other actors flush with large resources and little need to respect UNHCR's coordinating authority.[3]

An independent study commissioned by UNHCR to evaluate the agency's preparedness and response acknowledged that it had declined to collaborate with NATO's 1998 planning exercises. Legitimate concerns about jeopardizing its mission and credibility prevented a collaboration which might have promoted more elaborate contingency planning. International human rights groups might have gathered relevant information. By the time of the bombing, they had no one inside Kosovo and could only interview refugees to try to piece together what was happening.[4]

Prior commitments to internally displaced persons inside Kosovo also distracted UNHCR and others from preparing for outflows of refugees. In addition, no one—including NATO command —anticipated how long the bombing would continue, so it was impossible to predict the effects on the civilian population. Even close observers of the prior few years in the region would have anticipated internal displacement but not a mass refugee crisis.

## HUMANITARIAN WORKERS DURING THE WAR

Some humanitarian groups, notably the World Food Program (WFP) were able to respond more quickly than UNHCR. Facing a crisis situation, military leaders on-site pressed political leaders to produce a quick response. NATO peacekeeping troops stationed in

Macedonia were redirected to deal with the refugees. NATO was not itself fully prepared for a humanitarian effort.[5] NATO national troop contingents immediately carved up areas flooded with refugees in Macedonia and Albania and built refugee camps. The military commands, despite a lack of extensive experience in this activity, did not cooperate with UNHCR and WHO which tried to offer advice about how to set up refugee camps.

Competition developed among the different NATO governmental/military groups, and between them and the international humanitarian groups that the military perceived as slow and inefficient. Ultimately, national governments wanted to turn over the camps built by Italian, German, British, and French NATO contingents to their own national non-governmental groups. In that context, neither UNHCR nor any other international organization could play a coordinating role or even screen NGOs to ensure sufficient capacity and experience.

The arrival of NGOs on the scene was described by some as a "feeding frenzy" of crisis junkies. Some NGOs arrived to offer help without demonstrating experience or competence to serve the people they intended to help. Instead of defining their own missions and building on prior field experience, some providers sought to promise whatever donors were willing to underwrite.[6]

Several hundred non-governmental organizations became involved.[7] The difficulty arose not so much in the need to screen the groups but in failures to coordinate them.[8] The UNHCR, as the leader among UN agencies and potential leader of humanitarian groups, received much of the blame for the lack of coordination. Yet from the UNHCR perspective, the difficulty arose chiefly because the military—with their national troops and then their respective national NGOs—took over. Peter Morris of Medecins Sans Frontières commented that in Kosovo in 1999, "many governments made bilateral funding agreements with NGOs, greatly undermining UNHCR's ability to prioritize programs or monitor efficiency."[9] An independent group of experts concluded that

UNHCR was hampered by the blurring of humanitarian and military/political missions, institutional rivalries, and insufficient high-level staff to address difficult diplomatic challenges in the initial phase of the emergency.[10]

Nonetheless, after an initial period of chaos both the military and humanitarian organizations devised effective humanitarian responses. Humanitarian groups developed innovative methods to assist family reunification. Some used the Internet; others worked with Yugoslavian phone books to create a database. The International Rescue Committee (IRC) worked with the International Committee of the Red Cross (ICRC) on a common reunification approach. UNHCR eventually played the lead role in operations, but because it had been slower than the military in planning and deploying resources, NATO framed the initial humanitarian response. Even so, an independent expert team concluded that UNHCR effectively guided the movement of refugees out of Kosovo "with unprecedented speed and scale."[11]

In Albania the most significant assistance came from Albanian citizens, who hosted some 285,000 of the refugees. The World Food Program provided food and 40 NGO partners distributed it. The World Health Organization supported health needs for women, children and vulnerable groups. NGOs provided camp management, water, sanitation, and other services in camps while refugees with host families received less assistance. UNHCR offered cash to host families but was not able to deliver it before the time of repatriation. Typically refugees staying with host families paid their hosts at least in part for accommodation and food. Bilateral agreement between the Albanian government and NATO inhibited the UNHCR's ability to play an overall coordinating role. Both gaps and duplications occurred in service delivery.

In Macedonia, the government initially refused entry to refugees. Then during the initial stages of the emergency, government restrictions made it difficult for humanitarian aid to reach refugees. The Macedonian government required work on the refugee camps to also benefit the local community. This constrained the humanitarian agencies' ability to fulfill their own priority of pulling together a quick and temporary emergency response. NATO forces built several of the initial tent camps. Host families also provided shelter, while NGOs and the Macedonian Red Cross provided food and mattresses. UNHCR assisted with utility bills for host families.

The standards of treatment set in the Kosovar refugee camps exceeded what was generally offered, for instance, to refugees in Africa. Thus there were allegations of luxury and waste in the camps. Longtime participants in humanitarian aid criticize the camps as enormously and needlessly expensive for the numbers actually served, even though they filled an important symbolic function—especially for the Albanian and Macedonian governments—of demonstrating control and stabilizing efforts. In the context of global funding shortages any quick response to a crisis in one region requires curtailing efforts in another. Thus, the heightened international attention to Kosovo yielded an extraordinary humanitarian response even as aid budgets worldwide dwindled. This preferential treatment jeopardized the appearance and reality of commitments to impartial, universal humanitarian assistance.

The UNHCR's limited access to computers, radio and telephones in the early stages of the emergency curtailed its ability to collect and share information among humanitarian actors. The huge number of humanitarian actors arriving to assist the refugees, the early presence and initiative of NATO and the demands of local governments made coordination of the humanitarian response difficult. Enhancing and communicating shared guidelines for emergency preparedness and standards of assistance would help promote greater coordination among aid agencies and host governments and donors. In addition, UNHCR should join efforts to identify qualified NGOs in advance to reduce any waste of resources during a crisis.

## RETURN AND RESETTLEMENT OF REFUGEES

The Kosovar refugees wanted to return home as soon as the bombing ended, long before international observers thought it safe. Within days of the cessation of NATO bombing on June 10, 1999, literally hundreds of thousands of Kosovars left their refugee camps and shelters with families and friends in Albania and Macedonia, heading for the Kosovo border. Most returned to their home communities. By November, over 800,000 of the 850,000 refugees had returned, making this one of the largest and quickest refugee returns in modern history.

The lack of a civil infrastructure and basic civic order in many locales was an even more serious problem than the humanitarian challenges of delivering supplies or readying housing for these returnees. International groups underestimated the powerful desire for revenge that some of the returning Kosovar Albanians brought with them. Human Rights Watch reported in August 1999 that Serbs and Roma remaining in Kosovo faced harassment, intimidation, beatings, looting, and even some disturbing instances of abduction and murder.[12] Protection efforts by humanitarian groups were insufficient and under-prioritized, while NATO forces either could not or would not fill the void in civil policing. Some NATO forces began guarding some of the remaining Serbs, but practices varied enormously depending upon which national military force was responsible in a given area, until the situation stabilized. Humanitarian groups joined human rights groups in documenting abuses and calling for peace and order.

Some humanitarian groups remain especially critical of the responses inside Kosovo immediately after the bombing. Very few NGOS seemed willing to work with Serbs. Little was done by anyone in the field to establish foot patrols and enhance protection of all civilians. KFOR resisted taking on a protection function other than peacekeeping, with the exception of troops under the command of British General Sir Michael Jackson. Subsequently,

KFOR guarded enclaves of remaining Serbs. In general, the humanitarian groups emphasized relief activities over the protection of civilians during the return and resettlement period. This has prompted some internal deliberation and re-evaluation by some groups. UNHCR, for instance, is entrusted with a duty of protecting as well as assisting refugees.

Even in the absence of basic law, security and administration, humanitarian groups tried to provide aid and helped support the revival of a free press and other civil institutions. Moderate journalist Veton Surroi reopened his newspaper's office *(Koha Ditore)* in Prishtina/Pristina. Surroi courageously condemned the reprisals against Serbs. He received some international support for this stance, but not much domestic assistance.

At the time of writing, humanitarian and human rights groups still face the challenge of securing the release of at least 1500–2000 Kosovar Albanians abducted before and during the war who remain in Serbian prisons.[13] Their situation was ignored by the June 10, 1999, agreement ending the war. The ICG states in their well documented report that senior NATO and Pentagon officials have confirmed that the earliest drafts of the Kumanovo agreement — the basis for UNSC Resolution 1244 — include provisions regarding the Albanian prisoners but they were dropped by NATO. "Washington, eager to stop the bombing and cognizant of its allies' eagerness to bring the war to an end, decided to drop the provisions relating to the prisoners among others deemed objectionable by the Serbs."[14] These prisoners remain a central obstacle to peaceful co-existence between Kosovar Albanians and Serbs. Shukrie Rexha of the Associations of Political Prisoners explained: "There can be no rebuilding of civilian life in Kosovo unless we have our prisoners released."[15] The Serbian officials have not provided a full accounting of the prisoners nor permitted access to them by international humanitarian organizations, family members, or legal representatives of the prisoners' own choosing. In addition, rather than conducting trials according to international standards or releasing those wrongly held, the Serbian state is sanctioning ransoming of the detainees and conducing trials with fabricated evidence.[16] Humanitarian and human rights organizations have thus far not engaged in systematic or coordinated responses. ICG argue that UNSC should call for the prisoners' release in accordance with international law and that strong international pressure should be put on Belgrade to release the prisoners. The Commission concurs.

Humanitarian aid organizations need to prepare for revenge sentiments in these situations and develop strategies to promote coexistence. At a minimum, the distribution of humanitarian aid should not feed into simmering resentments. Simultaneously, working alongside military and government actors, humanitarian organizations should make protection a top priority while addressing assistance needs.[17]

## HUMANITARIAN ORGANIZATIONS AND THE MILITARY

The central humanitarian mission of protecting civilian life and safety is precisely what is under siege in military engagement. How can humanitarian organizations develop closer and more continuous working relationships with military organizations without compromising their mission? Can and should clearer demarcations be drawn to avoid "mission creep" by the military and ethical and political mistakes by the non-governmental organizations?

Relations between humanitarian organizations and the military are complex even when the military is engaged in a peace enforcement operation, as in Croatia or Bosnia-Herzegovina. Because NATO was a direct party to the military conflict in Kosovo, these relations became charged and difficult. UNHCR in particular risked undermining its impartiality and neutrality if it worked closely with NATO.[18] Some observers conclude that the humanitarian principle of impartiality was compromised during the crisis.[19]

The military/humanitarian frontier has grown increasing difficult to delineate, especially in humanitarian operations. Military forces have been increasingly involved in relief operations following natural disasters as well as political conflicts. Their significant capacity to provide both security and logistical assistance often make military partners welcome major partners together with humanitarian agencies. Starting in the early 1990s, a notion of complementary roles has evolved. The International Committee of the Red Cross (ICRC), for example, seeks to ensure that the rules of international humanitarian law apply to the parties in a conflict or war and also to engage in prevention and protection for victims of armed conflict.[20] Until 1988, though, the ICRC related to armed forces only in individual actions. Then, it began working with alliances of states and regional organizations. During the Bosnia-Herzegovina conflict, the ICRC developed closer relations with NATO in the hope of reducing risks to civilian populations and to ICRC staff and facilities from air strikes. The Dayton Peace Agreement assigned clear roles to each organization and clarified their relationship and coordination efforts.

ICRC is promoting the inclusion of humanitarian issues in NATO planning exercises and training. NATO wants to collaborate given the new shape of military and humanitarian missions, involving greater civilian risk, more military involvement in peacekeeping, but also potential military enforcement action. Humanitarian organizations must acknowledge the strategic implications of refugees and aid, which are both increasingly being manipulated as weapons of war.

What is needed are more precise definitions of each participant's tasks within a framework acknowledging their complementary roles. Mercier described the chief experience among humanitarian workers in Bosnia-Herzegovina as frustration. "[N]early four years of war in former Yugoslavia have shown that it is fatal to confuse the duties of politicians, soldiers and humanitarian workers. Merely adding these components together does not lead directly to a new golden age of peacemaking, and to think that it does is to underestimate the differences in structure, function and behavior of the forces involved."[21]

When military contingents are simultaneously fulfilling both humanitarian and war-making roles, the impartiality and universality of humanitarian aid is jeopardized. Political leaders often try to mobilize support — or cover — for planned military action from the humanitarian organizations. Before the NATO bombing action, President Clinton called together leaders of American NGOs active in Kosovo. Many participants sensed his agenda was to get the humanitarian community to go along with the administration's military plan. The humanitarian cover can facilitate the military operation, while the military effort can multiply the resources available for assistance needs, but the commitment to impartiality can be lost in the process.[22] The humanitarian effort is fragmented and weakened when the military actors treat humanitarian officers as technical implementers rather than as expert authorities with valuable contributions to give to policy-setting.[23] Clarifying lines of communication and responsibility between military and humanitarian organizations are crucial to producing more effective assistance and protection for civilians when crises do emerge. Coordination can and should be promoted when it is essential to civilian protection but the distinctions and independence between the military and humanitarian missions must be sustained.

Once the bombing war began, NATO was better prepared to deal with the emerging refugee crisis. UNHCR and private humanitarian groups quite properly put saving lives first and cooperated with NATO to provide aid to the refugees. Three specific difficulties emerged:

First, the early and commanding involvement of NATO allowed the military to skew decisions about what kinds of relief efforts would occur and to whom they would be assigned. This displaced the expertise and experience of UNHCR. One UNHCR official said, off-the-record, "NATO not only builds the refugee camps and ensures their security, it sets the humanitarian agenda."[24] NATO's role as both donor and warring party put humanitarian groups in an acutely difficult position. International guidelines seek to ensure that NGOs maintain a distance from any warring party in order to avoid any chance of prolonging the conflict or becoming tools of the disputing parties. The impartiality of humanitarian efforts involving NATO was in fact compromised. The distinction between military and humanitarian tasks could not be maintained as security efforts surrounding refugee camps also served the fight against Serbia.

Second, and perhaps even more troubling, civilians on the Serbian side faced both real and perceived risks of not getting the humanitarian aid they deserved. While refugees in Albania and Macedonia had video rooms and even better access to health care than Albanians and Macedonians themselves, the international community was unable to provide sufficient humanitarian assistance to Serbian Kosovars. Partiality was both the symbolic message and the fact.

Third, bilateral agreements between the Albanian government and national military contingents from NATO countries determined operations, leaving the UNHCR without adequate information and communication. This interfered with NGO efforts to work with civilians affected by the bombing and minority populations within Kosovo after the armed conflict subsided. National military contingents sought to involve their own national humanitarian organizations rather than treating UNHCR as the lead agency.

Military forces will increasingly be involved in humanitarian missions, peacekeeping operations, and even delivery of humanitarian aid. These problematic relationships between humanitarian organizations and military actors must therefore be reconciled. NATO's own planning process calls for civilian organizations to lead all humanitarian operations.[25] Yet military funding and planning capacities may replicate situations like Kosovo where

UNHCR and private humanitarian groups are less prepared than the military to deal with a humanitarian crisis. The risk that the military will be perceived as partisan by local warring parties jeopardizes humanitarian aid partners even when the military is not itself a party to armed conflict. The problem is exacerbated where the international military effort lacks UN Security Council authorization, as happened in Kosovo.[26]

Humanitarian organizations thus face new challenges in defining their own roles and relationships with military forces and governments. Institutionalized mechanisms for cooperation must be developed to avoid repeating the Kosovo experience where "the bride met the groom at the church."[27] Improved role definition and collaboration will require building basic trust to enhance communication, developing protocols for kinds of information that can be shared without jeopardizing each entity's distinctive mission, and enhancing respect for the experience of humanitarian organizations in activities that military actors are beginning to undertake.[28] This calls for joint training, joint planning, and support at the highest political levels for cooperation between military and civilian humanitarian aid. The humanitarian groups are understandably cautious about the inherent power imbalance in a cooperative relationship with an institution like NATO. This caution is further encouraged by the unwillingness of military institutions to engage in real negotiation and compromise with civilian counterparts. But this cautiousness cannot be resolved by seeking to remain "pure" and out of the loop, and consequently, as in Kosovo, too late to play a pivotal role in relief. Mutual education and training sessions in peacetime are vital to develop more effective coordination in times of crisis.

## IMPROVING RESPONSES AFTER A CRISIS

After the war, a void in civil governance including the absence of ordinary policing, judicial systems, and administrative management jeopardized safety and the transition to peace. Humanitarian and human rights organizations in the future are likely to encounter similar circumstances of resettlement prior to the establishment of indigenous governance and adequate security. Besides helping peacekeeping forces and working to fill in the gaps in basic infrastructure, NGOs may have important roles to play in informing the international community of difficult circumstances and helping to muster sufficient political will and resources to promote the development of civil society and civil administration.

International agencies need better and earlier planning for post-conflict management. This requires communication among agencies, participation by refugees, and cooperation with local actors to implement resettlement and reconstruction projects. Before refugees return home, a lead agency to coordinate assistance and protection should be identified.

A valuable focus for international support would be higher education in Kosovo and for Kosovars. Cooperative efforts between universities in other nations and those rebuilding in Kosovo and scholarship opportunities for Kosovars to study elsewhere in the region and internationally would strengthen potential leadership and civil society in the future. Similarly, programs for youth — especially ones that offer experiences with coexistence across ethnic lines — deserve international support.

When there are large numbers of internally displaced people, humanitarian groups should anticipate and prepare for the risks of a large outflow of refugees.

The heightened international attention to Kosovo yielded an extraordinary level of humanitarian response even as worldwide aid budgets dwindled. The result, while admirable in many respects, jeopardized the appearance and reality of commitments to impartial, universal humanitarian assistance.

UNHCR was unable to adequately screen aid organizations, to coordinate the humanitarian response, and to ensure impartiality in the distribution of aid in part because it was caught unprepared for the crisis, and in part because the military took over and many governments made bilateral agreements with NGOs.

To ensure more even-handed impartial response to humanitarian crises, to promote preparedness and coordination, and to assist in reducing waste, international donor states should provide more funds for UNHCR and assist its coordinating and planning capacities.

Protection of internally displaced peoples deserves high priority alongside assistance work. Humanitarian organizations should work with donor nations to assist asylum seekers in the context of massive human rights violations.

UN and human rights groups must address the release of Kosovar Albanians in Serb prisons and the identifying of remaining missing persons.

A lead agency needs to be identified and empowered to coordinate aid and protection before refugees return home. UNHCR and private humanitarian organizations need to follow-through after resettlement of refugees to promote coexistence and to assist the reconstruction of civil society.

UNSC should call for the release of Kosovar Albanian prisoners in accordance with international law.

International organizations need to undertake better and earlier planning for post-conflict management. This requires communication across agencies, refugee participation, and collaboration with local actors to implement resettlement and reconstructive projects.

Priority in social reconstruction efforts should be placed on higher education and programs for youth.

Humanitarian organizations and military organizations need to develop more precise definitions of their roles and tasks in responding to humanitarian crises and should also work during peacetime to develop basic trust that can enhance appropriate communication, information sharing, and mutual respect.

Human rights organizations should, where possible, collaborate in data collection to assist the investigatory activities of the International Criminal Tribunal for the Former Yugoslavia (ICTY) and other tribunals to protect evidence and witnesses and to permit reliable aggregation of data. Human rights organizations, humanitarian organizations, and the ICTY should collaborate to find ways to use transparent methodologies and where possible, coordinate data collection

UN and humanitarian groups need to make arrangements to protect local staff in case of expulsions from places of conflict.

\*\*\*

## THE ROLE OF THE MEDIA

Before the conflict erupted into large-scale violence, international media attention was lacking. Simmering conflicts are less "newsworthy" than boiling ones, and all eyes were focused on Bosnia-Herzegovina. Major media outlets tended to have only a few correspondents in the former Yugoslavia, and could not pull someone away from Bosnia and Croatia to visit Kosovo. Not until early 1999 did the Western media increase its reporting of abuses against individuals in Kosovo. Even the Recak/Racak massacre received only limited review with little historical context.

### NATO AND THE MEDIA

An issue of critical importance is the degree to which Western media became a weapon of war during the NATO bombing campaign. Maintaining public support for the NATO campaign was vital. NATO leaders realized that their media and public relations campaign was inadequate for the task. The press spokesman's operation was too small; the lag between some "collateral damage incident" in the theater of operations and a public information response from the Brussels headquarters was too long. Most of all, the Serbian regime was having a measure of success with its information campaign, especially after downing an American plane in the first week of the war. The Serbian regime's attempt to portray itself as the innocent victim of unprovoked aggression, and as a David confronting Goliath was beginning to pay dividends, especially in NATO countries like Greece and Turkey where the war never enjoyed firm support. Aware that public opinion polls might begin to shift against the air operation, NATO leaders decided after the first week of the campaign, to vastly increase the resources and staff available to the NATO and SHAPE press operations, and to mount a full-time information counter-offensive against what was termed Serbian "propaganda." The enormous attention devoted to the information war has led some commentators to conclude, in the words of a BBC Television documentary on the subject, that "the war was won by being spun." The key question is whether a supposedly independent and impartial Western media allowed itself to become a willing party to this NATO information battle; whether it devoted sufficient resources to independent verification of NATO assertions; whether it allowed moral sympathy, for example, for the plight of the refugees, as they streamed across the border from Kosovo into Macedonia and Albania, to make them less critical than they should have been of NATO military tactics and operations.

There is the related issue of whether NATO spokesmen, either intentionally or unintentionally, misled the press and the NATO electorate about the air campaign. It does seem that exaggerated claims were made about the accuracy of the bombing campaign.[29] Subsequent military accounting of the accuracy rates of the bombing campaign indicate that the Western press and public were led to believe that the bombing was more "surgical" and accurate than it actually was. In addition, claims about its impact on Yugoslav field forces have been shown to be inaccurate by NATO's own bomb damage studies conducted once hostilities ceased. Far fewer tanks, artillery pieces and other offensive and defensive weapon systems were destroyed from the air than NATO initially claimed.[30]

The Commission is not in a position to know whether these distortions were deliberate or not, i.e. whether NATO spokesmen exaggerated claims in respect of accuracy and impact, knowing that they were untrue. War is conducted in a fog, and at the time, it is consistent with what we know about their mode of operation that NATO spokesmen engaged in good faith attempts to establish the accuracy of their public claims. Certainly, NATO spokesmen insisted throughout the campaign that they were not knowingly engaged in propaganda and that they attempted to disclose the full truth in a timely fashion. This was both a moral and a prudential commitment, i.e. they believed they ought to tell the truth, and they believed that if they didn't they would eventually be found out anyway, chiefly because Western media had access to competing sources of information, mostly in Belgrade. Still, the aftermath of the war has made it clear that even if the distortions of truth were not intentional, they have left a bad aftertaste, raising doubts, ex post facto, about the legitimacy of NATO's media operation.

The Commission concludes that in any public information campaign related to a self-described humanitarian intervention, military forces and their spokesmen are under an even stricter obligation than in normal military operations to disclose all facts relevant to the public's right to know, and that only strict military necessity can ever justify withholding or distortion of publicly released information on the conduct of operations. Just as the Commission has concluded that the conduct of military operations in humanitarian interventions should obey stricter rules of engagement than those followed in normal military operations, so it concludes that media operations must be conducted under especially stringent rules of full disclosure. The reasons for this are evident: humanitarian interventions depend for their legitimacy on the continuing democratic consent of the electorates whose elected leaders authorize them. In the nature of things, humanitarian interventions are controversial since they are unconnected to national survival. Hence they are likely to be debated keenly in the societies which have authorized them. If the public and the media feel they are being manipulated, and even lied to, consent and support for these operations will quickly dissipate.

The Commission commends the NATO press operation for being aware of these distinctive conditions of public consent, but urges them to review their operations to ensure that claims in respect of accuracy and impact can always be justified, at the time, with the best available information. Warfare has always strained the objectivity and impartiality of journalism. Journalists are dependent on combatants for access to the sites of conflict, and this dependency can breed credulity and weaken journalistic impartiality. Moreover, wars mobilize emotions, and journalists end up taking sides, losing their ability to ask critical questions on behalf of the public. None of these features are new. The Kosovo air campaign was extremely hard to cover objectively: the vast majority of Western journalists covering the war were captives of the daily briefings at NATO headquarters and were almost entirely dependent on NATO information. Few journalists had access to the pilots and those that did fly on missions found it difficult to do anything more than admire the skill and dedication of the flyers. Almost no Western journalists had access to Kosovo, and those that did were escorted in and out of the province on tours organized by the Serbian government. This did not prevent a small number of journalists, from the Los Angeles Times, the New York Times as well as some Yugoslav stringers for foreign agencies, from presenting on the spot reports from Prishtina/Pristina during and after NATO attacks and during and after the mass expulsions of Kosovars.

Yet the basic charge — that journalists allowed themselves and consequently the public at large to be "spun" by NATO media manipulation — seems unfounded. The reality was that there was vigorous public debate about the conduct of the war throughout the NATO countries, and NATO never enjoyed the kind of easy ride with public opinion that is assumed in the argument that the war was won by being spun. Indeed, as "collateral damage incidents" multiplied, as the promised short, sharp campaign turned into a gruelling 68 day battle of wills, Western public opinion became, if anything, more critical of the conduct of the war.

NATO never dominated the propaganda war, and this enabled Western journalists and public opinion in general to form an independent view of its conduct. The basic reason for this was that Western journalists continued to operate in Belgrade throughout the conflict, and while their reports were censored and their access to damage sites was heavily controlled, they were able to convey critical reports to the Western public of what the bombing of a European city had accomplished. This access to the "enemy side" is a crucial precondition for the ability of the media to subject military operations to scrutiny. Indeed, without such access, "humanitarian intervention" would all but escape public scrutiny and accountability. The Commission strongly believes that open access to both sides of any humanitarian intervention is critical if military operations, on both sides, are to be kept under effective public scrutiny.

## THE FRY AND THE MEDIA

Belgrade interfered constantly with free press rights. International support for independent media, notably radio stations, was essential before, during, and after the conflict. Substantial levels of suppression in Belgrade intensified even further when the bombing began.[31] In March 1999, the Yugoslav government shut down *Koha Ditore*, the largest and most influential Albanian-language newspaper (and web-site) in Kosovo, although it was able to resume publishing from Macedonia in April. Alternative media within Serbia largely shared the view that Kosovo was "ours" or else did not focus on Kosovo.

Nonetheless, in the context of Serbian repression, journalists performed remarkably. The Serbian government directly aimed its repression against independent Serbian journalists, activists, and politicians in the summer of 1999, and yet individual journalists continued to speak out even when imprisoned. Serbia also expelled all NATO-country journalists on March 25, the day after the first NATO bombs, then rescinded the expulsion but arrested or expelled specific journalists. Many reporters moved to refugee camps and reported from there. Some, such as John Kifner of the New York Times, ably reconstructed the massacres from refugee accounts.[32] Sam Kiley reported effectively from Kukes for the [London] Times. Paul Watson of the Los Angeles Times became the last North American still reporting on the bombing directly from Kosovo and continued to report there despite frustration that the military on all sides were not giving trustworthy information.[33]

The Commission believes there is no case for restricting the ability of journalists to operate in theatres of conflict where humanitarian interventions are taking place. The Commission strongly condemns the attempts by the Serbian government to place restrictions on their own media's coverage of the war and its aftermath, especially the detention of Miroslav Filipovic for his interviews with FRY soldiers who took part in operations in Kosovo and for his publication of their admission of atrocities and war crimes. The Commission believes that this detention violates universal norms of press freedom and cannot be justified for reasons of military necessity or security, especially since the reports were conducted after the conclusion of military operations. The Commission calls for Mr. Filipovic's immediate and unconditional release.

## ATTACKS ON THE MEDIA

An additional and vital issue about press freedom in the Kosovo operation concerns the question of whether attacks on media installations can be justified under the Geneva Conventions. Serbian television was attacked in the early hours of April 16. A studio and office block were destroyed and fifteen journalists and media workers were killed. None of the victims appeared to have been in uniform or to have been directly under military command or in any direct way related to the conduct of military operations. While Serbian nationals were targeted by the attack, foreign nationals who were using the facilities to transmit international news reports were given advance warning to clear the building.

The arguments advanced by NATO for the attack were that the facility was re-broadcasting military signals, and that it was broadcasting war propaganda to the Serbian civilian population. The Commission is unable to assess the truth of the first claim. As to the second, it makes the controversial claim that nations whose constitutions contain formal commitments to press freedom are entitled to strike the press facilities of nations at war when they believe that the content of these broadcasts amount to propaganda. This justifies military operations on the basis of an inherently subjective assessment of the propaganda content of a broadcast. The Commission concludes that strikes on media targets, within the context of a humanitarian intervention are both politically unwise and legally dubious. They are politically unwise because they are controversial and jeopardize the perceived legitimacy of military operations. They are legally dubious because they are not strictly military targets and the attempt to construe them as being of military significance on the basis of their broadcast content is tendentious. The Commission recommends that in any future military operations under a mandate of humanitarian intervention, such attacks on media installations be avoided.

## THE MEDIA AND THE NGOS

Western media coverage neglected practical matters like lack of shelter in order to focus exclusively on the details of violence. This raises questions about how the press read or used information from NGOs and humanitarian organizations, whether the information was shared, and whether it had any impact. Humanitarian and human rights groups were able to obtain and disseminate on-the-ground information because of direct phone contact and Internet access.[34] E-mail from contacts assisted NGOs in detecting errors in wire service reports.[35] This resource had limited impact, however, on broader media coverage of events and perspectives on the conflict.

During the armed conflict, media and NGO cooperation produced detailed reports of violence in Gjakove/Djakovica, Drenice/Drenica, and elsewhere. In April, 1999, R. Jeffrey Smith, William Drozdiak, and others began reporting evidence of Serbian groundwork behind the mass expulsion of Kosovar Albanians.[36] Then, when NATO bombs struck refugees in a convoy on the Gjakove/Djakovica road, considerable international attention emerged. The military did not produce accurate information for five days, but then at a press conference a NATO spokesman expressed deep regret and admitted responsibility for mistakenly shelling the convoy.[37]

Subsequently, the media offered insufficient analysis of the political and security aspects of the attacks on Kosovar Serbs by returning refugees. To this day, almost entirely missing from media coverage are the issues of missing persons and war prisoners. The media coverage of the ICTY unfortunately contributed to politicizing its activities. The Tribunal itself missed the opportunity presented by media interest occasioned by the Kosovo conflict. This was an opportunity to use the media to educate the public about the Tribunal's work, but more aggressive efforts by the Tribunal would have been necessary to encourage the coverage to focus on the place of international human rights norms and institutions in responding to the conflict and to the processes guiding the Tribunal's work.

## MEDIA ISSUES AFTER THE WAR

After June 10, 1999, when the UN Security Council established the International Mission, there was a widely shared understanding that media behavior could impact the prospects for democratic development. A free press may be one of the pillars of democratic civil society, but media control in the hands of chauvinistic forces could quickly undermine the fragile stability of the transition. UNMIK was thus clearly mandated to exercise media control. At a very early stage, however, bureaucratic misunderstandings and infighting characterized management of emerging media by the International Mission. A particularly messy debate developed over how much temporary international control and content regulation would be necessary to ensure fair access and standards of fair reporting, and whether any content regulation or development of standards amount to censorship. The UN's chief administrator (SRSG), Dr. Bernard Kouchner, sought to restrain the ethnic Albanian media in order to restrict violence, and temporarily closed a daily newspaper for inciting vigilantism.[38] The OSCE plan to tutor local Kosovar media in responsible standards received sharp criticism from media watchdog groups.[39] The SRSG issued a regulation in February 2000 against hate speech with a sanction of up to 10 years' imprisonment. This controversial measure runs the risk of inviting political manipulation, but it has essentially not been enforced. Efforts to promote self-regulation among journalists have been inhibited by conflicts between the SRSG and the OSCE, and by the unwillingness of Serb journalists to participate. The perception of censorship was especially charged in light of continuing Serbian repression of independent media and governmental media propaganda after the war.

The international mission developed its own mission broadcasting through UNMIK's Blue Sky and KFOR's Radio Galaxy. Critics say they diverted resources, including local journalists, generating resentment (chiefly concerning Blue Sky). But these efforts remain vital to the extent that they created quality programming and perhaps the sole setting for interethnic conversation/listening (through KFOR Radio Galaxy).

Satellite provision was proposed and subcontracted by European Broadcast Union; and the Japanese government offered to restore the land network by 2001. Reconstructing media after mass violence should be given great priority by international governments and NGOs. The role of international donors has been crucial to support the return of independent media, but there have been serious coordination problems, with many funders directing aid to the same outlet while other outlets struggle to get underway. A joint effort by the Open Society Institute and OSCE has improved matters, but there are still difficulties getting reliable information about recipients to donors.

The long-term quality and sustainability of a free press and mass media in Kosovo is important. This has special immediacy in relation to forthcoming elections. A new Media Resource Center in central Prishtina/Pristina gives domestic journalists access to the Internet and information. Sponsored by the Institute for War and Peace Reporting and the Internet provider IPKO, with support from the Ford Foundation, the project is open to both Kosovar Albanian and Serb journalists. Kosovo journalists also contribute to the web-based Balkan Crisis Report produced by the Institute for War and Peace reporting.[40]

Map of the region.
© 1999maps.com

# 8

# KOSOVO:

# THE REGIONAL DIMENSION

A decade of war has just come to an end in the Balkans with a quarter million dead and millions of refugees. Among the main casualties, however, were ideas of a multi-ethnic society and of regional cooperation. Indeed this might be the appropriate moment to examine past obstacles and to present opportunities for the development of regional cooperation, which, in the long run, remains a necessary precondition for peace and stability in southeastern Europe. As this chapter will show, the European Union (EU) has a major role to play in the transition from intervention to integration.

The Yugoslav wars affected the entire Balkan region.[1] Just as the war in Kosovo cannot be understood in isolation from its broader regional context, so will the success or failure of postwar recovery and reconstruction also depend on the capacity of local actors and the international community to develop a coherent regional approach. The landscape after the battle is increasingly diversified. There are encouraging developments in the northern tier — in Croatia after Tudjman, and in Bosnia after the municipal elections of April 2000. But there has been a steady deterioration in the remnants of Yugoslavia (Serbia and Montenegro) and a mixed picture concerning Kosovo's neighbors (Albania, Macedonia).

A year after the NATO intervention, the Balkan region is at a crossroads. There is still potential for conflict, albeit on a more limited scale. But there is also an opportunity to create, in post-conflict southeastern Europe, a zone of stability and regional co-operation. Both options will require considerable international involvement to ensure security and help provide incentives and a framework for economic recovery and democratic change. The degree of international involvement in 1999, as well as the coop-eration of the governments of the region during the intervention, generated high expectations in southeastern Europe *vis à vis* the West. So far, such expectations have not been met.

When considering two of the main common features of poli-tics in the Balkans—the vigor of nationalism and the weakness of democracy and civil society—one must consider the dual lega-cies of the Ottoman and Habsburg Empires on one hand and the communist system on the other. Both represent past failures of imposed supranational integration. The post-imperial legacy is still with us, to the extent that the process of nation-state build-ing and of redrawing state boundaries is by no means completed. The post-communist legacy remains present in the weakness of democratic alternatives to nationalism. Both account, at least in part, for the derailment of democratic transitions by nationalist agendas and authoritarian regimes.

The wars of the former Yugoslavia exemplified both the un-finished business of post-1918 nation-state building and the role of post-communist political elite using nationalist tensions to perpetuate their hold on power. During the Kosovo intervention the international community and the states of the region wanted to deal with the latter—i.e. with Milosevic—while the Kosovar Albanians were interested in the former—i.e. correcting the boundaries of the 1912 London conference. Milosevic wanted to deal with neither.

# THE REGIONAL DIMENSIONS
# OF THE KOSOVO CONFLICT

Concerns for the stability of the Balkans were an important motive for the NATO intervention. Like the intervention in Bosnia in 1995, the Kosovo intervention itself avoided a spillover to neighboring countries. Nevertheless, the immediate effects proved to be highly destabilizing for some of them. This destabilization, apparently part of Milosevic's strategy, can be assessed in three concentric circles:

1   the fragmentation of the residual part of Yugoslavia (Serbia, Montenegro, Vojvodina);
2   the direct destabilization of Kosovo's immediate neighbors (Macedonia, Albania);
3   the negative impact on other regional actors concerned (Bulgaria, Romania, Greece etc).

The Yugoslav wars of the last decade focused on two major epicenters of conflict in the Balkans: the "northern tier" conflict, surrounding Bosnia and involving Serbia and Croatia; and the "southern tier" conflict in Kosovo, involving Serbia, Macedonia, and Albania, but also, indirectly, Bulgaria and Greece. Although there was little direct interaction between the two spheres of conflict, Milosevic's Serbia provided a common denominator. Solutions proposed or imposed in one case had an impact on expected solutions in the other. The stabilizing impact of Dayton for Bosnia and the Serbo-Croatian relationship produced destabilizing effects in Kosovo because it was immediately seen as a precedent. Why should the Kosovar Albanians settle for less than was granted to the defeated Bosnian Serbs? If Dayton could establish a would-be state composed of two entities with separate institutions and having the right to a "special relationship" with a neighboring state, one could not expect the Kosovars to accept the de facto apartheid imposed on them by Milosevic after abolishing their autonomy in 1989.

The debates and future answers concerning the final status of Kosovo will have important implications for its neighbors (particularly Macedonia and Albania) and could also be seen as precedents for Bosnia. The influential "regional contagion" argument essentially applies a "domino theory" to the Balkans: If Kosovo goes independent Macedonia might implode. Ethnic Albanians there might want either to join the new Kosovo state or demand nothing less than a "federalization" of Macedonia — a move strongly opposed by the majority Macedonian Slavs). If Macedonia implodes, Serbia, Bulgaria and perhaps even Greece are unlikely to remain passive. The second dimension of the "domino theory" is that an independent Kosovo would be seen as a legal precedent: if Kosovo can separate from Yugoslavia, why should not Republika Srpska separate from Bosnia-Herzegovina? The "domino effect" thus reinforces the process of "Balkanization," i.e. fragmentation, which affects the region. While the "regional contagion" argument had been abundantly used to justify paralysis on the Kosovo status issue through most of the 1990's, regional stability considerations were also put forward to support the decision to intervene in the Spring of 1999. A year later, it is time to assess the differentiated impact of the NATO intervention.

## THE "FINAL STAGE" OF THE DISINTEGRATION OF YUGOSLAVIA

SERBIA * The future of Serbia remains important to the whole of the Balkan region, both as a source of tension and conflict as demonstrated by the Milosevic regime during the past decade, and as a precondition for lasting peace and regional cooperation. The outcome of the NATO intervention has been ambiguous: the Serbian regime was defeated and had to retreat from Kosovo, but it remains in power in Belgrade. To make a historical parallel with all its limitations: this is not like Germany after World War II when, after a complete defeat, democracy was imposed from outside, but more like Germany after World War I: an ambiguous defeat left to fester internally and sowing potential seeds of another conflict. Related to that outcome is the ambivalence of the Serbian opposition: it still is not clear whether it criticizes Milosevic for embarking on a war, or merely for having lost it.

Perhaps the most striking feature of the Milosevic regime, confirmed since the Kosovo war, is its knack of making alternatives to its rule either unavailable or ineffective. With selective repression against opposition groupings and a clampdown on the media, Milosevic has preserved power through fear on the one hand and through a mixture of apathy and exhaustion on the other. These repressive policies certainly did not start with the intervention in Kosovo. For example, in 1998 a new university law marked a crackdown on what the regime considered to be one of the intellectual centers of the opposition. The war merely accelerated the trend, and in particular the repression, against the remaining independent media. The crackdown on the independent media escalated on May 17, 2000, when the police stormed the offices of Studio B Television, Radio B2-B92, and the newspaper Blic. The escalation of violence in Serbia, with a series of killings that now reaches the ruling elite, is also a means of spreading a climate of fear among the real or potential opposition forces. The regime is deliberately stoking an atmosphere of arbitrary terror to justify the passing in June of an "anti-terrorist act." All of this could certainly herald a move from authoritarianism to outright dictatorship.

The escalation of internal violence since the spring of 1999 also points to the criminalization of a regime and of some sections of society. For a decade the Milosevic war machine has relied on the "mafiazation" of the economy to get around the sanctions. Likewise, the division of labor between the Army as an institution and the paramilitary forces has facilitated both ethnic cleansing and organized crime. There have been over 500 "non-elucidated" assassinations in Serbia since the beginning of the

Yugoslav wars, including businessmen, paramilitaries, media leaders, and opposition figures. Some of these assassinations seem related to settling of accounts in the lucrative oil smuggling business.[2] The parallel rise of criminal violence and institutionalized violence against the independent media, the academic community, and opposition forces point to the possibility of a dangerous scenario for Serbia: the transition from external war to internal civil war—or a combination of the two, given the possibility that Milosevic could use the brewing crisis in Montenegro as a means to save his regime through an external/internal "state of war." This pessimistic scenario is reinforced by three factors.

1  First, there is the weakness and fragmentation of the opposition. The credibility of opposition leadership has been shattered since the winter of 1997 when it led the most powerful opposition movement to Milosevic into a dead-end through a combination of rivalry, corruption, and, in the end, cooptation. Vuk Drazkovic, the most prominent of opposition leaders, subsequently joined Milosevic's government. To be sure, there are also encouraging developments in the civil society. Some provincial towns are now administered by the opposition parties. The powerful movement Otpor (Resistance), which started at the end of 1998 as a student movement, is fast becoming the primary rallying point for those opposed to Milosevic but distrustful of the leadership of the major opposition parties.[3]

   These positive developments should be encouraged by external support. They exemplify the possibility of political renewal from the periphery to the center, and from the civil society to the political society. These developments, assuming they will be successful among the Serbian population, will need time. The young student leaders in Otpor, for instance, are reluctant, and are not really in a position to replace the discredited leadership of the opposition; but new leadership is precisely what today's Serbian politics is desperately lacking.

2   The more credible option of a change from within the ruling establishment also seems to have faded away. At the end of 1998, Milosevic purged the head of the secret services, Stanisic, and the former army chief of staff, General Peresic, both of whom apparently advocated more flexible conflict management in Kosovo. Milosevic's praetorian guard now seems to be made up only of generals completely loyal to him, such as Pavkovic and Ognanovic.

3   With his indictment as a war criminal by the International Criminal Tribunal in the Hague, Milosevic has no "exit strategy." Those closest to power have everything to lose and nowhere to go. The bunker mentality of the regime could last for some time with the help of Chinese and Russian subsidies. There are also parallels with the *fin de règne* of the Ceausescu regime. Therefore, although the Milosevic regime is crumbling, its disintegration could take a long time and could lead to renewed violence in the most important piece of the Balkan puzzle.

The implications of this scenario for the stability of the region are worrying indeed. Since the West has no leverage left on Milosevic, he is not only likely to continue his policies of internal violence and repression, but might well attempt to exploit tension points with Montenegro or in the Presevo region in southern Serbia bordering with Kosovo, where KLA-backed rebels are advocating the attachment of several Albanian villages to Kosovo.

The NATO intervention was conducted under the implicit assumption that the Milosevic regime could not survive military defeat. A year later the positions, and the implicit divide between the Europeans and the USA, oscillate between two lines of argument.

The first claims that Western policy has been too mesmerized by Milosevic's Serbia and thus is essentially a short-term policy: to prevent Serbia from doing much damage to its the neighbors and hopes that, through international isolation of the country and tacit support for the would-be democratic opposition, Milo-sevic will have to go. (Thus, for instance, Madeleine Albright stated that she could not imagine Milosevic surviving another election.) Such statements, though, suggest a lack of imagination or information about the previous elections won by Milosevic associated with the ultra-nationalist Radical Party of Vojislav Seselj. And if this next election-focused policy is not successful, then what? A long-term approach would take into account that the opposition is not fundamentally different from Milosevic as far as the national question is concerned. This approach, then, says: (1) Stop worrying about Serbia so long as it is unable to stir trouble in the region; (2) Stay out of the Serbian political equation; (3) Don't bet on an illusory success of a weak, divided, and basically untrustworthy opposition; and (4) Disengage complete-ly from Vuk Drazkovic, who is more a part of the problem than part of the solution. Serbia's nationalist delusions require a long *"cure de désintoxication."* We should not wait but should move on now to deal with the final status of Kosovo, while simultaneously promoting all available forms of assistance to civil society in Serbia and to the reconstruction and development of regional co-operation.

The opposite line of argument, prevailing among European political elites, tends to argue that Serbia remains pivotal to Balkan stability. You might want to forget about Milosevic, but you do so at your own peril. You cannot ignore Serbia if you are serious about a regional approach to conflict prevention. The great problem is that isolating a criminal regime necessarily re-sults in isolating the entire society. Sanctions, the argument goes, are not working: they are reinforcing Milosevic's sources of power, strengthening the mafias on the one hand, while humili-ating a whole society through poverty and the exile of youth and educated elite (a quarter of a million since 1991). As a result, Serb society has turned older, more rural, and less educated over the last decade. The sanctions do not help to reverse this trend, and thus they weaken one of the sociological conditions for a democratic alternative. The answer thus should be "lift and engage": help Serbia's coalition of discontent find a focus by involving it in regional cooperation. Only then will a "Croatian scenario" of a democratic transition stand a chance in Serbia.

A change of regime in Serbia will ultimately depend on the capacity of Serbian society to recover and bring about democratic change. Hence, independent of the successes and failures of the opposition parties, the priority of external assistance should be to support the long-term project associated with the promotion of Serbian civil society, including NGOs, alternative or independent media, and the universities. This will also be the best basis for transnational contacts in the region. Postwar reconciliation does not have to wait for the green light from the government.

Flooding Serbian society with international contacts should go hand in hand with a sanctions program maintained and targeted to hurt the Milosevic regime and particularly its inner core. The sanctions program has already been scaled down to block only oil, weapons and money. Given that even the oil embargo has been lifted for the opposition cities, the sanctions have become essentially a political symbol. To lift them without conditions is to give a boost to Milosevic. The aim should thus be to keep them scaled down but more effectively targeted on the ruling elite, preventing their foreign travel and their access to bank accounts in Cyprus.

MONTENEGRO * With Kosovo detached, for all practical purposes, from the control of Belgrade, Montenegro was left as Serbia's last "partner" in the remnant of the Yugoslav federation after a decade of dissolution. "Partner," though, doesn't really describe the relationship that has existed since the 1997 presidential election, when Milo Djukanovic defeated Milosevic's protégé, Momir Bulatovic, and promptly embarked on a course of democratic reform and growing independence from Belgrade. The war, if anything, has accelerated both trends: it has turned Montenegro towards a bastion of opposition to the Milosevic regime and enhanced the momentum towards independence. Montenegro is strategically important for Serbia as its only access to the sea. Montenegro's neutral stance during the NATO intervention thus posed a major problem for Serbia. This stance did not spare the province from NATO bombing of some of the Yugoslav Army facilities in Montenegro, but neither did Belgrade use the war as an opportunity to recapture power in Podgorica, possibly because its army was divided on this issue and was otherwise engaged in Kosovo.

Since the end of the war, a double process has been underway: a "rampant independence" process in Montenegro, and a "rampant military coup" by Belgrade. The steps towards independence focused on currency separation—Montenegro adopted the Deutschmark—and on the prospect of a referendum on "sovereignty." The referendum question to be asked—*"Do you support a sovereign Montenegro associated with the sovereign state of Serbia?"* —suggests a confederation rather than outright independence. The method is prudent, but the pattern is familiar enough from Slovenia or Croatia: independence as a way to overcome an institutional deadlock.

Meanwhile Milosevic has stepped up the pressure, relying on the Yugoslav army stationed in Montenegro and the Seventh Police Battalion, which the Montenegrin Prime Minister calls a "para-army" loyal to Belgrade. By controlling the border with Croatia, Albania, and Republika Srpska, the Belgrade authorities are imposing a quasi-blockade aimed at economically isolating Montenegro. Djukanovic has openly warned that the II Yugoslav army is preparing an overthrow of the Montenegro government that could lead to the "fifth Balkan war."[4] Djukanovic has every reason to avoid such a scenario, knowing (as the recent municipal elections have shown[5]) that, although opposed to the Milosevic regime, the majority of the population in Montenegro is deeply divided on a possible break with Serbia. On July 6, 2000, Milosevic took a further step in the direction of confrontation with Montenegro by pushing through the Yugoslav Parliament amendments to the federal constitution which would allow him to run for the presidency again (in a direct election) and to downgrade the status of Montenegro in the federation. According to the Montenegrin Prime Minister, Filip Vujanovic, the changes amount to an attempt to "transform Yugoslavia in a Greater Serbia."[6] These developments make very unlikely the participation of the authorities in Montenegro in the federal Yugoslav elections in the fall of 2000[7]. All this provides Milosevic with a certain leverage and a conflict "opportunity" that, given the overwhelming imbalance between the two republics, he could "win."[8] In other words, over the last decade he has conducted wars against all the ex-Yugoslav neighbors of Serbia and lost them all. In Montenegro, Milosevic has a chance to defeat a much weaker, smaller adversary

In addition to military pressure, Milosevic has also escalated tension by calling for a federal election under a new set of electoral rules that essentially downgrade the status of Montenegro in the federation. Under the new electoral laws, Montenegro is no longer considered as the "partner" of Serbia in the federation but merely as part of the Yugoslav population at large, and thus only represented according to its demographic strength, which is no match for Serbia's.

Neither the USA nor the EU actually support Montenegro's independence because they fear it is likely to lead to a major outbreak of violence for which there are limited means or readiness to intervene. Montenegro independence also has implications for the status of Kosovo: if Montenegro declares independence, the legal entity called Yugoslavia would cease to exist.

Why does Montenegro, a province of less than 700,000 inhabitants, matter? First, it represents (as does Macedonia) an alternative to Milosevic's confrontational policies: a peaceful coexistence between the ethnic groupings of Montenegrins and Serbs (three-quarters of the population) and the Albanians (7% before the arrival of refugees, which doubled the figure) and Muslims/Bosniaks (14%). Second, it represents a democratic or democratizing alternative to the Milosevic regime. Given the state of the democratic opposition in Serbia, its democratic future may depend more on the resilience of small and more "backward" Montenegro, whose democratic hopes are lead by the former chief of the police Finally, if Montenegro goes, there will be no Yugoslavia left and therefore little point in telling the Kosovar Albanians that their future lies, according to the UN resolution, in Yugoslavia.

Although Montenegro, as part of FRY, is subject to sanctions and not eligible for financial assistance, it has received €20 million from the EU, resulting from a decision adopted by EU finance ministers on May 8, 2000. No less importantly, Montenegro should be an integral part of the European Stability Pact as a means to strengthen its democratic process and its capacity to resist economic, military, and political pressure from Milosevic's Serbia.

Unless immediate and concrete steps are taken by the international community offering political as well as economic support for Montenegro's institutions and security, the Republic may be slipping towards a violent conflict with Serbia—a major setback for the stabilization efforts in the region undertaken a year ago.

## KOSOVO–ALBANIA–MACEDONIA

Kosovo's relationship with neighboring Albania and Macedonia is of major importance to regional stability. Milosevic deliberately used the NATO intervention for an attempt (which almost succeeded) to destabilize the two smallest, poorest, and most vulnerable of Kosovo's neighbors. Also, crucial debates around the final status of Kosovo focus on its relationship with Albania (as an ethnic Albanian state) and Macedonia, a state with what is perceived to be a considerable and restive ethnic Albanian minority.

**KOSOVO-ALBANIA** ⋆ Among the major contributing factors to the Kosovo conflict was the collapse of the Albanian state at the beginning of 1997, which resulted in important stocks of arms finding their way to Kosovo at the very moment when the KLA was trying to establish itself as an actor to be reckoned with. The outbreak of violence in Albania had nothing to do with ethnic conflict in Kosovo. It was triggered by the collapse of several pyramid investment schemes (with connections to organized crime but also to the ruling party of President Sali Berisha), which affected over a third of the population. The conflict was, however, related to deep divisions in Albanian society stemming from old clan and regional rivalries, post-communist political polarization, and poverty. The slide into anarchy and the disintegration of the state offered the KLA a base in northern Albania for its activities in Kosovo. This in turn contributed to the instrumentalization of the KLA in Albanian politics, in the confrontation between the ex-communists (Fato Nano) and the right (Sali Berisha). Over time (and especially during the height of the Kosovo crisis in 1999), competing factions of the KLA have established "diversified" ties to Albanian political actors. Thaci seems to have established a working relationship with the present government in Tirana. Rugova, however, returned to Kosovo from his Italian exile not through Albania (where his safety could not be guaranteed) but through Macedonia.

Since 1997, therefore, there has been a trend towards the creation of an Albanian political space, with a growing degree of interaction between its three components: Prishtina/Pristina (Kosovo), Tirana (Albania), and Tetovo (Macedonia). This has given rise to fears, both within and outside the Balkans, that there would be an attempt by ethnic Albanians to create a "Greater Albanian state." Although the KLA political platform in 1998 did advocate a Greater Albania, there is little evidence that this is still the case or that an Albanian political space should be equated with general support for such a goal. Indeed, indications are very much to the contrary — the notion of a Greater Albania seems to have been abandoned, both by Albanian politicians and by the general population.[9] Although Albania would in all likelihood support independence for Kosovo, in Tirana such a declaration would not result in a drive for a Greater Albanian state.

When analyzing the relationship between Albanians and Kosovar Albanians, one can talk of "one nation — two societies" much like the "Ossies" and the "Wessies" in Germany. If anything, the Kosovars tend think of themselves as the Wessies. They have not only a higher standard of living, but also a stronger support in the Diaspora established in Western Europe over the last thirty years. Such economic, historical, and cultural differences between Albanians and Kosovar Albanians were merely accentuated when the two groups were forced together by the refugee crisis precipitated by the Kosovo war.

A counter-argument is now developing that, should Kosovo attain independence, it will try to resume its historical role as the leader of Albanian unity.[10] In other words, in some circles the "Greater Albania" fear is now being replaced by (or confused with) a "Greater Kosovo" fear.

Whatever the hidden agendas of political actors in Albania, Kosovo, or Macedonia, at least two arguments should be considered before drawing conclusions about Kosovo's relationship with Albania. First, it is not an easy or a particularly attractive proposition to merge with a failed state. This certainly goes a long way to dampen the ambitions of the most radical of would-be nationalists in Albania and Kosovo. Second, Kosovo self-government (not to mention independence) is essentially about institution building or state-building. This process creates institutional and political vested interests eager to preserve themselves and thus less inclined to seek a merger with dubious state institutions in the "mother" country (i.e. Albania). Thus the Kosovo state-building process, if successful, might ultimately be the best argument against a Greater Albania project.

This discussion suggests a paradox in the goals of the Kosovo protectorate as currently structured. The aims of reconstruction and the development of democracy and a market economy depend on the capacity to establish the rule of law and other essentially state-building institutions. Yet the explicit goal of the Kosovo protectorate is not to build a state, but rather to prevent its formation.

**KOSOVO-MACEDONIA** ✳ Macedonian society is permeated with ethnic divisions. There were thus good reasons to fear for Macedonia's stability as the ethnic conflict in Kosovo escalated. For example, much like Serbo-Albanian relations in Kosovo, there are no mixed marriages between Slavs and Albanians in Macedonia. The former (like the Kosovo Serbs) fear that the demographic balance will be tipped and that in a couple of decades they could become a minority in Macedonia, given the higher Albanian birth rate. In Macedonia it is said that a census is more important than an election. The 1994 census indicated that the Albanians represent a quarter of the population: the real figure is likely to be higher due to the influx of (not officially registered) ethnic Albanian population from Kosovo over the last decade.

During the 1990s there was a slow but steady influx into Macedonia of Kosovar Albanians escaping the repressive policies of the Serbian regime. One result of this was the militant demands made in 1994 for the creation of an Albanian University in Tetovo, precipitated by the closure of the University of Pristina in Kosovo. More generally, the influence of Kosovars was sometimes identified by the government in Skopje and in popular perception with growing tension between Macedonian Slavs and ethnic Albanians.

It was in this context that, in the spring of 1999, 276,000 Albanians refugees from Kosovo arrived in Macedonia, a country of 2 million inhabitants that did not even exist as a state a decade ago. Although this context does not justify some of the more recalcitrant Macedonian reactions to the refugees, it does help to explain the fears that prompted them. The Macedonian Slavs dreaded the spillover effect of the war in Kosovo (the KLA using the Tetovo region in Macedonia as a base) and, perhaps even more, the partition of Kosovo. This in their eyes would have created a precedent for a similar process in Macedonia, where ethnic Albanians had boycotted the 1991 independence referendum.

Despite the tensions brought about by the massive influx of refugees into Macedonia, it can be pointed out that Macedonia avoided the worst-case scenario of complete destabilization, such as may well have been part of the intention behind the expulsions. As one prominent Macedonian MP (Professor Nano Ruzin) quipped during the conflict: "If Macedonia had not been an independent country there would have been there the same conflict as in Kosovo and the refugees would be in Greece and Bulgaria." Indeed, under former president Gligorov (who managed an exit from Yugoslavia while avoiding a war with Belgrade) and now, somewhat differently, under a VMRO-led government, Macedonia has shown that a policy of including major Albanian parties in government can work. It has shown that the alternative to ethnic cleansing is the kind of coalition of Slav Macedonian and Albanian parties which over the years has achieved both an increasingly important position in Skopje politics and growing self-government over minority affairs.

Nevertheless, there are still deep-seated political problems in Macedonia, some of which have been caused by this increasing Albanian self-government. Slav Macedonians would countenance a "cantonization" of Macedonia, while Albanians hope for federalization. The only way to give Albanians a stake in the Macedonian State seems to be to take political risks that might also jeopardize it.

The collapse of Macedonia would impact on other key regional players. Serbia has been weakened and directly constrained by
the effects of the NATO intervention, while Macedonia's ruling
VMRO has closer ties to Sofia. Bulgaria might therefore reluctantly become involved. So could Greece, which had earlier imposed
an economic blockade on the country and which claims to own
the copyright on the very name of "Macedonia."

If Kosovo is one territory for two dreams, then Macedonia is
one territory for several nationalist dreams. Its very weakness, the
awareness of its vulnerability, has perhaps been turned into a reason to search for compromise. Macedonia has avoided the worst-
case scenarios and remains firmly opposed to any suggestion of
Kosovo independence. Thus, for Macedonia the international
protectorate over Kosovo is supposed to provide what Yugoslavia
no longer could: to keep a check on a potentially destabilizing
neighbor and, more generally, on the Albanian question. Paradoxically, the price it has to pay for attempting to establish itself
as an independent state is to become a semi-protectorate itself,
dependent for its survival on international support.

## BULGARIA, ROMANIA, AND GREECE

Perhaps the most striking feature of the broader regional reaction
to the NATO intervention in Yugoslavia was the deep gulf it revealed between pro-Western political elite and the rest of the
population in Bulgaria, Romania, and Greece. While ambivalence or reluctant support for the intervention prevailed among
the ruling political elite, solidarity with Serbia was dominant in
public opinion in all three countries. It is interesting to note that
the strongest opposition came from Greece, where 95% of the
population opposed the NATO intervention (and to which the US
president had to postpone his visit, since the authorities could
not guarantee his security); however, according to polls conducted at the beginning of the intervention, 75% of the population in

Romania, 70% in Bulgaria, and 65% in Hungary were also against the intervention. This hostility grew stronger as the intervention progressed. In Central Europe also a majority of the population seem, according to surveys, to have opposed the NATO intervention. This was the case, for instance, in both the Czech Republic and Slovakia. Only in Poland, among the newcomers to NATO, was there a majority of public support for intervention in Kosovo. Although there is no love lost for Milosevic and his regime in southeastern Europe, there was a widespread perception of the intervention in Kosovo as "big powers imposing their might on a small country." In southeastern Europe the intervention also seems to have revived the divide between the Orthodox countries and the West — only Turkey fully supported the intervention.

Thus, one of the first consequences of the intervention was to weaken the reform-minded, pro-Western political elite that had come to power in Romania at the end of 1996 and Bulgaria in the Spring of 1997. The parliaments of the two countries approved the overflight of their territory by NATO planes (but not ground transit) in the hope of enhancing their chances of joining NATO. In Bulgaria, President Petar Stolyanov and Prime Minister Ivan Kostov pushed the NATO request for an air corridor through the legislature against the Socialist (ex-communist) opposition.[11] In Romania President Emil Constantinescu and the government did likewise in the face of the main opposition parties. Both countries also refused to grant overflight permission to the Russian Air Force at the very end of the NATO intervention, thus possibly thwarting a Russian military plan to establish in a preemptive move their own sector in Kosovo.

The domestic political price to be paid by these countries for their support of NATO could be high, especially if no "peace dividends" are in sight. US Secretary of State Albright's statement in Sofia in June 1999, praising Bulgaria's behavior during the conflict as having "exhibited signs of being part of the NATO family" raised expectations that are unlikely to be met soon. In the meantime it will be the ex-communist opposition parties, and in Romania also the nationalists, who are likely to benefit. The party of former president Iliescu and the ultra-nationalist Romania Mare now have a majority in the polls looking towards elections that are due at the end of the year. Attitudes toward the NATO intervention are merely one aspect of the deeper dissociation between the political elite and the population. A recent Romanian survey shows that the three main issues for the country according to the media are the EU, NATO, and the IMF. These priorities are shared respectively by 5%, 7%, and 8% of the population; inflation, standards of living, and corruption are considered priority issues by the Romanian public opinion.

Part of the explanation lies in the regional economic situation, which has been worsened by disruption caused by the intervention. For the weakest states (Macedonia and Albania) this has accelerated the slide into dependence on assistance and semi-protectorate status. In other states the economic problems undermine the reform-minded coalitions which have been relatively successful in empowering national minorities in the political system (the Hungarian minority in Romania, the Turkish minority in Bulgaria). These governments stretched their pro-Western orientation to its limit during the NATO intervention, understanding the risk that this could erode their social base. Now they feel they have not been given any tangible reward for this gamble. They have clearly suffered economic losses with no corresponding substantial political gains. Unless this changes soon, there is a real danger of their losing political support and their countries sliding back into coalitions of ex-communists and neo-nationalists, which would be unlikely to further consolidation of democracy and stability in the region.

## ECONOMIC IMPACT OF THE NATO INTERVENTION

In assessing the impact of the 1999 Kosovo crisis on the Balkan region, it is important to bear in mind that it is the least economically developed in Europe. The consequences of the war have combined with the double legacies of backwardness and the uncompleted transition from the command economy. The combined GDP of Albania, Bosnia, Bulgaria, Romania, Macedonia, and Croatia is equivalent to that of the city of Hamburg. None of the countries in the region has yet regained the economic levels of 1989 (see Table 3).

The destruction during the war of bridges on the Danube, transit routes and railway links has made regional contact more difficult and virtually isolated the region from supplies and potential markets in Western Europe. The cost of alternative routes is prohibitive, and thus some industrial plants in Romania and Bulgaria have had to close down. (Macedonia is also severely affected because its main economic partner had previously been Serbia.) There have been varying assessments of the situation by the leading international institutions (IMF, World Bank, EBRD).

During the Kosovo intervention and its immediate aftermath, the neighboring countries often stated that its worst effect for

| | Population m | GDP/1989 | GDP/1999 |
|---|---|---|---|
| Albania | 3.8 | 100 | 91 |
| Bosnia | 4 | 100 | 14 |
| Bulgaria | 8 | 100 | 66 |
| Croatia | 5 | 100 | 56 |
| Macedonia | 2 | 100 | 22 |
| Romania | 22 | 100 | 74 |
| Yugoslavia | 8.5 | 100 | 10 |

Source: European Bank for Reconstruction and Development, 1999.

Table 3: Population in relation to GDP

|  | Imports from SE Europe | Exports to SE Europe | Imports from FRY | Exports to FRY |
|---|---|---|---|---|
| Albania | 6.3 | 2.3 | 0.2 | 0.1 |
| Bulgaria | 3.0 | 7.0 | 0.8 | 2.3 |
| Bosnia-Herzegovina | 30.8 | 29.5 | – | – |
| Croatia | 2.8 | 16.1 | – | – |
| Macedonia | 20.4 | 19.1 | 11.4 | 10.4 |
| Romania | 1.0 | 3.0 | 0.0 | 1.4 |

Source: IMF Statistics, May 2000

Table 4: Import and Export data from 1998 between the countries of southeastern Europe and the Former Republic of Yugoslavia (FRY)

them was the loss of the Yugoslav market for their exports and, more generally, the adverse effect on regional trade. A closer examination of the trade patterns before and after the intervention suggests that the effect of the war on regional trade was relatively insignificant. To understand why, it is important to note that prior to the crisis the main trading partner for each Balkan country was the EU, and that intraregional trade was fairly limited. The proportion of EU/Balkan exports for Albania is 87.4%/8.4%; for Bulgaria it is 43.2%/7.0%; for Romania 56.5%/3%; and for Croatia 49.1%/29.5%.[12] That trade within southeastern Europe is relatively unimportant for most countries is demonstrated in Table 4.

The data in Table 4 helps to put the regional economic impact of the Kosovo crisis into perspective, it reveals the structural weakness of regional trade accentuated by the geopolitical realignments of the last decade. However, the figures have to be qualified by two remarks. First, the general observation about the lack of trade between the Balkan states is less applicable to the countries of former Yugoslavia, which, with the exception of Slovenia, still trade substantially with each other. The "ex-Yugoslav market" makes up roughly a third of the exports for Serbia, Croatia, and Macedonia, and two-thirds of the trade for Bosnia-Herzegovina. To be sure, some of this is "involuntary trade": one cannot always afford to choose one's trading partners. But it is likely that positive political and economic change in Serbia would enhance this phenomenon further.

In addition, much of the regional trade goes unregistered. A decade of wars and sanctions has disrupted some regional patterns, but it has also helped to establish new, unofficial ones. Though it might be an exaggeration to say that this has become the prevailing trade pattern in the region, nevertheless, entire sectors of the regional economy have become criminalized. These sectors do not figure in the official statistics, but they certainly have major economic and political implications.

## DIRECT DAMAGE

The NATO intervention of 1999 inflicted most damage in Serbia proper, while the rest of the region was affected only indirectly and unevenly. Damage in FRY (Serbia and Montenegro) was concentrated primarily to infrastructure and industrial capacity. Bombs took out dozens of key bridges, as well as airports, telecommunications and industrial plants. 70% of the electricity production capacity and 80% of the oil refinery capacity was knocked out.[13] According to the "Group of 17," an independent economic think tank based in Belgrade, unemployment went up from 26.8% in 1998 to 33% in 1999. The Group estimates the total economic cost for Serbia at close to $30 billion. (Other estimates are considerably higher.) The effects of economic sanctions and the arrival of refugees (an estimated 100,000 Serbs from Kosovo to be added to well over half a million Serbian refugees from Bosnia-Herzegovina and Croatia) further exacerbates the severe impact the intervention has had on an already decaying Serbian economy.

The impact on the neighboring countries has, however, been less destructive than initially feared. The worst affected were

| | GDP growth | Export | Trade deficit | Employ-ment | Budget cost |
|---|---|---|---|---|---|
| Albania | –2 | – | – | –2 | |
| Bulgaria | –5 | –10 | +5 | – | +5 |
| Bosnia-Herzegovina | –2 | –10 | +20 | –2 | +2 |
| Croatia | –1 | –10 | +10 | –1 | +2 |
| Macedonia | –5 | –15 | +20 | –2 | +2 |
| Romania | 0.5 | –2 | – | – | – |

Source: V. Gligorov and N. Sundström, "The Cost of the Kosovo Crisis" WIIW, Country Analyses and Country Profiles no. 12 (April 1999)

Table 5: Estimates of the cost of the war for neighboring countries (%)

those most dependent on trade with the FRY (Bosnia and Macedonia) and those most burdened by the arrival of refugees (Macedonia, Albania). The relatively short-term effect of the latter and the importance of international aid have, however, helped to limit the damage. The loss of trade revenue and investments has contributed to the deterioration of an already difficult situation for some, and represents a setback for others at a moment when much-delayed reforms were being introduced.

## RECONSTRUCTION AND REGIONAL COOPERATION IN THE BALKANS

OBSTACLES TO REGIONAL COOPERATION ★ The breakup of Yugoslavia and associated nationalist fragmentation obviously constituted the major impediment to regional cooperation during the 1990s. Unresolved or reopened border and minority issues encouraged conflictual agendas rather than cooperation. Serbia thinks of itself as a regional power, yet after a decade under Milosevic it remains, to put it mildly, ill equipped to lead and ill-equipped to follow any kind of regional scheme. Without democratic change in Belgrade, only sub regional projects are likely to be feasible.

There are two further characteristics of the region that represent major obstacles to regional integration. The first is the crisis of the state and the absence of a rule of law. To a variety of degrees, we are dealing with weak states with weak institutional ties to weak societies. The existence of an authoritarian regime is not to be confused with the strength of a state. The development of weak or failed states has political and security implications as well as a socio-economic dimension. Most of the region can be described as comprising rent-seeking states, which run huge deficits and public debts and therefore rely on substantial international financial assistance.[14] Bosnia, Kosovo, Albania, and Macedonia all rely on this system of internationally financed dependency on one hand, and the criminalization of the economy on the other (drugs, arms, prostitution). Romania and Bulgaria exhibit the same dynamic to a lesser extent because they can rely on some direct investment. Serbia after Milosevic might also fit this pattern, heralded by the opposition leaders attending international donors' conferences'. Needless to say, failing states are hardly conducive to democratic polities. Political power in such states is catering to three constituencies: the international community, mafias, and the voters. The first provides financial aid; the second thrives on corruption; and the third, by no means the most important, relies on clientelism. These are "illiberal democracies" in a permanent crisis of legitimacy.

Political leadership can thus make a crucial difference in these societies. The Milosevic case clearly exemplifies the negative sense. But positive cases can also be seen, such as when Bulgaria demonstrated restraint over the Macedonian question under the leadership of Jelev. Now Prime Minister Stojanov is showing the will to introduce reforms. Macedonia's former President Kiro Gligorov is managing an uneasy modus vivendi between Slavs and Albanians, while President Djukanovic is moving Montenegro towards greater democracy.

The decade of war, including the Kosovo intervention, is both a consequence and a cause of this crisis of legitimacy.[15] It has made regional cooperation a difficult and unlikely proposition. As the international community role moves from intervention and "hard security" issues to reconstruction and "soft security," it must be increasingly prepared to confront not only ethnic conflict, but also issues such as the criminalization of the economy and the weakness of state institutions. Both require a regional approach.

This analysis leads to several possible recommendations. In the first place, the international community could do more to help non-state actors. It could help civil society not just to organize itself outside the corrupt structures of the state, but also assist in "state-building" (institutions, the rule of law, etc). Furthermore, there must be much greater international cooperation in fighting organized crime. Adequate legislation and enhancing enforcement capacity is essential. Perhaps the only truly functional transnational organization in the region is the mafia. But corrupt governance, as much as ethnic conflict, is a major obstacle to regional cooperation.

The second characteristic of the Balkans that is blocking the development of postwar regional cooperation schemes is the heterogeneity of the region, in terms both of internal development (different stages in the political and economic transition of the various states) and international status (especially the differences in their relationships to the EU). Serbia has become an international pariah. Croatia is anxious to be considered Central European rather than a Balkan country, and has until now been rather reluctant to get too involved in Balkan cooperation. Bulgaria and Romania have some political but little economic stake in regional cooperation. Bosnia and Kosovo are international "protectorates," while neighboring Albania and Macedonia could qualify as "semi-protectorates." Greece, a member of both NATO and the EU, has played an ambiguous and not entirely helpful role through much of the 1990s. Turkey would like to reclaim a regional role but is perceived by most of the Balkan countries as too big and potentially threatening to be granted such a role.

Within the region, people are apprehensive about the more ambitious cooperation schemes for two reasons. The first stems from seeing such schemes as an attempt fostered from outside the region, to recreate some kind of Yugoslavia. Nobody in Slovenia, Croatia, or Kosovo wants to hear about that. The second reservation stems from a fear that regional integration encouraged by West Europeans is a substitute for the real thing, i.e. integration into the EU. The former Macedonian president Kiro Gligorov, one of the region's most experienced and moderate leaders, declared in March 1998:

Relations among Balkan countries must be based on new European relations (...) There is limited opportunity for economic cooperation. The Balkan countries are small countries with small markets. To leave the region outside of Europe, to embrace the recommendation for a miniature Partnership for Peace, is not the answer. Macedonia does not shy away from regional cooperation. However, association and integration should not be of the region as a whole but of each country depending on the development of its democracy. Otherwise the least advanced—in terms of economy, legal systems, democracy, minority rights—will hold back the integration of other countries.

## A NEW SOLUTION: THE STABILITY PACT

It is against this background that the international community put forward in the aftermath of the Kosovo crisis, the Stability Pact for southeastern Europe. The novelty of the Pact, launched in Sarajevo at the end of July 1999, is twofold. First, it proposes a coherent regional approach, beyond conflict management in individual crisis spots such as Kosovo or Bosnia. Security, economic reconstruction, and democracy are presented as complementary aspects of a process aimed at enhancing the stability of the region. Second, although the Stability Pact is a broad international initiative, the EU has assumed a leading role, not only in its implementation, but also in providing a crucial political link between the process of regional security and cooperation on one hand and the prospect of European integration on the other. This new approach, connecting postwar reconstruction, regional cooperation, and long-term European future, not to mention the considerable financial means promised, accounts for the extremely high expectations generated by the Pact throughout the region.

The Pact certainly has had a positive effect in providing much needed investment in infrastructure projects and encouraging the awareness of regional interdependence. Until now, opting out of the Balkans was often seen as the quickest way for a Balkan state to join Europe. The connection between regional cooperation and a European future is an important departure from the dominant mindset of the past decade.

However, after one year, several problems associated with the concept and the implementation of the Pact have surfaced. First, the two processes of *political stabilization* and *economic reconstruction* should not be confused and "are not necessarily convergent."[16] The economic process does not automatically enhance the political one, especially if some key regional players (e.g. Serbia) are left out. Second, and more important, there is an implicit contradiction in the attempt to combine strategies based on *regionality* and *conditionality*. The Stability Pact is based on the principle of regionality, while the EU's Association Process is based on the principle of conditionality. The former stems from the reckoning that regional problems require regional solutions. However, given the political and economic segmentation of the region, such regional integration is implausible without a common European framework. On the other hand, the logic of the EU enlargement process based on conditionality creates a variety of relationships and thus a new differentiation: Slovenia, Romania, and Bulgaria (and soon perhaps Croatia as well) have already opened accession negotiations with the EU, which puts them in a very different situation from Albania or Macedonia, which started negotiations on Stabilization and Association Agreements, not to mention Bosnia or Kosovo, for which the EU membership is not seen as a realistic perspective. There is a danger of marginalizing the so-called Western Balkans as a powder keg contained only by a continued international military presence. Thus, according to some critics of the Stability Pact, "the EU is de facto dividing a region with the left hand, while promoting multilateral cooperation among the states of the same region with the right hand."[17] A dual approach is emerging: the logic of *integration and enlargement* of the EU, and the logic of *intervention and protectorates*. For implementation of the Stability Pact to be at all feasible, there must be a rethinking by the EU of the relationship between the differentiation involved in its pre-accession process and the objective of regional cooperation/integration.

One view as to how to overcome this contradiction is to revise and accelerate the EU enlargement process much along the lines of the promises made during the NATO intervention when the Stability Pact was conceived. Speaking in Sofia on May 17, 1999, Tony Blair stated: "We will show that we have a commitment and an obligation to help this region to a different type of future, one that is based on membership of the EU and NATO." Hence the proposals made at the end of the Kosovo crisis for an accelerated, partial membership status for the countries of the region. The Center for European Policy Studies advocated a bold approach by the EU with a "new associate membership" for the countries of southeastern Europe starting with the introduction of the euro in Kosovo.[18] Other proposed measures focused on a functional integration and were suggested to give some substance to the notion of a special or associate membership. These ranged from an European Economic Area to preferential access to EU markets for countries of the region.

This fast track approach represents a politically important breakthrough in that it combines political will with economic tools. There have, however, been credible objections to what some described as "enlargement light" — for instance, that the fast-track approach might discredit the enlargement process as a whole and be seen as unfair to the countries of Central Europe which were patiently involved in assimilating into their legislation the 80,000 pages of the "acquis communautaire." The best way to give credibility to the European policies in the Balkans, the argument goes, is similarly to accelerate the enlargement process with the countries of Central Europe that have been successful in their transitions to democracy and have built a stable and cooperative regional environment (the so-called Visegrad Group, including Poland, the Czech Republic, Hungary, and Slovakia).

The Stability Pact aims at developing a regional economic strategy. The March 2000 Donors Conference held in Brussels pledged some €2 billion for the financing of reconstruction projects. A "Quick Start" program selected these projects under the three tables covered by the Stability Pact: 84% earmarked for reconstruction projects, 12% for democratization, and 4% for security issues. Given the importance attached to the economic dimension, it is worth noting some of the problems associated with the regional economic strategy proposed.

First, the World Bank strategy paper presented on that occasion considers that "a major factor underlying the poor economic performance of the [southeastern Europe] region as a whole is the lack of progress in the transition towards a market-based economy."[19] The key to the success of the latter is privatization. Yet the whole point about the transition in the Balkans is not just that the starting point there is much lower than in Central Europe, but that the region already has to cope with the consequences of a failed transition. The key challenge therefore seems to be: to combine a "developing region" approach, building infrastructures with the necessary institution building, with the development of the rule of law that would allow the "second transition" to be more successful than the first. To simply advocate privatization in the present conditions in Kosovo (or Albania or Serbia) entails the risk of transferring a substantial part of the economy to the control of criminal elements.

Second, major infrastructure projects are clearly necessary, especially in developing communications. East–West communication, road and rail links are important to relieve some of the dependence on the North–South links most affected by the war. Yet it is support for small enterprises that is likely to be the most effective in addressing unemployment. Funding for such small-scale projects, however, has been virtually ignored.

Finally, there is the issue of free trade as part of a regional economic strategy. A development of a Free Trade Area for the Balkans and, no less importantly, the free access of the region to the EU markets are, no doubt, essential ingredients of regional economic integration. Yet postwar reconstruction in Kosovo points to some of the contradictions in the strategies followed by the Stability Pact: on the one hand it advocates regional trade liberalization, while on the other it recommends that Kosovo introduce customs duties in order to generate fiscal revenue for Kosovo's emerging administration.

The Stability Pact has generated high expectations, but has achieved relatively little in its first year. There is a risk of failure or of its merely fading into irrelevance if it remains essentially a concept imposed on the region from above in the aftermath of a military intervention, without adequate input from, and identification within, the region. The Stability Pact will remain an empty shell unless its projects are implemented from below, based on an identification of needs/issues on which projects must focus, and on local actors who will implement such projects. It will work only if the desire among southeast European political and economic elite to join Europe prevails over nationalist agendas and corrupt practices.

Analysis of the Stability Pact thus raises several forbidding questions. Can the EU model of a security community built on interdependence be transposed onto the Balkans through external constraint mixing conditionality and assistance? Can a model based on arbitration between interests, a culture of permanent negotiation and compromise, prevail over identity politics and the exploitation of fears and nationalist passions by post-communist elite who feel their power threatened by the logic of integration? Although solutions to these dilemmas may seem unattainable, the alternative is only too obvious: a region of failed states and long-term protectorates, an unstable and marginalized periphery of the continent eternally disappointed in the West, combining excessive expectations with exaggerated resentment towards Europe. Beyond the logic of conflict containment and humanitarian protectorates, the real test for the moral issues that legitimized the intervention in the Kosovo crisis will be the EU's ability to sustain a long-term commitment to help establish a European future for the Balkans.

OSCE staff in Kosovo are putting up posters
encouraging people to vote during the 28 October
municipal elections.
PHOTO: OSCE/LUBOMIR KOTEK

# 9

# THE FUTURE STATUS OF KOSOVO

Any discussion of Kosovo's future status has to consider four essential elements:

1  The relationship of the province to the FRY;
2  The relationship of Kosovar institutions of self-government to any continuing UN administrative presence, and to the NATO/KFOR security presence.
3  The nature of Kosovo's borders and its relationship to neighboring states.
4  The definition of Kosovo as an entity within the international community

The starting point for any discussion of Kosovo's future must begin with UN Security Council Resolution 1244 of June 1999. It created a unique political and institutional hybrid, a UN protectorate with unlimited powers whose purpose is to prepare the province for substantial autonomy and self-government. There is a tension between the unlimited nature of the authority vested in the UN Administration and its purpose, which is to devolve power to the people of the province. A key question about Kosovo's future status concerns how this tension should be managed: should the UN be trying to "do itself out of a job" or must it remain for an indefinite period until the people of Kosovo are ready for self-government?

A similar tension runs through the way 1244 envisages the future status of Kosovo. The Resolution reaffirms the territorial integrity of the FRY while promising "substantial autonomy and self-government" to the people of Kosovo. Yugoslav sovereignty over Kosovo is not abrogated or revoked, but it is suspended, and in its place the UN is accorded the authority to administer the province and prepare for "substantial autonomy and self-government" pending future negotiations on the final political status of the province. At the same time, even though suspended, Yugoslav sovereignty is still allowed expression within the province. Annex 2/6 of UNSC 1244 authorizes a continuing Serb and Yugoslav presence in the province in order to maintain contact with the UN and KFOR, to assist in mine clearance, to be present at key border crossings, and to protect "Serb patrimonial sites", like the monasteries at Gracanica/Ulpiana and Decane/Decani.

In the first year of the UNMIK mandate in Kosovo, the Secretary General's Special Representative (SGSR) has tried to get both majority and minority communities to participate in transitional institutions aimed at delivering substantial autonomy for the people of Kosovo. He has put forward an "agenda of coexistence" and has tried to move both majority and minority communities towards a recognition that democratic self-government by the Kosovar Albanian majority must be tempered by respect for minority rights and inclusion of minorities in the political process. The Kosovar political leadership has signed up for this "agenda for co-existence', but popular support for it remains grudging and reluctant. This reluctance to accept co-existence helps to explain the ongoing acts of terror against minority groups. The extremists responsible for these acts may only be small in number, but they enjoy the passive support of substantial numbers of the majority. Courageous attempts by a few Kosovar Albanian political and intellectual leaders to denounce these acts of terror have not succeeded in isolating the groups who commit them.

As for the minority community, in the year since their defeat, the Serbs remaining in Kosovo are still coming to terms with their historical defeat. They are a minority still unwilling to admit that they are a minority. The conditions they face within the enclaves under international protection are exceedingly difficult: they do not enjoy freedom of movement; they cannot work, and they continue to live in fear of attack. It should be no surprise that their leadership has been reluctant to take a full part in transitional institutions.

Given the level of inter-ethnic conflict in the province and the difficulty which the SRSG has experienced in getting Kosovar Albanians, Serbs and Roma to sit around the same table, it may seem premature to raise final status issues at all. It might be better to leave questions about the future in limbo, since a constructive ambiguity about the political future of the province might make it easier for all sides to overcome their reluctance to work together. The example of other peace processes suggests that deferring final status issues can facilitate their eventual resolution. The dialogue between Palestinians and Israelis, for example, has depended on postponing final status issues until other roadblocks could be overcome. There are occasions, in other words, where parties can be induced to take the first steps towards political reconciliation only if the final destination of the process is not disclosed prematurely.

There are also external reasons for deferring discussion of future status. At present there is no consensus in the UN Security Council on Kosovo's future. Sharp divisions remain between those permanent members who supported NATO military action in 1999 and those who opposed it. In June 2000, the Russians and Chinese approved a renewal of the UNMIK mandate but only so long as the SRSG activities remain consistent with 1244. But their future support cannot be taken for granted. Already the Russians have made public their unhappiness with actions taken by the SRSG which give the appearance of deviating from the spirit of 1244, notably the adoption of the Deutschmark and the failure to implement the provisions in Annex 2/6 providing for access by

FRY personnel to the province. Any proposals, including those made by this Commission, which seek to move beyond the 1244 framework might fracture the fragile consensus in the UN Security Council that is necessary to sustain future renewal of the UNMIK and KFOR mandates.

The Commission is keenly aware that future status is a highly sensitive subject and that there are strong arguments for deferring discussion of it altogether at this stage.

Nevertheless, the Commission believes it must discuss the issue in detail because a wise and timely framework for taking this issue forward will help determine whether Kosovo's current transition process is successful. The Commission believes that while Resolution 1244 has served as a useful common denominator of agreement in the UN Security Council, it is reaching the end of its useful life as a framework for the transition to autonomy and self-government. The transitional process, initiated by the SRSG, is creating a dynamic that will soon require clarification of the ultimate in which direction the process is headed. Municipal elections are currently scheduled for October 2000 and Kosovo-wide elections are scheduled for sometime in 2001. When elected officials assume their functions, they will demand to know what powers they are allowed to exercise and when the transition to full self-government will occur. Even though the SRSG will retain overall formal authority over locally elected officials, the UN cannot defer the issue of status once Kosovo possesses its own democratically elected leadership. Unless a systematic dialogue is opened up, with both majority and minority communities in Kosovo, there is a substantial risk that the whole transitional apparatus will begin to unravel into a conflict between a UN administration with transitional powers and a locally elected leadership determined to press on to take full authority. For this reason alone, the international community must anticipate this challenge with a clear answer to the question of where the transitional process now underway is actually headed.

Externally too, Resolution 1244 is reaching the end of its useful life as a framework for managing the future of the province. Its essential commitments to FRY sovereignty and Kosovo autonomy may not be incompatible in theory, but they have become incompatible in practice. After what they have experienced at the hands of the FRY authorities, Kosovar Albanians are all but unanimous in their refusal to accept any real and ongoing exercise of FRY sovereignty over the province. This is the essential reason why Carl Bildt, special envoy of the United Nations Secretary General to the Balkans, concluded in recent remarks to the UN Security Council that "a clear constitutional separation" between Kosovo and the FRY has become inevitable.[1] These remarks have encouraged the Commission to examine various options for a future status for Kosovo, which go beyond the current framework of 1244.

## FIVE POSSIBILITIES

In the Commission's opinion, there are five possible options for Kosovo's future. In what follows, we evaluate the strengths and weaknesses of four of them in turn and conclude by defining our recommended choice.

PROTECTORATE * In essence, this option takes the current status quo, the administration of Kosovo by UNMIK, and extends it indefinitely into the future. 1244 would be renewed from year to year, and under its authority, a UN administration would attempt to widen the ambit of local and province-wide self-government, within continuing FRY sovereignty over the province. The question of whether this sovereignty would remain entirely vestigial or whether the FRY security presence at the borders and over patrimonial sites within Kosovo would actually be asserted would depend on the UN's assessment of the security situation and on negotiations with the Serbian regime.

The autonomy and self-government exercised by officials elected in local and province-wide elections would increase over time, and the size and reach of UNMIK would be scaled down, but ultimate authority in the province would continue to rest with the SRSG and with the international administration.

The protectorate option essentially implies that despite what 1244 promised, the majority and minority communities in Kosovo are not actually ready to enjoy "substantial autonomy and self-government." The 1244 regime may promise these goals, but they cannot actually be delivered except in a limited and partial way, subject to international oversight by the UN administration. There is too much suspicion and animosity between ethnic groups to allow the majority to exercise full powers of self-government, and unless there is continual supervision by a protectorate regime, minorities will remain in danger.

An indefinite extension of the 1244 regime has some support within the Kosovar Albanian majority community, from those who doubt the capacity of the available local elite to handle full self-government. In addition, an indefinite international protectorate brings powerful economic benefits—salaries and employment for local people—and these local people naturally hope that such benefits will continue for as long as possible. Minority communities may not support the 1244 status quo, but they fear what would happen if the ethnic majority did secure more power, and they worry what would happen to their security if the international administrative and military presence were reduced.

The principle difficulty with an indefinite extension of the 1244 regime is that it frustrates the almost universal demand of the Kosovar Albanian majority to run their own affairs. Since the early 1990's, the demand for self-determination, whether couched as autonomy or as independence, has been the uniform demand of the entire Kosovar Albanian political spectrum. Any remaining support for a political future involving autonomy within the FRY vanished in March 1999 when FRY forces began expelling the entire Kosovar Albanian population. Even a substantial exercise of autonomous self-government is now regarded as insufficient. Most Kosovar Albanians view the NATO intervention in 1999 as a victory in a long struggle for national independence. Accordingly, they perceive the protectorate established by 1244 as a purely "transitional" arrangement, which must lead eventually to full self-rule by the majority. The language of 1244 certainly encourages the population to believe that UNMIK is a "transitional" order, due to be replaced by permanent institutions of self-government.

Transitional institutions depend for their effectiveness on the tacit consent of the Kosovo majority and the reluctant acquiescence of the minority. The longer the international community holds on to ultimate power in Kosovo, and the longer it defers effective self-government, the more likely it becomes that the representatives of the majority will withdraw from transitional institutions and either set up parallel ones of their own or attempt to render the province ungovernable. In other words, consent for transitional institutions cannot be sustained unless these are seen to be gradually delivering a real transfer of power from the UN to local people.

This is not to say that the international community must simply defer to the wishes of the Kosovar Albanian majority. They must also respond to the needs and fears of Kosovo's minorities. Both the UN Administration and KFOR have taken on substantial responsibilities for their protection, and the key factor in determining both the timing and extent of eventual Kosovo self-government is whether these minorities are secure. The fear that self-government in the form of majority rule would result in the deaths or expulsion of the remaining Roma and Serb population remains the chief reason for extending the protectorate indefinitely. Yet extending it indefinitely will irrevocably alienate the majority of the population. This is the essential contradiction which makes it impossible to simply extend the 1244 regime indefinitely. If it actually delivers substantial autonomy and self-government to the majority, the minority will be oppressed and quite possibly expelled. If in order to protect the minority, the UN administration remains and denies the majority substantial autonomy and self-government, their resistance will make indefinite UN administration impossible.

**PARTITION** ∗ Ongoing violence towards the minorities in Kosovo, together with the emergence in north Mitrovice/Kosovska Mitrovica and other towns in Kosovo of Serbian minority enclaves makes it logical to consider partition of the province as a possible long-term solution. Normatively, partition would acknowledge that the Serbian people have a historical claim to continue to live in Kosovo. In practical terms, a formal partition, negotiated between the Serbian authorities in Belgrade and representatives of the international community would ratify the de facto ethnic division of the province that has emerged since June 1999. It would presuppose that Serbs couldn't live side by side with Kosovar Albanians, either now or in the future. Partition would seek to consolidate the remaining Serbs in the province into a contiguous area north of the Iber/Ibar river in the region, adjacent to the frontier with Serbia. Partition would facilitate a divorce between the communities, ostensibly allowing them to create independent and separate political futures. By agreeing to partition, the FRY would renounce its claims to the portion of Kosovo south of the Iber/Ibar, and this would facilitate the transition of the remaining portion of Kosovo south of the Iber/Ibar to full independence outside the FRY. Special provisions in such a partition agreement would have to cover such matters as the protection of historical and cultural monuments, together with compensation for properties lost or abandoned as a consequence of population transfer. An international security presence would be required to monitor the border.

A formal partition would serve the interests of those Serbs already living in the north Mitrovice/Kosovska Mitrovica region, but it would face Serbs living south of the Iber/Ibar with the choice of continuing to live under Kosovar Albanian majority rule or departing northwards to Serbian areas of northern Kosovo or Serbia proper. Likewise, partition would probably result in the departure southwards of all remaining Kosovar Albanians still living in the north Mitrovica region. In other words, partition would result in substantial amounts of forced population movement for both communities. It would create two separate and ethnically homogeneous territories.

It is difficult to see how an international community, which refused to approve formal partition in Bosnia, could approve or initiate such a move in Kosovo. Partition would violate the normative commitment of the international community to avoid forced population displacements and to sustain the multi-ethnic and mixed fabric of Balkan communities. Given the extent of de facto partition, it has been difficult to sustain these normative commitments in Kosovo, but abandoning them now would require the UN administration to accept that its entire attempt to create transitional forms of multi-ethnic political cooperation had failed.

A more pressing political objection to partition is that it would be unacceptable to almost every fraction of the Kosovar Albanian majority, even if the quid pro quo were Serb recognition of independence for the rest of the province. Partition would deprive the majority population of the northern parts of the Trepce/Trepca mine complex. Even if the commercially exploitable mineral resources in this complex were less valuable than is popularly supposed, losing Trepce/Trepca would deprive an already poor province of a source of employment and revenue. Partition would thus reduce the economic viability of an independent Kosovo. While partition might end Serbian claims on Kosovo, it would also create a permanent source of grievance among the Kosovar Albanian majority that would sow the seeds of future conflict.

On these grounds the Commission believes that formal partition is an undesirable option. It also believes that the existing de facto partition of the province should be discouraged and that the authority of the international community must be re-established over the north Mitrovice/Kosovska Mitrovica region.

**FULL INDEPENDENCE** * Under this option, which is the expressed and long-standing desire of responsible political opinion in the majority community, Kosovo should proceed rapidly from substantial autonomy and self-government under UN administration to full-scale internationally recognized independence as a nation state. The process towards independence would begin with the proclamation of a referendum on independence by the first province-wide parliamentary assembly elected under the UN transitional administration. Once this referendum had produced the likely result, i.e. a substantial popular mandate for independence, independence would be proclaimed by the elected parliament. It would then have a mandate to negotiate the terms and timing of independence with the international community, through the UN Administration, the Contact Group governments and ultimately the UN Security Council. A Kosovo parliament, having secured international agreement for independence, would then proceed to set up a constitutional assembly to draft laws and establish institutions for the independent state, either by adapting such constitutional arrangements as had been set up under the UN administration or creating ones *de novo*. UN transitional administration would be phased out, although an international security presence would remain on Kosovo's borders with Serbia until Kosovo was capable of defending itself. In this scenario, Kosovar independence would be declared by her representatives, then ratified by authoritative international bodies. It would not be negotiated with the Serbs.

The political appeal of full independence is that it would meet the long-expressed demands of the Kosovar Albanian majority.

Independence would both end UN tutelage and abolish the increasingly fictional sovereignty of the FRY over Kosovo. It would enable the Kosovar Albanian majority to become masters at last in their own house.

Whatever its attractions to the Kosovar Albanian majority, the practical political difficulties that stand in the way of unlimited Kosovar independence are immense. Two permanent members of the UN Security Council, Russia and China, are adamantly opposed to it on the grounds that granting independence would reward a violent secessionist movement, the KLA, and set a precedent that might undermine the stability and integrity of their own large, multi-national, multi-ethnic states.

Kosovar independence also arouses anxiety in neighboring countries, who fear that an independent Kosovo would soon have designs on the territorial integrity of Albania, Macedonia and Montenegro. The expressed fear is that independence for Kosovo would set the stage for the eventual emergence of a Greater Albanian state in the region, which could only be achieved at the price of the dismemberment of neighboring states.

Finally, Serb and Roma minorities within Kosovo are adamantly opposed to independence on the grounds that it would be followed, sooner or later, by the forcible expulsion of their entire communities. Independence for Kosovo, when seen through the eyes of the minorities, looks like a recipe for ethnic majority tyranny.

**AUTONOMY WITHIN A DEMOCRATIC FRY** ★ This issue — the vulnerability of minorities in an independent Kosovo — is one principal reason why many Western governments also oppose full, unsupervised independence for Kosovo. Also, some of them share the Russian and Chinese concern about the kind of precedent that would be set by allowing a secessionist movement to achieve independence by violent means.

Opposition to independence helps to explain why many Western governments remain reluctantly convinced that the 1244 regime, substantial autonomy and self-government within nominal FRY sovereignty remain the best option for the foreseeable future. In addition, they hope that at some time in the future a post-Milosevic Serbia and a re-invigorated and democratized FRY federation, might make it conceivable for the Kosovar Albanian majority to consider a future within a Yugoslav federation as an autonomous republic, effectively self-governing internally, but allowing the federation to represent it internationally.

The problem with this scenario is that it presumes the possibility of two peoples who have been at war with each other, one day living inside the same state. After what Kosovar Albanians experienced at the hands of the FRY authorities, not just between March and June 1999, but at least since 1989, there seems to be no practical prospect, however desirable it may be in theory, of Kosovars being willing to submit to any form of Serbian or FRY sovereignty, however notional. It is not impossible to conceive of Kosovar Albanians, individually and collectively, establishing good working relations with the institutions of a democratic, post-Milosevic Serbia or even with a renewed FRY federation including Montenegro. But the possibility of good relations can only be premised, at least on the Kosovar side, on being under a self-governing authority of their own. It seems highly unlikely that Kosovar Albanians would ever consent, for example, to the presence of Serbian or FRY personnel on Kosovan soil as provided by Annex 2/6 of Resolution 1244. Nor is there any chance that they could ever exchange the Deutschmark for the Yugoslav dinar. This change seems as irreversible as it is economically advantageous.

In any event, the Commission's view is that it would be irresponsible of the international community to defer future status questions in order to wait for Serbia, Montenegro and the FRY to make their own transition to a post-Milosevic, democratic era. As matters currently stand, there is no immediate prospect of such a transition, and even if it was to occur, it will take many years. In the meantime, Kosovar Albanian frustrations with the indefinite deferral of their political future will make continued UN administration of the province increasingly difficult.

The Commission's view is that the international community cannot defer Kosovo's final status in expectation of positive change in the FRY. The essential reality that the international community must face is that, because of the FRY's systematic violation of Kosovar rights, substantial autonomy and self-government for Kosovo have become incompatible with continued Yugoslav sovereignty of the province, and will remain so even if Yugoslavia eventually makes a transition to democratic rule. The simple truth is that no Kosovar will accept to live under Serb rule, however notional, ever again.

**CONDITIONAL INDEPENDENCE** ★ The Commission firmly believes that all the people of Kosovo must be given the chance to determine their political future. Once local and Kosovo wide elections have been held, and a limited exercise of self-government is underway, elected Kosovar officials will inevitably demand a referendum on the province's political future. This demand is a legitimate one, and while its timing should depend on the SRSG's estimate of the security situation, it should be granted as expeditiously as is prudent. It would also be within the SRSG's powers to frame the referendum question on future status in consultation with elected representatives of majority and minority communities in such a way as to ensure that a genuine range of options, ranging from continued UN administration to independence, is offered, and that the question is framed with sufficient clarity to enable the result to give an unequivocal indication of majority sentiment on the political future of the province.

Were such a referendum undertaken, it is to be expected that the result would probably favor some form of independence for the province. It seems out of the question for the international community to ignore such an important expression of political preference, but it is legitimate for its representatives in Kosovo to then seek to define with, elected representatives of majority and minority communities, what precise form of independence is possible.

Conditional independence is the phrase that the Commission feels best describes the future status that is likely to emerge from such a consultation process. Full, unlimited and unconditional independence is impossible in the nature of things, because an independent Kosovan state lacks the key property of statehood, the means to defend itself against external attack. It remains dependent, and will continue to do so, on the KFOR military presence on the ground and on NATO air and sea power. Moreover, as the security situation in Kosovo since 1999 has made abundantly clear, Kosovo lacks the other capacities of statehood: the ability to guarantee internal order, domestic safety and inter-ethnic peace. For these functions normally exercised by states, Kosovo will remain dependent, for years to come, on some form of international security presence, both police and military.

In these senses, then, Kosovo can only aspire to a conditional form of independence. Both its external security and internal human rights regimes will have to be supervised by the international community and by a considerable military presence. As long as minorities in Kosovo are unsafe and unable to travel freely and participate fully in Kosovan institutions, some supervisory international presence, both administrative and military, will remain necessary to protect them.

If, therefore, a referendum decided on independence, negotiations would then have to ensue between the elected representatives of both majority and minority communities and the UN administration to determine a constitutional regime that would protect minority rights, guarantee some continuing international military and administrative oversight of these rights, while also transferring the effective administration of Kosovo into the hands of a national parliament, an executive and municipal administration run by local people.

Such a constitutional regime would have to be based on acknowledging and respecting the following basic principles:

a  The international community would respect the right of all the citizens of Kosovo to freely determine their political future.

b  The citizens of Kosovo would accept the role of the international community in providing external security and internal human rights protection.

c  All citizens of a free Kosovo, regardless of origins, would have full and equal rights of access and participation in the institutions of a free Kosovo.

d  All minorities in Kosovo would have internationally protected rights to government services in their own language, education in their own language, religious freedom and protection of religious sites, equality of employment rights and full mobility rights, including unimpeded travel to and from Serbia.

e  Assured minority participation in the judiciary, police, and the local and national government.

## DISCUSSION

The Commission commends the Lund principles on minority rights, developed by the OSCE Commissioner for the Rights of Minorities, and believes that they afford a clear and detailed basis for a constitutional rights regime in Kosovo which would reconcile majority rule with enforceable minority rights protection.[2] The type of constitutional regime the Commission envisages does not entail power-sharing between distinctive and self-governing majority or minority communities, but rather a minority rights regime that seeks to guarantee fairness, equality and full participation in common and shared institutions. The objective of the constitutional regime should be to move communities away from ethnically homogeneous enclaves or cantons into joint participation in common institutions.

Only if the negotiations to establish this constitutional regime of self-government were successful and the international community was satisfied that full self-government by the citizens of Kosovo was compatible with an internationally monitored minority rights regime and border security, would the UN Security Council then be asked to ratify Kosovo's conditional independence.

While conditional independence would effectively end FRY sovereignty over Kosovo, it would not immediately confer the full international legal personality of statehood either. The Commission has in mind a process in which Kosovo would gradually acquire the rights of a state as it demonstrates that its peoples can live in peace with each other and with the neighboring states in the region. As it did so, over a period of years, the international community would be able to reduce its security presence within Kosovo, provided that minorities were securely protected by Kosovo's own courts, police and parliament. Only as it established conditions of internal and external peace, would Kosovo earn recognition from other states as a fully independent international state.

Even then, as a small state, it would have to base its security and its economic viability on very close political, economic and security relationships with its neighbors in the region. Conditional independence for Kosovo is only a viable proposition within the context of a stability pact for all the small states in the region so that they can develop their infrastructure, trading ties, political and strategic partnerships within an enduring framework of peace. The European Stability Pact is a crucial step towards creating such a framework, but the Commission believes that the pact must acquire a political dimension as well as an economic one. It must develop a secretariat and a structure capable of reconciling political tensions in the region and above all, gradually guiding Kosovo to its proper place as a functioning state within the Balkan region. Such a pact should ensure, as its basic political principles, that all members respect the borders, territorial integrity and internal autonomy of its neighbors. This is of particular relevance in the case of Kosovo, since its independence arouses considerable fears in Macedonia, Albania and Montenegro that this would be is a prelude to the creation of a greater Kosovo or a greater Albania. A crucial condition of Kosovo's path to independence is that it fully respects the existing borders of its neighbors and that it refrains from any interference in their internal affairs. The Stability Pact's essential political dimension is to ensure that Kosovo complies with these conditions of international citizenship. Only when it does so is it likely to receive recognition from other states as a fully-fledged member of the international system.

The key challenge in developing a realistic path towards conditional and ultimately full independence for Kosovo lies in its relationship with Serbia. The Commission believes that it would be desirable to negotiate Kosovo's conditional independence with Serbian authorities, since peaceful recognition of each other's borders and integrity would constitute the critical guarantee of peace in the region. But neither the existing Serbian regime, nor any other regime that can be imagined is likely to negotiate the cession of Yugoslav sovereignty over Kosovo.

It is therefore a regrettable fact of life that Serbia is unlikely either to negotiate Kosovar independence or, in the short term at least, to recognize it once it has occurred. This fact, coupled with the reality of Serb defeat and the flight of substantial numbers of Serbs from Kosovo, may encourage the Kosovar Albanian majority to believe that it can simply ignore Serbia as it proceeds on its way towards conditional independence.

The Commission believes that it would be foolhardy to ignore Serbia or to refuse to seek to engage it first in dialogue and then in negotiations over the future of Kosovo. Peace in the Balkans ultimately depends on the integration of Serbia into a stability pact for the region, and Kosovo's external security depends critically on patiently establishing a modus vivendi with the Serbian state. To be sure, dialogue with the existing regime in Belgrade is both difficult and distasteful, but over the medium term, there cannot be a secure future for either Kosovo or Serbia until both sides accept separation and ratify each other's borders. Moreover, each side has further grievances that must be addressed for peace to be durable. These include the Kosovar Albanians currently held in Serbian prisons. On the Serbian side, there are property claims for assets seized from Serb refugees after June 1999. In addition, some Serb refugees currently in Serbia claim a right to return to their former homes.

Each side urgently needs to begin dialogue on these issues. This dialogue could proceed on the following principles:

1 Each side should agree to release political detainees of the other side, as well as prisoners of war.

2 An international compensation board would be established to hear claims, and to fund redress, for Serb loss of property in Kosovo and for Kosovar Albanians loss of property during Serbian occupation.

3 Each side acknowledges the right of each other's citizens to travel freely across each other's borders and for those who wish to do so to return to their homes. The security forces of the international community should supervise such returns.

4 Dialogue would eventually seek to establish terms of mutual recognition as states.

While the current regime remains in power in Belgrade, no negotiations along these lines are possible. But a change of regime, and a change of heart among the Serbian political elite, might make it possible to negotiate the terms of a lasting peace.

In the longer term, as Kosovo demonstrates its capacity to contribute to regional stability, it might secure international recognition as a sovereign state. That depends, in effect, on whether its leaders display the prudence and self-discipline to seek and maintain good relations with both their external neighbors and their internal minorities over the long term.

The Commission is aware that conditional independence exceeds what many members of the UN Security Council can accept. But the political point it wants to insist upon is that the 1244 consensus is unsustainable, because it is based on a fiction that nominal Serbian sovereignty can be maintained over a population once it has definitively withdrawn its consent. Moreover, the 1244 regime, envisaging as it does a long-term UN administration, is setting up an inevitable clash between a majority bent on self-rule and an international community struggling to hold on to its authority. The proper way out of the impasse of 1244 is to begin exploring the implications of conditional independence.

Obviously such an idea creates important and controversial precedents. It would effectively commit the international community to the proposition that national minorities have a right of secession when they have been subjected to a systematic abuse of their human rights, together with a systematic denial of their right to self-government. It would also commit the international community to the correlative principle that states can lose their sovereign rights over national minorities when their treatment of these minorities rises to the level of persistent and brutal suppression of both individual rights and collective rights of self-government.

Neither of these principles is securely established in international law. Indeed, there is very real confusion that the Commission believes it is urgent to dispel.

The Commission appreciates that creating these precedents is not an easy matter for they may appear to legitimize, or even encourage, secessionist struggles by national minorities. Yet the inescapable fact is that national minorities, faced with brutality and oppression, will engage in struggles for self-determination, whatever the state of international law. It is better, in our view, that the international community develop procedures to accord self-government to these groups under appropriate and justifiable conditions than to maintain an obsolete regime of unalterable state sovereignty. Indeed, one of the central messages of the whole Kosovo tragedy is that by defending its sovereignty in Kosovo at all costs and by rejecting every attempt to internationalize the human rights problem in Kosovo, Serbia ended up accelerating its loss of the province.

The Commission's recommendations in relationship to final status need to be seen in the context of its earlier recommendations about early intervention. It is not merely that early intervention might have prevented the tragic conflict; it is that early intervention might have made it possible to find a solution that would have kept Kosovo within the Federal Republic of Yugoslavia. The Commission takes it for granted that in every case it is preferable to reconcile claims for autonomy and self-government within the existing order of nation states. Accordingly, when conflicts arise, intervening states must always seek to assist parties to find solutions that first seek to reconcile state sovereignty with minority rights and self-government. Only when such forms of compromise are clearly shown to be impossible, can minorities reasonably claim a right of secession. The Commission's argument is that in Kosovo after a certain point, peaceful reconciliation of Yugoslav sovereignty and Kosovar rights was no longer possible. In such cases — and the Commission hopes they will be rare — the international community must not shrink from its responsibility to devise rules for secession and independence which allow persecuted groups to find a constitutional order which grants them security and self-government. But granting independence should not be unconditional. The Commission is seeking to devise a strategy for supervised independence which instead of granting immediate international legal personality to secessionist peoples makes such independence conditional on minority rights protection and respect for the territorial integrity of neighboring states.

The process by which a future status agreement is reached is as important as the agreement itself. For understandable political reasons, the representatives of the international community may be unwilling to share their private discussions on final status with anyone inside the province. Given the immense difficulty of making joint institutions work, it is understandable that the international community's representatives want to preserve their room for maneuver by keeping most of the discussions secret for as long as possible. At some point, early in 2001, however, it would be advisable for the international community to begin a careful debate on the future with leading representatives of all the communities inside Kosovo. Unless support for a future status regime is firmly anchored in Kosovo's civil society and political class, unless the terms of a "deal" are comprehensively reviewed and discussed, the process will soon exacerbate the already harmful divide between the "internationals" and the "locals." Local actors, many of whom have shown great resourcefulness and courage, need to take part as soon as possible, so that unrealistic dreams can be tested against hard realities and a gradual consensus can emerge to carry the negotiation process through to success.

# PART III

# CONCLUSION

*

Rebuilding Kosovo
PHOTO: NATO PHOTO

# 10

# CONCLUSION

Some of the Commission's findings are presented here in an effort to put them in a wider historical context and to make clear the linkages between the recommendations. Our intention is to help governments frame a policy of sustained engagement in the development of a peaceful Kosovo and to bring together the Commission's thinking on Kosovo as a precedent for future forms of humanitarian intervention.

The Kosovo conflict has to be seen as one act in the tragic history of state fragmentation and state formation in the Balkan peninsula since the death of Tito. This catastrophic process cost over two hundred thousand lives and drove millions from their homes. This crisis pitted the majority ethnic Albanian population of Kosovo against a FRY government bent on Serb domination using tools of terror and repression. The Kosovar Albanian population responded to this repression with an impressive nonviolent mobilization throughout the 1990s. But despite its significant achievements this mobilization and organization of a parallel society could not reverse the destructive FRY policies toward the region. This combined with the limited engagement of the international community, and specifically the failure of the Dayton negotiations to raise the Kosovo issue, created a frustration that encouraged the outgrowth of an armed rebellion under the KLA. Both the unarmed and armed resistance movement shared an unswerving commitment to complete independence from the FRY. At every phase of the conflict, the Kosovar Albanian population suffered severe abuses at the hands of FRY security forces and civil institutions.

Four wars have convulsed the Balkans since 1991: over Slovenia, Croatia, Bosnia-Herzegovina and Kosovo. Given the continuing tensions between Serbia and Montenegro and the inter-ethnic rivalries in Macedonia, the Kosovo conflict may not be the last of these Balkan wars. The emerging state structure in the Balkans is unstable and likely to remain so. The Commission is keenly aware that the goal of its recommendations, like the goal of responsible policy in all states with interests in the region, must be to ensure that the Kosovo conflict turns out to be the last of the Balkan wars.

In this spirit, it is essential to read the Commission's central recommendation—that Kosovo be placed on a path towards "conditional independence"—within the framework of a Balkan Stability Pact, which adds a security as well as a political perspective to the existing economic commitment. This is the context in which the international role within this quasi-independent Kosovo becomes meaningful. The conditionality extends beyond the provision of a security guarantee by NATO troops and continuing international oversight of Kosovo's human rights protection. It must also result in the integration of Kosovo into a regional pact which provides development funding, political collaboration with neighboring states and a road map towards eventual integration into the European Union.

The Commission is of course fully cognizant that an independent Kosovo is currently opposed by Serbia, Russia, and many of the neighboring Balkan states. It is our contention however, that the unsustainability of the current situation, and the potentially explosive consequences of not dealing adequately with the Kosovar demands for self-determination, require a reconsideration of these positions.

Kosovo's future depends on whether the powers that were prepared to go to war can muster the long-term commitment and cohesion to build a framework for peace in the whole Balkan peninsula. The Stability Pact is a first step towards this framework. But it must become something more than an economic development fund, and it must evolve into a forum for political and diplomatic cooperation. Above all, European governments must demonstrate a capacity for extended commitment to Balkan development, over at least a 15 year period. Nothing less is required if the region is to overcome its legacy of war, poverty and institutional weakness.

Even if, as this Commission recommends, Kosovo eventually joins Croatia, Slovenia, Bosnia-Herzegovina and Macedonia as one of the new states built on the ruins of the former Yugoslavia, its future will remain uncertain until Albania, Montenegro and Serbia are stabilized within a framework of democracy, independent civil society and an open market economy. Montenegro must be given guarantees of security and self-determination, preferably within a federation with a democratic Serbia, but if necessary outside it. Democratic forces in Serbia urgently need the international community to offer a road map outlining a path towards re-integration within the Balkans and Europe. With this map at its disposal, opposition forces within Serbia could then offer the electorate a credible way out of their country's isolation and decline.

The destination of the Balkans as a whole must be European integration. Obviously, other Eastern European states which have already taken their place in the line, must be integrated first. By steady stages the Balkan peninsula should gain full acceptance as part of Europe. The division of Europe was not ended in 1989 only to create new divisions.

The future of Kosovo, then, depends on the sustainability of the European idea and its supporting institutions. While the United States needs to remain engaged, militarily and diplomatically, the chief responsibility for integrating Kosovo into a peace-ful Balkan region must lie with the European nations themselves. The Kosovo conflict tested to the limit the capacity of NATO and the EU to sustain the military and diplomatic partnerships necessary to enforce peace on the southeastern flank of the continent.

The alternative to integration is disintegration and the return to violence. For this reason the peoples of the Balkans need to be given a prospect which combines incentives to regional cooperation with a European future. The Stability Pact has attempted to do precisely that and has thus raised considerable expectations. The EU has committed itself, through its sponsorship of the Stability Pact, to help overcome poverty and instability in the Balkans. This promise must not be marred by red tape and lack of commitment.

We are now at a critical juncture: Either peace, reconstruction and a cooperative framework for the region are established, or these efforts fail with disastrous consequences for the Balkans and Europe as a whole. The EU members must make the necessary effort to underpin peace in the region. Failure to sustain development investment, human rights monitoring and support for civil society in the area will almost certainly lead to a renewal of ethnic conflict, as well as large-scale and potentially uncontrollable movements of population out of the region.

In the end, the people of Kosovo have to solve their own problems, together with their neighbors. The international community can provide the framework for a Kosovo at peace but it is for the citizens of Kosovo to make it a reality. For too long, the people of the Balkan region have looked to outside powers to solve their problems, or have blamed their catastrophes on the malign influence of outsiders.

While the Commission commends the dedication and hard work of the UNMIK, it believes strongly that in a post-imperial age, it is wrong, as a matter of principle, for the UN or any outside authority to exercise protectorate powers over national communities anywhere in the long-term and indeed, very difficult, given the complexity of contemporary society. The international community's long-term objective should be to build local capacity and do itself out of a job. The people of Kosovo must take over the running of their affairs, first at the local level and then at the Kosovo-wide level. Kosovar people living abroad should be encouraged to invest in their homeland and make it a place worthy of the enormous sacrifices Kosovars have made for their freedom.

But the condition of freedom is tolerance. Tolerance need not mean amnesia, and tolerance is no substitute for justice. Those responsible for crimes against humanity in Kosovo must be punished, and the Commission strongly supports the efforts of the ICTY in the Hague to end the cycle of impunity throughout the Balkans, as well as the efforts by the UNMIK to set up courts to try those accused of crimes of inter-ethnic hatred. The Commission is also keenly aware of the security problems in Kosovo and the difficulty of maintaining a secure environment for all ethnic groups without adequate policing or an adequate judiciary. At the same time, justice is in vain and security cannot be guaranteed if it is not accompanied by tolerance.

In the Kosovo context, tolerance simply means the willingness to live side by side with former enemies and to collaborate with them politically to prevent violence from destroying Kosovo's future. No one on the Commission supposes that this will be easy, yet Kosovars must realize that the international community did not intervene to turn Kosovo over to another ethnic majority tyranny. By its intervention, the international community won the right to insist that an independent Kosovo must accord equal rights to all the peoples — of whatever origin — who chose to live there. Tolerance is the political and moral condition of self-determination. If the inter-ethnic violence in Kosovo does not stop, the momentum towards self-determination and independence will cease. The Kosovar majority has to understand a stark reality: that if it will not live in peace with other ethnic groups, it will not achieve its freedom. The minority populations in Kosovo must also come to terms with the fact that their best hope of a long-term future within Kosovo lies in full-scale participation in emerging institutions of self-government.

There is no chance of long-term international investment in the region, and hence no long term future for their children, unless the killing and intimidation, from whatever side, stop now.

The Commission believes that internal reconciliation will remain extremely difficult as long as Kosovar Albanians continue to harass and attack Serbs, as long as the current regime remains in Belgrade and as long as the Serbian minority in Kosovo fails to grasp the reality that the province will never return to Serbian administration. Still, the Commission believes that a dialogue of reconciliation between an independent Kosovo and a democratic Serbia are essential for peace in the region. Here courageous civil society groups can take the first steps, and contacts between governments can follow later. It would be naïve to expect such a dialogue to yield results in the short term, but enduring sources of bitterness — prisoners held in Serbia, property seized in Kosovo — cannot be addressed without face to face negotiations between the two sides. For the Kosovar majority to pretend that the other side no longer exists is a sure recipe for trouble in the future. The leadership on both sides must have the courage to talk, and eventually to recognize each other.

It is premature to judge the success or failure of the military and humanitarian intervention in Kosovo in 1999. Clearly, any Kosovar government or party that seeks to destabilize Albania or Macedonia in particular will only delay or even deny Kosovo's chances of independence. The test of success is whether an independent Kosovo becomes a genuinely democratic state and whether it establishes stable and peaceful relationships with its neighbors.

If the question of whether the intervention has been successful cannot be answered until Kosovo is securely at peace, the question of whether the intervention was legitimate has to be answered, especially since Kosovo may provide a precedent for further interventions elsewhere in the future. The Commission's answer has been that the intervention was legitimate, but not legal, given existing international law. It was legitimate because it was unavoidable: diplomatic options had been exhausted, and two sides were bent on a conflict which threatened to wreak humanitarian catastrophe and generate instability through the Balkan peninsula. The intervention needs to be seen within a clear understanding of what is likely to have happened had intervention not taken place: Kosovo would now still be under Serbian rule, and in the middle of a bloody civil war. Many people would still be dying and flows of refugees would be destabilizing neighboring countries.

While accepting the unavoidable nature of intervention, the Commission has criticized the way the intervention was conducted in several respects, including:

1  It was a serious misjudgment of NATO not to foresee that bombing would lead to severe attacks on the Kosovar Albanians. There was consequently a lack of anticipation or preparation for the refugee flows that accompanied the outbreak of international war.

2  Once hostilities began, the exclusive reliance on air power proved incapable of stopping civilian expulsions, ethnic cleansing and murder.

3  Insufficient emphasis was given to the protection of ethnic minorities once the military occupation of Kosovo was underway.

4  Insufficient intelligence-gathering and intelligence-sharing has impeded the post-war efforts of KFOR to root out the perpetrators of inter-ethnic attacks.

In short, the international community willed a humanitarian end in Kosovo, without willing sufficient or adequate means. Far from vindicating the use of military power for humanitarian ends, the Kosovo operation showed up the shortcomings of modern military power as a humanitarian instrument. This is not to question the dedication, skill and competence of the military forces deployed before, during and after the Kosovo operation, but to argue that their best efforts could not disguise the fact that Kosovo took Western military power into new and uncharted areas. What is striking about the air operation was its improvised character. No one imagined the conflict would extend for 78 days, and no one had thought through the implications of trying to stop ethnic cleansing from high altitudes. As a result, weapons ran short, mistakes were made, and above all, the military operation was unable to prevent the exodus of nearly a million refugees and the deaths of thousands of civilians at the hands of the Serbian authorities. Once ground forces were deployed in June 1999, it soon became clear that neither training for high-intensity warfighting nor low-intensity peace-keeping adequately prepared the soldiers for the actual challenges met on the ground.

The chief of these challenges was providing security for threatened ethnic minority populations and preventing the de facto partition of the province into ethnic enclaves. Until these military failures are directly addressed by national governments, justified humanitarian causes will continue to be compromised by inadequate rules of engagement, equipment, tactics and intelligence gathering.

The problems that Kosovo revealed are not confined simply to the dissonance between the military means employed and the moral ends in view. The intervention laid bare the inadequate state of international law. The intervention was not legal because it contravened the Charter prohibition on the unauthorized use of force. This is a troubling fact and one which the necessity and legitimacy of the action cannot conjure away. There is a standoff between incompatible principles, those safeguarding the territorial integrity of states and prohibiting the non-defensive use of force, versus those seeking to protect the human rights of vulnerable populations within these states.

The Commission believes that there is an urgent need to clarify the conditions under which justifiable humanitarian interventions in UN member states can be undertaken in the future. While the sovereignty of states is an essential element of human rights protection itself, sovereignty is frequently abused as a cover and justification both for abuse and for non-compliance with international norms. What is urgently needed is a code of citizenship for nations, which both protects states against unwarranted interference from outside powers, and guarantees their inhabitants remedies when their human rights are systematically abused. This ultimately implies changing the "default setting" of the UN Charter, revising the so-called inviolability of sovereign states so that sovereignty becomes conditional on observance of certain minimal but universal and clear standards of behavior.

The Commission fully appreciates that there is no international consensus among states on these issues, and that such a consensus cannot emerge without a protracted process of debate. The Commission is in no position to define this code of citizenship in detail, but it aligns itself firmly with an international process of free discussion among UN member governments, and among civil society institutions around the world about re-defining the rights and duties of citizens and states in the world community so that ordinary people can count on remedies when their lives are in danger from actions by their own states. Such a code of global citizenship may seem utopian now, but it is becoming ever more urgent to make it a reality.

The Commission has also concluded that additional UN reforms could address the growing gap between legality and legitimacy that always arises in cases of humanitarian intervention. The global credibility of the UN is undermined by the lack of representivity of the current structure of the UN Security Council. Expansion of the UNSC and of the permanent members will be an essential step toward regaining the credibility to maintain an effective role as guardian of world security.

As for humanitarian intervention itself, the Commission's approach has been to specify both the threshold and contextual principles that would justify armed humanitarian intervention when populations are at risk of their lives. The Commission takes it for granted that in all cases intervening parties must first secure the formal consent and approval of the UN Security Council. But there may be cases—and Kosovo was one—in which such permission will not be forthcoming. In this situation, the following principles should guide the determination of national governments as to whether they can or cannot join in a coercive military intervention to stop human rights abuses.

The Commission's recommended framework of principles is divided into two parts. The first suggests threshold principles that must be satisfied in order for any claim of humanitarian intervention to be legitimate. The second puts forward principles that enhance or diminish the *degree* of legitimacy possessed by forceful intervention. These "contextual principles" can be applied either before an intervention in order to determine whether force should be used, or to assess whether an intervention was justifiable. Unless it is apparent from the context that a principle is relevant only to instances of intervention without a UN mandate, these principles should be understood to be capable of application to coercive humanitarian intervention either by the UN, or by a coalition of the willing acting with or without the approval of the UN. It should further be kept in mind that the term "intervention" is not applicable to a situation where a government in power gives its consent to an international presence, given that, in such a situation, no legal problem arises regarding the legitimacy of the humanitarian participation.

## THRESHOLD PRINCIPLES

1  There are two valid triggers of humanitarian intervention. The first is severe violations of international human rights or humanitarian law on a sustained basis. The second is the subjection of a civilian society to great suffering and risk due to the "failure" of their state, which entails the breakdown of governance at the level of the territorial sovereign state.

2  The overriding aim of all phases of the intervention involving the threat and the use of force must be the direct protection of the victimized population.

3  The method of intervention must be reasonably calculated to end the humanitarian catastrophe as rapidly as possible, and must specifically take measures to protect all civilians, to avoid collateral damage to civilian society, and to preclude any secondary punitive or retaliatory action against the target government.

## CONTEXTUAL PRINCIPLES

4  There must be a serious attempt to find a peaceful solution to the conflict. This solution must ensure that the pattern of abuse is terminated in a reliable and sustainable fashion, or that a process of restoring adequate governance is undertaken.

5  Recourse to the UN Security Council, or the lack thereof, is not conclusive. This is the case if approaching the Council fails because of the exercise of a veto by one or more permanent members; or if the failure to have recourse to the UN Security Council is due to the reasonable anticipation of such a veto, where subsequent further appeal to the General Assembly is not practical. Effectively, the latter case suggests that the veto right be superseded by a 2/3 or better majority determination by a "coalition of the willing" that a humanitarian catastrophe is present or imminent.

6 Before military action is taken, lesser measures of mediating and coercive action, including sanctions, embargoes and non-violent methods of peace observation, must have been attempted without success. Further delay must be reasonably deemed to significantly increase the prospect of a humanitarian catastrophe;

7 Recourse to the threat or use of force should not be unilateral, but should enjoy some established collective support that is expressed both by a multilateral process of authorization and the participation of countries in the undertaking;

8 There should not be any formal act of censure or condemnation of the intervention by a principle organ of the United Nations, especially by the International Court of Justice or the UN Security Council.

9 There must be even stricter adherence to the laws of war and international humanitarian law than in standard military operations. This applies to all aspects of the military operation, including any post cease-fire occupation.

10 Territorial or economic goals are illegitimate to justifications for intervention, and there should be a credible willingness on the part of intervening states to withdraw military forces and to end economic coercive measures at the earliest point in time consistent with the humanitarian objectives.

11 After the use of armed force has achieved its objectives, there should be energetic implementation of the humanitarian mission by a sufficient commitment of resources to sustain the population in the target society and to ensure speedy and humane reconstruction of that society in order for the whole population to return to normality. This implies a rejection of prolonged comprehensive or punitive sanctions.

These principles are not designed to let the genie of human rights imperialism out of the bottle, but to prevent a doctrine of intervention from becoming a license for the unprincipled exercise of great power politics.

## FINAL COMMENTS

The Commission takes it for granted that military intervention should always be a strategy of last resort, when all other peaceful means of responding to human rights violations have been exhausted. The Commission also believes that military intervention is a poor second best, and that non-coercive forms of early engagement with societies in the midst of human rights crisis are not only superior to military intervention, but actually might make the resort to force unnecessary. One of the major lessons of Kosovo is that greater early engagement with a region in crisis with a view to preventing conflict is invariably a more effective response than late intervention using force. Early engagement means not only making clear representations to defaulting governments condemning their human rights abuses, but also lending support to democratic and non-violent groups in civil society who are seeking to change government policy in the country concerned. A further lesson of the Kosovo story is that an outside presence — monitors, observers, peace-keeping forces — introduced with the consent of all parties can play an essential role in reducing human rights abuses and in ensuring transparency and assigning responsibility for those that do occur. If the international community had been conscientiously engaged with the developing Kosovo crisis from 1989 onwards, and if the Belgrade government had shown the foresight to internationalize its human rights problem in Kosovo, the whole downward spiral towards a tragic and costly military intervention might have been avoided. This might appear to be a counsel of perfection — and therefore useless — were it not for the fact that governments can now avail themselves of an early warning capability, in the form of human rights monitoring from a host of competent non-governmental organizations (NGOs), who did not exist 25 years ago. If governments were to listen more carefully to the human rights warnings of NGOs and use their political and diplomatic influence on abuser states at an earlier stage, the focus of international intervention could shift towards prevention, with long-term benefits for vulnerable communities everywhere. Yet it must always be remembered that early preventive engagement with countries in the midst of a human rights crisis is only possible when the government in question is prepared to engage. Some regimes, and certainly Serbia is one of them, are much more resistant than others to the internationalization of their problem. In the long run this may have made an eventual coercive intervention unavoidable.

If the intervention was ultimately unavoidable, its legitimacy was and remains questionable in non-Western eyes. In the majority of countries of the world there is a much stronger commitment to the protection of their sovereignty than currently exists in the West.

At a seminar held by the South African Institute of International Affairs and the University of Witwatersrand in cooperation with the Commission on August 25–6, 2000 in Johannesburg, South Africa, former president Nelson Mandela, criticized the double standards in humanitarian intervention (his remarks are published at the beginning of this book), giving the examples of Kosovo, where intervention took place and Sierra Leone, where it did not. However, most African as well as non-African participants emphasized the defense of sovereignty and criticized the new doctrine of humanitarian intervention as a tool of Western powers.

Given the dual history of colonialism and the Cold War, there is widespread concern about Western interventionism. The global power of NATO and specifically the United States creates a feeling of vulnerability in other parts of the world, especially in a case such as Kosovo where NATO claimed a right to bypass the UN Security Council.

At the same time, some aspects of the intervention demonstrated unmistakable partiality in the protection of supposedly universal human rights norms. The international community intervened in Kosovo in 1999, but did not intervene in for example Rwanda. The Commission, composed as it was of citizens of many non-European, non-Western societies, is keenly aware that for non-Europeans the intervention was less a demonstration of moral universalism than further proof that European lives and liberties command a more immediate and substantial response from the international community than non-European ones.

All of these facts point to the need for a further strengthening of the United Nations. These inequities support the case for creating a United Nations standing army, with a robust full-time capability to rescue civilian victims of gross human rights abuses. Such a force would help to equalize the currently unequal distribution of military capability in the humanitarian field. But there are enormous political difficulties in the way of creating such a force and vesting its command and control within the UN system. Until these problems can be overcome, humanitarian intervention will be plagued with legitimacy problems which derive essentially from inequalities in military and political capabilities among UN member states.

If, therefore, we stand back from the Kosovo intervention, it becomes clear that it did not so much create a precedent for intervention elsewhere as raise vital questions about the legitimacy and practicability of the use of military force to defend human rights and humanitarian values in the 21st century. It exposed the limitations of the current international law on the balance between the rights of citizens and the rights of states; it demonstrated the difficulties that ensue when even the most sophisticated and professional military forces are deployed to achieve humanitarian goals; it showed, in the UN administration's difficulties in Kosovo, the immense obstacles that lie in the path of creating multi-ethnic cooperation in societies torn apart by ethnic war. Far from opening up a new era of humanitarian intervention, the Kosovo experience seems, to this Commission at least, to teach a valuable lesson of scepticism and caution. Some-times, and Kosovo is such an instance, the use of military force may become necessary to defend human rights. But the grounds for its use in international law urgently need clarification, and the tactics and rules of engagement for its use need to be improved. Finally, the legitimacy of such use of force will always be contro-versial, and will remain so, so long as we intervene to protect some people's lives but not others.

# ANNEXES

\*

1.
Documentation on Human Rights Violations • 301

2.
Kosovo—Facts and Figures • 319

3.
The Rambouillet Agreement—a Summary • 320

4.
The Ahtisaari-Chernomyrdin Agreement—a Summary • 324

5.
UN Resolution 1244 • 325

6.
The Commission's Work • 331

7.
End notes • 342

8.
Literature on Kosovo and the Crisis • 364

9.
Acronyms • 367

10.
Index • 369

Looking for a future.

During the course of its work, the Independent International Commission asked ABA/CEELI to set up a team of experts to compile data on violations of human rights and humanitarian law before, during and after the NATO campaign. The team was set up and organized by executive director Mark Ellis, ABA/CEELI. The members of the team were Scott Carlsson, director of the Kosovo and War Crimes Documentation Project for ABA/CEELI; Charles Rudnick, assistant dean of International Law at the Chicago-Kent Collage of Law; Randy Clark, the Chicago-Kent Collage of Law; Wendy Betts, assistant director of the Kosovo and War Crimes Documentation Project for ABA/CEELI (hereafter called the Team). The Commission extends its warm thanks to ABA/CEELI and its Team.

This annex is the report of the Team. It sets forth supporting documentation for chapter two, Internal Armed Conflict: February 1998–March 1999; chapter three, International War Supervenes: March 1999–June 1999; and chapter seven, Humanitarian Aid and Media.

The section on *Gathering Evidence* provides a comprehensive list of organizations whose public and non-published information were reviewed by the Team in support of its findings on human rights violations prior, during and after the conflict. Particular focus is placed on the difficulties of obtaining precise quantification of human rights violations prior to NATO's air campaign.

The section on *Violations of Human Rights and Humanitarian Law* in Kosovo, sets out a detailed review of the human rights violations, particularly those perpetrated during the period of March 24, 1999 and June 10, 1999. The section includes a discussion of the methodologies used by the Team in documenting the number of killings during this period.

Finally, in the section on *A Need For A New Approach for Documenting Human Rights Violations*, the Team calls for the coordination of NGOs and government entities in adopting a common and comprehensive set of standards that would enhance human rights data collection. This includes the development of an atrocities documentation database in the form of software that would be shared free of charge with interested parties. This will allow disparate groups to gather data in a format suitable for larger analyses with greater accuracy.

### Gathering Evidence

The Team reviewed either public or non-published information from the following organizations: Albanian Human Rights Group, Albanian Center for Human Rights, The Center—Peace Through Justice, Center for Peace and Tolerance, Council for Defense of Human Rights and Freedoms, Humanitarian Law Center, Kosovo Helsinki Committee, Mother Theresa Society, Serb Helsinki Committee, American Bar Association Central and East European Law Initiative (ABA/CEELI), Amnesty International, Berkeley Center for Human Rights, Committee for the Protection of Journalists, European Roma Rights Center, Human Rights Watch, International Committee of the Red Cross, International Crisis Group, International Organization for Migration, Interrights—International Center for the Legal Protection of Human Rights, IPLS/American Association for the

Advancement of Science, Lawyers Committee for Human Rights, Medicins Sans Frontiers, Physicians for Human Rights (PHR), Society for Threatened Peoples, Federal Republic of Yugoslavia Federal Foreign Ministry, Kosovo Diplomatic Observer Mission (KDOM), Organization for Security and Co-operation in Europe (OSCE)/Kosovo Verification Mission (KVM), United Nations Children's Fund (UNICEF), United Nations High Commissioner for Refugees (UNHCR), United Kingdom Ministry of Defense, US Federal Bureau of Investigation (FBI), Albanian Prosecutor, International Criminal Tribunal for the Former Yugoslavia (ICTY), US Department of State, US Department of Defense. While some relevant organizations did not respond to the Team's requests for information, the Team is confident that the missing data would not alter the clear trends identified in this Chapter.

A wide variety of reports have been issued by many international, governmental, and non-governmental organizations. Most of the information is narrative. However, several organizations conducted statistical studies including, Physicians for Human Rights; American Association for the Advancement of Science (AAAS); Centers for Disease Control; and a cooperative effort between the ABA/CEELI, Human Rights Watch, PHR, AAAS, and the Center for Peace Through Justice.

The findings of these reports support many of the conclusions drawn from the descriptive accounts. However, the statistical studies employed techniques, such as scientific sampling, which added rigor to and countered many of the biases often associated with the collection of narrative information. In addition, the methodology used in these analyses allows for projections as to the scale of abuses Kosovo-wide, whereas most narrative descriptions highlight representative cases.

To address the criticism that much of the information regarding human rights abuses in Kosovo exaggerated the situation, the Team gathered data from a wide variety of sources. While giving weight to all viewpoints, the Team analysis of this information has attempted to avoid relying on materials that contained significantly unsubstantiated claims or which clearly contradicted a preponderance of other reliable evidence. Where differences emerged on specific points among reliable sources, they have been noted in the report and annex.

As noted above, the Team has made a serious effort to collect and analyze all data relevant to human rights violations in Kosovo. During the buildup to the armed conflict, there were a variety of human rights abuses. However, it is important to note here that an accurate and comprehensive tabulation of the number of killings is difficult if not impossible to establish for the period preceding 1998. During this May–August period of escalation, a precise quantification of the violence against civilians is inhibited by the lack of detailed; verified data was not readily available.

With that in mind, the Team also notes that the human rights organizations assembling such data were, by and large, not focusing on statistics as a primary goal. Rather, they were interested in portraying the nature and variety of human rights abuses present to galvanize public opinion. To accomplish this goal, they chose the narrative approach, which puts a human face on the tragedy as it unfolded. This approach is undoubtedly important and useful.

A consistent theme among major human rights monitoring organizations was the need for greater rigor in the collection and presentation of Kosovo data. Beginning in 1997, the International Crisis Group (ICG) commented on the need for more precision in the presentation of human rights data. The ICG noted with regard to a report by CDHRF:

> [O]f the 2263 overall cases of "human rights" violations in the period from July to September 1997, they cite 3 murders, three "discriminations based on language" and 149 "routine checking's." By collating minor and major offenses under the same heading, the statistics fail to give a fair representation of the situation.[1]

Similarly, Amnesty International devoted an entire report to highlighting the need for additional rigor concerning the documentation of the July conflict in Rrahovec/Orahovac.[2] According to Amnesty, the goal of the report was to:

> look[ ] at the conflicting reports, said to be based upon the testimonies of witnesses, by journalists, human rights monitors and others, and the arguments over the truth behind the events in the latter half of July, arguments which have raged in a climate of significant misreporting, unverified published data and deliberate disinformation promoted at times by both sides of the conflict and their supporters.[3]

This Amnesty report, published in August 1998, closed with a series of recommendations, including a specific admonition that the Serb authorities should cooperate with ICTY investigations and prosecutions and permit long-term OSCE observers within Kosovo itself.[4]

In future settings of this type, the Team hopes that both narrative and statistical reporting will be developed more in tandem as suggested at the end of the annex. New technology and the lessons from this conflict give room for optimism.

### Violations of Human Rights and Humanitarian Law in Kosovo During the March 24–June 10 1999 Period

During the course of its work, the Team benefited from the significant assistance of a team of researchers who made an exhaustive effort to compile data on violations of human rights and humanitarian law before, during and after the NATO campaign.[5] One of the most significant aspects of this process was its effort to promote collaboration among the broad variety of international governmental and non-governmental agencies that had compiled such data. The result is, we believe, the single most integrated and thorough report.

What follows is an analysis of narrative evidence of human rights violations in Kosovo based upon data and reports provided to the Team by international, governmental, and non-governmental organizations. Collection of narrative data from sources within Kosovo was difficult during the NATO campaign. After withdrawal of the OSCE-KVM Mission on March 22, 1999, virtually all on-ground monitoring of human rights violations in Kosovo by international governmental organizations and NGOs ceased. Some local NGOs attempted to continue monitoring activities in-country during this period.[6] However, most of the narrative information about human rights violations during the NATO campaign was acquired through interviews with refugees conducted outside of Kosovo at the time, or with returned refugees after the conclusion of the bombing campaign.[7] These interviews were usually conducted in refugee camps or host family homes in Albania, Macedonia, and Fort Dix, New Jersey. Other organizations and governmental agencies relied on post-conflict forensic data,[8] published news reports,[9] independent investigations,[10] or military/intelligence information[11] in evaluating the human rights situation in Kosovo during the NATO air campaign. Still other groups collected potentially relevant data that has not been made public in any form.[12]

The extensive human rights violations[13] in Kosovo during the period of March 24–June 10, 1999 can be grouped into the following ten categories: forced displacement; killings; rape/sexual assault; arbitrary detention and violation of the right to fair trial; destruction, looting, and pillaging of civilian property; human shields and placing civilians at risk of harm; violations of medical neutrality; torture, cruel and inhuman treatment; confiscation of documents; and violations by NATO.

### Forced Displacement

Approximately 863,000 refugees were displaced from Kosovo during the NATO air campaign,[14] leading to an estimated total of "at least one million" persons who left the province from March 1998 through the end of the armed conflict.[15] Most of these refugees ended up in refugee camps or with host families in Albania, Macedonia, Montenegro, and Bosnia and Herzegovina. Approximately 80,000 were transferred to other countries in Europe, the United States, and elsewhere. In addition, over 590,000 became internally displaced persons (IDPs) within Kosovo.[16] Taken together, these figures demonstrate that over 90% of the estimated Kosovar Albanian population in 1998 were displaced from their homes.[17]

The substantial planning and coordination of these mass deportations are illustrated by the fact that before March there were two regular daily trains between Prishtina/ Pristina and the Macedonian border, usually with three carriages each. During deportations there were three to four extra trains were added each day, each with between thirteen to twenty carriages. One report recounts a train with twenty-eight carriages crammed full of people leaving Prishtina/Pristina for Macedonia.[18]

There were a number of challenges in quantifying the exodus. What is clear is that much of the ethnic Albanian population of Kosovo left their homes during the conflict, particularly between March 23 and April 6, 1999.[19] Collection of information from refugees departing Kosovo was complicated by a number of factors including chaotic wartime conditions surrounding their departure, the overwhelmingly sensitive nature of the information requested during refugee interviews, potential bias of refugees reporting information, and after the fact accounts of information that was traumatic and confusing when it occurred.

Despite these factors, a number of organizations did collect extensive amounts of information either from departing refugees, from refugees in camps or with host families outside of Kosovo during the conflict, or from returned refugees in Kosovo after the conflict. These organizations include the OSCE, KVM, KDOM, Physicians for Human Rights, The Lawyers Committee, the Council For Defense of Freedoms, ABA/CEELI in cooperation with The Center for Peace Through Justice (Tirana), UNHCR, and many others. Basic information, including name, home municipality and village, and departure date was collected by customs and border monitoring officials in neighboring Macedonia and Albania.

Two types of findings can be extracted from the gathered information; compilations of narrative information, and statistical conclusions derived from specific analysis of refugee reports. Many organizations provided reports of the first type, compiling narrative information by date, region where events described occurred, and nature of events described.[20] The American Academy for the Advancement of Science (AAAS) produced what is to date the only statistical analysis of information derived from refugee flow data.

The statistical analysis of forced displacements performed by AAAS shed some light on the reasons why the majority of refugees and IDP's left their homes. The report analyzes information gathered by Albanian government officials registering refugees crossing the Albania/Kosovo border at Morine/Morina. Similar information gathered by Macedonian border officials at the Blace border has been requested by the Team, in hopes of assembling a more comprehensive statistical analysis. The AAAS report correlates refugee departure dates and home locations with NATO bomb attacks and locations of mass killings. From this correlation, the report demonstrates that refugee flow patterns do not match NATO bombing or mass killing location patterns, and, therefore, neither bombings nor mass killings directly caused refugee flows. The report then analyzes refugee departure locations and border arrival dates. It finds that refugees departed in three distinct waves from each of three regions of Kosovo. The regularity with which each wave of refugee arrivals builds up and drops off before the next wave begins suggests that the ethnic Albanian population was systematically expelled from with a carefully planned and orchestrated operation.[21]

Narrative information gathered by a number of non-governmental organizations sheds light on the conditions surrounding most refugees' departure form Kosovo. Virtually all of those displaced were Kosovar Albanians who were forced to leave their homes by members of the Yugoslav Armed Forces, Serbian police, or armed paramilitary units.[22] Witnesses from municipalities across the province reported a similar pattern of expulsions.[23] Serb forces would surround a village or town and attack it with grenades or artillery shelling, forcing many people to hide in basements or flee to the surrounding hills. Serb forces would then move into the village, frequently shooting into the air, and forcibly enter any Kosovar Albanian home. Any remaining occupants were threatened and usually given a brief period of time—several minutes or a few hours—within which they had to collect any belongings and leave. This process was usually accompanied by physical abuse, extortion, and killing. Once the village inhabitants were expelled, the Serb forces would loot and burn homes and businesses, and kill livestock. In some locations, such as Prishtine/Pristina, inhabitants were forced to board trains or buses that would transfer them across the border. Others traveled on tractor, car, cart, or on foot. In other cases, people were allowed to take cars and tractors and ordered to follow a prescribed route to the border. Many residents of municipalities east of the main North–South railroad were forced to walk to railway stations and were taken by trains to the Macedonian border.

## Killings

Summary and arbitrary killings became widespread during this period. The international community has not yet reached agreement on the precise number of people killed during the Kosovo conflict. The OSCE has declined to estimate a figure. ICTY Chief Prosecutor Carla Del Ponte reported to the UN Security Council that the ICTY had received reports of 11,000 people killed, with exhumations of 2108 bodies as of November 1999.[24] The US State Department has estimated that 6000 people were killed and buried in mass graves, and puts the total number killed at approximately 10,000.[25]

While there are limited reports of Serbs having been summarily executed by the KLA,[26] the overwhelming number of summary and arbitrary killings were reported to have been carried out by Serb forces against Kosovar Albanians. These killings took many forms. During forced expulsions, Serb forces would sometimes arbitrarily execute a Kosovar Albanian as an "example" in view of other village inhabitants and family members. Also during the forced expulsions, the Serb forces would usually separate the men from the women. In numerous cases, the group of men would be gathered together and killed. People traveling in convoys to the borders after expulsion were similarly victimized. Serb forces would also occasionally surround groups of IDPs hiding in the hills or forests and kill them. Also, children were specifically targeted for murder.[27]

In addition to arbitrary executions, there was apparently a pattern on the part of the Serb forces in which prominent members of Kosovar Albanian society were targeted for killing. One of the most widely reported such killing was of the leading human rights attorney Bajram Kelmendi and his sons. However, other lawyers, doctors, and political leaders were reportedly targeted as well.[28]

Usually the victims of arbitrary and summary killings were shot.[29] There are reports, however, of individual and mass killings carried out by burning people alive in locked homes, and beatings that led to death. In addition, many civilians were killed by the shelling and bombardment of villages, and indiscriminate gunfire by Serb forces.[30]

Reports during the period of the NATO air campaign indicate that Serb forces attempted to minimize evidence of mass killings by destroying and/or exhuming mass graves.[31] There is also evidence that Serb forces would leave dead bodies decomposing in the open for days or weeks, and sometimes prevented Kosovar Albanians from burying the dead in compliance with their religious customs.[32]

ABA/CEELI and the American Association for the Advancement of Science (AAAS) with the cooperation and support of like-minded human rights NGOs, including The Center for Peace Through Justice (Center), Physicians for Human Rights (PHR), and Human Rights Watch (HRW) undertook a statistical analysis of documented accounts of killings during the Kosovo conflict.[33] Each of these organizations conducted extensive interviewing of Kosovar concerning what happened during the conflict. In total, there were 3353 interviews included in the study.

AAAS statisticians estimate that approximately 10,500 Kosovar Albanians were killed between March 20–June 12, 1999. This estimate tracks closely the early numbers suggested by the US Department of State and the ICTY. Furthermore, it is based upon established statistical methods that would be defensible in a court of law.[34]

Because the estimate of 10,500 killed was generated from samples of the population and not the entire population itself, a range must be computed that represents a margin of error for the estimate due to the sampling methods and the estimation technique. Using a 95% confidence interval, AAAS statisticians estimated the number of Kosovar Albanians who were killed during this time period to fall between 7494 and 13,627 (see Figure 1). This confidence interval indicates that if this study were repeated 100 times using different but independent lists of data, one would expect that in 95 of the 100 studies, the estimate would fall in the range 7494–13,627 killings.[35]

This confidence interval is most significant because it establishes that the 10,500 estimated killed is consistent with the findings of other scientific estimates of the number of killings. In September 1999, the Center for Disease Control (CDC) conducted a two-stage cluster survey among the Kosovar Albanian population in Kosovo. They collected retrospective mortality data, including cause of death, for the period from February 1998 to June 1999. Their report concluded that approximately 12,000 Kosovar had died in the conflict with a confidence interval of from 5500 to 18,300.[36] In addition, PHR[37] estimated that there were 9,269 Kosovar Albanians killed in the year prior to interview (the majority of these killings occurred during 1999). A 95% confidence interval for the PHR estimate results in a range of killings between 6911 and 11,627. Note that the ABA/CEELI-AAAS study's estimate of 10,500 fits within the confidence intervals from the PHR and CDC studies, and that both the PHR and CDC estimates. Thus, there is a general convergence of the ABA/AAAS estimate with other scientific estimates.[38]

With this cross comparison, it is now possible to assert that there is strong scientific evidence to support early ICTY and US Department of State estimates. While further data could provide refinements in the overall estimate, the ABA/CEELI-AAAS estimate would likely increase slightly with additional data, as opposed to decrease. Thus, the estimate of 10,500 killed should be viewed in terms of a minimum total number killed.[39]

While an accurate estimate of the total number killed is an important issue with geopolitical consequences, an equally compelling point of inquiry is an examination of the timing of the killings. These findings reveal that a majority of documented killings[40] occurred between late March and mid-April. This timing correlates in substantial part with refugee flows. Building upon past AAAS research on refugee flows, the results of this study support the proposition that there was a systematic campaign conducted against the Kosovar Albanian population.[41]

An analysis of the documented killings by time indicates that there was a peak in killing in late March, followed by another in mid-April. Reports also indicate a smaller, but sustained peak in late April to mid-May, after which the number of documented killings tapered off. This pattern of peaks corresponds with the pattern of refugee flows that occurred during these times. In the AAAS study Policy or Panic (2000), refugee flows out of Kosovo are described as having occurred in three distinct phases: March 24–April 6, April 17–23, and April 24–May 11. During the beginning of each phase, the flow of refugees was relatively light. The number of refugees leaving Kosovo would rise to a high point (a peak, group of peaks, or plateau) during the middle of the phase, before tapering off toward the end of the phase.[42]

By comparing the estimated numbers of people who left each municipality over time to the times when NATO bomb attacks occurred, the AAAS study concludes that only a small fraction of Kosovar Albanians fled Kosovo as a direct result of NATO bombing raids. It also concludes that the mass exodus of refugees from Kosovo occurred in patterns so regular that they must have been coordinated. In the context of qualitative accounts given by refugees, the most likely explanation for the migration is the implementation of a centrally organized campaign to clear at least certain regions of ethnic Albanians.[43]

This last proposition is supported by the timing of reported killings seen in these analyses. Killing patterns mirror refugee flows extremely closely. If killings are a means of intimidation used to facilitate mass forced evictions then refugee flows are a logical result of killings. The close correspondence between the rise and fall of numbers of refugees leaving their homes and reported killings is wholly consistent with that postulate. Furthermore, the fact that the increases in the number of reported killings fluctuate in unison with refugee flows is consistent with the proposition that there was a centrally organized campaign targeting ethnic Albanians.[44]

The patterns of people killed in Kosovo over time and across space are similar to the refugee migration patterns and imply coordination. Narrative reports from refugees interviewed by ABA/CEELI-Center, PHR, and HRW attributed the vast majority of the killings to Yugoslav government and Serb paramilitary forces. This claim is consistent with the information collected by other organizations such as the International Crisis Group[45] and OSCE.[46] In light of the qualitative sources' attribution of a wide range of violations of international humanitarian law to Yugoslav forces, and given the conclusion that patterns of violations suggest central coordination, the ABA-AAAS report concludes that the patterns in the data imply that Yugoslav forces provided the central coordination of the documented violations.[47]

### Rape/Sexual Assault

Occurrences of rape and sexual assault during the air war were merely a continuation of a trend begun by Serb forces a decade earlier. Many local and international NGOs reported cases of rape in the time period prior to the bombing. However, the majority of these incidents have not been corroborated.[48] It is also unclear precisely how many women were raped during the March 24–June 10 time period, primarily because the stigma attached to this form of violence in traditional Albanian society likely led to the underreporting of rape in Kosovo. HRW confirmed 96 documented cases, but note that due to women's reluctance to report sexual assault, this figure represents only a fraction of the actual incidents.[49] The reported cases demonstrate that Serb forces engaged in rape across the province between March 24 and June 10 as described below.

Rapes frequently occurred during forced expulsions, when men and women were separated. Serb forces would occasionally gather the women in a home and subject them to multiple rapes.[50] Sometimes, individual women were taken from their families to a separate home or village, where they were raped and then often returned a few hours later. Serb forces would also rape women or girls in front of their families or in view of the public, either in their homes, outside during expulsions, or on the side of the road during convoys. Some groups of women were reportedly taken to hotels or army camps, where they were held for extended periods and subjected to multiple rapes. The threat of rape was also used by Serb forces as a means of extorting money from the families of women and girls.

### Arbitrary Detention and Violation of Right to a Fair Trial

Arbitrary arrests and detention were widespread in Kosovo during the period of the NATO bombing campaign, particularly following the adoption of an emergency criminal procedure code by the Yugoslav government.[51]

During forced expulsions, when the men and women were usually separated, Serb forces would often detain Kosovar Albanian men of "fighting age," which could range from 14 to 65 years old. Similar treatment would frequently be encountered by men in IDP convoys. Those detained would often be taken to ad hoc detention facilities in schools or factories, or to prisons and jails. The most commonly used facilities were located in Istog/Istok, Lipjan/Lipljan, Vushtrri/Vucitrn, Prishtina/Pristina, Peje/Pec, and Gjakove/Djakovica.

Those detained would frequently be beaten and tortured, and forced to sign documents admitting their involvement with the KLA. After commencement of the NATO air campaign, there was little pretense of providing a fair trial to detainees. The rights of those arrested to appear before a judge were routinely violated.[52] Many were killed, and many were transferred to detention facilities located in Serbia at the conclusion of the NATO air campaign. The ICRC has estimated that approximately 2500 people disappeared during the period of the NATO bombing campaign. Of those, approximately 2000 were seized by Serb forces.[53]

The KLA was also involved in arbitrary detention and arrests of Kosovar Serbs and policemen, and established its own judicial system to handle the detainees. Although it is unclear to what extent this continued during the NATO air campaign, ICRC has estimated that 370 of those still missing from the entire conflict were seized by the KLA.[54]

### Destruction, Looting, and Pillaging of Civilian Property

Attacks on civilian property were one of the defining characteristics of the period of the NATO bombing campaign. The vast majority of refugees reported incidents of destruction of civilian property, looting, or pillaging.[55] Over 500 villages were reported to have experienced burning, with 54 of them identified as having been mostly or entirely destroyed by burning.[56]

The attacks were conducted almost exclusively by Serb forces against Kosovar Albanian property, usually during the forced expulsion process. Sometimes, civilian homes would be destroyed by the shelling that would normally precede the forced expulsion. More often, once the inhabitants of a village had been expelled, Serb forces would move in, pillaging and looting the homes of Kosovar Albanian citizens. There were reports that Serb forces sometimes used lists of wealthy Kosovar Albanians to identify targets for looting.[57] Shops and businesses were almost always targeted. In rural areas, livestock was often killed,[58] and the corpses sometimes placed in wells.[59] Following looting and pillaging, the homes and businesses were often burned. In addition, there were many reports of the Serb forces targeting religious buildings, especially mosques, as well as buildings of historical or communal significance.

The Serb forces would also confiscate personal property, money, and automobiles at police checkpoints or random searches of IDP convoys. They would often extort money by threatening to kill or rape a family member.

### Human Shields and Placing Civilians at Risk of Harm

During the period of the NATO air campaign, Serb forces reportedly used Kosovar Albanians as "human shields" on numerous occasions. Some refugees reported being forced to accompany Serbian military convoys, as deterrence to NATO air attacks.[60] It is also possible that groups of IDPs were forced to remain in the vicinity of potential NATO targets by Serb forces, thereby acting unknowingly as human shields.[61] It is difficult to estimate the precise extent of these activities, in part because the victims may not have been aware of the risk. Moreover, there were incidents in which Serb forces escorted groups of IDPs where the Kosovar Albanians were not being used as human shields.

Reports also include incidents in which Serbian forces compelled Kosovar Albanians to wear Serbian military uniforms, and placed groups of Kosovar Albanians inside likely NATO targets to try to generate civilian casualties. Serb forces also used civilian locations, including private homes, to conceal ammunition, weapons, and military vehicles.

There are reports of detained Kosovar Albanians being forced to conduct labor under dangerous circumstances. At least two incidents include reports of detainees being forced to walk across fields to see if they were mined, resulting in injuries to four Kosovar Albanian men.[62] This does not appear to have been a widespread phenomenon.

### Violations of Medical Neutrality

The period of the NATO air campaign brought with it a broad range of violations of medical neutrality by Serb forces against the Kosovar Albanians. These violations included the expulsion of Kosovar Albanian doctors and patients from hospitals; targeting and murdering of physicians; denial of health care to Kosovar Albanian patients, including those seriously wounded;[63] harassment of Kosovar Albanian physicians; and positioning of military equipment on the roofs or grounds of medical facilities.[64] Serb forces also used hospitals to store ammunition. There were reports that the Serbs destroyed approximately 100 hospitals, clinics, and pharmacies.[65]

### Torture, Cruel and Inhuman Treatment

Torture and ill treatment took place across Kosovo during the period in question. Refugee interviews demonstrate that virtually every municipality experienced incidents in which civilians were deliberately targeted for cruel, inhuman or degrading treatment.[66] These incidents were overwhelmingly reported to have taken place against Kosovar Albanians at the hands of Serb forces.

Victims were most often subjected to this treatment while being held in police stations, prisons, or other detention facilities. During interrogation, detainees would often be beaten, either by hand or with wooden clubs and baseball bats. Electric shocks were administered through electrical cables. Finger and toenails were removed, and needles were placed under finger and toenails. There were reports of knives being used to carve designs into victims' skin.[67] Men would sometimes be beaten in the genital area, and often required to strip naked, both in public and while in detention. Such incidents also took place during forced expulsions, both within private homes and during IDP convoys. Often the ill treatment was accompanied by extortion of money and other valuables.

## Confiscation of Documents

This phase saw an extensive series of incidents in which the identification papers belonging to Kosovar Albanians, including passports, identification cards, or identification papers, were confiscated by Serb forces. The overall number of such incidents is unclear, but one survey of nearly 1200 refugees found that 60% had experienced or observed the confiscation or destruction of identity papers.[68]

Destruction of identification documents usually took place during forced displacement or when IDPs were about to cross borders into Albania or Macedonia. Serb forces also confiscated large numbers of automobile license plates, registration papers, land titles, and other forms of documentation.

## A Need For A New Approach for Documenting Human Rights Violations

Acknowledging the diverse purposes of human rights reporting could promote clarity and effectiveness in the uses of the reports. At least three distinct purposes are at work, and each justifies its own methodology.[69] The first is to obtain in-depth eyewitness accounts of specific human rights violations to provide definitive, reliable, and compelling information for domestic and international audiences. Exemplified by the work of Human Rights Watch, in Kosovo this approach called upon field staff to develop trusting relationships with witnesses and to work quickly and flexibly to enable real-time reporting.

The second is to gather the kind of quantifiable information that can establish the scale and time frame of the human rights violations. In Kosovo, Physicians for Human Rights exemplified this kind of work. In conflict situations with incomplete access to information, this process faces many methodological hurdles. Ensuring the reliability of data aggregated across collecting groups is difficult when the methods for collecting data differ across different groups. Random sampling helps control for bias but it is not always easy to undertake in crisis situations. Cluster surveys and other population-based methodologies require standardization and technical expertise.[70] Testimonial and interview data do not lend them to the same kind of quantification and extrapolation as do measures of refugee flow. Selection bias limits the usefulness of interview data for epidemiological purposes even though such information can be vital in establishing the nature and course of particular human rights violations.

Finally, data can be sought to identify witness testimony to assist the ICTY. This kind of work in Kosovo was exemplified by ABA/CEELI and the International Crisis Group (ICG), which cooperated in developing standard interview forms as guides for interviewers, based on the information required by the ICTY and designed to connect with a database that could absorb information gathered by varied groups in varied settings.[71]

Additional information might be available from humanitarian groups, which inevitably gather stories in the midst of providing aid and protection. However, their neutrality could be compromised if they share their information with human rights reporting efforts. Perhaps improved communications among the two kinds of groups could reduce tensions and promote more constructive points of connection. Similarly, humanitarian groups should cooperate with human rights groups and the ICTY to provide family support and liaison in conjunction with field investigations because such investigations to date lack family support.

Coordinating methods for data collection offers some real benefits for each of these purposes, but there are also compelling reasons to ensure that each group can pursue its own methodology. Coordination, especially if imposed, can be bureaucratizing and inefficient; it can also founder in the face of rivalries and the possessive attitudes of individual groups; it can make operating field missions even more difficult; and it can impair the prospects for timely reportage. Specific coordination among human rights groups, humanitarian groups in the field and the ICTY is crucial, however, so that potential sources of evidence for criminal prosecutions are not tampered with and potential witnesses are not exhausted by repeating their stories to multiple interviewers. For this work, it is vital that information about how to locate the witness in the future be obtained, that a consistent form be used, and that interviewees be respected as potential witnesses in a criminal tribunal. The ICTY itself should clarify its position regarding the use of human rights and humanitarian organizations in gathering information to be used by the Tribunal. Sometimes, it has ignored organizations despite their offers to help and at other times it has attempted to force organizations to hand-over information. Standardization of methods by ICTY investigators would overcome such inconsistencies.

At the same time, rigorous standards developed by some non-governmental groups could inform and improve the forensic field investigations performed for the ICTY.[72] More generally, sharing at least a common vocabulary can strengthen the capacity of human rights reporting efforts to inform the media, the public, governments, and tribunals. Ideally, human rights organizations can find ways to share data sources, use transparent methodologies, and where feasible, coordinate data collection to permit more effective and wide-scale reporting. Improved training of field staff would improve data collection and coordination.[73]

Human rights organizations were a key focal point in the Kosovo conflict. Their reporting proved to be a decisive condition precedent for international intervention. In the slow build up to international intervention, there were numerous reports of large scale human rights abuses, but the international community responded cautiously, linking the degree of involvement to the assembly of quantifiable data of these alleged abuses. Given the debate surrounding the question of intervention generally, it is likely that the international community will continue to insist upon an increasingly sophisticated body of documentation for human rights abuses upon which to base their decisions. The political significance, for instance, of the massacre in Recak/Racak, was greatly magnified due to the speed with which a third party, OSCE-KVM, was able to catalogue and report the events. International resolve to act hardened immediately thereafter.

However, access to better information for the international community to use in determining its response is only one benefit of enhanced human rights data collection methods. There is also a need for more reliable data in order to hold perpetrators responsible for their actions. Statistical studies can be of particular use in this endeavor as they can identify patterns and trends in abuses that may not necessarily be gleaned from anecdotal information alone. Knowledge of these patterns can help to place responsibility on people in authority positions by helping to identify abuses that result from official policies. For example, the American Association for the Advancement of Science (AAAS) study, Policy or Panic, provides a powerful basis for asserting that Yugoslav authorities executed a coherent program of ethnic cleansing, in contradiction to their repeated official statements. Future conflicts would benefit from more of this type of information and analysis.

Comprehensive analyses of the pattern of human rights violations cannot be achieved without the cooperation and participation of the organizations devoted to collecting the data, and we urge the relevant organizations to work together to enable such comprehensive analyses in the future. In addition, where possible, groups pursuing both in-depth interviews and statistical overviews can train their staff also to obtain witness contact information to assist the ICTY. Groups pursuing statistical overviews can and should work together on common standards to promote reliability in aggregation and estimation.

To ensure that such analyses are readily available, it is important for the international community to support NGO efforts to facilitate and expand the collection of this type of information. One promising area involves the development and use of electronic databases. Currently, ABA/CEELI, in collaboration with the Chicago-Kent College of Law and the AAAS, is developing an atrocities documentation database. The design of this database is directly informed from the experience of these organizations in Kosovo and elsewhere. The goal of this database will be to provide a piece of software free of charge that will allow interested NGOs to gather data in a format suitable for statistical processing. Furthermore, the format and structure will allow disparate groups to merge some or all their data to conduct larger analyses with greater accuracy. Ideally, in future conflicts, NGOs could arrive on the scene equipped with the proper software and understanding of the power of collaboration.

## Footnotes

1   International Crisis Group, Kosovo Spring (March. 1998).
2   Amnesty International, Orahovac, July–August 1998, Deaths, Displacement, Detentions: Many Unanswered Questions, in Kosovo A Decade of Unheeded Warnings, (May 1999).
3   Id.
4   Id.
5   The team was assembled by the American Bar Association Central and East European Law Initiative (ABA/CEELI) and the Chicago-Kent College of Law. The materials contained herein represent the findings of researchers and should not be construed to be the view of ABA/CEELI or the Chicago-Kent College of Law, or any of the other contributing organizations.
6   The Humanitarian Law Center, for example, based in Belgrade with an office in Pristina, operated in Pristina sporadically throughout the air campaign.

7 These interviews were conducted by a wide range of organizations, including the Kosovo Verification Mission of the Organization for Security and Co-operation in Europe (OSCE-KVM), the War Crimes Documentation Project of the ABA/CEELI WCDP, Physicians for Human Rights (PHR), Medecins sans Frontieres, and The Center, Peace Through Justice, a coalition of Albanian NGOs.

8 See US State Department, Ethnic Cleansing in Kosovo: An Accounting (1999) (which relies on forensic data collected by the ICTY and KFOR).

9 See, e.g., reports by the Society for Threatened Peoples.

10 See, e.g., reports by Human Rights Watch.

11 See, e.g., US Department of Defense, Kosovo/Operation Allied Force After-Action Report to Congress (2000).

12 The International Committee of the Red Cross and the United Nations High Commissioner for Refugees.

13 The term, "human rights violation", is used here to include violations of international human rights standards, international humanitarian law, and war crimes.

14 UNHCR figures.

15 US State Department, Fact Sheet (1999).

16 UNHCR estimate as of May 1999, cited in OSCE, Kosovo/Kosova As Seen, As Told 98 (1999). The UCK estimate of internally displaced persons was 650,000.

17 US State Department, Ethnic Cleansing in Kosovo: An Accounting 7 (1999); OSCE, Kosovo/Kosova As Seen, As Told ix (1999).

18 OSCE, Kosovo ... p.111

19 AAAS Study: 236,201 of 387,185 that left Kosovo during the conflict via the Morina border left during this time period.

20 The OSCE's two-volume report, "As Seen As Told", is the predominant report based on collected narrative information. Other reports of this type were produced by The US State Department, Physicians for Human Rights, The Lawyers Committee, The Center for Peace and Tolerance, The ABA/CEELI, The Center, Peace Through Justice (Tirana).

21 AAAS, Policy or Panic (2000)

22 Members of the Kosovar Roma population have also been identified by many Kosovar Albanians as collaborators of the Serb forces in a number of human rights violations. These include forced displacement, looting and pillaging, and the transportation and burying of bodies in mass graves. OSCE, Kosovo/Kosova As Seen, As Told 39, ch. 20 (1999).

23 See The Center, Peace Through Justice, in Preliminary Compilation of Data, Report to the Independent International Commission on Kosovo 13 (Apr. 2000) (summarizing refugee interviews story of the attack on the village of Dobrolluk/Dobra Luka), preliminary compilation on file at ABA/CEELI. See also Society for Threatened Peoples, Preliminary Compilation of Data, Report to the Independent International Commission on Kosovo 57 (Apr. 2000) (describing forced expulsions), preliminary compilation on file at ABA/CEELI; US State Department, Ethnic Cleansing in Kosovo: An Accounting 51, 69, 71 (1999); OSCE, Kosovo/Kosova As Seen, As Told ch. 14 (1999). Also, see Amnesty International news service

reports: "FRY — Kosovo: the plight of refugees must not be ignored," April 7, 1999; "Federal Republic of Yugoslavia: Killings in the Kacanik area," April 9, 1999; "Killings and beating on the journey to Albania — Amnesty International reports from the field," April 21, 1999; "Federal Republic of Yugoslavia–Kosovo: Amnesty International reports from the field," April 30, 1999.

24 ICTY Prosecutor Report to the Security Council, November 10, 1999. See also US State Department, Ethnic Cleansing in Kosovo: An Accounting (1999).

25 US State Department, Ethnic Cleansing in Kosovo: An Accounting 3 (1999). Also, the Council for Defense of Human Rights and Freedoms reports more than 7,500 killings between January 1, 1999 and December 31, 1999, and estimates the total number of killings to be at least 11,000.

26 The Society for Threatened Peoples noted that a UCK leader, Jakub Krasniqi, admitted that the UCK carried out some executions. Society for Threatened Peoples, Preliminary Compilation of Data, Report to the Independent International Commission on Kosovo 58 (Apr. 2000), preliminary compilation on file at ABA/CEELI. See also US State Department, Ethnic Cleansing in Kosovo: An Accounting 15 (1999).

27 OSCE, Kosovo/Kosova As Seen, As Told VIII, 38-9 (1999).

28 See Physicians for Human Rights, Preliminary Compilation Of Data, Report to the Independent International Commission on Kosovo 52 (Apr. 2000), preliminary compilation on file at ABA/CEELI. See also OSCE, Kosovo/Kosova As Seen, As Told VIII (1999).

29 The US State Department has estimated that there are approximately 500 mass graves throughout Kosovo. US State Department, Ethnic Cleansing in Kosovo: An Accounting 7 (1999).

30 See The Center, Peace Through Justice, in Preliminary Compilation of Data, Report to the Independent International Commission on Kosovo 11 (Apr. 2000) (A witness saw residents of Malisheve/Malisevo killed by grenade during Serb attack on that town), preliminary compilation on file at ABA/CEELI.

31 US State Department, Ethnic Cleansing in Kosovo: An Accounting 4-5 (1999).

32 OSCE, Kosovo/Kosova As Seen, As Told 42 (1999).

33 ABA/CEELI and AAAS, political killings in Kosova/Kosovo, March–June 1999 (2000).

35 Id. at 8.

36 The Spiegel and Salama study included 1,197 households comprising 8,605 people. From February 1998 through June 1999, 67 (64%) of 105 deaths in the sample population were attributed to war-related trauma, corresponding to 12,000 (95% CI 5,500-18,300) deaths in the total population. The crude mortality rate increased 2·3 times from the pre-conflict level to 0·72 per 1,000 a month. Mortality rates peaked in April 1999 at 3·25 per 1,000 a month, coinciding with an intensification of the Serbian campaign of "ethnic cleansing." Men of military age (15-49 years) and men 50 years and older had the highest age-specific mortality rates from war-related trauma. However, the latter group was more than three times as likely to die of war-related trauma than were men of military age (relative risk 3·2).

37 The data in the PHR Study is distinguishable from the HRW and ABA/CEELI-center

data in that it was collected using statistical sampling methods. The HRW and ABA/CEELI-center data was collected in narrative form without a sampling methodology. Consequently, it had to be "cleaned" and coded to be used in this study.

38 ABA/CEELI and AAAS, supra note 33, at 9.

39 Id at 10.

40 While estimates of total killings are possible, the data is insufficient to make estimates of the total number of people killed in each municipality for each sub-period of the conflict. There are killings that were not reported to the ABA/CEELI-Center, HRW or PHR researchers, and estimates of unreported killings are not included in discussions of the killings breakdown by date and geography.

41 ABA/CEELI and AAAS, supra note 33, at 10–16.

42 Id at 10–12.

43 Id at 11.

44 Id at 15.

45 See, International Crisis Group, Reality Demands: Documenting Violations of International Humanitarian Law in Kosovo (1999).

46 See, OSCE, Kosovo/Kosova as Seen, as Told (1999)

47 ABA/CEELI and AAAS, supra note 33, at 15.

48 Human Rights Watch, Kosovo: Rape as a Weapon of "Ethnic Cleansing" (2000).

49 Human Rights Watch, Kosovo: Rape as a Weapon of "Ethnic Cleansing" (2000). This figure includes cases reported to local and international NGOs and confirmed by HRW.

50 US State Department, Ethnic Cleansing in Kosovo: An Accounting 11 (1999) (citing refugee interviews reporting that women were taken to the Hotel Karagac in Pejë/Pec, and to a Serb army camp near GjakovëDjakovica). Also, Amnesty International reports at least one incident in which Serb forces in a village in Suhareke/Suva Reka detained women and raped them repeatedly over a three-day period. See also OSCE, Kosovo/Kosova As Seen, As Told 58-9 (1999) (included an account in which a group of women were abducted from a village and detained as sexual slaves).

51 Decree on Application of the Law of Criminal Procedure during the State of War, Official Gazette of the Federal Republic of Yugoslavia, vol. VIII no. 21, April 4, 1999, cited by OSCE, Kosovo/Kosova As Seen, As Told 74 (1999).

52 OSCE, Kosovo/Kosova As Seen, As Told 66 (1999). See also Society for Threatened People, Preliminary Compilation of Data, Report to the Independent International Commission on Kosovo 57 (Apr. 2000), preliminary compilation on file at ABA/CEELI.

53 Red Cross Appeals for Information on 3300 Missing From Kosovo Conflict (June 7, 2000) <www.cnn.com>.

54 Red Cross Appeals for Information on 3300 Missing From Kosovo Conflict (June 7, 2000) <www.cnn.com>.

55 The OSCE noted that "of the nearly 800 refugee statements taken by the OSCE-KVM in this period, very few were without mention of such experience." OSCE, Kosovo/ Kosova As Seen, As Told 91 (1999). See also Council for Defense of

Human Rights and Freedoms, Preliminary Compilation of Data, Report to the Independent International Commission on Kosovo 21 (Apr. 2000) (citing more that 41,000 homes and flats destroyed or burned), preliminary compilation on file at ABA/CEELI.

56  US State Department, Ethnic Cleansing in Kosovo: An Accounting 2 (1999).

57  See, e.g., OSCE, Kosovo/Kosova As Seen, As Told 92 (1999) (eyewitness account alleging that a group of Serb civilians and soldiers beat and robbed the interviewee's uncle because they had a list of names that helped them identify the uncle as wealthy.)

58  OSCE, Kosovo/Kosova As Seen, As Told 91 (1999). See also The Center, Peace Through Justice, in Preliminary Compilation of Data, Report to the Independent International Commission on Kosovo 12 (Apr. 2000), preliminary compilation on file at ABA/CEELI.

59  There are also reports that Serb forces used human corpses to poison local water supplies. See, e.g., US State Department, Ethnic Cleansing in Kosovo: An Accounting 28 (1999).

60  US State Department, Ethnic Cleansing in Kosovo: An Accounting 10 (1999).

61  OSCE, Kosovo/Kosova As Seen, As Told 94 (1999) (stating that the restricted movement of IDPs by the Serb forces "had at least the appearance of protecting military objects, sites or personnel.").

62  These incidents occurred in Trnoc/Trnavce and Ferizaj/Urosevac, according to refugee interviews. OSCE, Kosovo/Kosova As Seen, As Told 96 (1999)

63  OSCE, Kosovo/Kosova As Seen, As Told 86 (1999).

64  OSCE, Kosovo/Kosova As Seen, As Told ch.11 (1999); US State Department, Ethnic Cleansing in Kosovo: An Accounting 5 (1999); see also Physicians for Human Rights, in Preliminary Compilation of Data, Report to the Independent International Commission on Kosovo 52 (Apr. 2000), preliminary compilation on file at ABA/CEELI.

65  US State Department, Ethnic Cleansing in Kosovo: An Accounting 12 (1999); see also Physicians for Human Rights, in Preliminary Compilation of Data, Report to the Independent International Commission on Kosovo 51 (Apr. 2000), preliminary compilation on file at ABA/CEELI.

66  OSCE, Kosovo/Kosova As Seen, As Told 47 (1999) ("Examples of torture and ill-treatment can be found in every part of the section of recorded events in Kosovo's municipalities"). See also The Center, Peace Through Justice, in Preliminary Compilation of Data, Report to the Independent International Commission on Kosovo 8 (Apr. 2000), preliminary compilation on file at ABA/CEELI, preliminary compilation on file at ABA/CEELI; Society for Threatened People, in Preliminary Compilation of Data, Report to the Independent International Committee on Kosovo 56 (Apr. 2000), preliminary compilation on file at ABA/CEELI.

67  OSCE, Kosovo/Kosova As Seen, As Told 46 (1999).

68  See Physicians for Human Rights, in Preliminary Compilation of Data, Report to the Independent International Commission on Kosovo 53 (Apr. 2000), preliminary compilation on file at ABA/CEELI.

69 This discussion is informed by an interview with Kenneth Roth, Executive Director, Human Rights Watch, May 16, 2000.

70 See Paul B. Spiegel and Peter Salama, War and Morality in Kosovo, 1998-99: An Epidemiological Testimony, The Lancet, vol. 355, June 24, 2000, at 2204-09.

71 See 15 International Crisis Group, Reality Demands: Documenting Violations of International Humanitarian Law in Kosovo 1999 (2000).

72 Interview with Len Rubenstein, Executive Director, Physicians for Human rights, May 8, 2000.

73 Interview with Diane Paul, formerly with Human Rights Watch, May 12, 2000.

| | |
|---|---|
| Area: | 10,887 square kilometres (12.3% of Serbian Republic) |
| Population 1981 (latest census): | 1.9 million (175/sq.km) |
| | 77.5% Albanians |
| | 13.2 % Serbs |
| | 3.7% (Bosnian and Montenegrin) Muslims |
| | 2.2% Roma |
| | 1.7% Montenegrins |
| | 0.8% Turks |
| | 1.1% Others |
| Population 1998 (est.): | 2.2 million (>200/sq.km) |
| | 90% Albanians |
| | 7% Serbs |
| Languages: | Albanian, Serbian |
| Religions: | Islam, Serbian Orthodox |
| Administrative status: | De jure province in the Serbian republic of the Federal Republic of Yugoslavia (FRY). Enjoyed a certain degree of autonomy within Serbia during 1974–90. |
| | De facto under interim UN administration since June 1999. |
| Province capital: | Prishtina/Pristina (more than 300,000 inhabitants) |
| Other major cities: | Prizren/Prizren (70,000), Peje/Pec (60,000), Mitrovice/Kosovska Mitrovica/ (58,000), Gjakove/Djakovica (46,000), Gjilan/Gnjilane (40,000) |
| Pre-war GDP≤/capita: | USD 400 (est., not accounting for the large informal sector). About one third of the average GDP/capita in FRY. |
| Natural resources: | Lead and zinc (mines at Trepce/Trepca), copper, silver, gold, brown coal |
| Agricultural products: | Wheat, corn |
| Major rivers: | Sitnica, Drini i Bardh/Beli Drim |
| Highest mountain: | Gjeravica, 2522 meters |

This is a summary of the final draft of the proposed Interim Agreement for Peace and Self-Government In Kosovo reached at Rambouillet on the 23 February 1999. The full text is available on a number of internet sites, for example www.usip.org/library/pa/kosovo/kosovo_rambtoc.html. The text contains a framework and eight chapters.

**The framework** establishes equal rights for all citizens in Kosovo, special provisions and legal equality of the national communities, as long as these special provisions do not endanger the rights of other national communities or "the sovereignty and territorial integrity of the Federal Republic of Yugoslavia" (a wording which is used several times in the text). It also provides the right to democratic self-government for citizens in Kosovo. The framework states that use of force in Kosovo shall cease immediately and that all persons have the right to return to their homes and recover their property. It specifies the right of access for international aid agencies. Persons held without charge or "in connection with the conflict" shall be released (within 3 weeks according to Chapter 7) and the work of the International Committee of the Red Cross shall be facilitated. With the exception of persons "having committed serious violations of international humanitarian law" a general amnesty shall be granted and no one shall be prosecuted for crimes related to the conflict. Press freedom shall be ensured.

    **Chapter 1, Constitution**, states that "Kosovo shall govern itself democratically", although FRY will retain authority in the areas of: territorial integrity, maintaining a common market within the Federal Republic of Yugoslavia, monetary policy, defense, foreign policy (although Kosovo shall have authority to conduct foreign relations within its areas of responsibility equivalent to the power provided to Republics under the FRY Constitution), customs, federal taxation, federal elections, and "other areas specified in this Agreement". It outlines the structure of Kosovo's self-government: an Assembly with 120 members (80 elected directly, 40 by national communities according to a certain definition; laws adopted by the Assembly shall not be changed or modified by Federal or Republican authorities), a President of Kosovo elected by the Assembly, a Prime Minister and a Government approved by the Assembly, Administrative Organs where national communities shall be "fairly represented at all levels", a Chief Prosecutor, a court system consisting of a Constitutional Court with judges from all national communities and partly selected from a list drawn up by the President of the European Court of Human Rights, a Supreme Court, District Courts and Communal Courts. The chapter specifies the duties of these organs. It further elaborates on the rights of national communities, including the rights to elect "institutions to administer its affairs in Kosovo", to "preserve and protect their national, cultural, religious, and linguistic identities" in certain specified ways and with reference to "international standards and the Helsinki Final Act", to have access to media and to finance their activities by levying contributions from their members. The chapter further outlines the rights and responsibilities of Kosovo's communes. It also establishes a minimum representation for Kosovo citizens in the Federal Assembly and in the National Assembly of Serbia.

**Chapter 2, Police and Civil Public Security,** stipulates that all law enforcing agencies shall act according to international standards of human rights and due process. It gives OSCE and its implementation mission (see Chapter 5) a central role in monitoring and supervising law enforcement including the right to issue binding directives. Primary responsibility for law enforcement shall lie with communal police units led by communal commanders. Policemen shall be recruited at the local level. A Criminal Justice Administration shall be established, as well as a Police Academy, Criminal Justice Commissions both on a Kosovo-wide and a communal level with the task to review and make recommendations on the work of the police. Federal and Republic law enforcement officials may only act within Kosovo in cases of hot pursuit of a person suspected of committing a serious criminal offence and under certain specified conditions. Serbian Border Police and federal customs officers will remain at international border crossings. The chapter specifies rules for arrest and detention.

**Chapter 3, Conduct and Supervision of Elections,** sets the conditions for elections and requests the OSCE to supervise the preparation and conduct of elections both at a Kosovo-wide and communal level and to establish a Central Elections Commission. The president of this Commission shall decide the timing and order of elections, but the first elections shall be held within nine months of the agreement. The Commission shall adopt rules and regulations for the electoral process. Responsibilities of the Commission are further specified, as well as its composition — a president appointed by the Chairman-in-Office of the OSCE and representatives of all national communities and of political parties in Kosovo.

**Chapter 4, Economic Issues,** starts by establishing that the economy shall function in accordance with free market principles. The chapter lays down principles for tax collection. It outlines responsibilities for the federal authorities in distributing to Kosovo a proportionate share of federal resources, in ensuring the free movement of persons, goods, services and capital to and from Kosovo, and in concluding international contracts for reconstruction projects if required. It deals with the reallocation of ownership and resources in accordance with the changed distribution of power between federal and Kosovo level, and provides for a Claim Settlement Commission to solve disputes in this regard. The chapter also deals in general terms with the framework for humanitarian assistance, reconstruction and economic development. It refers to EC coordination of international assistance, the UNHCR's lead role in humanitarian assistance, and details areas where international assistance shall be provided, e.g. reconstruction of housing and infrastructure, development of the institutional and legislative framework, social welfare and a revival of the local economy.

**Chapter 5, Implementation I,** outlines the structure and process for the civilian implementation of the agreement. The OSCE in cooperation with the European Union are invited to constitute an Implementation Mission (IM). The tasks of the IM shall be to supervise and direct the implementation of civilian aspects of the agreement, to take part in donor meetings, to coordinate the activities of civilian organizations assisting in the implementation, and to carry out functions pertaining to police and security forces. The Chief of the IM shall head a Joint Commission with representatives from Federal and Republic level, from each national community in Kosovo, from the office of the

President of Kosovo and from the Assembly of Kosovo. Joint Councils can also be established "for informal dispute resolution and cooperation" on province level and local level. The chapter repeats the electoral provisions of Chapter 3 and the osce's role. It further requires federal authorities to conduct, under osce supervision, a census of the population in Kosovo. All laws and regulations in effect which are compatible with the agreement shall remain in effect "unless and until replaced by laws or regulations adopted by a competent body". Martial law is revoked.

**Chapter 6, Ombudsman,** stipulates that there shall be an Ombudsman to monitor human rights protection and the rights of members of national communities. The Ombudsman, who shall be nominated by the President of Kosovo from a list of candidates prepared by the President of the European Court of Human Rights and elected for a three-year period by the Assembly, shall not be "a citizen of any State or entity that was a part of the former Yugoslavia, or of any neighbouring State". He or she may act either on his or her own initiative or in response to an allegation of violation of the rights mentioned above, and issue findings in the form of a published report. A procedure is set for how non-compliance with recommendations from the Ombudsman shall be treated.

**Chapter 7, Implementation II,** contains provisions for military implementation. A reference is made to the sovereignty and territorial integrity of the fry. The Chapter starts by inviting the un Security Council to pass a Chapter VII resolution endorsing the chapter, including the creation of a multinational military implementation force (kfor). It invites nato to lead the force while other states may assist. The Parties agree to refrain from all hostilities. The international border of fry shall be demilitarised except for border guards. The chapter specifies how forces present in Kosovo shall be redeployed, withdrawn or demilitarised. Yugoslav army forces shall, within five days, be redeployed to 13 cantons within Kosovo, further specified in an appendix to the chapter. Within 30 days a detailed plan for their withdrawal from Kosovo shall be provided. Within 90 days half the men and material and all "designated offensive assets" shall be withdrawn. By 90 days authority for storage sites shall pass to kfor, and within 180 days all army forces shall be withdrawn. Border guards will be the only remaining Yugoslav forces with restrictions on their numbers, location, tasks and equipment. Yugoslav air and air defence forces shall be withdrawn within ten days. The chapter also has a timetable for the cantonment (at 37 sites, specified in Appendix A) and withdrawal of Yugoslav security forces with a final deadline after one year, which can be extended for up to an additional year by the kfor commander. "Other forces" (basically meaning uck) are required to "refrain from all hostile intent, military training and formations, organization of demonstrations, and any movement in either direction or smuggling across international borders or the boundary between Kosovo and other parts of the fry", not to carry weapons in certain specified areas and to demilitarise on terms to be defined by the kfor commander. Within 5 days they shall abandon all fighting positions and establish weapon storage sites, where within 30 days all larger weapons shall be stored. Within 120 days total demilitarisation shall be completed. 30 days after the entry into force of the agreement, personnel who are not of local origin shall be withdrawn from Kosovo.

Further, the mandate of KFOR is defined, generally to "take all necessary action to help ensure compliance" with the chapter. This includes the right to "respond promptly to any violations and restore compliance, using military force if required". KFOR is also given the task to support other agencies in implementing other parts of the agreement, including the creation of secure conditions. The legal status, rights and obligations of KFOR are specified in an appendix ("B"). These include the obligation to respect FRY laws, exemption from passport and visa regulations, the right to wear uniforms and NATO/national flags, legal immunity, exemption from taxes and duties, free use of infrastructure and communication facilities and the right to hire local personnel. The appendix also contains the clause that "NATO personnel shall enjoy, together with their vehicles, vessels, aircraft, and equipment, free and unrestricted passage and unimpeded access throughout the FRY".

The "sole authority to establish rules and procedures governing command and control of the airspace over Kosovo as well as within a 25 kilometre Mutual Safety Zone" is given to NATO.

A Joint Military Commission, chaired by the KFOR commander or his representative and consisting of a Yugoslav military commander, the Federal and Republican Ministers of Interior, military representatives of other forces, a representative of the Implementation Mission and "other persons as COMKFOR shall determine, including one or more representatives of the Kosovo civilian leadership", shall be established. It shall advise the KFOR commander and address any military complaints, questions, or problems that require resolution by the commander.

**Chapter 8** describes how amendments to the agreement can be made and states that an international meeting shall be convened after three years "to determine a mechanism for a final settlement for Kosovo, on the basis of the will of the people, opinions of relevant authorities, each Party's efforts regarding the implementation of this Agreement, and the Helsinki Final Act". The meeting shall further "undertake a comprehensive assessment of the implementation of this Agreement" and "consider proposals by any Party for additional measures".

## ANNEX 4 ★ THE AHTISAARI-CHERNOMYRDIN AGREEMENT — A SUMMARY

The agreement — or peace plan — was presented on 3 June 1999 to the FRY leadership by Finland's President Martti Ahtisaari, representing the European Union, and Viktor Chernomyrdin, the Russian president's special representative. It was accepted by both the federal government of FRY and the Serbian assembly, and formed the basis for the detailed provisions of UN Security Council Resolution 1244 adopted on 10 June 1999.

It is a short document listing the ten principles necessary for an agreement to be reached. The principles are summarized as follows:

1 An immediate and verifiable end to violence and repression in Kosovo.

2 The rapid withdrawal of military, police and paramilitary forces.

3 An international civil and security presence under the auspices of the UN.

4 Substantial NATO participation in the security presence, under a unified command and control, authorised to establish a safe environment for all people in Kosovo and facilitate the return of all displaced persons and refugees.

5 An interim administration "under which the people of Kosovo can enjoy substantial autonomy within the Federal Republic of Yugoslavia".

6 A small, agreed number ("hundreds, not thousands" according to a footnote) of Yugoslav and Serbian personnel may return to liase with the international mission, to mark/clear minefields and to maintain a presence at Serb patrimonial sites and border crossings.

7 Safe and free return of all refugees and displaced persons under UNHCR supervision.

8 A process towards an interim framework agreement providing for substantial self-government, taking full account of the Rambouillet accords, the principles of FRY sovereignty and the demilitarisation of the UCK.

9 A comprehensive approach to economic development and stabilization of the region, including a stability pact for southeastern Europe.

10 The rapid conclusion of a military-technical agreement, which will specify, among other things, procedures for withdrawal and modalities for personnel returning in accordance with principle 6. The withdrawal shall be completed within seven days; air defence weapons shall be withdrawn within 48 hours outside a 25-kilometre safety zone.

## ANNEX 5 ★ RESOLUTION 1244 (1999)

Adopted by the Security Council at its 4011th meeting, on 10 June 1999

*The Security Council,*

*Bearing in mind* the purposes and principles of the Charter of the United Nations, and the primary responsibility of the Security Council for the maintenance of international peace and security,

*Recalling* its resolutions 1160 (1998) of 31 March 1998, 1199 (1998) of 23 September 1998, 1203 (1998) of 24 October 1998 and 1239 (1999) of 14 May 1999,

*Regretting* that there has not been full compliance with the requirements of these resolutions,

*Determined* to resolve the grave humanitarian situation in Kosovo, Federal Republic of Yugoslavia, and to provide for the safe and free return of all refugees and displaced persons to their homes,

*Condemning* all acts of violence against the Kosovo population as well as all terrorist acts by any party,

*Recalling* the statement made by the Secretary-General on 9 April 1999, expressing concern at the humanitarian tragedy taking place in Kosovo,

*Reaffirming* the right of all refugees and displaced persons to return to their homes in safety,

*Recalling* the jurisdiction and the mandate of the International Tribunal for the Former Yugoslavia,

*Welcoming* the general principles on a political solution to the Kosovo crisis adopted on 6 May 1999 (S/1999/516, annex 1 to this resolution) and welcoming also the acceptance by the Federal Republic of Yugoslavia of the principles set forth in points 1 to 9 of the paper presented in Belgrade on 2 June 1999 (S/1999/ 649, annex 2 to this resolution), and the Federal Republic of Yugoslavia's agreement to that paper,

*Reaffirming* the commitment of all Member States to the sovereignty and territorial integrity of the Federal Republic of Yugoslavia and the other States of the region, as set out in the Helsinki Final Act and annex 2,

*Reaffirming* the call in previous resolutions for substantial autonomy and meaningful self-administration for Kosovo,

*Determining* that the situation in the region continues to constitute a threat to international peace and security,

*Determined* to ensure the safety and security of international personnel and the implementation by all concerned of their responsibilities under the present resolution, and *acting* for these purposes under Chapter VII of the Charter of the United Nations,

*1. Decides* that a political solution to the Kosovo crisis shall be based on the general principles in annex 1 and as further elaborated in the principles and other required elements in annex 2;

*2. Welcomes* the acceptance by the Federal Republic of Yugoslavia of the principles and other required elements referred to in paragraph 1 above, and *demands* the full cooperation of the Federal Republic of Yugoslavia in their rapid implementation;

*3. Demands* in particular that the Federal Republic of Yugoslavia put an immediate and verifiable end to violence and repression in Kosovo, and begin and complete verifiable phased withdrawal from Kosovo of all military, police and paramilitary forces according to a rapid timetable, with which the deployment of the international security presence in Kosovo will be synchronized;

*4. Confirms* that after the withdrawal an agreed number of Yugoslav and Serb military and police personnel will be permitted to return to Kosovo to perform the functions in accordance with annex 2;

*5. Decides* on the deployment in Kosovo, under United Nations auspices, of international civil and security presences, with appropriate equipment and personnel as required, and welcomes the agreement of the Federal Republic of Yugoslavia to such presences;

*6. Requests* the Secretary-General to appoint, in consultation with the Security Council, a Special Representative to control the implementation of the international civil presence, and *further requests* the Secretary-General to instruct his Special Representative to coordinate closely with the international security presence to ensure that both presences operate towards the same goals and in a mutually supportive manner;

*7. Authorizes* Member States and relevant international organizations to establish the international security presence in Kosovo as set out in point 4 of annex 2 with all necessary means to fulfil its responsibilities under paragraph 9 below;

*8. Affirms* the need for the rapid early deployment of effective international civil and security presences to Kosovo, and *demands* that the parties cooperate fully in their deployment;

*9. Decides* that the responsibilities of the international security presence to be deployed and acting in Kosovo will include:

(a) Deterring renewed hostilities, maintaining and where necessary enforcing a ceasefire, and ensuring the withdrawal and preventing the return into Kosovo of Federal and Republic military, police and paramilitary forces, except as provided in point 6 of annex 2;

(b) Demilitarizing the Kosovo Liberation Army (KLA) and other armed Kosovar Albanian groups as required in paragraph 15 below;

(c) Establishing a secure environment in which refugees and displaced persons can return home in safety, the international civil presence can operate, a transitional administration can be established, and humanitarian aid can be delivered;

(d) Ensuring public safety and order until the international civil presence can take responsibility for this task;

(e) Supervising demining until the international civil presence can, as appropriate, take over responsibility for this task;

(f) Supporting, as appropriate, and coordinating closely with the work of the international civil presence;

(g) Conducting border monitoring duties as required;

(h) Ensuring the protection and freedom of movement of itself, the international civil presence, and other international organizations;

*10. Authorizes* the Secretary-General, with the assistance of relevant international organizations, to establish an international civil presence in Kosovo in order to provide an interim administration for Kosovo under which the people of Kosovo can enjoy substantial autonomy within the Federal Republic of Yugoslavia, and which will provide transitional administration while establishing and overseeing the development of provisional democratic self-governing institutions to ensure conditions for a peaceful and normal life for all inhabitants of Kosovo;

*11. Decides* that the main responsibilities of the international civil presence will include:

(a) Promoting the establishment, pending a final settlement, of substantial autonomy and self-government in Kosovo, taking full account of annex 2 and of the Rambouillet accords (S/1999/648);

(b) Performing basic civilian administrative functions where and as long as required;

(c) Organizing and overseeing the development of provisional institutions for democratic and autonomous self-government pending a political settlement, including the holding of elections;

(d) Transferring, as these institutions are established, its administrative responsibilities while overseeing and supporting the consolidation of Kosovo's local provisional institutions and other peace-building activities;

(e) Facilitating a political process designed to determine Kosovo's future status, taking into account the Rambouillet accords (S/1999/648);

(f) In a final stage, overseeing the transfer of authority from Kosovo's provisional institutions to institutions established under a political settlement;

(g) Supporting the reconstruction of key infrastructure and other economic reconstruction;

(h) Supporting, in coordination with international humanitarian organizations, humanitarian and disaster relief aid;

(i) Maintaining civil law and order, including establishing local police forces and meanwhile through the deployment of international police personnel to serve in Kosovo;

(j) Protecting and promoting human rights;

(k) Assuring the safe and unimpeded return of all refugees and displaced persons to their homes in Kosovo;

*12. Emphasizes* the need for coordinated humanitarian relief operations, and for the Federal Republic of Yugoslavia to allow unimpeded access to Kosovo by humanitarian aid organizations and to cooperate with such organizations so as to ensure the fast and effective delivery of international aid;

*13. Encourages* all Member States and international organizations to contribute to economic and social reconstruction as well as to the safe return of refugees and displaced persons, and *emphasizes* in this context the importance of convening an international donors' conference, particularly for the purposes set out in paragraph 11 (g) above, at the earliest possible date;

*14. Demands* full cooperation by all concerned, including the international security presence, with the International Tribunal for the Former Yugoslavia;

*15. Demands* that the KLA and other armed Kosovar Albanian groups end immediately all offensive actions and comply with the requirements for demilitarization as laid down by the head of the international security presence in consultation with the Special Representative of the Secretary-General;

*16. Decides* that the prohibitions imposed by paragraph 8 of resolution 1160 (1998) shall not apply to arms and related *matériel* for the use of the international civil and security presences;

*17. Welcomes* the work in hand in the European Union and other international organizations to develop a comprehensive approach to the economic development and stabilization of the region affected by the Kosovo crisis, including the implementation of a Stability Pact for South Eastern Europe with broad international participation in order to further the promotion of democracy, economic prosperity, stability and regional cooperation;

*18. Demands* that all States in the region cooperate fully in the implementation of all aspects of this resolution;

*19. Decides* that the international civil and security presences are established for an initial period of 12 months, to continue thereafter unless the Security Council decides otherwise;

*20. Requests* the Secretary-General to report to the Council at regular intervals on the implementation of this resolution, including reports from the leaderships of the international civil and security presences, the first reports to be submitted within 30 days of the adoption of this resolution;

*21. Decides* to remain actively seized of the matter.

## Annex 1

Statement by the Chairman on the conclusion of the meeting of the G-8 Foreign Ministers held at the Petersberg Centre on 6 May 1999.

The G-8 Foreign Ministers adopted the following general principles on the political solution to the Kosovo crisis:

- Immediate and verifiable end of violence and repression in Kosovo;
- Withdrawal from Kosovo of military, police and paramilitary forces;
- Deployment in Kosovo of effective international civil and security presences, endorsed and adopted by the United Nations, capable of guaranteeing the achievement of the common objectives;
- Establishment of an interim administration for Kosovo to be decided by the Security Council of the United Nations to ensure conditions for a peaceful and normal life for all inhabitants in Kosovo;
- The safe and free return of all refugees and displaced persons and unimpeded access to Kosovo by humanitarian aid organizations;
- A political process towards the establishment of an interim political framework agreement providing for a substantial self-government for Kosovo, taking full account of the Rambouillet accords and the principles of sovereignty and territorial integrity of the Federal Republic of Yugoslavia and the other countries of the region, and the demilitarization of the KLA;
- Comprehensive approach to the economic development and stabilization of the crisis region.

**Annex 2**

Agreement should be reached on the following principles to move towards a resolution of the Kosovo crisis:

1 An immediate and verifiable end of violence and repression in Kosovo.

2 Verifiable withdrawal from Kosovo of all military, police and paramilitary forces according to a rapid timetable.

3 Deployment in Kosovo under United Nations auspices of effective international civil and security presences, acting as may be decided under Chapter VII of the Charter, capable of guaranteeing the achievement of common objectives.

4 The international security presence with substantial North Atlantic Treaty Organization participation must be deployed under unified command and control and authorized to establish a safe environment for all people in Kosovo and to facilitate the safe return to their homes of all displaced persons and refugees.

5 Establishment of an interim administration for Kosovo as a part of the international civil presence under which the people of Kosovo can enjoy substantial autonomy within the Federal Republic of Yugoslavia, to be decided by the Security Council of the United Nations. The interim administration to provide transitional administration while establishing and overseeing the development of provisional democratic self-governing institutions to ensure conditions for a peaceful and normal life for all inhabitants in Kosovo.

6 After withdrawal, an agreed number of Yugoslav and Serbian personnel will be permitted to return to perform the following functions:

· Liaison with the international civil mission and the international security presence;

· Marking/clearing minefields;

· Maintaining a presence at Serb patrimonial sites;

· Maintaining a presence at key border crossings.

7 Safe and free return of all refugees and displaced persons under the supervision of the Office of the United Nations High Commissioner for Refugees and unimpeded access to Kosovo by humanitarian aid organizations.

8 A political process towards the establishment of an interim political framework agreement providing for substantial self-government for Kosovo, taking full account of the Rambouillet accords and the principles of sovereignty and territorial integrity of the Federal Republic of Yugoslavia and the other countries of the region, and the demilitarization of UCK. Negotiations between the parties for a settlement should not delay or disrupt the establishment of democratic self-governing institutions.

9 A comprehensive approach to the economic development and stabilization of the crisis region. This will include the implementation of a stability pact for South-Eastern Europe with broad international participation in order to further promotion of democracy, economic prosperity, stability and regional cooperation.

10 Suspension of military activity will require acceptance of the principles set forth above in addition to agreement to other, previously identified, required elements, which are specified in the footnote below.1 A military-technical agreement will then be rapidly concluded that would, among other things, specify additional

modalities, including the roles and functions of Yugoslav/Serb personnel in Kosovo:

*Withdrawal*
- Procedures for withdrawals, including the phased, detailed schedule and delineation of a buffer area in Serbia beyond which forces will be withdrawn;

*Returning personnel*
- Equipment associated with returning personnel;
- Terms of reference for their functional responsibilities;
- Timetable for their return;
- Delineation of their geographical areas of operation;
- Rules governing their relationship to the international security presence and the international civil mission.

*Notes*
1  Other required elements:
- A rapid and precise timetable for withdrawals, meaning, e.g., seven days to complete withdrawal and air defence weapons withdrawn outside a 25 kilometre mutual safety zone within 48 hours;
- Return of personnel for the four functions specified above will be under the supervision of the international security presence and will be limited to a small agreed number (hundreds, not thousands);
- Suspension of military activity will occur after the beginning of verifiable withdrawals;
- The discussion and achievement of a military-technical agreement shall not extend the previously determined time for completion of withdrawals.

The Commission members have convened five times. The first meeting was in September 1999 in Stockholm. It was also at this meeting that the Mission Statement was agreed upon.

The second meeting in December 1999 was held in New Your. Prior to this meeting a seminar was hosted and organized by the New York University School of Law.

The Commission's third meeting was held in Budapest where the Central European University and Open Society hosted and organized a seminar.

The fourth meeting was held in Florence at the invitation of the New York University. The fifth and final meeting was held in Johannesburg. The South African Institute for International Affairs and the University of the Witwatersrand hosted and organized a seminar where the opening speaker was Dr. Nelson Mandela.

In addition to the meetings, the Chairman and the Co-chairman have traveled extensively to visit and talk to key players in the conflict. Two meetings were organized in Kosovo.

Meetings have also been organized by e.g. The Carnegie Endowment for International Peace, the American Peace Foundation and the London School of Economics with representatives of neighboring countries as well as NGOs active in Kosovo.

**Mission Statement**

The Independent International Commission on Kosovo will examine key developments prior to, during and after the Kosovo war, including systematic violations of human rights in the region. The Commission will present a detailed, objective analysis of the options that were available to the international community to cope with the crisis. It will focus on the origins of the Kosovo crisis, the diplomatic efforts to end the conflict, the role of the United Nations and Nato´s decision to intervene militarily. It will examine the resulting refugee crisis including the responses of the international community to resolve the crisis. The effect of the conflict on regional and other states will also be examined. Furthermore, the Commission will assess the role of humanitarian workers, NGOs and the media during the Kosovo war. Finally, the Commission will identify the norms of international law and diplomacy brought to the fore by the Kosovo war and the adequacy of present norms and institutions in preventing or responding to comparable crisis in the future.

In addition the Commission will take up: The future status of Kosovo, Lessons learned for Kosovo, and Lessons learned for the future.

**The Members of the Commission**

CHAIRMAN

**Richard Goldstone,** South Africa ★ Born 1938. Graduate from the University of the Witwatersrand 1962 then practiced as an advocate at the Johannesburg Bar. In 1976 appointed Senior Counsel and in 1980 Judge of the Transvaal Supreme Court. In 1989 appointed Judge of the Appellate Division of the Supreme Court and in July 1994 appointed a Justice of the Constitutional Court of South Africa. In 1991–1994 he served as chairperson of South Africa's Commission of Inquiry regarding Public Violence and Intimidation. From August 15, 1994 to September 1996 Chief Prosecutor of the United Nations International Criminal Tribunals for the former Yugoslavia and Rwanda.

CO-CHAIRMAN

**Carl Tham,** Sweden ★ Born 1939. Graduated Stockholm University 1963, in Literature and History. 1969–1976 Secretary General of the Swedish Liberal Party. Member of Parliament 1976 to 1982, State Secretary at the Ministry of Labor 1976–1978, and Minister of Energy 1978–1979. Between 1979 and 1981 Special Advisor to the Minister for Foreign Affairs, and 1981–1982 State Secretary at the Ministry of Foreign Affairs, responsible for Development Assistance. In 1983 Director General of the Swedish Energy Agency, 1985 Director General of SIDA, The Swedish Agency for International Assistance. 1994 to 1998 Minister of Education and Science in the Social Democratic government. At present Secretary General of the Olof Palme International Center. Publications include: The New-Old Left, 1967, 1969; The Universities in the Knowledge Society 1971, The Conditions of Welfare, 1971, The Equality that Disappeared, 1973, The Turn of the Tide, 1994

MEMBERS:

**Grâce d'Almeida,** Benin ★ Grâce d'Almeida, 1951. Degree in Private Law, a Masters in Private Law, and a Diplôme d'Etude Approfondie in African Law from the University of Paris. 1978 Attorney at Law in Benin. 1990 founder and President of the Association of Female Lawyers of Benin. Member of the High Council of the Republic of Benin 1990–1992 Professor of Law since 1993 Attorney General of the Republic of Benin and Vice President of the Superior Council of Judges 1995–1996,1996 Professor of Law at the University of Benin. Research and papers on studies of children's rights in Benin, the establishment of Legal Aid Centers in francophone Africa, and "Structural Impediments to the Improvements of Women's Living Conditions in Benin" (for the World Bank).

**Hanan Ashrawi,** Palestine[1] ★ Hanan Mikhail-Ashrawi born in Nablus, Palestine, on October 8, 1946. B.A. and M.A. in English American University of Beruit, and a Ph.D. in English (Medieval and Comparative Literature) University of Virginia, Charlottesville. Faculty member of Birzeit University in the Israeli-occupied West Bank 1973–1995 Established and chaired the Department of English 1978–1984. Member of the Inifada Political Committee 1988–1993, the Official Spokesperson of the Palestinian Delegation to the Middle East Peace Process 1991–1993, Head of the Preparatory Committee, founder, and Commissioner General of the Palestinian Independent Commission for Citizens Rights 1993–1995. Elected member of the Palestinian Legislative Council in 1996 and served as Minister of Higher Education

---

1    Unfortunately commitment to peace initiatives in the Middle East has prevented Dr Ashwari from participating in more than the first of the Commission's meetings and she is, therefore, not associated with the report.

and Research 1996–1998. 1998 founder and Secretary General of the Palestinian Initiative for the Promotion of Global Dialogue and Democracy "Miftah". Publications include "This Side of Peace", "From Intifada to Independence", and "Contemporary Palestinian Poetry and Fiction".

**Akiko Domoto,** Japan ★ Akiko Domoto born in 1932 in California, and received a BA in Social Sciences from Tokyo Women's Christian College in 1955. From 1959–1989 producer, director, and newscaster for the Tokyo Broadcasting System, producing documentaries such as "The Baby Hotel Series" (1980–1981), and "The Age of Child Slavery" (1989). Received 1991 the Japanese Citizen's Broadcasting League Award, the Conference of Japanese Journalists Award, and the Special Award from the Japanese Cultural Broadcasting Foundation. Member of the House of Councillors of Japan in 1989 and continues to serve in that capacity. Founder of the International Children's Network in 1991 and Japan Women's Global Environment Network International in 1992. 1994 Councillor for IUCN-The World Conservation Union and now serves as an IUCN Regional Councillor and Vice President and President of the Global Legislators Organization for a Balanced Environment (GLOBE). Publications include "The Rise of the Earth's Citizens: Linking NGOs and Politics"(1995) and "Threats of Global Warming to Biological Diversity" (co-editor, 1997).

**Richard Falk,** USA ★ Richard Falk is Albert G. Milbank Professor of International Law and Practice and Professor of Politics and International Affairs at the Woodrow Wilson School, Princeton University, Princeton, New Jersey. Born in New York City on November 13, 1930. B.S. (Economics) from the Wharton School, University of Pennsylvania, in1952, L.L.B.from Yale Law School in 1955, and a J.S.D. Harvard University in 1962. Member of the Independent World Commission on the Oceans; counsel to Ethiopia and Liberia in the Southwest Africa Case before the International Court of Justice; research director of the North American Team in the World Order Models Project; research director of the Coming Global Civilization Project; and is honorary vice president of the American Society of International Law. Major publications include: On Humane Governance: Toward New Global Politics; Revolutionaries and Functionaries; The Promise of World Order; Indefensible Weapons (co-author); Human Rights and State Sovereignty; A Study of Future Worlds; This Endangered Planet; Crimes of War (co-editor); Legal Order in a Violent World; and The Vietnam War and International Law (four volumes, editor and contributor).

**Oleg Grinevsky,** Russia[2] ★ Ambassador Oleg Grinevsky, diplomat, reciding in Monterey Institute of International Studies, USA. Born in Moscow on June 3, 1930 Graduate and post-graduate doctoral studies from the Moscow Institute for International Affairs. Entered diplomatic service 1957. Participating in the negotiations on the Test Ban Treaty of 1963 and the Nuclear Non-Proliferation Treaty of 1968, Served as Deputy Head of the Soviet Delegation to the SALT I and ABM

---

2   Unfortunately ill-heath prevented Ambassador Grinevsky from participating in more than the first of the Commission's meetings and he is not associated with the report.

Negotiations in 1968–1972. Director of the Middle East Department and in 1984 the Head of the Soviet Delegation to the Stockholm Conference on Confidence and Security-building Measures. In 1989 appointed head of the USSR delegation to the Vienna conference on Conventional Armed Forces Reductions in Europe (CFE), and the European Conference on Confidence and Security-building Measures in Vienna. In 1991–1997 Russian Ambassador to Sweden. Publications include two books on the diplomacy of Peter the Great and three books on Soviet foreign policy.

**Michael Ignatieff,** Canada ★ London-based writer, historian and broadcaster. Born in Toronto, Canada in 1947. Doctorate in history at Harvard, senior research fellowship at King's College, Cambridge and visiting professorships and lectureships at St. Antony's College, Oxford, the University of California at Berkeley, Notre Dame, the University of London and the London School of Economics. Publications include a trilogy of books on ethnic war and the dilemmas confronting Western intervention: "Blood and Belonging: Journeys into the New Nationalism" (1993); "The Warrior's Honor: Ethnic War and the Modern Conscience", (1998), and "Virtual War: Kosovo and Beyond" (2000).

**Mary Kaldor,** UK ★ Mary Kaldor was born on March 16, 1946. BA in Politics, Philosophy, and Economics from Oxford in 1967. Scholar at the Stockholm International Peace Research Institute 1967–1969, and Consultant 1969–1971. Since 1969 various positions of Research Fellow, Associate Fellow, and Senior Fellow at the Institute for the Study of International Organisation, the Institute of Development Studies, and the Science Policy Research Unit, University of Sussex. 1999 Director of the Programme on Global Civil Society at the Centre for the Study of Global Governance, London School of Economics. Co-Chair of the Helsinki Citizens Assembly and Governor of the Westminster Foundation for Democracy. Publications include: "The Arms Trade and the Third World" (1971) (principle co-author), "The Imaginary War: Understanding the East-West Conflict" (1990), and "New and Old Wars: Organised Violence in a Global Era" (1999).

**Martha Minow,** USA ★ J.D. from Yale, Ed.M. from Harvard, and A.B. from the University of Michigan. Professor of Law at Harvard Law School. Teacher at Harvard since 1981. Previously law clerk for Justice Thurgood Marshall, and for Judge David Bazelon. On the boards of many non-profit organizations and foundations, including Facing History and Ourselves, a teacher-training and curriculum development organization that seeks to prevent intergroup conflict and hatred. Publications include "Between Vengeance and Forgiveness: Facing History after Genocide and Mass Violence" (Beacon Press, 1998); "Not Only for Myself: Identity, Politics, and Law" (The New Press, 1997); and "Making All the Difference: Inclusion, Exclusion, and American Law" (Cornell University Press, 1990).

**Jacques Rupnik,** France ★ Born on November 21, 1950. History at the Sorbonne and politics at the Institut d'Etudes Politiques de Paris, M of A in Soviet Studies from Harvard University (1974), and Doctorat en Histoire in the History of International Relations from the University of Paris (1978). Research Associate at the Russian Research Center at Harvard University 1974–1975, specialist in Eastern Europe at the BBC World Service 1977–1982, and Director of Research at the Fondation nationale des sciences politiques (Centre d'études et de recherches internationales) and Professor at the Institut d'Etudes Politiques de Paris 1982–1996. Executive Director of the International Commission for the Balkans at the Carnegie Endowment for International Peace 1995–1996. Visiting Professor at the College of Europe in Bruges and one of the editors of the quarterly Transeuropéennes. 1990–1992 advisor to Czech President Vaclav Havel. Publications include "Histoire du parti communiste tché-coslovaque" (1981), "The Other Europe" (1989), "De Sarajevo à Sarajevo: l'échec you-gloslave" (1992), "Les Balkans, paysage après la bataille" (1996); He was a drafter of "Unfinished Peace" (1996).

**Theo Sommer,** Germany ★ Born in 1930 in Constance, Germany. Studied History, Political Science and International Relations in Sweden, at Tübingen University and the University of Chicago; PhD thesis on "Germany and Japan be-tween the powers 1935–1940" (published 1962). In 1960 participant in Henry Kissinger's International Summer Seminar, at Harvard University. Between 1967 and 1970 Reader in Political Science at the University of Hamburg. Appointed Foreign Editor of "Die Zeit" in 1958, and became Deputy Editor in 1968. Chief of the Planning Staff at the Ministry of Defense in 1969-70; Returned to "Die Zeit" as Editor-in-Chief in 1973 and became Publisher on October, 1 1992. Writes mainly on international affairs, strategic questions, German and European problems. Publications include "The Chinese Card" (1979), "Changing Alliance?" (1982), "Look Back Into the Future" (1984), "Journey to the Other Germany" (1986).

**Jan Urban,** the Czech Republic ★ Born in Hradec Kralove, Czechoslovakia on March 27, 1951. Graduated 1974 in history and philosophy from Charles University in Prague. One of the founders of the only international network connecting dissident journalists at that time in Czechoslovakia, Poland, Soviet Union, Hungary, Yugoslavia and the German Democratic Republic. One of the founders "Lidove noviny" in 1987. Active in the Civic Forum movement that brought the change of the regime in November 1989 and served as its leader during the last four months before the first free elections in June, 1990. Left political functions one day after the victorious elec-tions. Visiting Fellow at the New School for Social Research in New York in 1990 and at the Cambridge University Immanuel College Global Security Programme in 1992, as well as German Marshall Fund Visiting Professor in 1994.

ASSISTING THE COMMISSION:

The American Bar Association Central and East European Law Initiative (ABA/CEELI) generously seconded its director, Mark Ellis, to act as the legal advisor of the Commission. Mr. Ellis will as of January 1, 2001, take up the post of Director for the International Bar Association in London. The Director of the Commission Secretariat is Pia Övelius, a senior member of the office of the Swedish Prime Minister who was generously seconded by the Prime Minister to assist the Commission. The media and public relations work for the Commission was directed by Anki Wood, a freelance journalist. The final report was edited by Liam Mahony, a lecturer at Princeton University. The Commission would like extend a special thanks to Liam Mahony who, at a very short notice agreed to undertake the editing of the full report.

In Johannesburg, the researchers in the chambers of Justice Goldstone at the Constitutional Court of South Africa assisted with administrative work of the Commission and with the editing of this report — Nicole Fritz, Estelle Dehon and Tung Chan. Statistical team in Washington: Scott Carlsson, Director of the Kosovo and War Crimes Documentation Project for ABA/CEELI; Charles Rudnick, Assistant Dean for International Law at the Chicago-Kent Collage of Law; Randy Clark, the Chicago-Kent Collage of Law; Wendy Betts, Assistant Director of the Kosovo and War Crimes Documentation Project for ABA/CEELI.

The Commission extends its warm thanks to all these people and others who have made this report possible.

FINANCIAL AND OTHER CONTRIBUTIONS

A large financial contribution came from the Government of Sweden. This has been complemented by financial contributions from the Government of Canada, the Ford Foundation, the Carnegie Foundation, the Sasakawa Peace Foundation. Contributions by way of hosting Commission meetings and holding seminars for the Commission have been made by the Swedish Cooperative Union, New York University School of Law, the Carnegie Endowment for Peace, the Soros Foundation, the Central European University, ABA/CEELI, the United States institute for Peace, the University of the Witwatersrand, and South African Institue of International Affairs

FOLLOW UP

After the presentation of the report to the Secretary General of the United Nations, Mr. Kofi Annan on 23 October 2000 and to Prime Minister Göran Persson on 24 October 2000, the Commission will organize further seminars to discuss the reception of the report. The Commission's work formally ends on 31 December 2000.

SPECIAL CONTRIBUTIONS BY

The Commission expresses its special thanks to a number of persons that have provided help, advice and/or reports to the Commission.

Professor Diane Orentlicher, Princeton University, USA; George Wood, webmaster; Magnus Engelbrektsson, researcher; Head of Section Jan Lundin, Swedish foreign Office; Oleg Levitin, Kings College London; Susanne Woodward, senior fellow Kings College London; second secretary Jonas Weiss, Swedish Embassy in Moscow; vice-president Ildikó Nagy Moran, Central European University, Budapest; Ken Kidd, New York University, School of Law; Tracey Mitchell-Björkman, designer of logotype; univ. lektor Inger Österdahl, Uppsala University, Sweden; Cindy Thermoshusien and Laura Samartin who assisted senator Domoto, Mari Peterson, free-lance journalist, Sue Hughes, copy editor and Josh Kaldor-Robinson.

CONSULTATIONS:

Fisnik Abrashi, BBC, Kosovo

Ljubica Z. Acevska, Macedonian ambassador, USA

Mr. Erahman Ahmeti, Rezalla/Rezala, Kosovo

Svedie Ahmeti, Committee for the Protection of Women and Children, Kosovo

Martti Ahtisaari, President, Finland

Mr Yasushi Akashi, Japan Centre for Preventative Diplomacy

Sven Alkalaj, Bosnia-Herzegovinian ambassador, USA

Dr. Abdullah Al Ashaal, Visiting scholar, NYU School of Law

Kerstin Asp-Johnson, Swedish ambassador, Finland

Mr Lloyd Axworthy, Foreign Minister of Canada

Yll Bajraktari, The Forum, Kosovo

Patrick Ball, AAAS, USA

Nina Bang-Jensen, Coalition for International Justice

Göran Berg, Swedish ambassador, Italy

Håkan Berggren, Swedish ambassador, Denmark

Mats Bergquist, Swedish ambassador, UK

Isuf Berisha, KFOS

Örjan Berner, Swedish ambassador, France

Sidney Blumenthal, the White House, USA

Tiziana Boari, Giornalista, Italy

Alexander Boraine, New York University School of Law, South Africa

Tony Borden, Institute of War and Peace Reproting (IWPR)

Mark Bowden, Foreign and Commonwealth Office, uk

Jan Braathu, Ministry for Foreign Affairs, Norway

Frau Sandra Breka, Aspen Institute Berlin

Alice Brown, Ford Foundation

Ambassador Peter Brückner, Royal Danish Embassy, Japan

Barbara Burns, Inside the Law

Petrit Bushati, Albanian ambassdor, USA

Filoretta Bytygi, Lawyer, Kosovo

Vincenzo Camporini, Capo Terzo Reparto, Italy

Richard Caplan, Jesus College, Oxford, UK

Andrea Carcano, UN War Crimes Project

Thomas Carothers, Carnegie Endowment for International Peace

Viktor S. Chernomyrdin, Member of the State Duma, Russian Federation

Vladimir A. Chizhov, Ministry of Foreign Affairs of the Russian Federation

Flemming Christensen, Swed. Bat. KFOR, Sweden

Svend Aage Christensen, Director, DUPI, Denmark

Derek Christian, South African Navy

Jonathan Cima, UN War Crimes Project

Counsellor Gregory Cooney, Canadian Embassy, Japan

K. Coster , Wits University, South Africa

Jock Covey, dep. Head of UNMIK

Jeff Crisp, UNHCR

David Crocker, Univ. of Maryland

Hans Dahlgren, ambassador, Swedish Delegation to the UN

Lars Danielsson, State-Secretary, Prime-minister's office in Sweden

David Dasic, Trade Mission to the USA, Republic of Montenegro

Maarta Dassù, CeSPI, Italy

Mr. Umer Delilu, Abrija/Obrija, Kosovo

Betula Destani, Historian, Kosovo

Philip Dimitrov, Bulgarian ambassador, USA

Joly Dixon, Deputy Special Representative, UNMIK

Ambassador Jim Dobbins, State department, United States of America

Senator Robert J. Dole, Washington

Ambassador Mitsuro Donowaki, Special Assistant to the Minster of Foreign Affairs, Japan

Prof. Norman Dorsen, NYU School of Law, USA

Vjosa Dreshaj, The Forum, Kosovo

John Dugard, University of Leiden, the Netherlands

Rolf Ekéus, Swedish ambassador, the United States of America

H.E.E. Eliades, Cyprus High Commission, South Africa

Glynne Evans, Foreign and Commonwealth Office, UK

Can Everts, Head of Mission, OSCE

Peter Fabricius, Independent Foreign Service, South Africa

Mient Faber, IKV

Nicolo Figa-Talamanca, UN War Crimes Project

Jacques Forster, Vice President, International Committee of the Red Cross

William Friis-Möller, Ambassador of Denmark to Sweden

Dr Akiko Fukushima, International Cooperation Department, NIRA

Senior Deputy Director Yoshitaro Fuwa, FASID

H.E. Naela Gabr, Egyptian Ambassador to South Africa

V Dianna Games, Business in Africa

Mircea Geoana, Rumanian ambassador, USA

Mario Giro, Communauté de Sant'Egidio, Italy

Misha Glenny, journalist, historian, UK

Vladimir Gligorov, Vienna Institute for International Economic Studies

Ettore Greco, Instituto Affari Internazionali, Italy

Ms. Janne Haaland-Matalry, the State Secretary of the Norwegian Foreign Ministry

Deputy Foreign Minister, Peter Hain, the UK

Jeremy Harding, London Review of Books

Andrew Harper, UNHCR

Florence Hartmann, France

Pierre Hassner, Institut Francis des Relations Internationales

Amb. Jorge Heine, University of Chile

Mats Hellström, Swedish ambassador, Germany

Jeffry Herbst, Princeton University, USA

Phillip Heymann, Harvard Law School, USA

Sven Hirdman, Swedish ambassador, the Russian Federation

Kossar Hjasein, UN War Crimes Project

Quinton Hoare, The Bosnian Institute, UK

Captain François Hugo, Defense Secretariat, South Africa

Connie Huntsman, ABA/CEELI, USA

Anna Husarska, journalist, CERI, France

Ylber Hysa, Koha Ditore, Kosovo

Wilbert J.E.M.van Hövell tot Westerflier, Deputy to DSRCG, UNHCR, Kosovo

Olatokunbo Ige, International Commission of Jurists

Gordana Ignic, IWPR

Dr Masako Ikegami, Uppsala University, Sweden

Adesola Ilemobade, Wits University, South Africa

Wolfgang Ischinger, State Secretary, Foreign Ministry, Germany

Leonid Ivachov, Ministry of Defense, the Russian Federation

Pierre Jacquet, Institut Francais des relations internationales

Bianca Jagger

Sanna Johnsson, Olof Palme International Center

Lynn Jones, psychiatrist working in Kosovo and Bosnia

Emyr Jones-Perry, Political Director, Foreign and Commonwealth Office, UK

Dr. Chantal de Jonge Oudraat, Carnegie Endowment for Peace

Claude Kabemba, Centre for Policy Studies

K. Kak, Institue for Defense Studies and Analyses

Natasha Kandic, Humanitarian Law Center, Serbia and Kosovo

Jan Kickert, political Adv. to Mr. Kouchner, UNMIK

Prof. Benedict Kingbury, NYU School of Law, USA

Ms Miho Kitshitani, JEN Japan Emergency NGOS

Ms Eri Komukai, Environment, WID and Other Global Division, Planning Department, JICA

Dr. Bernard Kouchner, UN Chief Administrator in Kosovo

O. Kovalchik, Charge d'Affairs at the Russian Embassy, South Africa

Ms Mariko Koyatsu, The Japan Institute of International Affairs

Garentina Kraja, The Forum, Kosovo

Jakup Krasniqi, Secretary General of the Party of Democratic Prosperity

Justice Kriegler, Constitutional Court, South Africa

Radha Kumar, Council on Foreign relations

Director Satoru Kurosawa, Environment, WID and Other Global Division, Planning Department, JICA

Anthony C. Land, UNHCR, Kosovo

Colonel Robert Laloux, Belgian Embassy, South Africa

Frédéric Baleine de Laurens, Directeur général adjoint, Ministere des Affaries Etrangeres

Alison Lazarus, Center for Conflict Resolution, South Africa

Dominique Lebastard, French Trade Commission

Stefan Lehne, Council of the European Union

Allan Little, BBC, UK

Edward Llewellyn, European Commission, Brussels

Eckard Lohse, Frankfurter Allgemeine Zeitung, Germany

George Lugalambi, Makerere University

Vladimir P. Lukin, Deputy Speaker of the State Duma, Russian Federation

Faik and Ragip Luta, BBS World Service

Björn Lyrvall, Swedish Foreign Office

Shyqri Malaj, Director of School, Rezalla/Rezala, Kosovo

Noel Malcolm, historian, UK

Eddie Maluleka, Constitutional Court, South Africa

Giulio Marcon, Italian Consortium of Solidarity, Italy

Luciano Massetti, Italian Joint Operations Command

Jessica Mathews, Carnegie Endowment for International Peace

Errol P. Mendes, Director, University of Ottawa, Canada

Gian Giacomo Migone, Senato della Repubblica, Italy

Paul Miller, Amnesty International

Greg Mills, SAIIA, South Africa

Michael Montgomery

Pascale Moreau, UNHCR, Kosovo

Prof. Madeleine H. Morris, Duke University, USA

Rudina Mullahi, Counselor of the Albanian Embassy, USA

Aleksey Nikiforov, Ambassador of the Russian Federation, Sweden

Sgaren Naidoo, Institute for Global Dialogue, South Africa

Mr Jim Nickel, Canadian Embassy, Japan

Aleksey Nikiforov, Ambassador of the Russian Federation, Sweden

Jill O'Hara, UN War Crimes Project

Andreas Gordon O'Shea, University of Durban-Westville, South Africa

Rory O'Sullivan, the World Bank, Brussels

Jane Olson

H. Onoria, Makerere Univesity

Prof Ryo Oshiba, Professor, Hitotsubashi University

Joseph Otteh, Access to justice

Mr Toshiro Ozawa, The Japan Institute of International Affairs

Patsy Palmer, ABA/CEELI,USA

Michelle Parlevliet, Center for Conflict Resolution, South Africa

Marina Pavlova-Silvanskaya, Carnegie endowment for International Peace, the Russian Federation

Martina Pavolva-Silvanskaya, Carnegie Moscow Center

Executive Director Lulzim Peci, the Kosovar Civil Society Foundation.

Sören Jessen Pedersen, Assistant High commissioner, UNHCR

Bo Pellnäs, Sweden

Friis Arne Petersen, Director, Ministry for Foreign Affairs, Denmark

Nadan Petrovic, Italian Consortium of Solidarity, Italy

Professor James Pettifer, UK

Anu Pillay, African Women's Anti War Coaliton

Misha Piro, Open Society Foundation for Albania

Barney Pityana, Human rights Commisison, South Africa

Carla Del Ponte, Chief Prosecutor of the UN War Crimes Tribunal for the former Yugoslavia

Helen Popovic, Libération, France

Dr Aleksander Prlja, Ambassador of the FR of Yugoslavia to Sweden

Nebi Qena, The Forum, Kosovo

Emmanuela C. del Re, European University Institute, Italy

Klaus Reinhardt, General, KFOR

Peter Ricketts, Director for International Security at the Foreign and Commonwealth Office, UK

Lord Robertson, Secretary General of NATO

Mary Robinson, High Commissioner for Human Rights, UNHCR

Jeremy Root, Inside the Law

Herr John Roper, Prof. Univ. of Birmingham, UK

General Len le Roux, Defence Secretariat, South Africa

Dr Ibrahim Rugova, LDK (Democratic League of Kosova), Kosovo

Martin Rupiya, Univesrity of Zimbabwe

Bonaventure Rutinwa, Dar es Salaam University

Robert Rydberg, Swedish Foreign Office

Albie Sachs, Constitutional Court, South Africa

Father Sava, Serb Orthodox Monastery in Ulpiana/Gracanica, Kosovo

Prof. Michael Scharf, New England Law School

Albrecht Schnabel, UN University

Maxie Schoeman, RAU

Robert Schrire, University of Cape Town, South Africa

Ms Sachiko Seya, FASID, International Development Research Institute, Japan

John Sefton, NYU School of Law, USA

Blerim Shala, Editor "Zeri", Kosovo

William Shapcott, Council of the European Union

Director Takashi Shinozuka, International Cooperation Department, NIRA

Deputy Director-General Takahiro Shinyo, MOFA, Japan

Amananth Singh, Financial Mail

Laura Silber, Financial Times, USA

Betsie Smith, Department of Foreign Affairs, South Africa

Stephen Smith, American Radio Works

Hussein Solomon, University of Pretoria, South Africa

Jonathan Steele, The Guardian, UK

Michael Steiner, Foreign Policy Advisor to the Bundeskansler, Germany

Frau Dr. Constanze Stelzenmüller, Die Zeit, Germany

John Stremlau, Wits University, South Africa

William A. Stuebner, United States Institute of Peace

Ms Megumi Suezawa, Research Fellow, The Japan Institute of International Affairs

Veton Surroi, Koha Ditore, Kosovo

Roland Svensson, Managing Director, the Swedish Cooperative Union, Sweden

Dr Kazuo Takahashi, FASID, International Development Research Institute

Terence Taylor, Assistant Director, the International Institute for Strategic Studies

Hashim Thaqi, chairman of the PPDK party, Kosovo

Roberto Toscano, Secreatry General, Ministero Affari Esteri, Italy

Kim Traavik, director, Ministry for Foreign Affairs, Norway

Mr Susumu Ueda, Central and Eastern Division, MOFA

Magnus Valquist, Swedish ambassador, Norway

Ivan Vejvoda, fund for an Open Society, Belgrade, FRY

Mr Masato Watanabe, Central and Eastern Division, MOFA

Rob de Wijk, Clingendael, Holland

Martin Woollacott, Guardian, Foreign Affairs, UK

Jeta Xharra, student, Kosovo

Tetsuya Yamada, Japan

Ditron Zhubi, The Forum, Kosovo

Jeremy Zucker, Journal of International Law and Politics

Miomir Zuzul, Croatian ambassador, USA

*The Commission apologizes for any oversight or inaccuracy in this list.*

## Preface

1  There is also a summary document prepared by the International Committee of the Red Cross under the title *Fundamental Rules of International Humanitarian Law Applicable in Armed Conflicts*. These texts can all be found in Burns Weston & others, *Documents: International Law and World Order* (3rd ed. 1997); the direct documentary references would be more professionally correct.

## 1. The Origins of the Kosovo Crisis

1  Rankovic was a Stalinist rather than a nationalist who strongly favored centralization.

2  See interviews in Julie Mertus, Kosovo: *How Myths and Truths Started a War*, University of California Press, 1999.

3  According to official statistics more than 700 people had been arrested by 1982 for "anti-Yugoslav, Albanian nationalist-irredentist activity" and 320 had been put on trial. By October 1983, some 595 individuals had been sentenced to prison in connection with the demonstrations. Quoted in Mertus

4  GMP or Gross Material Product is based on manufacturing and agricultural output. GNP also includes services.

5  See Gramoz Pashko, "Kosovo: Facing Dramatic Economic Decline", in Thanos Vermemies and Evangelos Kofos, *Kosovo: Avoiding Another Balkan War*, ELIAMEP, University of Athens, 1998.

6  The survey results can be found in Marina Blagojevic, "Kosovo: In/Visible Civil War" in Veremies and Kofos, op.cit. Interviews undertaken by Mertus, indicate similar experiences.

7  Later, Martinovic confessed to the commander of the garrison where he worked as a clerk that the wound was self-inflicted, an act of "self-satisfaction", and this was the view of the Prishtina/Pristina clinic where he was first treated. However, the authorities later gave conflicting opinions and the case was never decisively established. Martinovic again changed his story and claimed that his confession had been forced, whereupon the commander of the garrison, himself a Serb, sued him for libel, (see Mertus). Serb nationalists seized upon the case as evidence of the "genocide" theory and as a metaphor for all injustices meted out to Serbs in history. In particular, a parallel was drawn with the Turkish practice of impalement described by Ivo Andric in his book *Bridge over Drina*. A book about the case sold 50,000 copies. As Julie Mertus has put it, "The power of the Martinovic case lay in its ability to invoke the primary imagery of Serbian oppression: the Turkish brutality of impaling, Jasenovac (the wartime concentration camp where Serbs and Jews were killed), 'for sale' sign on the property of Kosovo Serbs" (Mertus, p.112). Mertus quotes an Albanian woman as saying: "I am ashamed to think that Albanians could have done this. The expert testimony conflicted so we don't know what happened for sure. Where I take offence is that Serbs automatically accused all of us of being there with the perpetrators. It was as if we had all done the attack" (Mertus, p.106).

8   Quoted in Tim Judah, *The Serbs: History, Myth and the Destruction of Yugoslavia,* Yale University Press, 1997, p.159.

9   Mertus, p.109.

10  Quoted in Noel Malcolm, *Kosovo: A Short History,* papermac, London, 1998.

11  Quoted in Mertus, p.185

12  Mertus, p179.

13  See International Helsinki Federation for Human Rights, IHF Special Report: *The Past 10 Years in Kosovo: Autonomy, Colonization, Genocide,* July 1999.

14  For example, in Prizren/Prizren, "League of Prizren" street became "King Peter the Liberator" street. The Museum of the League of Prizren, which had been declared a world heritage site by UNESCO, was looted and turned into a hostel for Serb refugees from Croatia. See International Crisis Group (March 1998) Kosovo Spring.

15  Humanitarian Law Center, *Human Rights 1991–5,* 1997 p.61.

16  Judy Dempsey, "Serbian authorities step up pressure in Kosovo", Financial Times, July 13, 1992, p.3.

17  Amnesty International has published reports dated as early as 1981. The International Helsinki Federation and the Council for Defense of Human Rights and Freedoms began monitoring the situation in 1989, Human Rights Watch in 1990, OSCE in 1991, United Nations in 1992, and the Humanitarian Law Center in 1993.

18  Some 7000 Albanian schoolchildren became ill. There was no definitive account of what happened to the children, but most experts seem to accept the theory of mass hysteria; there have been similar occurrences in situations of heightened tension.

19  Quoted in Tim Judah, "Kosovo's Road to War", Survival, Summer 1999, p.120.

20  Andrew March and Rudra Sil, The "Republic of Kosova" (1989–1998) and the Resolution of Ethno-Separatist Conflict in the Post-Cold War Era, University of Pennsylvania Press, Forthcoming.

21  Ibid.

22  Interview with Sonja Licht, Director of the Open Society Foundation, Belgrade.

23  Shkelsen Maliqi, *Kosovo: Separate Worlds,* MM, Pristina, 1998.

24  Pashko, Gramoz (1998) *"Kosovo: Facing Dramatic Economic Decline"* in Veremis and Kofos.

25  Quoted in Mertus, p. 204.

26  Quoted in Stephan Troebst, *Conflict in Kosovo: Failure of Prevention, an Analytical Documentation,* European Centre for Minority Issues, Flemsburg, 1999, p. 27.

27  Quoted in Tim Judah, *Kosovo: War and Revenge,* Yale University Press, 2000, pp. 79–80. Revealingly, presumably because the possibility of a solution to Kosovo which accommodated Belgrade was beginning to circulate in the form of speculation and rumors, the KLA (whom few Kosovar Albanians had even heard of at the time) was reportedly issuing death threats in 1996 directed at any Albanian leader who attempted to reach an autonomy deal with Belgrade.

28  Maliqi, Shkelsen (1998) *"Kosova: Separate World: Reflections and Analyses"* MM, *Pristina.*

29  Judah, *Kosovo*, 2000, p.81.

30  Maliqi, 1998.

31  Quoted in Richard Caplan, "International Diplomacy and the Crisis in Kosovo", International Affairs, Volume 74, no. 4, October, p.752.

32  Quoted in Veremis and Kofos, 1998, p.36.

33  Ibid.

34  Humanitarian Law Center, Spotlight Report No. 25, 1998, p.30.

35  Humanitarian Law Center, Human Rights, 1991–1995 (1997).

36  Guy Dinmore, "Uneasy Peace in Kosovo May be Coming to an End", Financial Times, Nov. 4, 1997, p. 4.

37  Quoted in Judah, *Kosovo*, 2000, p.152.

38  Economist Intelligence Unit, Country Profile: Yugoslavia (Serbia-Montenegro) Macedonia 1997–8, London, New York and Hong Kong, 1997, p.14.

39  Quoted in Judah, *Kosovo*, p.74.

40  "President Bush's message was specific and clear. We are prepared to respond against Serbia in the event of a conflict in Kosovo caused by Serbian action. Secretary of State Christopher has reiterated this message." Quoted in Troebst.

41  The Kosovar Albanians were invited as observers and not as participants. "If you are planning to be in London at the time of the conference", Lord Carrington wrote to Rugova, it would be possible to have some meetings, but "for practical and other reasons" it would not "be possible to grant your delegation access to the conference (…) We are making strenuous efforts to ensure that the views of Kosovar Albanians are heard. If you are interested in participating on this basis, I should be grateful if you would contact the secretariat … with details of your proposed delegation and accommodation in London (quoted in Judah, *Kosovo*, pp. 92–3).

42  The Contact group is an informal ad-hoc group consisting of representatives from the USA, the UK, France, Italy, Germany and Russia. It was originally formed for consultations on Bosnia but has now expanded to questions relating to Western Balkans.

43  Quoted in Troebst, p.26.

44  Quoted in Judah, Kosovo, p. 125.

45  Interview with director Sonja Licht, OSF.

46  See Mary Kaldor, *New and Old Wars, Organized Violence in a Global Era*, Polity Press, Cambridge (UK), 1999.

47  Interview with Aryeh Neier, Soros Foundation/Open Society Institute, May 1, 2000.

## 2. Internal Armed Conflict: February 1998–March 1999

1   ICG, Kosovo Spring, March 1998, p. 30.

2   The subsequent chapter analyzes the international response in greater detail.

3   Stefan Troebst, *Conflict in Kosovo: Failure of Prevention*, European Centre for Minority Issues, No. 1, 1998, p. 3.

4   Tim Judah, pp.138–40. The Humanitarian Law Center stated that among the dead there was a large number of women and children. They also noted that people were shot while trying to surrender, (Humanitarian Law Center, *Police Operation in the Drenica Area*, March 5–6, 1998).

5   Human Rights Watch, *Humanitarian Law Violations in Kosovo*, Oct. 1998, p. 18.

6   Ibid., p. 19.

7   Ibid., pp. 1–74.

8   Ibid., p. 75.

9   Donji Prekazi/Prekaze, "Serbs Declare Kosovo Crackdown Over; Ethnic Albanians Allege that the Lull in Fighting is Designed to Deceive the West, Only Timed to Coincide with a Meeting of World Powers in London on Peace in the Balkans," Minneapolis Star Tribune (AP Wire), Mar. 9, 1998, p. 4A.

10  Jeffrey Smith, "Eerie Quiet Follows Assault in Kosovo; Ruins, Refugees, Death Left in Serbian's Wake," Washington Post, Mar. 9, 1998, p. A13.

11  "Major Powers Demand Urgent Action on Kosovo," Toronto Star, Mar. 9, 1998, p. A1.

12  Office of the Prosecutor, Press Release, CC/PIO/302-E, March 10, 1998. The Prosecutor also announced that the ICTY was "currently gathering information and evidence in relation to the Kosovo incidents and would continue to monitor any subsequent developments." The Prosecutor's remarks concluded with a statement that she expected the "full cooperation" of Serb authorities.

13  SC Resolution 1160 UN SCOR, UN Doc S/RES/1160 (1998).

14  "UN Hits Yugoslavia with Arms Embargo; Security Council Hopes to Force Peace in Kosovo," Toronto Star, Apr. 1, 1998, p. A11.

15  Thus, for instance, leaders chosen to represent the KLA at peace talks even as late as the spring of 1999 met one another for the first time during their flight to the negotiation sessions.

16  Philip Smucker, "Young Kosovars Await Order for Border Assault; Expatriate Kosovans Have Begun Returning to their Homeland to Fight Serbs," Sunday Telegraph, Apr. 26, 1998, p. 34.

17  Humanitarian Law Center, Kosovo: Disappearances in Times of Armed Conflict, Report No. 27, 1998, pp. 6–7.

18  Amnesty International, "Ljubenic and Poklek: Extrajudicial Executions, Excessive Use of Force, and Disappearances," in *Kosovo: A Decade of Unheeded Warnings*, Apr. 2, 1999, p. 20.

19  Ibid., pp. 3-6.

20  Elizabeth Neuffer, "NATO Weighs Raids to Slow Serbs in Kosovo; Aides Gather in Brussels Today to Consider Options," Boston Globe, June 11, 1998, p. A2.

21  Ibid.

22  Ibid.

23  Ibid.

24  OSCE, 156th Permanent Council, PC. DEC/218 (1998).

25  Memorandum from Tim Isles, deputy head, OSCE Presence in Albania, to chairman of the Permanent Council, Vienna, July 13, 1998 (citing shelling of villages in Decane/Decani, Serb soldiers torching houses in Potok Morine/Potok Morina, and desertion of 5 Serb soldiers, as well as reporting on the visit of German Minister of Foreign Affairs Kinkel).

26  According to Robert S. Gelbard, special representative of the President and the

secretary for implementation of the Dayton Peace Agreement, in a statement before the House International Relations Committee, Washington, DC, on July 23, 1998, "One aspect of Ambassador Hill's mission has been to work with the Kosovar Albanian side to promote the development of an authoritative negotiating team that represents the full spectrum of political opinion in the Kosovar Albanian community, including extremist elements. Unless the views of those on the Albanian side engaged in the fighting are represented, it is unlikely that either a cessation of hostilities or a comprehensive political settlement can be negotiated. That is why we have opened a dialogue with the UCK. The UCK is a reality on the ground, and however much we condemn the use of violence by either side, they will have to be a party to any cessation of hostilities."

27  Kosovar journalist, (name withheld upon request), in an interview by the Commission in Budapest, Apr. 2, 2000.

28  Memorandum from Tim Isles, op. cit.; OSCE Albania Spot Report, July 18, 1998 (citing a Serb ambush of 700 UCK, leading to as many as 450 killed or captured); OSCE Albania Spot Report, July 24, 1998 (citing heavy artillery shelling from the direction of Rrahovec/Orahovac during a two hour period on July 21).

29  Human Rights Watch, *Humanitarian Law Violations in Kosovo*, Oct. 1998, p. 39.

30  Amnesty International, "'Disappeared' and 'Missing' Persons: The Hidden Victims of the Conflict," in *Kosovo: A Decade of Unheeded Warnings*, Apr. 1999, p. 11.

31  See The Center — Peace through Justice, "Preliminary Compilation of Data: Report to the Independent International Commission on Kosovo," Apr. 2000, p.13. Preliminary compilation on file available at ABA/CEELI

32  Smith, "Eerie Quiet," op. cit.

33  Statement by the president of the Security Council, Aug. 24, 1998, S/PRST/1998/25.

34  Office of the Prosecutor, Press Release, CC/PIU/329-E, July 7, 1998.

35  Ibid.

36  James Hooper, "UN Prosecutor Must Go to Kosovo," Toronto Star, Sept. 16, 1998.

37  Justice Louise Arbour, "Prosecutor Won't Play Politics in the Balkans," Toronto Star, Sept. 22, 1998. It is worth noting that this response upon the part of the Chief Prosecutor was foreshadowed publicly in April 1998. Speaking at a conference on War Crimes Tribunals: The Record and the Prospect, held at American University in Washington, DC, she stated: "I am not sure that personally going there [Kosovo] is likely to advance my investigations a great deal" Audience Questions, 13. Am. U. Int'l L. Rev. 1495, 1505 (1998).

38  Memorandum from Tim Isles, deputy head, OSCE Presence in Albania, to chairman of the Permanent Council, Vienna, Oct. 1, 1998; memorandum from Ambassador Daan Evert, head, OSCE Presence in Albania, to chairman of the Permanent Council, Vienna, Sept. 24, 1998 (citing expulsion of 3500 refugees from Montenegro); memorandum from Ambassador Daan Everts, head, OSCE Presence in Albania, to chairman of the Permanent Council, Vienna, Sept. 9, 1998 (citing over 100 explosions and machine gun fire within 4 kilometers of Gjakove/Djakovica).

39  SC Resolution 1199, UN SCOR, UN Doc. S/RES1199 (1998).

40 Jane Perlez, "Serb Pullback May Forestall NATO Attack," New York Times, Oct. 5, 1998, p. A1.

41 Organization for Security and Cooperation in Europe (OSCE), "Kosovo/Kosova As Seen As Told," 1999, p. 6.

42 William Drozdiak, "NATO Approves Airstrikes on Yugoslavia; Milosevic is Given Ultimatum; Key Demands Reportedly Met," Washington Post, p. A1.

43 SC Resolution 1203, UN SCOR, UN Doc. S/RESI203 (1998).

44 Vernon Loeb, "End of Fighting in Kosovo May Be Within Sight, Holbrooke Says," Washington Post, p. A38.

45 SC Resolution 1207, UN SCOR, UN Doc. S/RES/1207 (1998).

46 Office of the Prosecutor, Press Release, CC/PIU/351-E, October 7, 1998.

47 Human Rights Watch, Detentions and Abuse in Kosovo, Report No. 10 (D), Dec. 1998.

48 Ibid.

49 Humanitarian Law Center, *Spotlight on: Human Rights in FR Yugoslavia*, Report No. 28, 1998, pp. 20-5.

50 Report of the Secretary-General Prepared Pursuant to Resolution 1160 (1998), 1199 (1998) and 1203 (1998) of the Security Council, UN Doc. S/1998/1068, Nov. 12, 1998.

51 Ibid., p. 3.

52 Marc Weller, *The Crisis in Kosovo 1989–1999: From the Dissolution of Yugoslavia to the Rambouillet and the Outbreak of Hostilities,* vol. 1, Cambridge University Press, 1999, p. 286.

53 Memorandum from Tim Isles, deputy head, OSCE Presence in Albania, to chairman-in-office, Dec. 2, 1998 (citing machine gun fire from a FRY border post into the nearby village of Gorozhup/Gorozup); memorandum from Ambassador Daan Everts, head, OSCE Presence in Albania, to chairman-in-office, Dec. 19, 1998 (citing Serb shelling of Albanian villages of Gegaj and Padesh and Kosovar village of Prejlep/Prilep and Serb border incursions); memorandum from Ambassador Daan Everts, head, OSCE Presence in Albania, to chairman-in-office, Dec. 24, 1998 (citing shelling of Vrbnica and border incursions).

54 Nicole Veash, "Bitter Welcome in Kosovo No Place to Call Home," Observer, Dec. 6, 1998, p. 15.

55 Report of the Secretary-General Prepared Pursuant to Resolution 1160 (1998), 1199 (1998) and 1203 (1998) of the Security Council, UN Doc. S/1998/1221, Dec. 24, 1998, p. 3.

56 UN Inter-Agency Report, *Update on Humanitarian Situation in Kosovo,* Dec. 24, 1998.

57 On December 10, 1998, Finnish forensic pathologists, accompanied by the Finnish ambassador, were not allowed to proceed to Obri e Eperme/Gornje Obrinje without a substantial armed accompaniment (two busloads of security personnel and eight armored vehicles). Due to the risk of KLA attack accompanying movement of a military convoy of that size, the Finnish team declined to travel to Obri e Eperme/Gornje Obrinje and protested the conditions imposed by the Yugoslav government. The minister of justice of Serbia then promised that such a situation

would not happen again. Thereafter, the pathologists discussed the security situation with KLA and Serb authorities who both suggested that investigations be targeted at safer locations. The Finnish pathologists determined that it would not be possible to conduct fieldwork at these other locations either, and left on December 20, 1998. These difficulties were raised in meetings between EU officials and Serb authorities, who expressed a willingness to address the issue only after the pathologists had returned to Yugoslavia, (Special Report of the Secretary-General Prepared Pursuant to Resolutions 1160 (1998), 1199 (1998), and 1203 (1998) of the Security Council, UN Doc. S/1999/99, 1999, p. 5).

58 Judah, op. cit., p. 230. Serbian analyst Braca Grubacic, editor of Belgrade's English-language newsletter, VIP, offered the following analysis of Milosevic's expectations after the Holbrooke deal: "He thought the US would close the border with Albania to prevent arms smuggling, that the US would freeze the KLA's assets and make arrangements to terminate the KLA's influence... When Milosevic understood that Holbrooke would not fulfill such a promise he went for war."

59 Interviews with UNHCR and KVM personnel on the ground in Prishtina/Pristina, Kosovo, Aug. 1999.

60 In the October Agreement, Milosevic agreed not to place more than three company sized units in the field in Kosovo at any one time and not to use heavy weapons. All training exercises had to be announced to the OSCE KVM mission in advance to allow proper monitoring presence. The presence of paramilitary units was prohibited, as was the arming of civilians.

61 OSCE, "Kosovo/Kosova," op. cit., p. 354.

62 Ibid. p. 36.

63 Ibid., p. 354.

64 Office of the Prosecutor, Press Release, CC/PIU/379-E, 20 January 1999.

65 Ibid.

66 Security Council Press Release SC/6628, Jan. 19, 1999; OSCE Press Release, Jan. 1999, no. 10/99.

67 Ibid.

68 Letter Dated 23 March 1999 from the Secretary-General Addressed to the President of the Security Council, UN Doc. S/1999/214 (1999).

69 OSCE, "Kosovo/Kosova," op. cit., p. 7.

70 OSCE Press Release No. 24/99, March 19, 1999.

## 3. International War supervenes: March 1999–June 1999

1 Weller, op. cit., page 498.

2 House of Commons, Select Committee on Foreign Affairs, Fourth Report, para 77.

3 See, e.g. House of Commons, op.cit., and Adam Roberts, "NATO's Humanitarian War Over Kosovo", Survival, vol. 41, no 3, Autumn 1999.

4 See Barry Posen, "The War for Kosovo", International Security, vol. 24, no. 4 , Spring 2000.

5 Judah, op. cit., p.282; OSCE, "Kosovo/Kosova" op. cit., p.25.

6 Interview with Sejdiu Pleurat, Prishtina/Pristina, Nov. 1999.

7 House of Commons, Select Committee on Foreign Affairs, Fourth Report, op. cit., para 115.

8 The OSCE concluded that "the violations inflicted on the Kosovar Albanian population after 20 March were a continuation of actions by Yugoslav and Serbian military and security forces that were well rehearsed, insofar as they were already taking place in Kosovo well before 20 March". OSCE, "Kosovo/Kosova" op. cit., p. viii.

9 US State Department, "Ethnic Cleansing in Kosovo: An Accounting" Washington, DC, 1999.

10 House of Commons Select Committee on Foreign Affairs, Fourth Report, op. cit., para 105., paragraph 105.

11 See also ICG Reality Demands, Documenting Violations of International Humanitarian Law in Kosovo 1999.

12 OSCE, "Kosovo/Kosova" op. cit., p111.

13. "Kosovo's Killing Fields — a myth?" Mail and Guardian, August 25 to 31, 2000.

14 ICG Report no 85: Albanians in Serbian Prisons, p. 3.

15 Figures from NATO, quoted in ICTY, Final Report to the Prosecutor by the Committee Established to Review the NATO Bombing Campaign against the Federal Republic of Yugoslavia, op. cit., p. 17.

16 See summary in Posen, "The War for Kosovo" op. cit.

17 Europe Information Service, Brussels, Euro-Est, op. cit., July 1999.

18 The "G8" comprises the United Kingdom, Canada, France, Germany, Italy, Japan, the United States, and Russia.; the G7 is the above, bar Russia.

19 Judah, op. cit., p. 271.

20 Copy of the Peace Plan Approved by the Serb Parliament, Associated Press, June 3, 1999.

21 SC. Resolution. 1244, UN. SCOR, UN. Doc. S/RES1244 (1999).

## 4. Kosovo Under United Nations Rule

1 The Resolution was passed by a vote of 14 in favor, no votes against. China abstained from the vote.

2 Leonard J. Cohen, "Kosovo: Nobody's Country", Current History, March 2000, pp. 117-23.

3 Under the North Atlantic Council authorization of Operation Joint Guardian, the international force was to:

- establish a security presence in Kosovo, as authorized by the UN Security Council Resolution (UNSCR) 1244 and further defined in the Military Technical Agreement (MTA) signed by military authorities from the Federal Republic of Yugoslavia and NATO;
- verify and enforce the terms of the MTA;
- establish a secure environment in which refugees and displaced persons can return home in safety;
- establish a secure environment in which the international civil presence can operate, a transitional administration can be established and humanitarian aid can be delivered;

- help achieve a self-sustaining secure environment which will allow public secu-rity responsibilities to be transferred to appropriate civil organizations.

4 See the letter from Nikolay Ryzhkov, chairman, State Duma Commission for Assistance to the FRY on the Elimination of the Consequences of NATO Aggression, to Kosovo Commission Chairman Richard Goldstone on July 5, 2000, and the attached list, "Non-implementation of the UN Security Council Resolution 1244," Moscow, June 27, 2000.

5 Force levels have not varied dramatically since then. Three months after the end of hostilities, KFOR consisted of a total troop strength of 40,000 soldiers. By June 12, 2000 — the first anniversary of KFOR's advance into Kosovo — its strength had dwindled to 37,000 soldiers.

6 For General Reinhardt's comments, see Süddeutsche Zeitung, June 26, 2000.

7 Full text of Resolution 1244 appears in annex 5.

8 Kouchner is former French Health Minister and co-founder of Médecins Sans Frontières.

9 Report of the Secretary-General on the United Nations Interim Administration Mission in Kosovo, June 6, 2000, p. 1.

10 Süddeutsche Zeitung, June 26, 2000.

11 Report of the Secretary-General on the United Nations Interim Administration in Kosovo, 6 June 2000, p.6.

12 Ibid., p. 22

13 Lord Robertson, as quoted in the Financial Times, July 18, 2000.

14 Report of the Secretary-General on the United Nations Interim Administration in Kosovo, June 6, 2000, p. 22.

15 Ibid., p. 6

16 UNMIK, Administrative Department of Justice, The Justice System of Kosovo, p. 3.

17 House of Commons Select Committee on Foreign Affairs, Fourth Report, May 23, 2000, pp. 191-92.

18 Report of the Secretary-General on the United Nations Interim Administration in Kosovo, 6 June 2000, p. 294.

19 Since February 20, 2000, the European Agency for Reconstruction.

20 Report of Secretary-General on UNMIK, 6 June 2000, pp. 19 f.

21 The Stability Pact can be described as a declaration of intent between the coun-tries of Southeastern Europe and interested parts of the international community. It was introduced at a meeting with EU foreign ministers in Cologne, June 10, 1999. The Stability Pact offers to the countries of the region the perspective of in-tegration into European and Euro-Atlantic structures. In return, the countries of the region must commit themselves to regional cooperation as well as institutional reform.

22 For the official record of achievement, see Special Representative Bernard Kouchner, "UNMIK Marks Six Months in Kosovo," press briefing, December 13, 1999, and Report of the Secretary-General on UNMIK, June 6, 2000.

23 Carl Bildt, remarks to UN Security Council, June 23, 2000, p. 4.

## 5. The Diplomatic Dimension

1 Ivo Daalder, presentation to the Commission in Washington, DC, February 8, 2000. See also Ivo Daalder and Michael O'Hanlon, *Winning Ugly,* Brookings Institution, Washington, 2000; Noam Chomsky and Norman Davies, "Is This Really a Grand NATO Victory?" New Statesman, June 14, 1999, pp. 11–16.

2 Bill Frelick, in a meeting with the Commission, February 8, 2000. See also "The Kosovo Refugee Crisis," testimony of Bill Frelick, senior policy analyst of the US Committee for Refugees before the US Senate Committee on the Judiciary Subcommittee on Immigration, April 14, 1999. On p. 4, he states: "Had President Milosevic intended to ethnically cleanse Kosovo all along? It certainly was a wish, but not necessarily a plan. He is the consummate opportunist, and will take what he can get away with. Last year, his strategy did not appear to be ethnic cleansing per se — the magnitude of that task and its prospects for success too daunting. So, he followed a classic counter-insurgency strategy, in the process of which his forces displaced about 300,000 people within Kosovo. We can debate whether this would have become ethnic cleansing by slow bleeding in the absence of NATO bombing, instead of the hemorrhage that occurred after March 24. My guess is that it may well have happened. However, I also think the hemorrhage could have been avoided if a significant number of NATO troops had been deployed in the region during the Rambouillet negotiations (…)" See also Michael MccGwire, "Why Did We Bomb Belgrade?" International Affairs, January 2000, pp. 1-23, and US Department of State, Erasing History: Ethnic Cleansing in Kosovo, May 1999). This report states: "In late March 1999, Serbian forces dramatically increased the scope and pace of their efforts, moving away from selective targeting of towns and regions suspected of KLA sympathies toward a sustained and systematic effort to ethnically cleanse the entire province of Kosovo."

3 For instance, the political party of Seselj, the elected vice Prime Minister of Serbia in February 1998, had such a platform.

4 The US State Department did apparently investigate the legality of interdicting financial support for the KLA, but no such steps were implemented.

5 Statement on Kosovo of the Contact Group Foreign Ministers, New York, September 24, 1997.

6 Stefan Troebst, *Conflict in Kosovo: Failure of Prevention,* European Center for Minority Issues Working Paper no. 1, 1998, p. 32, citing the Draft Resolution, "Recent Developments in the Federal Republic of Yugoslavia and their Implications for the Region," Report to the Political Affairs Committee of the Parliamentary Assembly of the Council of Europe, Doc. 7986.

7 Contact Group Statement on Kosovo, Moscow, February 25, 1998.

8 Jeffrey Smith, "U.S. Assails Government Crackdown in Kosovo; Administration Seeks Support for Sanctions," Washington Post, Mar. 5, 1998, p. A23.

9 Anne Swanson, "Diplomacy and Fear Follow Killing in Kosovo; West, Russia Agree on Sanctions for Belgrade: Albright Calls Steps A Satisfactory Response," Washington Post, Mar. 10, 1998, p. A13.

10 "Major Powers Unlikely to Back Either Intervention or Sanctions for Kosovo," Irish Times, Mar. 9, 1998, p. 15.

11 Statement on Kosovo, London Contact Group meeting, March 9, 1998.

12 "Finally, we learned in Bosnia, and we have seen in Kosovo, that President Milosevic understands only the language of force" (statement by Secretary of State Madeleine K. Albright, "Remarks and Q & A Session at the US Institute of Peace," Washington DC, February 4, 1999).

13 According to Albright, "(...) Kosovo is not Bosnia because we have learned the lessons of Bosnia — and we are determined to apply them here and now (...) Simply put, we learned in Bosnia that we can pay early, or we can pay much more later." "(...) we have reached the stage where diplomacy, to succeed, requires the backing of military force. And it reflects wide agreement that NATO successfully acted beyond its borders in Bosnia to bring a deadly conflict to an end, and that it can do this again in Kosovo" (see statement by Secretary of State Madeleine K. Albright, "Remarks and Q & A Session at the US Institute of Peace," Washington DC, February 4, 1999. See also Secretary of State Madeleine K. Albright, "Statement at the Contact Group Meeting on Kosovo," Bonn, Germany, March 25, 1998: "Think of all the peace plans that were advanced during the Bosnian war. How many times did one party or another appear to accept our proposals, only to walk away? We saw then that in the former Yugoslavia, promises mean little until they are implemented with safeguards. Incentives tend to be pocketed; warnings tend not to be believed. Leaders respond not to the distant threat of sanctions, but to the reality of sanctions." Albright also stated, in an interview with Frontline, Public Broadcasting System, on February 22, 2000, "We all knew that he [Milosevic] best understood the use of force. He didn't see the light in Bosnia until the NATO bombing, and then he agreed to the Dayton Accords". In contrast, according to Mary Kaldor, "What went wrong in Bosnia was the reluctance to risk the lives of peacekeepers. It is the same syndrome in Kosovo. NATO credibility will never be restored unless NATO succeeds in stopping the violence in Kosovo. And that means troops on the ground to protect civilians" (Mary Kaldor, "Kosovo Crisis: Bombs Away! But to Save Civilians We Must Get In," Guardian, March 25, 1999, p. 19.

14 Resolution 1160 called for the Secretary-General to make "recommendations for the establishment of a comprehensive regime to monitor the implementation of the prohibitions (...) " seeking cooperation from all states. In his first report back to the Council, the Secretary-General wrote: "The establishment of a comprehensive regime to monitor the implementation of the prohibitions imposed by Security Council resolution 1160 (1998) would require the deployment of teams composed of qualified experts (...) It should be noted that the United Nations is unable, within existing budgetary resources, to establish and administer the requested comprehensive monitoring regime (...) I believe that OSCE, with contributions and assistance from other regional organizations, as necessary, would be in a position to carry out the requested monitoring functions effectively. Those regional organizations might include the European Union, the North Atlantic Treaty Organization, and the Western European Union" (Report of the Secretary-General Prepared Pursuant to Security Council Resolution 1160 (1998), UN Doc. S/1998/361 (April 30, 1998), p. 2).

15 Report of the Secretary-General Prepared Pursuant to Resolution 1160 (1998) of the Security Council, UN Doc. S/1998/834 (September 4, 1998), p. 3.

16 UN Security Council Resolution 1203, UN Doc. s/RES1203 (1998).

17 Tim Judah, Kosovo: *War and Revenge*, Yale University Press, 2000, pp. 187–90. With respect to China's position, see statement by Guofang Shen, UN Security Council Press Release sc/6597, 3944th meeting, November 17, 1998. "Chinese Official, at Yugoslav Parliament, Denounces NATO," New York Times, June 13, 2000, p. A13.

18 Oleg Levitin, "Inside Moscow's Kosovo Muddle," Survival, vol. 42, no. 1, spring 2000, p. 137.

19 This agreement opened the way for the installation of the Kosovo Diplomatic Observer Mission (KDOM).

20 Levitin, op. cit., p. 132. Levitin also argues: "One should not overestimate the leverage that Moscow possessed. But there was at least one lever that could have been used and, occasionally, was used: for example, in June 1998 at the Moscow summit meeting when Boris Yeltsin told Milosevic unequivocally that he could not rely on Russian support in the conflict if he ignored advice from the Kremlin."

21 Contact Group Statement, Bonn, Germany, July 8, 1998.

22 Albright stated on October 8: "But if force is necessary, then we will not be deterred by the fact that the Russians do not agree with that" (Secretary of State Madeleine K. Albright, Press Conference on Kosovo, Brussels, Belgium, October 8, 1998). With respect to the US interpretation of Belgrade's unreliability as a negotiating partner except when coerced, Albright stated on October 27: "We must consider Milosevic's track record, his long-standing unwillingness to negotiate seriously and the accumulated barbarity of the past months. Time and again, Milosevic has taken half steps to avoid the consequences of his actions. We are not interested in further promises, only continued compliance. We assume that Milosevic will act responsibly only when all the other alternatives have been exhausted" statement by Secretary of State Madeleine K. Albright, "Remarks on Kosovo," Washington, DC, October 27.

23 Robert Gelbard, Press Conference, Belgrade, February 23, 1998

24 Judah, op. cit., p. 154.

25 Catherine Guichard, "International Law and the War in Kosovo," Survival, vol. 41, no. 2, Summer 1999.

26 The exact and full nature of the Holbrooke–Milosevic agreements (and their informal understandings) is not disclosed in open sources. Its interpretation is based on the best existing evidence, including interviews with many of the principals, but remains at this point somewhat circumstantial, and to some extent conjectural. See R. Jeffrey Smith, "Kosovo Rebels Plan for Renewal of War; Guerrillas Say They Will Strike if Government Troops do not Withdraw as Pledged," Washington Post, October 22, 1998, p. A30: "Many officials in Washington essentially have agreed with Belgrade that Kosovo Liberation Army demands no longer carry weight because the group is not strong enough to play a spoiling role in negotiations being set up between the Serbian authorities and the more moderate, elected

ethnic Albanian leadership headed by Ibrahim Rugova. Special US envoy Richard C. Holbrooke did not, for example, consult with guerrilla representatives during his nine days of talks with Yugoslav President Slobodan Milosevic that ended Oct. 12 with a series of accords aimed at resolving the crisis. Deputy Secretary of State Thomas Pickering reflected a common view when he said on Oct. 14 that "this overwhelming use of military power on the part of Milosevic has driven most of the armed fighters either underground or out of the country or out of the picture." Also see statement by Secretary of State Madeleine K. Albright, "Remarks on Kosovo," Washington, DC, October 27, 1998: "To support these negotiations, we have also delivered a clear message to the leadership of the KLA: there should be no attempt to take military advantage of the Serb pull-back. Neither side can achieve military victory in Kosovo. The message is starting to have an effect. In recent days, we've seen a new degree of restraint on the part of the KLA, which has been willing to negotiate the disengagement of forces in several key areas (...) "

27  Magnusson, Kjell, *Rambouilletavtalet*, Uppsala University, 1999, page 76.

28  Rubin, press briefing, Rambouillet, Feb. 21 (Weller, page 451), Albright Press Conference February 23, 1999, http://secretary.state.gov/www/state-ments/1999/990223.html.

29  Judah, op. cit., p. 207.

30  Weller, op. cit., pp. 229-30.

31  In the October and November drafts it was said in more general and vague terms that in three years the sides would undertake an assessment of the agreement and consider proposals by either side for additions steps "which will require mutual agreement." These words disappeared in the January version (Magnusson, *Rambouilletavtalet*, Uppsala, 1999).

32  Judah, op. cit., p. 213.

33  Weller, page 410.

34  See also the Parliamentary Report of the House of Commons, Select Committee on Foreign Affairs Fourth Report, para. 62-5, for a discussion of the impact of the military annex.

35  Statement by Secretary of State Madeleine K. Albright, Press conference on the Kosovo peace talks, Rambouillet, France, February 20, 1999.

36  Judah, op. cit., p. 220.

37  Judah, op. cit., p. 220. Also, according to Braca Grubacic, Milosevic felt quite threatened by the provisions: "He thought the only goal was NATO in Kosovo, and after Rambouillet, when he saw that the West wanted to allow NATO to pass through Yugoslavia he was afraid that someone like [William] Walker would turn up and say: "You are no longer president.' "

## 6. International Law and Humanitarian Intervention

1  Final Report to the Prosecutor by the Committee Established to Review the NATO Bombing Campaign against the Federal Republic of Yugoslavia.

2  Uniting for Peace Resolution, adopted by the UN General Assembly, 3 Nov. 1950, G.A. Res. 337A, IN Do. A/1775 (1951).

3   The Treaty of Washington, article 5 states:
    The Parties agree that an armed attack against one or more of them in Europe or
    North America shall be considered an attack against them all and consequently
    they agree that, if such an armed attack occurs, each of them, in exercise of the
    right of individual or collective self-defence recognised by Article 51 of the Charter
    of the United Nations, will assist the Party or Parties so attacked by taking forth-
    with, individually and in concert with the other Parties, such action as it deems
    necessary, including the use of armed force, to restore and maintain the security of
    the North Atlantic area.
    Any such armed attack and all measures taken as a result thereof shall immediately
    be reported to the Security Council. Such measures shall be terminated when the
    Security Council has taken the measures necessary to restore and maintain inter-
    national peace and security.

4   See Oscar Schachter, "In Defense of International Rules on the Use of Force,"
    University of Chicago Law Review 53:113 (1986); Louis Henkin, "Force,
    Intervention, and Neutrality in Contemporary International Law," Proc. ASIL 147,
    166 (1963); P. Jessup, The Modern Law of Nations 164–67 (1948)

5   In that decision the majority of the Court clearly held that customary internation-
    al law, independent of the Charter, now imposes on states as restrictive an ap-
    proach to the use of force as does the Charter, Military and Paramilitary Activities
    in and against Nicaragua (Nicaragua v United States) 76 ILR 349. For a range of
    views on the case see Appraisals of the ICJ's Decision: Nicaragua v United States
    (Merits), G Maier (ed) in 81 Am. J. Int'l L. 77 (1987).

6   Such argumentation is relied upon by Ruth Wedgewood, "NATO's Campaign in
    Yugoslavia", included in "Editorial Comments", NATO's Kosovo Intervention", 93
    Am. J. Int'l L. at 835

7   Julie Mertus, "Reconsidering the Legality of Humanitarian Intervention: Lessons
    from Kosovo", 41 Wm. & Mary L. Rev. 1743 (2000).

8   See especially Kofi Annan's 1999 "Report of the Secretary General on the Work of
    the Organisation" made at the 54th session of the General Assembly.

9   See Michael J. Glennon, "The New Interventionism", 78 Foreign Affairs. (1999),
    on the need to revise the UN, or abandon its authority.

10  Among the many books, perhaps the strongest indictment is that of David Rieff,
    "Slaughterhouse: Bosnia and the Failure of the West", Vintage, London, 1995.

11  This suspicion was reiterated to the Commission by many participants at its final
    seminar in Johannesburg, South Africa, August 25–26, 2000.

12  See comment on this in David Cartright & George Lopez, eds., The Sanctions
    Decade: Assessing un Strategies in the 1990s (Boulder, CO: Lynne Rienner, 2000);
    Anthony Arnove, ed., Iraq under Siege (Cambridge, MA: South End Press, 2000);
    for general background see Lori Fisler Damrosch, "Enforcing International Law
    Through Non-forcible Measures," Recueil des cours, 269:13–250 (1997).

13  For an overview see Anthony Clark Arend and Robert J. Beck, International Law
    and the Use of Force, New York, Routledge, 1993; for a balanced view on these issues
    see Rosalyn Higgins, Problems and Process: International Law and How We Use It,
    Oxford University Press, 1994, pp. 254-266.

14 Michael Reisman Kosovo's Antinomies included in Editorial Comments: NATO's
Kosovo Intervention, op. cit., p. 867, has argued this most persuasively. See also
Reisman, Article 2(4): The Use of Force in Contemporary International Law,"
Proc. ASIL 74-87(1984); Reisman, "Coercion and Self-Determination: Construing
Charter Article 2(4)," AJIL 78: 642(1984).

15 For an overview supporting such an approach, see Myres, McDougal and
Feliciano, *Law and Minimum Public Order: The Legal Regulation of International
Coercion,* New Haven, CT, Yale University Press, 1961.

16 Article 53 of the UN Charter provides:
"(1) The Security Council shall, where appropriate, utilize such regional arrangements or agencies for enforcement action under its authority. But no enforcement
action shall be taken under regional arrangements or by regional agencies without
the authorization of the Security Council, with the exception of measures against
any enemy state, as defined in paragraph 2 of this Article, provided for pursuant to
Article 107 or in regional arrangements directed against renewal of aggressive policy on the part of any such state, until such time as the Organization may, on request of the Governments concerned, be charged with the responsibility for preventing further aggression by such a state.
"(2) The term enemy state as used in paragraph 1 of this Article applies to any
state which during the Second World War has been an enemy of any signatory of
the present Charter."

17 Article 39 of the UN Charter provides:
"The Security Council shall determine the existence of any threat to the peace,
breach of the peace, or act of aggression and shall make recommendations, or decide what measures shall be taken in accordance with Articles 41 and 42, to maintain or restore international peace and security."

18 Article 51 of the UN Charter provides:
"Nothing in the present Charter shall impair the inherent right of individual or
collective self-defense if an armed attack occurs against a member of the United
Nations, until the Security Council has taken measures necessary to maintain
international peace and security. Measures taken by Members in the exercise of
this right of self-defense shall be immediately reported to the Security Council
and shall not in any way affect the authority and responsibility of the Security
Council under the present Charter to take at any time such action as it deems necessary in order to maintain or restore international peace and security."
[But there were other reasons for legal concern about even this mandate. See
Ismael and Ismael for a collection of articles critical of the UN approach; also the
remark of Boutros Ghali in Agenda for Peace that never again should a mandate
to use force be so open-ended and without continuing Security Council supervision.)

19 Resolution 1160 (1998) of March 31, 1998, Resolution 1199 (1998) of September 23,
1998, and Resolution 1203 (1998) of October 24, 1998.

20 Deep concern at the massive influx of Kosovo refugees into Albania, the former
Yugoslav Republic of Macedonia, Bosnia and Herzegovina, and other countries, as

well as by the increasing numbers of displaced persons within Kosovo, the Republic of Montenegro and other parts of the Federal Republic of Yugoslavia activated sc Resolutions 1199 (1998) and 1239 (1999).

21  See the Report of the Secretary-General pursuant to General Assembly Resolution 53/35 (1998) and also the Report of the Independent Inquiry into the Actions of the United Nations during the 1994 Genocide in Rwanda.

22  On the latter see *Mad Dogs: the US Raids on Libya* edited by Paul Anderson and Mary Kaldor (Pluto Press: London, 1986)

23  On March 26, by a vote of 3 in favor (China, Namibia, Russian Federation) to 12 against, the Security Council rejected a draft resolution demanding an immediate cessation by NATO of the use of force against the Federal Republic of Yugoslavia. The draft had been submitted by Belarus, the Russian Federation, and India.

24  See Thomas Franck, Lessons of Kosovo included in Editorial Comments: NATO's Kosovo Intervention, op. cit., at p. 864, on "exception" versus Glennon, op. cit., on "obsolescence".

25  See criticism by Dennis McNamara as cited in Steven Erlanger, "As UN's Kosovo Role Ebbs, an Official has Caustic Advice", International Herald Tribune, July 4, 2000.

26  1899 Hague Declaration 2 Concerning Asphyxiating Gases; 1899 Hague Declaration 3 Concerning Expanding Bullets; 1907 Hague Convention IV Respecting the Laws and Customs of War on Land; 1907 Hague Convention V Respecting the Rights and Duties of Natural Powers and Persons in Case of War on Land; 1907 Hague Convention VI Relating to the Status of Enemy Merchant Ships at the Outbreak of Hostilities; 1907 Hague Convention VII Relating to the Conversion of Merchant Ships into Warships; 1907 Hague Convention VIII Relative to the Laying of Automatic Submarine Contact Mines; 1907 Hague Convention IX Concerning Bombardment by Naval Forces in Time of War; 1907 Hague Convention XI Relative to Certain Restrictions with Regard to the Exercise of the Right to Capture in Naval War; 1907 Hague Convention XIII Concerning the Rights and Duties of Neutral Powers in Naval War; 1949 Geneva Convention I for the Amelioration of the Condition of the Wounded and Sick in Armed Forces in the Field; 1949 Geneva Convention II for the Amelioration of the Condition of Wounded, Sick and Shipwrecked Members of the Armed Forces at Sea; 1949 Geneva Convention III Relative to the Treatment of Prisoners of War; 1949 Geneva Convention IV Relative to the Protection of Civilian Persons in Time of War; 1977 Geneva Protocol I Additional to the Geneva Conventions of 12 August 1949, and Relating to the Protection of Victims of International Armed Conflicts; 1977 Geneva Protocol II Additional to the Geneva Conventions of 12 August 1949, and Relating to the Protection of Victims of Non-International Armed Conflicts.

27  France apparently intends to ratify shortly. The most important Protocol I provisions have been incorporated into the US Military Code of Conduct which is supposed to guide the behavior of its armed forces.

28  This view of the content of Additional Protocol I is supported by the ICTY's Final Report, op,. cit., par. 15.

29  See e.g. *Crimes of War: A Legal, Political-Documentary and Psychological Inquiry into the Responsibility of Leaders, Citizens and Soldiers for Criminal Acts in Wars,* edited by R. Falk, G. Kolko and R. Lifton (New York: Random House, 1971).

30  See Section 4:11, "NATO/Federal Republic of Yugoslavia: "Collateral Damage' or Unlawful Killings? Violations of the Laws of War by NATO during Operation Allied Force," AI Index EUR 70/18/00, June 2000.

31  ICTY, Final Report, op. cit., par. 5.

32  ICTY, Final Report, op. cit., par. 5.

33  Article 1 of the Convention on the Prohibition of the Use, Stockpiling, Production and Transfer of Anti-Personnel Mines and on Their Destruction, 18 September 1997, provides:

"1. Each State Party undertakes never under any circumstances:

To use anti-personnel mines;

To develop, produce, otherwise acquire, stockpile, retain or transfer to anyone, directly or indirectly, anti-personnel mines;

To assist, encourage or induce, in any way, anyone to engage in any activity prohibited to a State Party under this Convention.

2. Each State Party undertakes to destroy or ensure the destruction of all anti-personnel mines in accordance with the provisions of this Convention."

34  This is especially so given the recently leaked internal report from the British Ministry of Defense, which admitted that 60% of the Royal Air Forces' cluster bombs missed their intended target or remain "unaccounted for". R. Norton-Taylor, "MoD Leak Reveals Kosovo Failure" The Guardian August 15, 2000.

35  AI Index EUR, op. cit., p 25. Commendably, NATO made some adjustments to the Rules of Engagement governing bombing after the civilian damage arising from the attack near Gjakove/Djakovica on April 14, 1999 and the bombardment of the Barbarin/Barbarin bridge on May 30, 1999.

36  ICTY, Final Report, op. cit., par 56.

37  "The Kosovo Conflict: Consequences for the Environment and Human Settlements".

38  ICTY, Final Report, op. cit., par 14.

39  ICTY, Final Report, op. cit., par 26.

40  Legality of Nuclear Weapons, AO, icj 1996, 242

41  Article2(7) of the UN Charter provides:

"Nothing contained in the present Charter shall authorize the United Nations to intervene in matters which are essentially within the domestic jurisdiction of any state or shall require the Members to submit such matters to settlement under the present Charter; but this principle shall not prejudice the application of enforcement measures under Chapter VII."

42. See Report of the Secretary-General Pursuant to General Assembly Resolution 53/35, op. cit.; Organization of African Unity, Report of the International Panel of Eminent Personalities to Investigate the 1994 Genocide in Rwanda and the Surrounding Events, July 7, 2000.

43  See Rieff, op. cit.

44  See the Convention on the Suppression and Punishment of the Crime of

Apartheid, General Assembly resolution 3068 (XXVIII) of November 30, 1973, which entered into force on July 18, 1976.

45 Special Report of the International Panel of Eminent Personalities to Investigate the 1994 Genocide in Rwanda and the Surrounding Events. July 7, 2000.

46 Report of the Secretary-General pursuant to General Assembly resolution 53/35, The Fall of Srebrenica. November 15, 1999.

47 *Humanitarian Intervention: Legal and Political Aspects,* Danish Institute of International Affairs, Copenhagen, 1999, pp. 106–11.

## 7. Humanitarian Organizations and the Role of Media

1 The following persons have been consulted in connection with this chapter: Nina Bang-Jensen, Coalition for International Justice, John Faucett, previously with Coalition for International Justice, Karen Koning Abuzayrd, UNHCR Washington Office, Aryeh Neier, Open Society, Diane Paul, formerly with Human Rights Watch, Len Rubenstein, Executive Director, Physicians for Human Rights.

2 Tim Judah, *Kosovo: War and Revenge,* Yale University Press, 2000, p. 240 (citing House of Commons, International Development Committee, Fourth special Report: Government Response to the Third Report from the Committee, Session 1998-99: *"Kosovo: the Humanitarian Crisis"*, London, 1999, p. xi).

3 Astri Suhrke, Michale Barutciski, Peta Sandison, Rick Garlock, UNHCR Evaluation and Policy Analysis: *The Kosovo Refugee Crisis: An Independent Evaluation of UN-HCR's Emergency Preparedness and Response,* February 2000, chapter 5, para. 322.

4 Physicians for Human Rights, War Crimes in Kosovo, A Population-Based Assess-ment of Human Rights Violations Against Kosovar Albanians, Boston, 1999.

5 NATO/EAPC Ad Hoc Group, Report from a Seminar on Kosovo Experience With Regard to Compendium on Humanitarian Aspects of Peacekeeping, Brussels, October 21, 1999, (Civil-Military Cooperation in Humanitarian Efforts during the Kosovo Crisis: NATO Lessons Learned).

6 The Economist begins a story about NGOs by describing a newcomer whose NGO will do whatever a funder will fund. See "NGOs: Sins of the Secular Missionaries", The Economist, Jan. 29, 2000, p. 25. As the article notes, "The focus of such NGOs can easily shift from finding solutions and helping needy recipients to pleasing their donors and winning television coverage." Id., at 26. And "Personnel and re-sources were even shifted [to Kosovo] from worse wars and refugee crises in Africa" apparently to get media recognition. Id., p. 27.

7 The larger trend is the escalating number of humanitarian organizations in exis-tence. The number of humanitarian aid agencies registered with the U.S. Agency for International Development expanded from 144 to 418 between 1983 and 1992; the number of NGOs in the North registered with the Organization for Economic Cooperation and Development grew from 1660 to 2970 between 1980 and 1993. See Jennifer Leaning, I*ntroduction, in Humanitarian Crises: The Medical and Public Health Response (*Jennifer Leaning, Susan M. Briggs, and Lincoln C. Chen eds., Harvard University Press, Cambridge, 1999, pp. 1 and 4.

8 The problem is increasingly present in complex humanitarian crises. See Marc

Lindenberg, Complex Emergencies and NGOS: The Example of Care, in Humanitarian Crises, supra note 7, pp. 211, 216. After the crisis, UNMIK issued regulation 1999/22 to govern the registration and operation of non-governmental organizations in Kosovo as an effort to better coordinate private initiatives.

9   Quoted in "NGOS: Sins of the Secular Missionaries", The Economist , Jan. 29, 2000, p. 27.

10   UNHCR, Evaluation and Policy Analysis, supra note 3; see also UNHCR, Independent Evaluation of UNHCR's Kosovo Response Released, www.balkan-info.com, May 12, 2000.

11   UNHCR, Evaluation and Policy Analysis, supra note 3; see also UNHCR, Independent Evaluation of UNHCR's Kosovo Response Released, supra note 10.

12   Human Rights Watch, Abuses Against Serbs and Roma in the New Kosovo, Aug, 1999.

13   Susan Blaustein, consultant with International Crisis Group, Congressional Testimony Before Helsinki Commission, Feb. 28, 2000 (calling for response to continued detention affecting one in 100 Albanian families and left out of the June 10 military-technical agreement ending the war); ICG Balkans Report, No. 85, Albanians in Serbian Prisons: Kosovo's Unfinished Business, Washington/Pristina, Jan. 26, 2000. According to the International Committee of the Red Cross (ICRC) there were, as of March 21, 2000, 1571 Kosovar Albanian prisoners in Serb prisons, held for "sedition" or similar offences.

14   ICG: Albanian in Serbian Prisons, January 26, 2000, page 6

14   ICG interview, Oct. 29, 1999, quoted in ICG Balkans Report, No. 85, supra note 13, p.25.

15   ICG Balkans Report, No. 85, supra note 13, p. 17-20.

16   UNHCR Evaluation and Policy Analysis supra note 3, chapter 6.

17   Id. Chapter 7, para. 519.

18   Toby Porter, The Partiality of Humanitarian Assistance-Kosovo in Comparative Perspective (focusing on response to the refugee crisis in Albania and Macedonia, between March and June 1999).

19   Thierry Germond, NATO and the ICRC: "A Partnership Serving the Victims of Armed Conflicts", NATO Review, May/June, 1997, 45: pp. 30–32).

20   Michele Mercier, Crimes Without Punishment: Humanitarian Action in Former Yugoslavia, Pluto Press, London, 1994. [first published as "Crimes sans chatiemen", Bryulant, Brussels, 1994], p. 168.

21   Private humanitarian and human rights groups themselves diverged over how much to call for or endorse particular governmental action and specifically, military intervention. After the Recak/Racak massacre in January 1999, Physicians for Human Rights became the first human rights group to call for some kind of intervention; and it tried to work with a coalition of other NGOs, but the groups disagreed over whether to support military intervention and indeed, over whether to support governmental action.

22   Steven Mufson, "Report: Infighting, Poor Intelligence Plague U.S. Relief Efforts", Washington Post, May 9, 2000, p. A27 (reporting on interagency U.S. report, co-chaired by Morton H. Halperin and James Michel).

23 Quoted in Guardian, June 10, 1999 (cited in Porter, supra note 18).

24 NATO/EAPC Ad Hoc Group, Report From a Seminar On the Kosovo Experience With Regard to Compendium on Humanitarian Aspects of Peacekeeping, supra note 5.

25 Jennifer Leaning, Introduction, in Humanitarian Crises, supra note 7, pp. 1, 9.

26 Id.

27 Cedric Thornberry, "Learning to Live With the Military", Refugees Magazine, Issue 116, 1999.

28 I.e. "Aiming Off over Kosovo", Guardian, August 15, 2000.

29 For an extensive report on the media and the war, see "The Kosovo: News and Propaganda War", International Press Institute, Vienna, 1999. In a critical introduction Peter Goff sharply criticizes NATO's "lies, spin and rumors".

30 Human Rights Watch, Curtailing Dissent: Serbia's Campaign of Violence and Harassment Against Government Critics, March, 2000.

31 Kevin McAuliffe, Kosovo: A Special Report, Columbia Journalism Review, May/June, 1999,

32 Leslie Heilbrenn, "Honor Roll: Alone in the War", Brills' Content, July/August, 1999.

33 Michael Ignatieff, Virtual War: Kosovo and Beyond, Henry Holt & Co, 2000, pp. 137–141.

34 Id.

35 R. Jeffrey Smith and William Drozdiak, "The Anatomy of a Purge: Milosevic's Intimate Understanding of His Enemies Facilitates His Campaign of Terror Against the Kosovars", Washington Post, April 11, 1999, p. A1.

36 OSCE, Kosovo/Kosova: As Seen, as Told, Part V, pp. 10–11.

37 Llazar Semini, "Kosovo's Vigilante Journalism", (author from Institute for War & Peace Reporting).

38 Steven Erlanger, NATO Peacekeepers Plan a System of Controls for the News Media in Kosovo, N.Y. Times, Aug. 16, 2000,

39 Humanitarian Aid, www.balkan-info.com.

## 8. Kosovo — The Regional Dimension

1 The term "southeastern Europe" or "the Balkans" used in this chapter includes Albania, Bosnia-Herzegovina, Bulgaria, Croatia, Macedonia, Romania, Greece, and the Federal Republic of Yugoslavia (Serbia and Montenegro).

2 For example, Zoran Todorovic, close to Milosevic' wife Mira Markovic and head of the petrol industry; more recently the assassination of the director of JAT, the Yugoslav airlines; possibly even the Zeljko Raznatovic (Arkan) assassination in January of this year.

3 The founders of Otpor were activists from the 1996–97 student movement, although only 10% of present day members were active then. It has at first received influential support of leading artists and writers now broadening its support in the population at large. Otpor thrives on not being a political party and thus not being compromised or corrupted by the struggles for power. Yet at the same time it has no better option than to give its backing to a broad coalition of all political parties

(and their discredited leaders) in order to help to bring about an electoral defeat of Milosevic's regime. Cf. www.OTPOR.com.

4   International Herald Tribune, March 29, 2000.

5   Christophe Châtelot, "Un scrutin partiel montre UN Monténégro divisé entre pro et anti-Milosevic", Le Monde, June 13, 2000.

6   "Le Monténégro refuse les modifications de la Constitution fédérale décidéees à Belgrade", Le Monde, July 9–10, 2000, The resolution of the Montenegrin Parliament states: "The parliament invites citizens of Montenegro, citizens and democratic forces of Serbia and the international community to help resolve the problem between Montenegro and the state authorities of Serbia and the federation peacefully." See also "Montenegro Rejects Yugoslav Move," International Herald Tribune, July 8–9, 2000.

7   This report went to press shortly before these elctions, and could thus not take into account the results.

8   Carlotta Gall, "Montenegrin Leader Warns of Coup Plan," International Herald Tribune March 29, 2000.

9   This was the overwhelming viewpoint presented by the participants from Albania at the second seminar of the Kosovo Commission, hosted by the Central European University in Budapest (April 2000).

10  The League of Prizren established at the end of the nineteenth century is often considered as the founding moment of Albanian nationalism.

11  Answering allegations to this effect in Parliament in the early phase of the NATO intervention, Prime Minister Kostov declared that Bulgaria had never put its air space at the disposal of NATO. The minister of internal affairs Bogomil Bonev even threatened that court proceedings could be initiated against journalists or politicians who were spreading rumors that could stir up negative disposition against Bulgaria in war-stricken Yugoslavia, (according to a report by Dimitri Filipov, AIM, April 2, 1999).

12  Based on national statistical yearbooks cited in Daniel Heimerl, Yorgos Rizopoulos, and Nebojsa Vukadinovic, "Contradictions et limites des politiques de reconstruction dans les Balkans " Revue d'études comparatives Est-Ouest, vol. 30, 1999, n. 4, p. 213.

13  Euro-Est, no. 79, Europe Information Service, Brussels, July 1999.

14  Presentation by Vladimir Gligorov to the Independent International Commission on Kosovo at the Central European University, Budapest, April, 2000.

15  "The Real Winners of the Kosovo War is the Mafia" Washington Quarterly, Spring 2000.

16  Daniela Heimrl, Yorgos Rizopoulos, Nebojsa Vukadinovic, Contradictions et limites des politiques de reconstruction dans lesBalkans" in Revue d'études comparatives Est-Ouest, 1999, vol.30, no. 4, pp 201–44.

17  Bertelsman Foundation, Strategy paper for the Club of Three and the Balkans, presented to the Stability Pact chief Bodo Hombach, Brussels, June 29-30, 2000, p. 19.

18  M. Emerson and D. Gross, The CEPS Plan for the Balkans, Center for European

Policy Studies, Brussels, 1999.

19  The World Bank Strategy Paper released to coincide with the Stability Pact fund-
     ing conference is analyzed by Vladimir Gligorov, "Strategies and Instruments",
     Balkan Eye (Newsletter of the Balkan Reconstruction Observatory), London, no.
     1, June 2000, pp. 3–4.

## 9. The Future Status of Kosovo

1   Remarks to the UN Security Council, by Mr. Carl Bildt, Special Envoy of the
     Secretary-General for the Balkans, June 23, 2000

2   OSCE, The Lund Recommendations on the Effective Participation of National
     Minorities in Public Life, (The Hague: Foundation on Inter-Ethnic Relations,
     1999).

**Books, reports and articles**

Aspen Institute Berlin and Carnegie Endowment for International Peace
Unfinished Peace, Report of the International Commission on the Balkans
(Washington: The Brookings Institution Press, 1996)
Particularly the chapter

Abrahams Fred and Andersen Elizabeth, *Humanitarian Law Violations in Kosovo*,
Human Rights Watch, 1998

Amnesty International, Ljubenic and Poklek: Extrajudicial Executions, Excessive Use
of Force, and Disappearances, in *Kosovo: A Decade of Unheeded Warnings*, Apr. 2 1999

Amnesty International, Orahovac, July–August 1998, Deaths, Displacements,
Detentions: Many Unanswered Questions, in Kosovo: *A Decade of Unheeded
Warnings*, May 1999

Ash Timothy Garton, *Anarchy & Madness*, N.Y. Review of Books, Feb 10, 2000

Aspen Institute Berlin and Carnegie Endowment for International Peace, *Unfinished
Peace, Report of the International Commission on the Balkans*, The Brookings
Institution Press, 1996

Bildt Carl, *Winning the Peace in Kosovo*, Financial Times, January 19, 2000

Bildt, Carl, *Uppdrag fred.* Stockholm, 1997 (Swedish)

Blagojevic Marina, Kosovo: *in/visible civil war*, in Veremis and Kofos.

Caplan Richard, *International Diplomacy and the Crisis in Kosovo,* International Affairs,
Volume 74, No.4, October

Carpenter Ted Galen, editor, *NATO's Empty Victory*, Cato inst, 2000

Chalmers Malcolm, Kosovo: *The crisis and beyond* Saferworld, London, 1999

Chomsky Noam, *The New Military Humanism: Lessons from Kosovo*, Common Courage
Press, Monroe, 1999

Cohen Leonard J., *Kosovo: Nobody's Country*, Current History, March 2000

Daalder Ivo H. and O'Hanlon Michael E., *Winning Ugly: NATO's War to Save Kosovo*,
Brookings institute, 2000

Elsie Robert, editor, *Kosovo*, East European Monographs, 1997

*Ethnic Cleansing in Kosovo: An Accounting*, US State Department, 1999,

Fromkin David, *Kosovo Crossing. American Ideals Meet Reality on the Balkan Battlefields*,
The Free Press, 1999

Glenny Misha, *The Balkans: Nationalism, War and the Great Powers 1809–1999* Penguin
USA, 2000

Goff Peter, editor, *The Kosovo News and Propaganda War*, International Press Institute,
2000

Guichard Catherine, *International Law and the War in Kosovo*, Survival, vol. 41, no. 2, 1999

Hartmann Florence, *Milosevic–la diagonale du fou*, Denoel, Sodis, 1999

House of Commons Select Committee on Foreign Affairs, Fourth Report, May 24, 2000

Human Law Center, *Human Rights 1991–1995*, 1997

Human Law Center, *Spotlight* Report, no. 25, 1998

Human Law Center, *Kosovo: Disappearances in Times of Armed Conflict*, Report no. 27, 1998

Human Law Center, *Spotlight on Human Rights in FR Yugoslavia*, Report no. 28, 1998

Human Rights Watch, *Humanitarian Law Violence in Kosovo*, October 1998

Human Rights Watch, *Detentions and Abuse in Kosovo*, Report no. 10 (D), December 1998

Human Rights Watch, *Abuses Against Serbs and Roma in the New Kosovo*, Aug. 1999

Human Rights Watch, *Civilian deaths in the NATO air campaign*, Volume 12

Human Rights Watch, *Curtailing Dissent: Serbia's Campain of Violence and Harassment Against Government Critics*, March 2000

Human Rights Watch, *Rape as a Weapon of "Ethnic Cleansing"*, 2000

Ignatieff Michael, *Virtual War: Kosovo and Beyond*, Henry Holt & Co, 2000

Judah Tim, *The Serbs — History, Myth & the Destruction of Yugoslavia*, Yale University Press, 1997

Judah Tim, *Kosovo's Road to War*, Survival, Summer, 1999

Judah Tim, Kosovo: *War and Revenge*, Yale University Press, 2000

Kaldor Mary, *New and Old Wars, Organised Violence in a Global Era*, Polity Press, 1999

Kissinger Henry, *Doing Injury to History*, Newsweek, April 5, 1999

Kosovo Liberation Army, Strategic Comments Volume 5 Issue 4, May 1999

*Kosovo/Kosova — As Seen, As Told*, OSCE, Vienna, 1999

*Kosovo/Operation Allied Force After-Action Report*, Department of Defense, Washington D.C., January 31, 2000, available on

*Kosovo: The Humanitarian Crisis*, Third Report of the House of Commons International Development Committee, London, May 11, 1999

Levitin Oleg, *Inside Moscow's Kosovo Muddle*, Survival, vol. 42, no. 1, 2000

Loquai, Heinz, *Das Kosovo-Konflikt. Wege in einer vermeidbaren Krieg*. Institut fur Friedensforschung, Universitet Hamburg, DSF Band 129, 2000

Magas Branka, *The Destruction of Yugoslavia: Tracking the Break-Up 1980–1992*, Verso, 1993

Malcolm Noel, *Kosovo–a Short History*, Papermac, London, 1998

Maliqi Shkelsen, *Kosovo: Seperate Worlds*, MM, Pristina, 1998

March Andrew and Sil Rudra, *The "Republic of Kosova" (1989–98) and the Resolution of Ethno-Separatist Conflict in the Post-Cold War Era*, University of Pennsylvania, forthcoming

Mertus Julie, *Kosovo: How Myths and Truths Started a War*, University of California Press, 1999

Mertus Julie, *Reconstructing the Legacy of Humanitarian Intervention: Lessons from Kosovo*, 41 Wm&Mary L. Rev. 1743, 2000

Motes Mary, *Kosovo-Kosova: Prelude to War 1966–1999*, Redland Press, 1999

OSCE — Organization for Security and Cooperation in Europé, *Kosovo/Kosova As Seen As Told*, monthly reoports based on collected narrative information, 2000

Pashko Gramoz, *Kosovo: Facing Dramatic Economic decline*, in Veremis and Kofos.

Pond Elisabeth, Kosovo: *Catalyst for Europe*, The Washington Quarterly, autumn 1999

Posen Barry, The War for Kosovo, International Selection, vol.24, no.4, 2000

Ramet Sabrina Petra, Balkan Babel: *The Disintegration of Yugoslavia From the Death of Tito to the War for Kosovo*, Westview Press, 1999

*Report of the Secretary-General Prepared Pursuant to Resolution,* 1160 (1998), 1199 (1998) and 1203 (1998) of the Security Council, UN Doc. S71998/1068, Nov. 12, 1998

*Report of the Secretary-General, resolution 53/35, The Fall of Srebenica,* November 15, 1999

*Report of the Secretary-General on the United Nations Interim Administration in Kosovo,* 6 June, 2000

Rieff David, *Slaughterhouse: Bosnia and the Failure of the West,* Vintage, London, 1995

Roberts Adam, *NATO's "Humanitarian War" over Kosovo,* Survival, vol 41, no. 3, autumn 1999

Schnabel Albrecht and Thakur Ramesh, *Kosovo and the Challenge of Humanitarian Intervention,* United Nations University Press, 2000

Schwartz Stephen, *Kosovo: Background to a War,* Anthem Press, 2000

*The Economic Consequences of the Kosovo Crisis: An Updated Assessment,* IMF, May 25, 1999

*The Kosovo Conflict — Consequences for the Environment & Human Settlements* (UNEP and UNHCR, Geneva 1999

*The Kosovo News & Propaganda War,* International Press Institute, Vienna, September 1999

*The Kosovo refugee crisis: an independent evaluation of UNHCR's emergency preparedness and response,* published by UNHCR, 2000

Thomas Robert, *Serbia under Milosevic,* Hurst & Co, London, 1999

Troebst Stephen, *Conflict in Kosovo: Failure of Preventio, an Analytical Documentation,* European Centre for Minority Issues, Flensburg, 1999

Veremis Thanos and Kofos Evangelos, *Kosovo: Avoiding Another Balkan War* ELIAMEP, University of Athens, 1998

Vickers Miranda, *Between Serb and Albanian: A History of Kosovo,* Columbia University Press, 1998

Weller Marc, *The Crisis in Kosovo 1989–1999,* Documents & Analysis Publishing Ltd, Cambridge 1999

de Wijk, Rob, *Pyrrus in Kosovo* (dutch) Mets en Schilt, Amsterdam 2000

Wolfgang-Uwe Friedrich, editor, *The Legacy of Kosovo: German Politics and Policies in the Balkans,* The American Institute for Contemporary German Studies, 2000

Woodward Susan L., *Balkan Tragedy. Chaos and dissolution after the cold war,* The Brookings institution, Washington D.C. 1995

Various reports from International Crisis Group, to be found on www.intl-crisis-group.org/projects/sbalkans/kosovo.htm#reports

Internet sources

A plethora of websites present news and views on Kosovo. Three useful guides to these sources are:

United States Institute for Peace Library: Kosovo Crisis Web Links www.usip.org/library/regions/kosovo.html

Resolution and Ethnicity (INCORE) guide to Internet sources on conflict and ethnicity in Kosovo www.incore.ulst.ac.uk/cds/countries/kosovo.html Initiative on Conflict

The Independent International Commission on Kosovo: www.kosovocommission.org

| AAAS | American Association for the Advancement of Science |
| ABA/CEELI | American Bar Association Central and East European Law Initiative |
| BBC | British Broadcasting Cooperation |
| CDHRF | Council for the Defense of Human Rights and Freedoms |
| CIA | Central Intelligence Agency |
| CIMIC | Civilian Military Cooperation |
| COE | Council of Europe |
| DU | Depleted uranium |
| ECOMOG | West African Peace Monitoring Force |
| EU | European Union |
| FRY | Federal Republic of Yugoslavia |
| G7 | Group of seven. Heads of State or government from France, the United States, the UK, Germany, Japan, Italy and Canada, meeting annually |
| G8 | Group of eight. G7 plus Russia. |
| GDP | Gross Domestic Product |
| HLC | Humanitarian Law Center |
| HRW | Human Rights Watch |
| ICFY | International Conference on Former Yugoslavia |
| ICG | International Crisis Group |
| ICJ | International Court of Justice |
| ICRC | International Committee of the Red Cross |
| ICTY | International Criminal Tribunal for the Former Yugoslavia |
| IDP | Internally Displaced People |
| IICK | Independent International Commission on Kosovo |
| IMF | International Monetary Fund |
| IOM | International Organization for Migration |
| IRC | International Rescue Committee |
| JIAC | Joint Interim Administrative Council |
| JIAS | Joint Interim Administrative Structure |
| KDOM | Kosovo Diplomatic Observer Mission |
| KFOR | Kosovo (International Security) Force |
| KLA | Kosovo Liberation Army |
| KPC | Kosovo Protection Corps |
| KPS | Kosovo Police Service |
| KTC | Kosovo Transition Council |
| KVM | Kosovo Verification Mission |
| LDK | League for a Democratic Kosovo |
| LPK | Levizja Popullare e Kosoves |
| MP | Member of Parliament |
| MTA | Military-Technical Agreement |
| MTV | Music Television |

| | |
|---|---|
| MUP | Military Uniformed Police |
| NATO | North Atlantic Treaty Organization |
| NGO | non-governmental organization |
| OAU | Organization of African Unit |
| OSCE | Organization for Security and Cooperation in Europe |
| OSCE-KVM | OSCE Kosovo Verification Mission |
| OSF | Open Society Foundation (of Belgrade) |
| SC | Security Council |
| SCR | Security Council Resolution |
| SFOR | Stabilization Force (Bosnia) |
| SRSG | Special representative of the (UN) Secretary-General |
| UCK | Ushtria Clirimtare E Kosoves (English: KLA) |
| UK | United Kingdom |
| UN | United Nations |
| UNSC | United Nations Security Council |
| UNEP | UN Environment Program |
| UNESCO | UN Educational, Scientific and Cultural Organization |
| UNHCR | UN High Commissioner for Refugees |
| UNICEF | UN Children´s Fund |
| UNMIK | UN Interim Administration Mission in Kosovo |
| UNPREDP | United Nations Dag Hammarskjöld Library United Nations Preventive Deployment Force |
| UNSC | UN Security Council |
| UNSG | UN Secretary-General |
| USA | United States of America |
| USAID | US Agency for International Development |
| USIA | US Information Agency |
| USIS | US Information Service |
| VJ | Yugoslav armed forces |
| VMRO | A Macedonian political party |
| WFP | World Food Program |
| WHO | World Health Organization |
| WIIW | The Vienna Institute for International Economic Studies |

A

administrative committee 124
Agami, Fehmi 48–49
Ahrens, Geert 57
Ahtisaari, Martti 95, 324
Albania 74, 103, 172
Albright, Madeleine 56, 153
Amnesty International 42, 53, 60, 72,
    178–184
Annan, Kofi 14, 20–22, 85, 98, 107–108,
    123, 141, 169, 183
Arbour, Louise 69, 75
Artemije, Bishop 115
Autonomy 269

B

Barbarin/Barbarin 180
BBC 78, 216
Belgrade 29, 34, 37–65, 136–161
    government 29, 86–97, 219, 230
    intellectuals 34, 39
    Koha Ditore 219
    monitoring meetings 73
    Serbia 34
Berisha, Sali 51, 239
Bildt, Carl 126, 263
Blair, Tony 73, 254
Blewitt, Graham 73
Blue Sky 224
Bosnia-Herzegovina 34, 284–285
British House of Commons 86, 89
budget 2000 122–124
Bujko 47
Bukoshi, Bujor 46, 59
Bulgaria 172
Bush, George, President 56

C

Lord Carrington 55–57
Ceku, Agim 87
Central Election Commission 116
Chernomyrdin, Viktor 95, 324

China 69, 168
Chinese 142–145, 163, 175, 233, 261, 269
Chinese embassy 94
Cirez/Qirez 68
Civil Registry 116
Civilian Military Cooperation (CIMIC)
    120
Clark, Wesley 76, 81, 95
Clinton 85–86, 147
cluster bombs 180
Communita di Sant'Egidio 50, 60
conditional independence 271–279, 284
Contact Group 57, 69, 137–161, 268
Council for the Defense of Human
    Rights 42, 53, 83
Croatia 34, 284–285

D

Danish Institute of International Affairs
    192
Dashinovc/Dasinovac 72
Dayton Agreement 50, 57–65, 104, 139,
    146–161, 209, 229, 283
    Clinton 210
    Peace Agreement 209
    UN Security Council 212
Demaqi, Adem 47, 50
demographics 38
depleted-uranium (DU) 182
Despic, Aleksandr 50
Deutsche Welle 78
Deutschmark 103, 121, 236, 261, 270
Diaspora 45–65, 240
diplomacy, failure of 25
Djakovica/Gjakove 73–75, 222
Djukanovic, Milo 235–236, 250
Drazkovic, Vuk 232
Drenice/Drenica 67, 68–69, 70, 137, 222

E

economic levels 246
ethnic conflict 33

European [Union] Community
    Conference on Former Yugoslavia 57
European Agency for Reconstruction
    121, 124
European Stability Pact 238
European Union (EU) 55–65, 101, 103,
    121–127, 133, 227–257, 284–286

F
Federal Republic of Yugoslavia (FRY)
    59–65, 69–83, 96, 153
Filipovic, Miroslav 220
Forum 47
four pillars 100
Fushe Kosove/Kosovo Polje 33, 40, 79

G
Gelbard 146–147
Gjakove/Djakovica 73–75, 222
Gjilan/Gnjilane 103, 110–111
Gornje Obrinje/Obri e Eperme 75
Gornji i Ratis/Ratishi i Eperme 72
Gracanica/Ulpiana 109
Grdelica 180

H
Helsinki Summit 58
Hill, Chris 153–161
Holbrooke 76–80, 142–150
Human Rights Watch 42, 53, 60, 68, 77,
    94, 180, 206
Humanitarian Law Center (HLC) 53, 72,
    77, 91
Humanitarian Law Fund 60

I
ICFY 57–58
Identification Commission 116, 120
Independence 268
Institute for Civil Administration 117
internally displaced people 69, 74, 202,
    213–214
International Committee of the Red
    Cross (ICRC) 77, 91, 142, 204, 209

International Criminal Tribunal at The
    Hague 140, 233
International Helsinki Federation for
    Human Rights 53
International Mission 223
International Rescue Committee (IRC)
    204

J
Jashari, Adem 55, 68, 147
Joint Interim Administrative Council
    (JIAC) 116
Joint Interim Administrative Structure
    (JIAS) 115

K
KFOR 100–127, 206–207, 224, 259–262,
    272, 289
Kinkel, Klaus 73
Koha Ditore 47, 110
Korishe/Korisa 94
Kosovo 34
Kosovo crisis 23
Kosovo Diplomatic Observer Mission
    (KDOM) 73
Kosovo Liberation Army (KLA) 67–83,
    104
Kosovo Polje/Fushe Kosove 33, 79
Kosovo Protection Corps (KPC) 107, 118
Kosovo Protection Force 123
Kosovska Mitrovica/Mitrovice 43
Kouchner, Bernard 98, 99–115, 223
kvm 76–83, 85, 150

L
League for a Democratic Kosovo (LDK)
    45–65, 104
League of Prizren 36, 40
Levizja Popullare e Kosoves (LPK) 51
Liksoshan/Likosane 68
Luan/Luan 180
Lubeniq/Ljubenic 72

M

Macedonia 34, 51, 74–83, 87, 90, 103, 172,
    200, 227–257, 284–285
Mandela, Nelson 14, 296
Martinovic, Djordje 39
Medecins Sans Frontières 203
Media Resource Center 224
Mercy Corps 60
Military–Technical Agreement (MTA)
    101–104
Milosevic 34–65, 69–83, 131–161, 163–164,
    228–257
Milutinovic, Milan 152
Mitrovice/Kosovska Mitrovica 43, 103,
    106, 108–117, 267, 268
Montenegro 34, 74

N

NATO 72–83, 133, 148, 222, 259–262, 272,
    289
NATO Secretary-General 85
non-governmental organizations (NGOs)
    46–47, 57, 60–65, 203–205
Novi Poklek/Poklek i Ri 72

O

Obri e Eperme/Gornje Obrinje 75
Odalevic/Veljko 69
Open Society Foundation of Belgrade
    (OSF) 60–61
Open Society Institute 224
Operation Horseshoe 88, 201
Operation Joint Guardian 101, 103
Orahovac/Rrahovec 74, 109
organized crime 51–53
Organization of Security and
    Cooperation in Europe (OSCE)
    56–65, 78–83, 85–97, 101, 105, 107,
    133–148, 223–225
    The Permanent Council 73
OSCE-KVM 87
Otpor 232
Owen, David 57–58

P

Panic, Milan 48–49
Peje/Pec 67, 68, 78–80, 103, 110–111
Podujevo/Podujevo 79–80, 80–82
Poklek i Ri/Novi Poklek 72
Poland 244
Polish Solidarity 44
Post-Pessimist Club 47
Prekazi/Prekaz 55, 68, 147
Primakov 143
Prishtina/Pristina 35–37, 43, 68–69, 90,
    102, 103, 110–111, 124, 207, 224, 239
Prizren/Prizren 33, 35–37, 73–75, 103,
    110–111
Protectorate 263
Protocol I–III 30–31, 166

Q

Qirez/Cirez 68
Qosja, Rexhap 50

R

Radio Galaxy 224
Radio TV Belgrade 40
Rambouillet 82, 86–87, 97, 100, 104, 145,
    151–161, 320–323
rape 3, 11, 39, 91, 97
Ratishi i Eperme/Gornj 72
Recak/Racak 81, 83, 159, 215
Reconstructing media 224
referendum 271
Reinhardt, Klaus 105
Resolution 1160 140–141
Resolution 1199 75–76
Resolution 1203 142
Resolution 1244 96, 99–127, 163, 172, 207,
    259–269, 325–330
Roma 104, 109, 116–117, 164, 206, 265, 269
Rrahovec/Orahovac 74, 109
Rubin, James 153
Rugova, Ibrahim 43–65, 70, 83, 104, 147,
    239
Russia 73, 95–97, 168, 284

Russian 102–103, 137–161, 163, 175, 233, 244, 261, 269
Rwanda 159, 170, 185–198, 297

S
sanctions program 235
Serbia 284
Serbian television 221
Seselj, Vojislav 54
78-day campaign 89, 92, 97, 290
sexual violence 91
Shterpce/Strpce 80
Shtime/Stimlje 81
Slovenia 34, 284–285
Special Envoy of the un Secretary-General for the Balkans 126
Special Group on Kosovo 57
Stability Pact 124–125, 252–257, 274–275, 284–286
Supreme Court 112
Surroi, Veton 44, 50, 110, 207

T
targets 179
Territorial Defense law 80
Tetovo 239
Thaci, Hashim 104, 239
The Council for the Defense of Human Rights 46
The Government of the Republic of Kosova 104
The Provisional Government of Kosova 104
"three republic" proposal 51
Tirana 239
Tito 34–37, 43
Turkey 244

U
Ulpiana/Gracanica 109
UN 78, 133
UN Charter 75, 139, 166, 291
UN General Assembly 59, 190
UN Secretary-General 78

UN Security Council 56, 59, 69–83, 96, 99, 138–143, 223, 291–293
Unemployment 37
UNESCO 59
UNHCR 101, 107, 127, 138, 140, 142
UNICEF 59
United Nations (UN) 56
United Nations High Commissioner for Refugees (UNHCR) 201–225
United Nations Interim Mission in Kosovo (UNMIK) 100–127, 191, 223–224, 259–264
US 103, 137–138

V
Vance, Cyrus 57
Veljko/Odalevic 69
Victim Recovery 116, 120
Voice of America 77–78
Vojvodina 34
Vollebæk, Knut 82
Vushtrri/Vucitrn 74, 80

W
Walker, William 81
war criminal 233
WHO 59
women 47, 61, 91, 116–117
World Bank 121, 124–125, 246, 255
World Food Program (WFP) 202, 204
World Health Organization 204

Y
Yeltsin 73, 144
youth 61
Yugoslav Red Cross 60

Z
Zeri 47

Gjakove/Djakovica July 5, 1999.
A Roma woman wails as her home burns.
Italian KFOR soldiers help to put out the fire,
which was allegedly set by Kosovar Albanians.
PHOTO: RUTH FREMSON/PRESSENS BILD